Contents

THE HUMAN CONSEQUENCES OF GROWTH FOR THE ECONOMY'S SAKE

GALWAY COUNTY LIBRARIES

KT-394-320

Introduction

John Jopling

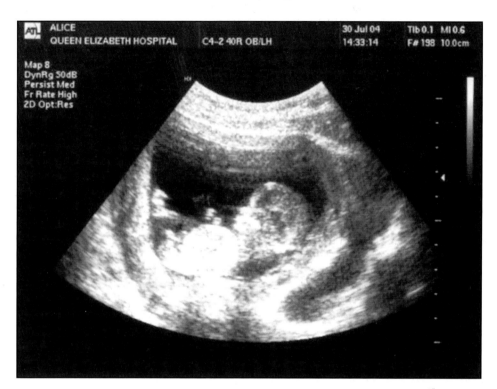

I have just been informed that my niece is pregnant: when born, her baby will be my parents' first great-grandchild. I hope he or she will share my good fortune and live a healthy life in a secure and supportive society. But what are the prospects for this?

The prospects for any unborn child depend to a crucial extent on the economic system within which he or she lives. So, to broaden the question: does our increasingly global economic system offer all newborn children everywhere excellent prospects of good health, societal support and economic security? In other words, is the world economic system just and sustainable?

And if it isn't, the next question has to be: what can be done to make it so?

This is the issue with which Feasta concerns itself. It was founded in 1998 out of the conviction that the current economic system is so seriously flawed that it threatens us all, but the poor, and future generations, most of all. The purpose of the *Feasta Review* is to present in a permanent form some of the ideas about what might be done to improve the system that have been developed or discussed within Feasta since the last issue appeared.

A core issue for Feasta has always been that of economic growth. Humans, we are told, already consume 40% of the planet's primary production, leaving the remaining 60% for the other seven million species. No wonder we are causing widespread extinctions. No wonder we are pulling innumerable threads from the fabric of nature. No wonder we using up the resources on which human life itself depends. How can we sensibly talk of growth if achieving it means consuming even more resources and thus accelerating the pace of destruction?

Very few economists seem to appreciate that growth is not necessarily a good thing because it can be uneconomic as well as economic. One who does is Herman Daly, who is well known for promoting the concept of a zero-growth, 'steady-state' economy. Feasta therefore picked him to give the first Feasta Lecture in 1999. In his talk, Daly said that growth was bound to become uneconomic eventually because, beyond a certain point, it begins to use or destroy more resources than it creates and thus actually makes us poorer. And he went on: "If growth really is uneconomic now, then we have to face very radical solutions to fundamental problems." The lecture was reproduced in the first *Feasta Review*, published in 2001.

Growth is closely linked with energy use and the growth achieved in the past 200 years has been heavily dependent on the use of fossil fuels. Two consequences of this will have a massive influence on our lives and those of future

>>> *the recent doubling of national income was achieved at great cost*

generations: climate change induced by the release into the atmosphere of carbon dioxide and other 'global warming' gases produced by the combustion of fossil fuels; and the imminent peak in the amount of energy that humanity will be able to obtain from oil and gas because the reserves are being used up much faster than new ones are being found. Climate change was the subject of several papers in the first *Feasta Review* and is currently a hot issue within Feasta as you'll see from our website www.feasta.org.

Since the British Government's chief scientist, Sir David King, has warned that Antarctica could be the only continent suitable for mammalian life by the end of the century if greenhouse gas emissions continue unchecked, to continue with growth fuelled by oil and gas must surely be extremely irresponsible. But suppose the supply of oil and gas can no longer be expanded, what happens then? What if the amount of energy available to the world from fossil fuels reaches a peak and then starts to contract? The question is far from academic. In the first *Feasta Review*, the petroleum geologist Colin Campbell predicted the imminent peak of world oil production. And hasn't he been proved right? A peak in global gas output will follow within a few years. In the same issue David Fleming described the serious

economic contraction and destabilisation that will inevitably result from the decline in energy availability following these peaks.

Fleming also looked at the consequences of oil and gas depletion in his 2001 Feasta Lecture, the text of which is reproduced here. He told us that energy scarcity would cause the market economy not just to cease growing but to collapse. The collapse was unavoidable, he said, and public policy should therefore concentrate on laying the foundations for a transformed political economy that could rise from the ashes.

Since energy availability is so crucial, Feasta held a three-day conference in October 2002 on oil and gas supply prospects and the time scale available for making the transition to renewable forms of energy. The conference concluded, as you will see from reading the book that emerged from it, *Before the Wells Run Dry*, that the only sustainable economy is one based on renewables, and that such an economy would look very different from the present one.

One of the key differences would be the potential for growth. In an energy-constrained economy, the potential for economic growth is very limited. *Before the Wells Run Dry* reports the results of a run of a computer model of energy flows in the Irish economy commissioned by Feasta. This showed that Ireland's plentiful supply of renewable resources, even if fully developed, would allow only modest economic growth.

If the consequences of growth fuelled by fossil energy are so adverse, and the feasibility of its continuing are so limited, why are governments so keen on it? Here we come back to the design of the economic system. As Feasta explained in a paper it submitted to the Irish Government in December 2001 in the run-up to the World Summit on Sustainable Development held in Johannesburg the following year, one of the major flaws in the current system is that it has to grow each year if it is not to collapse. Here's what we wrote:

> Sustainability needs to be achieved in two time-frames. One is short-term, largely economic and very demanding. We need to eat tonight. Employees have to be paid at the end of the week. Interest has to be paid at the end of the half-year. With its focus of competitiveness, this is the time frame which has occupied Ireland's attention almost exclusively so far. Actions required to achieve sustainability in the second

time-frame seem less urgent but are no less important. The natural environment has to be preserved. Capital equipment, buildings and infrastructure have to be kept up. Health has to be maintained. Knowledge and skills have to be preserved and passed on. And social structures such as families, friendships and neighbourhoods have to stay strong. Unfortunately, in almost every country, the achievement of immediate, short-term sustainability has made it difficult if not impossible to take serious steps towards attaining the longer-term type. Only by changing the economic system can countries get the freedom and the resources to attend to longer-term sustainability.

In short, the system compels those running it to put immediate economic sustainability - the achievement of growth to avoid an economic collapse - far ahead of social and environmental sustainability. So far ahead, in fact, that they ignore the human, social and environmental costs of generating growth until those costs begin to have a serious impact on the immediate growth prospects.

Just how far governments are prepared to allow human health and societal strength to deteriorate in their pursuit of growth is illustrated by the first article in the present volume. Extensive research undertaken by Dr. Elizabeth Cullen (as, initially, a project for the Feasta Indicators working group) shows that the recent rapid doubling of national income per person in Ireland was achieved at great cost to the population's mental and physical health. This was because of the increase in inequality which came about not just because of the economic system's inherent tendency to concentrate wealth but also because the Irish government aggravated that tendency in order to make the economy more competitive internationally and thus increase the rate at which the country grew. Rapid growth meant rapid change: many Irish people felt stressed and took refuge in comfort eating or in alcohol, both with serious consequences. Very similar results have been reported from other countries. Indeed, beyond a certain point, growth should be seen as a cancer right here in the body of our society. In future, it should be accompanied by a health warning unless steps are taken to ensure that it leads to a reduction in inequality, rather than the reverse.

Feasta has therefore been searching for ways in which the economy could be restructured so that, when rapid economic growth comes to a halt, it does not collapse but instead develops along a more sustainable path. Our search area has been wide since, unlike organisations which limit their recommendations to those the current mainstream will accept or at least listen to, we are quite prepared to be radical. However, to ensure that our proposals are relevant, we insist that they have to be 'doable'.

One of our concerns has been with the discipline of economics as such. The current system seeks to maximise the return investors get on their capital. Should the aim of the system, instead, be to maximise human welfare as measured by human health, subject to sensible environmental constraints? Frank Rotering has been working on this question and you can find in this issue a summary of a paper of his which we discussed over several months on a dedicated e-list set up for the purpose. I think it's fair to say that most of those who took part in the discussion thought that Frank was trying to bring too many economic tools over from the present flawed system and was thus infecting the new one with harmful attitudes and characteristics from the old. A more serious problem was whether it was going to be possible to compile the data required to enable anyone to work out exactly when health was being maximised. Still, those who took part learned from it and Frank was helped to take his ideas forward.

For many of us, it is the way that money is put into circulation that creates the growth-or-collapse problem, rather than the system's profit-maximising goal. You will therefore find several articles about aspects of money in this Review. For example, James Robertson's contribution says that we must redesign money so that rather than being an instrument of growth and ever greater inequality it becomes a way of fairly sharing common resources. And the new design he sets out is very 'doable' – far simpler than the extremely complicated arrangements currently needed for the money supply, taxation and subsidies.

The country to benefit most from the present money system is, not surprisingly, the richest country, the USA, because its currency, the dollar, is used around the world as if it was an international currency rather than a national one. Europe, with the euro, has the potential to benefit the same way and in his article, Coilin Nunan describes the fascinating competition between the two currencies. An earlier article on the dollar and euro which Coilin wrote for circulation on the Feasta e-list in January 2003 "Oil, Currency, and the War on Iraq," was selected as a finalist for the Project Censored "Most Censored" News Stories of 2003 Awards. Out of the 900 news stories nominated for the award, Coilin's was ranked number nineteen.

Some people think that, rather than the debt-based nature of our current money system, it is the charging of interest which is responsible for the economy's growth compulsion. Ana Carrie went to Sweden on behalf of the Feasta money group to study a bank there which neither charges interest on its loans nor pays interest to its depositors. Ana's article in this issue explains exactly how the bank works. From a sustainability perspective, however, the big advantage of the bank is not that it doesn't charge interest, but rather that it does not take in money from poor areas and lend it out in richer ones.

The 2002 Feasta lecturer, Stan Thekaekara, is particularly concerned about the way both property ownership and the international trading system take from the poor and give to the rich. Inspired by the attitudes of the tribal people with whom he works in Southern India, he has devised a trading system, Just Change, which links producers and consumers across the world in a jointly-owned co-operative as an alternative to leaving their relationships to be governed by market forces. Trading in tea has already started and, as we go to press, trading in rice is about to begin.

My co-editor, Richard Douthwaite, is also concerned about the global system's built-in tendency to polarise wealth in the hands of the better-off. On top of that, he says, the world economy is inherently unreliable and puts excessive pressures on the environment. His article therefore suggests that we should attempt both to change the way it works and to build regional (that is, sub-national) alternatives to it.

As radical economic change is unlikely to come about without equally radical changes in our political systems, Feasta has become increasingly interested in identifying the sorts of changes we should advocate in the way the political system works. The Schumacher Briefing I wrote with Roy Madron on this topic is reviewed by John Barry in this issue. But there are many other approaches and we also print a paper by Mark Garavan spelling out what could be done to reform the way government works in Ireland without even changing the constitution.

So, all in all, there are plenty of novel possibilities for transforming the present system to make it more equitable and sustainable. And thus improve the life chances for the babies to be born in years to come.

Unprecedented growth, but for whose benefit?

Elizabeth Cullen

Fifteen years ago, most of us thought that it would be a marvellous thing to double the average income of everyone in Ireland. So, now that a doubling has happened, why has it seriously damaged the nation's health and the bonds between its people? The answer is – because of the way the growth was generated. In order to bring it about, the government used the tax system to aggravate the tendency of the free market system to increase inequality.

Elizabeth Cullen is a medical doctor with a particular interest in public health. She currently attends NUI, Maynooth, studying the likely effects of climate change on Irish health. She is a trustee of Feasta and a committee member of the Irish Doctors' Environmental Association. She lives in Co. Kildare. health@feasta.org

For the politicians who claimed to have bred it, the Celtic Tiger was a matter of great pride. After all, it had been hailed as 'one of the most remarkable economic transformations of recent times' by *The Economist* magazine. 'Mr. President,' the Taoiseach, Bertie Ahern, boasted[1] to President Clinton and members of the Oireachtas during the American leader's visit to Ireland in 2000, 'in the eight years of your presidency, Ireland has changed, and changed very fast. We've a new economy and a modern society. The economy is now in its seventh year of sustained growth. It has grown by over 9 percent per annum in the last three years.'

Certainly, the pace of Irish economic growth had been remarkable. As figure 1 shows, in just thirteen years, between 1989 and 2002, the population's average income had doubled, which meant that it had grown by as much as it had increased in all the 8,000-odd years since the first settlers moved into the country as the ice sheets retreated.[2]

Irish incomes double

GDP/Capita & GNP/Capita 1985-2002 (1995 Prices)

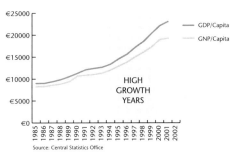

Source: Central Statistics Office

Figure 1: *Gross Domestic Product (GDP) measures the value of all the goods and services produced in a country in the course of a year, whereas Gross National Product is the value of the goods and services the inhabitants of the country actually consume. The growing gap between the two shown above is largely due to the fact that the profits made by foreign companies based in Ireland are included in GDP but not GNP and that these have increased more rapidly than other incomes. Nevertheless, the value at 1995 prices of the goods and services available to the average Irish resident (the lower line above) doubled between 1989 and 2002. Most of that growth took place between 1994 and 2000, the shaded area on the graph.*

This rate of growth was at least three times faster than in comparable countries. To achieve it, the way people lived and earned their incomes had had to change significantly. Many more people were going out to work than before and unemployment, which began to fall in 1993, dropped from almost 16% to just under 4% in 2001, as depicted in figure 2. It has risen slightly since.

By 2003 Ireland had become the world's 'most globalised' country thanks to its high level of foreign trade, multinational investment and the large number of telephone calls to the rest of the world[3]. The Central Statistics Office's *Statistical Yearbook of Ireland 2003* reported that manufacturing industry production more than doubled between 1995 and 2002 and the output of the distribution, transport and communications sectors expanded by almost as much during the same period. By contrast, the traditional base of the economy, agriculture, forestry and fishing, only grew by 7% during those years.

Unemployment Rate 1985-2002 (%)

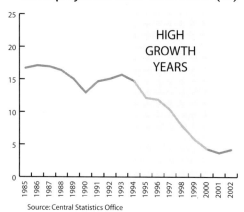

HIGH
GROWTH
YEARS

Source: Central Statistics Office

Figure 2: The percentage of people unemployed fell sharply in the high growth period between 1994 and 2000, and then began to rise a little once the growth rate slowed. The fall was perhaps the major benefit of the Celtic Tiger years but many of the jobs created were poorly paid.

Dramatic fall in unemployment

The beneficial effects of the reduction in unemployment must not be underestimated. Many studies have found that unemployed people consistently show higher levels of psychological distress than employed people living on the same level of income. There is also a lot of evidence that unemployment is associated with increased illness and mortality. However, it may have been that other changes during the period offset much or all of the benefit of reduced unemployment, particularly as many of the jobs created were poorly paid. We will be discussing some of these changes in this article.

Apart from the lower unemployment, what benefits did the rapid growth bring? Was the Taoiseach's pride justified? Were people happier,

less stressed and more content? Did their health improve? Or the physical and social environment in which they lived? Or did the distribution of income change markedly, leaving some badly behind?

This report will attempt to answer these and similar questions. It is divided into two parts. First we will look at how the changes affected people's health and the way they felt about themselves. Then, in part two, we will explore the effects that growth had on society. However, as we will see, the health and societal aspects of life are closely linked.

Part One. How the Celtic Tiger affected the nation's health

A. The quality of life

Did the increase in incomes fulfill their advertised promise and make people happier, less stressed and more content? Or, to put this another way, did the increase enable their quality of life to improve? Unfortunately, the quality of life, like happiness and contentment, cannot be measured directly and it is very difficult to measure trends in the quality of life over time. Nevertheless, many recent surveys clearly show that during Ireland's high growth years a deterioration took place in many of the factors that make up the quality of life.

One of these factors was the **level of stress** under which people found themselves. Several reports show that this increased significantly. For example:

- A survey of 1,000 people carried out in 2001 on behalf of the Mental Health Association of Ireland[4] found that 73% reported finding life more stressful than five years previously; 19% of the respondents said they were smoking more and 17% said they were drinking more in order to cope with their stress.
- A National Health and Lifestyle Survey of 6,539 people in 1999 to ascertain what people believed would best improve their health[5] found that the majority reported 'less stress' regardless of their age, sex and social background. A follow-up report in 2001 also reported that stress was the most common answer for both males and females.
- In an online survey[6] in 2001, a sample of 2000 students was asked if they thought that the level of stress experienced by the general Irish population had increased. Over two-

thirds said that it had increased a lot, 30% said it had a little and only 3% said not at all.

- The 2004 Amarach report[9] found that between 2001 and 2004, the proportion of people who said they suffered from stress 'often', rose from 9% to 14% and half the population suffer from stress 'sometimes or often', up from 41% just three years previously. Furthermore, the proportion of people who thought that the pace of change in Irish society was too fast had almost trebled since the mid-1990s.
- A 2002 study[7] of attitudes in the workplace found that 77% of respondents said that the economic boom had not improved their quality of life. Almost half of the sample of 344 people interviewed at work felt that they were caught up in a rat race; a third said they were continually tired and over a quarter complained of excessive stress levels. The main cause of their absences from work was found to be the stress they experienced while they were there. Almost a quarter of them said that they suffered 'great stress from bullying, back biting and other forms of aggressive behaviour and intimidation'. Over a half reported that they did not have a satisfactory balance between the demands of their work and the time that they devoted to their personal lives.

Longer working hours may partially explain this lack of balance. The hours Irish people worked increased substantially during the high growth period. As shown in Figure 3, Ireland came third highest out of 23 countries in terms of the increase in hours worked between 1995 and 2003. A survey in August 2002 on behalf of the National Economic and Social Forum[8] found that 83.5% of respondents said that they would like to meet up with family and friends more often. The greatest single barrier to this was reported to be lack of time due to paid work. This makes it unsurprising that the 2004 Amarach report[9] found that almost a half of all workers said that they would like to retire before the age of 55, compared with one third in 2001.

Working hours increase

Hours Worked % Change 1995-2003

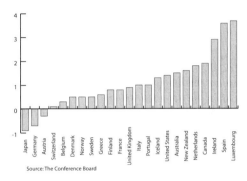

Source: The Conference Board

Figure 3: *A small amount of the increased incomes people received was due to their working longer hours. Between 1995 and 2003, the average hours worked by Irish employees rose by almost 3%, one of the biggest increases in the OECD. This left less time for other activities and almost certainly led to increased stress. Working hours fell slightly in two countries with rising unemployment, Germany and Japan.*

More depressive disorders: In 2003[10], research involving a representative sample of 12,702 women in four European countries found that women in Dublin were more susceptible to depressive disorders than those in similar cities in other countries. One in three suffered from depression. One of the authors, Professor Patricia Casey commented 'This [study] was conducted at a time of economic boom, when you would expect depressive disorders to reduce'[11].

The 2004 Amarach report found that although there was a positive relationship between feeling less miserable and increased GDP, the measure of life satisfaction has fallen steadily in recent years, returning to levels last seen in the mid 1980s.

Satisfaction with life drops by half

Trend in Irish GDP per capita as % of EU Average and % of Irish who are 'Not Satisfied' with their lives

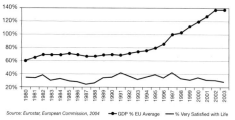

Source: Eurostar, European Commission, 2004 ◆ GDP % EU Average ━ % Very Satisfied with Life

Figure 4: At the end of the high growth period during which Irish GDP climbed in relation to the EU average, only half the number of people said that they were very satisfied with their lives as had done so before growth took off.

In view of these studies, it is not surprising that one of the EU's regular Eurobarometer surveys[12], showed that only 30% of Irish people reported themselves to be very satisfied with their lives in spring 2002 compared with 42% in 1997[13]. Nor that the Mid Western Health Board reported[14] in January 2004 that 60% of the men randomly selected in a survey it had carried out agreed with the statement, 'that the lot of the average man is getting worse'. A third of the men surveyed believed that they had little control over their lives and 4% had actually planned their own suicide. In short, there seems little doubt that for many, rapid economic growth, longer hours and higher pay led to less satisfying, more stressful lives.

No increase in life satisfaction

Life Satisfaction, Ireland (1993-2003)

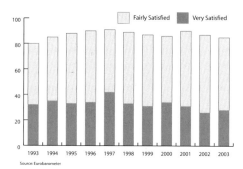

Source: Eurobarometer

Figure 5: Each year, the EU's Eurobarometer team asks a random sample of the inhabitants of each member state whether or not they are satisfied with their lives. The results for Ireland show that the number of people expressing themselves as very satisfied has fallen from a peak in 1997, despite the massive rise in average incomes.

It has to be said, though, that not all surveys were negative. The 2002 Amarach report[15] *Quality of Life in Ireland* found that the proportion of all respondents reporting feeling stressed 'often or sometimes' declined from 48% in 1999 to 41% in 2001. Moreover, 77% of people believed that the quality of life in Ireland had improved over the previous five years. On the other hand, one in ten adults thought it had worsened. Those thinking this way were predominantly 'in the older age groups and the lower social classes'. This group also reported that their personal quality of life had worsened.

B. How did the distribution of income in Ireland change?

As one might expect in a period in which the average income doubled, the number of people living in conditions of basic deprivation fell from 15% in 1994 to 5.5% in 2003. This was very good, since basic deprivation means not being able to afford to have some of the things that most of us would regard as essential, like heating on a very cold day, a waterproof coat, a change of shoes, and at least one substantial meal each day. In short, it means absolute poverty.

But there is another form of poverty, too, and that increased. It is relative poverty, This was defined in the 1997 National Anti-Poverty Strategy as living on income and resources (material, social and cultural) which are so inadequate as to preclude people "from having a standard of living which is regarded as the norm for other people in society". It is generally accepted that living on less than half the median income (that is, less than half income that the middle person received if everybody in the country lined up according to their earnings) involves relative poverty. This more than doubled, from 6% in 1994 to 12.9% in 2001.[16] The National Anti-Poverty Strategy concentrates on reducing absolute poverty and does not have targets to reduce relative poverty. To those who believe that relative poverty does not cause stress and despair, Padraig O'Morain[17] says 'Tell that to the lone parent who is so in debt that she is afraid to answer the door, but whose child wants a €35 pair of Nike runners and will not wear a perfectly adequate €15 pair of non-Nike runners from a department store'.

Figure 6 shows that the incomes of those at the top of society increased strongly as a result of the growth, while those at the bottom were left behind. It divides the Irish population into ten groups of equal size on the basis of their incomes. The groups range from the poorest 10% of the population on the left to the richest 10% on the right. The chart shows that between 1994/95 and 2000, seven out of the ten groups (deciles) saw their share of the national income fall in relation to the other three groups. While the 5th decile saw its share increase slightly, the most significant feature was the gains made by the top 20% and particularly the top 10%, which stand in marked contrast to the experience of the rest of the population. The chart was prepared by Micheal Collins of Trinity College, Dublin, for the Conference of Religious in Ireland[18] a body which has followed recent changes in the distribution of income with some care. Collins found that the gap between the top and bottom of the income distribution widened for three reasons. These were: the segmentation of the labour market into high and low skills; in that highly skilled people did very well, low-skilled people badly; tax cuts that gave most benefit to those with higher earnings, and the fact that social welfare payments grew more slowly than average incomes.

The rich get much richer

Change in Decile Divisions of Disposable Income, Ireland 1994-2000 (%)

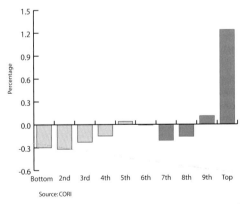

Source: CORI

Figure 6: In the high growth years between 1994 and 2000, the share of national income going to the top 20% of the Irish population grew at the expense of almost everyone else. The top 10% did particularly well.

Roughly three times as many adults were living in relative poverty in 2001 as had been the case seven years earlier. As Table 1 shows, the deterioration was worst among the elderly, whose incomes did not keep up with the rest of the population. The percentage of people over the age of 65 living in relative poverty increased over sixfold in the years 1994-2001. If the numbers of people on old age pensions are categorized as being under the 60% median income line, approximately one in twenty were below this limit in 1994; by 2001, it had risen to almost one in two[19].

As Table 2 shows, carers, the old and the ill were also amongst those left behind economically. There was almost a sixfold increase in the percentage of people in relative poverty who were ill or had a disability. There was a similar increase in the percentage of people categorized as 'performing home duties' and a threefold increase among people who had retired living in relative poverty. Table 2 also shows that almost five times the proportion of employees were in relative poverty in 2001 compared to 1994, reflecting the deterioration in the position of less-skilled workers. In short, not everyone has gained from the economic growth.

More poverty in old age

	1994	1997	1998	2000	2001
	%	%	%	%	%
Adults	4.3	6.4	8.1	10.8	12.4
Aged 18-64	4.6	7.1	8.6	10.6	11.3
Aged 65 or more	2.8	2.6	5.7	12	18.2
Children (under 18)	9.4	13.8	14.2	15.1	14.2

Table 1 shows the percentages of the people in each age category who received an income of less than half the national median income. The figures clearly show that, during the high growth years, increasing numbers of people saw their incomes fall behind.

Source: *Monitoring Poverty Trends in Ireland* 2003, ESRI

Carers, the sick and the old lose out

	1994	1997	1998	2000	2001
	%	%	%	%	%
Employee	0.6	1.2	0.4	2.3	2.9
Self-employed	9.9	10.7	12.6	12.7	10.6
Farmer	10.2	6.2	5.5	17.1	12
Unemployed	19.1	39.8	41	37.3	33.8
Ill/have a disability	10.1	27.5	43.6	45.3	59
Retired	4.0	2.1	6	12.1	15.3
Home duties	5.7	8.9	21.2	24.8	31.2
All	6.0	8.4	9.9	12	12.9

Table 2 shows the proportion of people in each employment category who received incomes less than half the national median income. As the Celtic Tiger ran its course, carers, the retired, the unemployed and the sick and disabled got progressively worse off in comparison with the rest of society. Many employees' incomes fell behind too.

Source: *Monitoring Poverty Trends in Ireland 2003*, ESRI

In an earlier study, the ESRI[20] found that 1 in 10 of those who had lived below the relative poverty line for a year had sunk into absolute poverty while after five years below the line, the proportion had risen to a half.

Impact on children

Children were also badly affected by the income changes. As table 1 shows, the percentage of children living in relative poverty increased from 9.4% in 1994 to 14.2% in 2001. Other observers drew similar conclusions:

- In 2003, the Combat Poverty Agency described the level of child poverty in Ireland as 'relatively high', with 6.5% per cent of children at risk of consistent poverty and nearly a quarter of all those under 18 living in low income households[21]. In its 2003 pre-budget submission, the St. Vincent de Paul society noted that '70,000 children did not necessarily have enough food, warmth or a second pair of shoes'[22] implying that they lived in homes in absolute poverty.

- A UNICEF survey[23], published in 2000, of the extent of child poverty (which the researchers defined as being brought up in a household where less than 50% of the national median income was coming in), placed Ireland sixth worst out of 23 countries, as it had 16.8% of children living in such households whereas the average for the countries involved was 11.87%. Mexico and the United States had the worst records. The report warned that 'many of the most serious problems facing today's advanced industrialized nations have roots in the denial and deprivation faced by many in childhood.'

- A Combat Poverty Agency[24] (CPA) survey of low income families in late 2000 found that only a quarter of children living in poverty were happy with their lives; they had concerns about 'fitting in' and had a fear of being different. A quarter of the deprived children were being bullied in school, causing some to leave early. One in three reported health problems. 'By allowing child poverty to continue in this country, we are denying over a quarter of a million children their basic rights to fulfill their talents and potential,' Hugh Frazer, the then director of CPA commented. 'How children live today powerfully influences how they will live tomorrow. Poverty has negative effects on the health and development of children. Those who grow up in poverty are likely to do less well educationally, have fewer recreational, social and cultural opportunities and are more at risk of being involved in crime and anti-social behaviour.'

The Chief Medical Officer, Dr. Jim Kiely, stated in his annual report *The Health of Our Children 2002*, that 300,000 children under 14, one in four, were being brought up in a home where the income was less than €175 a week, and that 17 per cent were experiencing chronic poverty. The CMO admitted that this proportion was higher than in most European Union countries[25] and added that the socio-economic conditions in which children lived were among the key determinants influencing their health.

Despite his recognition that poverty causes illness in children, he noted that the data on how it does so and the extent to which it does were very limited. 'We have some way to go before we have the information available which enables us to produce a comprehensive picture of the health of our children' the CMO wrote. 'There are considerable gaps such as information from out-patient and primary care, mental health information and chronic disease information.'

He was right. The data collected on child health in Ireland are not coded by socio-economic group[26], even though international research has indicated that adverse socio-economic circumstances in childhood are associated with stroke, heart disease, respiratory disease and stomach cancer in later life[27 28] and that the level of infant mortality is directly proportional to the degree of income inequality[29].

Farmers suffer

Another group to be badly hit by the changes in the high-growth years were farmers and 35,000 of the 275,000 working the land in 1998 had left it by 2002. A major factor in their decision to leave farming was that between 1996 and 2002, agricultural output prices fell by 5% while input prices rose by over 9%[30]. It is not surprising then that the *Living in Ireland* survey found that farmers made up a significant proportion of those living in relative poverty. 'There is no getting around the fact that there is a feeling of an occupation in decline,' commented Mike Magan of Agri-Aware[31]. 'There is huge uncertainty and great worry, and that can make people feel very isolated'. As one farmer put it[32] 'If 20% of the people expand to survive, another 50% will be put out of business. What will happen to them?'

After farmers had donated €28,000 to the Samaritans in 2003 to help the organization combat loneliness and depression in rural areas, Paul O'Hare of the Samaritans commented that farmers were subject to uncertain seasonal factors and were looking at reduced incomes.[33] As a result, they could find themselves under considerable stress particularly if they were trying to support a family.

C. Psychological stress of poverty

Not only has research clearly established that living in relative poverty damages both physical and psychological health, studies have also found that, not surprisingly, the damage is proportional to the degree of poverty. For example, the ESRI[34] found that people who were consistently poor suffered more psychological distress than those who were categorized as potentially poor, who in turn appeared to suffer to a greater degree than those who were in neither category. ('Consistently poor' referred to people who were living below 60% of the mean income and experiencing basic deprivation in relation to a standard set of items while 'potentially poor' was defined as living below 60% of the national mean income and not having one of five stated luxury items). There was also, not surprisingly, a strong relationship between the degree of fatalism felt and the number of years the person had been poor. The authors write 'we found a clear relationship with the sense of control over one's life decreasing as the period of income poverty increased.'

Several studies have shown that continual stress (which includes psychological distress) weakens disease resistance. For example, stress has been found to influence cardiovascular and immune disorders[35], ulcers[36], and strokes[37], but not cancer[38]. A longitudinal study [39] published in the Proceedings of the National Academy of Sciences established a link between long-term stress and the release of chemicals involved in both immune system regulation and the development of cardiovascular disease and myocardial infarction, adult-onset diabetes, osteoporosis, arthritis and congestive heart failure. Researchers have found that greater job stress is associated with higher cholesterol, a person's body mass index 5 to 10 years later and cardiovascular mortality regardless of factors such as age, exercise habits and smoking. In a 28 year study[40] of workers in Finland, Kivimäki and colleagues found that work stress doubled the risk of cardiovascular death.

People who suffer from clinical depression have been found to have a three- to fourfold increase in the risk of a heart attack[41]. A correlation was also found[42] between long-term work stress and high blood pressure. 'Work woes could contribute to problems with blood clotting or insulin resistance, a precursor to diabetes, which in turn is a major risk factor for heart disease and stroke,' the study added. Other researchers have shown[43] that the heart conditions of men who show stress-induced blood pressure reactivity and who report high job demands deteriorate more rapidly than those in less stressful situations. This finding was independent of other known risk factors and suggests that the traditional medical advice about cardiovascular health - stop smoking, cut down drinking, eat less fat, and engage in physical activity - needs to be supplemented by reducing stress at work.

D. The effects of stress on health

We saw earlier that people complained about increased stress during the period of very rapid economic growth between 1994 and 2002 and that relative poverty also increased during that time - a change which would have created great stress in the groups that lost out. We've also seen evidence that stress weakens the body's immune system and leads to increased illness. Accordingly, although it might take some years for the full effects of the stress to show up in the statistics, I thought it worthwhile to check whether health in Ireland did in fact deteriorate during that period, or at least improve less than in other similar but less-stressed countries.

Life expectancy is one measure of health. It is a broad measure and does not take into account life expectancy in different groups in society. Nevertheless, I found that Irish life expectancy is very low and getting worse in comparison with our EU partners. In 1997, Irish life expectancy at birth for Irish males was 73.5 years and 79.2 for females, the second lowest in the EU[44]. But by 2001, the changes during the high-growth period seem to have made the situation worse and Ireland had[45] the lowest life expectancy of all EU countries, being three years less than the EU average for both males and females (male life expectancy had fallen to 73 and female to 78.5 years). The most recent Central Statistics (2004) report states that life expectancy in Ireland rose in 2002, to 75.1 for males and 80.3 for females[46], and 'the most dramatic increase in life expectancy for both sexes occurred in the past 6 years'. Even so, in 2002, life expectancy for both sexes was lower than the EU 15 average, for both life expectancy at birth and life expectancy at age 65.

Table 3: *Life expectancy at birth 2002*

	Males	Females
Ireland	75.1	80.3
EU 15	75.8	81.6

Source CSO

Table 4 *Life expectancy at age 65*

	Males	Females
Ireland	15.4	18.7
EU 15	16.3	19.9

Source CSO

World Health Organization figures show that Ireland, at 46 per 100,000, has by far the highest death rate for heart disease for those under 65 in the countries in the European Union, the EU average being just 25[47]. In fact, the Department of Health's own website shows that for all major disease groups apart from stroke and motor vehicle accidents, Irish mortality rates are higher than the EU-15 average. This can be seen in Table 5.

Irish death rates compare badly with other EU states

per 100,000 population

	Ireland	EU-15 average
All causes	734.3	687
Ischaemic heart disease	160.2	107.6
Lung cancer	39.4	38.5
Breast cancer	35.2	28.2
Suicide	11.5	10.7
All circulatory diseases	286.8	266.82
All cancers	197.2	187.6
Meningitis	0.4	0.2 males 0.1 females
Stroke	60.9	67.2
Road Traffic Accidents	9.0	10.7

Table 5: *Irish mortality rates are worse than the EU average for almost all diseases except strokes. No allowance has been made in this comparison for the age distribution of the different countries' populations. If this were done, Ireland, with a relatively young population, would fare even worse. The Irish data is for 2001 while the EU data is for 1998*

Source: Department of Health website 2003

E. Health and Relative Income

Before looking at more data to see what actually happened to health in Ireland during the high-growth years, let's look more closely at what researchers have found out about the relationship between health and relative income.

One's health depends on the interplay of many factors. Robin Stott in the Schumacher briefing, *The Ecology of Health* [48] suggests that 80% of our health is determined by factors outside the scope of the conventional healthcare sector. Socio-economic influences on health have been comprehensively explored by Richard Wilkinson of the Trafford Centre for Medical Research at the University of Sussex[49] since the mid-seventies. 'The distribution of income is the single most important determinant of levels of health in the developed world' he writes. 'It has now been demonstrated [many] times using different measures of income distribution from different countries at different dates. About two-thirds of the variation in life expectancy between these countries is related to differences in their income distribution.' This can be seen in figure 8.

Higher national incomes don't always mean better health

GDP per Capita and Life Expectancy OECD Countries, 2000

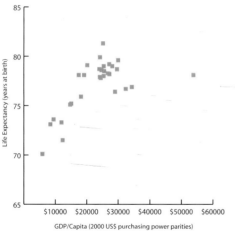

Source: UNDP Human Development Indicators

Figure 7: This graph uses more up-to-date data than that used by Wilkinson. It shows that life expectancy at birth does tend to be longer in countries with higher average incomes per head but that countries with an enormous range of average incomes per head (ranging from less than $20,000 to almost $60,000 in the graph) can have the same life expectancy and that countries with the same or greater average incomes can differ in life expectancy by five or six years. Those countries with the longer life expectancies tend to have smaller income differences between rich and poor as shown in Fig. 8

Wilkinson found that there was no link at all between GDP per capita and life expectancy in twenty-one OECD countries and that the proportion of national income going to the poorest 70 per cent of families explained most of the international variations. Even the proportion of national income devoted to health care had a negligible explanatory effect: He writes:

> Since the early 1970s, Japan has gone from the middle of the field in terms of life expectancy and income distribution to the top in both. Japan now has the highest recorded life expectancy and the most egalitarian income distribution in the world. On the other side of the coin, while Britain's income distribution worsened dramatically during the eighties to produce the largest inequalities for over a century, its relative position in terms of life expectancy has also worsened. Each year since 1985 mortality rates among both men and women between the ages of 16 and 45 have actually risen - a trend which is not attributable to deaths from AIDS[50].

Greater income equality means longer lives.

Income Distribution and Life Expectancy Selected OECD Countries, 2000

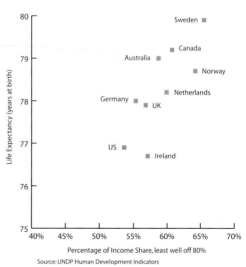

Source: UNDP Human Development Indicators

Figure 8 shows that the more equally national income is distributed, the longer people tend to live. Sweden, which reduces relative poverty by taking a very high proportion of its citizen's incomes in tax and redistributing a lot of that to the less well-off, enables its citizens to live longer than equally rich countries with a bigger gap between rich and poor.

Wilkinson is certain that differences in absolute poverty do not account for the differences in death rates among rich countries. He maintains, for example, that the improvement in the health of people in Japan could not be explained by dietary changes, smoking and other behavioural factors affecting health, in health services and other preventive health policies.

> We are not dealing with the effects of residual poverty in the developed world - there are too few people in absolute poverty in each of the developed countries for their death rates to be the decisive influence (on the overall statistics). Some people in rich countries were unable to eat properly even though they had incomes which were theoretically adequate to cover the cost of essentials because they were forced to buy 'inessentials' like rounds of drinks if they were to participate in ordinary activities in their communities. Others had to live in damp housing. However, neither of these circumstances could account for most of the increase in the gap between death rates. These differences were found after controlling for the effects of average personal disposable income, absolute levels of poverty, smoking, racial difference, and various measures of public or private provision of medical services.

He further states that health inequalities within countries cannot be understood in terms of selective social mobility, genetic differences, and inequalities in health care or health-related behaviour. 'Relative poverty is a demeaning and devaluing experience and a sense of relative deprivation will reduce people's sense of self-worth and self esteem,' which then affected their health. 'What people feel about their housing, he writes, their financial and social circumstances and what that does to their morale is likely to be more important [to their health] than their objective conditions.' Relative poverty, he writes, leads people:

> To feel depressed, cheated, bitter, desperate, vulnerable, frightened, angry, worried about debts or job and housing insecurity; to feel devalued, useless, helpless, uncared for, hopeless, isolated, anxious and a failure: these feelings can dominate people's whole experience of life, colouring their experience of everything else. It is the chronic stress arising from feelings like these, which does the damage. The material environment is merely the indelible mark and constant reminder of the oppressive fact of one's failure, of the atrophy of any sense of having a place in a community, and of one's social exclusion and devaluation as a human being.

This leads him to suggest that health statistics could be used as an indicator of the subjective aspects of the quality of life.

Wilkinson is by no means alone in stressing the importance of relative income to health. Ichiro Kawachi writes[51] in his book The Health of Nations: Why Inequality is harmful to your health 'The degree of income inequality in society explains about three quarters of the variation in life expectancy across countries, whereas by itself, the absolute size of the economic pie (measured by per capita GNP) accounts for less than 10%.' He adds that income inequality and poverty rates could together explain about one quarter of the differences between countries in overall mortality rates, as well as just over half of the variation in murder rates.

Many studies[52] confirm Wilkinson's view that changes in income relationships have profound effects on the health and life expectancy of those experiencing them, with the winners becoming healthier and living longer and the losers doing the reverse.

In The Growth Illusion, Richard Douthwaite[53] reported the adverse health effects associated with economic growth in Britain:

> Elsie Pamuk, who investigated changes in Britain in the mortality rates of men in 143 occupations that could be consistently identified for the span from 1921 to 1971 found that mortality rates for occupations in social class V (such as labourers), tended to improve more rapidly than those for social class I (doctors, accountants, lawyers) in the period up to 1951, when war, economic depression and government policies pushed relative incomes in favour of the less well-off.

> After 1951, however, there was a concentration of national income around the middle of the distribution – both the richest and the poorest 10% lost in relative terms to the middle group although their actual incomes increased. Pamuk's study showed that when the various classes' incomes ceased to converge, the difference between mortality rates ceased to converge as well. This was largely because the absolute death rate of class I people continued to fall while the Class V death rate behaved erratically, even worsening from time to time'.

Later work[54] has shown that the mortality gap between the classes continued to widen until 1991 at least. Douthwaite also reported that Pamuk found that wives' mortality rates moved in parallel with those of their husbands. 'Another study, published by the British Department of Health and Social Security[55] in 1984, showed that children were affected too:

the difference in height between eight-year-old children from the five social classes which had been converging until 1950 remained on a plateau until the end of the 1970s and then began moving apart' he wrote.

How the British income gap has widened since 1960

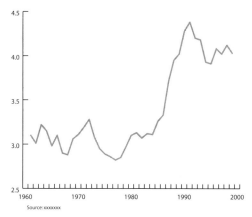

Source: xxxxxx

Figure 9 shows how the income gap between rich and poor in Britain has widened since 1960. The vertical axis measures the ratio between the income received by the highest-paid 10% of the population in comparison with that received by the poorest 10%. It will be seen that in the 1960s and 1970s, the rich earned about three times more than the poor. However, after Mrs. Thatcher came into office in 1979, there was a rapid increase in the incomes of the better-off and now they earn around four times more than the least well-off. Source: Institute for Fiscal Studies.

Anna Lee, chairperson of Combat Poverty Agency in 2000 stated the situation quite clearly ' Poor people get sick more often and die younger than the well-off.... The scale of income difference, the bigger the gap in inequality, the more life expectancy drops'[56].

F. The problems with Irish statistics

Anyone wishing to investigate whether the recent changes in relative incomes have affected Irish health faces enormous problems mainly due to a lack of data. Irish health data is grossly inadequate. This is admitted officially. In relation to children, the Chief Medical Office wrote in The *Health of our Children,* a report published in 2002:[57] 'The description and analysis of the health determinants, health status and service utilization pattern among children given in the report are necessarily limited due to the lack of comprehensive data.'

Nor is the adult situation any better. The following year Dr. Kiely wrote: 'There is increasing interest in the scale and nature of inequalities in health in Ireland. But the discussion is hampered by the lack of quality information. While a substantial amount of data on the Irish health service is collected, drawing inferences on inequalities is not straightforward, primarily because of weaknesses in the data collection systems used.'

The Institute of Public Health agrees. 'The poor quality of occupational data on death records on the island, particularly among people outside the working years and amongst females, severely limits our ability to explore the relationship between socio-economic circumstances and mortality. The absence of other data items such as ethnicity and country of origin imposes further limitations' it stated[58] in 2002 in its publication *Inequalities in Mortality.*

'You will know of those who are <<< poor in the midst of riches, which is the worst of poverties'

Seneca Epistles to Lucilius 88.28, as quoted in The Health of Nations

When data is collected by the health system, no link is usually made between the patient's income, the health problem and the treatment outcome. Only the patient's occupation is recorded so that he or she can be assigned to a socio-economic group. The latter can, of course, be used by researchers as a proxy for a person's income but this may lead to erroneous conclusions. For example, those who are unemployed are categorized according to their previous employment and occupations traditionally associated with low pay, such as hotel work, hairdressing and farm labouring do not have a separate entry in the occupational statistics classification.

Nevertheless, even the limited data shows a marked discrepancy in health status between the socio-economic groups. *Inequalities in Mortality* examined mortality data between 1989 and 1998. It found that mortality from all causes in the occupational classes associated with lower

What a difference one's income makes

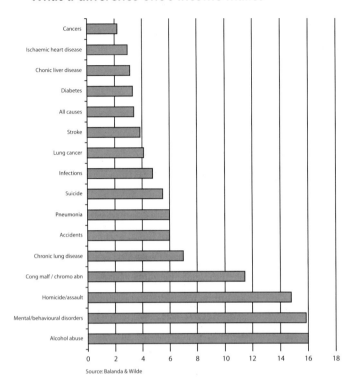

Source: Balanda & Wilde

Figure 10 This graph, showing data from the years 1989-1998, compares the death rates from various diseases of the richest and poorest socioeconomic groups. It shows, for example, that the poorest have twice the likelihood of dying from cancer and 16 times the chance of dying from alcohol abuse as the most prosperous members of our society.

Source: K. Balanda and J. Wilde in *Health in Ireland – an unequal state* Public Health Alliance Ireland, Institute of Public Health, 2004

rates of pay was 100-200% higher than the rate in the occupational classes associated with higher pay. For circulatory diseases it was 120% higher, for respiratory diseases it was over 200% higher, for injuries and poisoning, it was 150% higher and for cancers it was 100% higher. The overall all-cause mortality rate in the Republic was 6% higher than the North. Unfortunately, this study amalgamated data for the years 1989-1998, making it impossible to distinguish trends during this period of massive economic change and to ascertain if there was a link with income. There are no plans to repeat this analysis using data from the most recent census[59].

Even the results in *Inequalities in Mortality* may be underestimating the problem. A 2001 study by the Department of Community Health at Trinity College, Dublin[60] found that the socio-economic group with the highest mortality rates was 'unknown'. It accounted for 14% of all deaths in 1981, rising to 24% in 1996. This category had a higher standardized mortality ratio for all-cause mortality, ischaemic heart disease, cancer, injuries and poisoning than every other socio-

economic category. Over a third of people who were admitted to a psychiatric hospital had a classification of 'unknown' socio-economic group. The authors state that this could reflect either a lessening of standards in data coding and collection, or a genuine increase in the number of people in very poor health whose socio-economic group could not be identified.

Low birth-weight

The standard of data compilation and publication has certainly fallen in one key area – the perinatal statistics. It has been established that, in general, the incidence of low birth-weight is higher in babies born to poorer mothers than in babies born to more affluent ones. Consequently, one of the first effects of an increase in inequality could be a rise in the number of low birth-weight babies. Unfortunately information on birth-weights is not published promptly. The 1999 figures were only published in 2002 and the figures for 1993-1998 have not been compiled at all, although the data was collected. This has made it very difficult to follow trends during the high-growth period.

This matters because research by Professor David Barker,[61] an epidemiologist at Southampton University, has shown that underweight babies are much more likely to develop heart disease, high blood pressure, diabetes and kidney and liver problems in later life. This may be because their bodies diverted the poor supply of nutrients their mothers provided in the womb away from their vital organs to ensure that their brains, at least, developed fairly well. Some workers think, however, that their brains could be permanently locked in 'fight or flight' mode. If true, this could partially explain the high incidence of crime and behavioural problems among deprived groups.

From the national point of view, the birth of an underweight baby is a double tragedy. It is bad for the community, who will have to shoulder the expense of providing medical (and possibly custodial) care for the new individual for a lot of his or her life. It is worse, however, much worse, for the family and the baby concerned, as it will have to put up with chronic illnesses and never develop its full potential.

In 1998, research by the Southern Health Board[62] found that the high infant mortality figures for Cork City were caused by low birth-weight, congenital abnormalities and infant death syndrome. It associated these with the high levels of social deprivation in the city. The report found that despite 'significant overall improvements in infant mortality in the SHB area, infants born into the lower socio-economic area (Cork City) continue to experience higher relative risks of mortality in comparison with those born in the higher socio-economic areas'.

In the absence of official national low birth-weight statistics from 1994-1998, I compared the birth-weights of babies born to mothers who were confined in public wards (as a proxy for mothers on lower incomes) and who tend to have a higher proportion of babies with low birth-weight, with the birth-weights of babies born to mothers who were confined in private wards in a large Irish maternity hospital over the years 1995 to 2000. One fifth of the babies born to women in the public wards weighed less than 3kg, in 1995, and this remained the same in 2000, while the percentage of low birthweight babies in the private wards had fallen from 14.8% to 10.6%. In other words, economic growth and the reduction in absolute poverty did nothing to reduce the number of low birthweight babies being born to the poorer section of the population.

This result was confirmed by the publication in 2002 of the 1999 perinatal statistics, which showed that the proportion of babies born in 1999 with low birth-weight was significantly higher than in the early 1990s. Furthermore, the perinatal mortality figures for babies from poorer homes had worsened seriously since that time. In 1993, the perinatal mortality rates for single babies born to fathers who were classified as being manual unskilled workers and unemployed were 6.2 and 7.9 per thousand respectively. By 1999, the corresponding figures were 10.7 and 11.4. The figures for babies with fathers classified as higher professionals had improved, however, falling from 5.0 in 1993 to 3.5 in 1999. So the gap I had been trying to measure in one Dublin hospital had clearly widened in the country overall. Again, economic growth was clearly not benefiting everyone equally.

More underweight babies

1990	4.18
1991	4.23
1992	4.13
1993	4.18
1999	4.99

Table 6 shows that the percentage of babies born with low birth-weights increased by 20% between 1993 and 1999. The increase appears to have been concentrated in babies born to parents on lower incomes.

Figure 11 shows that the decline in infant mortality after 1990 stopped during the high growth years and may have resumed since. The ESRI data suggests that the plateau may have been due to the fact that the survival rate of children born into affluent families continued to improve while the death rate in poor families worsened, the two trends canceling each other out.

The 2003 edition of the report *Better Health for Everyone* from the Department of Health states that the infant mortality rate in Ireland is second highest in the EU-15 at 6.2, the EU-15 average being 5.2. Only Greece is worse. However, the reasons for infant mortality are complex and the report suggests that 'variations in practice relating to the registration of deaths' might be

194557

GALWAY COUNTY LIBRARIES

responsible. The same report states that the Irish perinatal mortality rate at 10.00 is the highest in the EU-15, the average being 7.7. Part of the difference here however, could be due to the fact that abortion is not carried out in Ireland on babies with serious congenital malformations who may then die after they are born.

No improvement in proportion of babies dying at birth

Infant and Perinatal Mortality per 1,000 live births (1991-2002*)

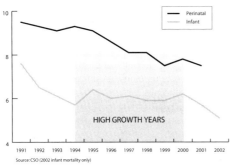

Source: CSO (2002 infant mortality only)

Figure 11 shows that, although the proportion of babies dying at or near birth (perinatal deaths, the upper line above) continued to improve between 1994 and 2000, the long run improvement in Ireland's infant mortality figures marked time during the high growth period.

Other data problems

Here's a round-up of some of the other statistical difficulties I came across in the course of this research:

1. The National Disease Surveillance Centre is concentrating on infectious diseases which caused only 0.6% of deaths in 1999, the last year for which such information is available. They do not collect information on income.

2. Ireland does not have national registers for asthma, diabetes, depression, arthritis, and most other common disorders despite the fact that they account for a high proportion of all healthcare activity. This means that we can neither assess the incidence of these diseases nor examine an association with income.

3. The Irish National Cancer Registry does not record income.

4. HIPE (Hospital In-Patient Enquiry), which reports activity in Irish hospitals, does not note socio-economic status or income.

5. Data on prescriptions is only analyzed for medical cardholders, whose income is extremely low. This prevents investigations into the differences in health status between people on low incomes with medical cards and those on higher incomes who don't.

6. Although farmers are one of the groups worst affected by relative poverty, those compiling the report *Inequalities in Mortality* were unable to analyze their mortality figures because of inadequacies in the data.

7. Although the height of British schoolchildren was found to track their socioeconomic circumstances, it is not possible to follow height trends of Irish schoolchildren because, although they were being measured regularly by the schools medical service, measuring methods do not appear to be standardized and accurate socio-economic details are not recorded. As a former schools doctor, I was particularly interested in following this issue up and wrote to the Department of Health to ask if the data had been analyzed in any way. I received no reply.

8. No income records are kept on people who are eligible for the long-term illness card scheme.

9. The Census Office changed the way it assigned the living to socio-economic groups in 1996 without a corresponding change being made in the death classifications. This highlights the need for a coordinated approach to addressing the issue of monitoring trends in health.

In summary, although income inequality plays a significant role in determining illness and mortality, the relevant data is not collected routinely.

G. What the available statistics do show

There are no long-run, consistent time-series showing trends in the nation's overall health in a way that can be related to trends in the distribution of income. There are however two Irish studies on the issue. One is a study[63] from the European Foundation for the Improvement of Living and Working Conditions, which relates self-assessed health in Ireland to income. This was published in 2002 and compares the proportion of the poorest fifth of the population saying they were experiencing bad health with that of the richest fifth. The results were shocking. Those in the lowest fifth (quintile) in Ireland were over eight times more likely to say that they had bad or very bad health compared to those in the top quintile, far higher than any other EU country. The Irish figure of 8.3 compares with 4 in Denmark, 2.6 in France and 1.6 in Germany. The next worst figures after Ireland were from Greece at 5.7. Furthermore, a recent study from the Irish Institute of Public Health[64] found that people on the lowest incomes are 52% less likely to be very satisfied with their health compared with people on the highest incomes.

Suicide

If people feel badly about themselves they may think of suicide and the rate at which suicide is increasing among young Irish men is the fastest in the world[65]. It trebled in adolescents in the past decade[66] to become the most common cause of death among 15-24 year olds. Since 1997, all deaths by suicide have been consistently higher than the number of deaths from road traffic accidents[67]. Ireland has the second highest young male suicide rate in the world[68] and is the only EU country where youth suicide continues to rise.[69] Concern has been expressed that suicide may still be under reported.[70] The national chairperson of the mental health association GROW, Jean Hasset, stated in the organization's annual report for 2001 that high suicide rates 'did not represent the full extent of the despair that is rampant among Ireland's men and women and were little more than a record of those who had succeeded'[71]. Rates of suicide in young women doubled in past ten years, and violence and aggression in young women were cited as possible reasons.[72]

The experience of being a young Irish person in 2002 is one of 'personal loneliness, lack of purpose and engagement' according to a draft report from the National Economic and Social Forum.[73] In a youth poll, carried out by *The Irish Times* and published[74] in September 2003, it was found that 55% of those aged 15-24 knew somebody in their age group who had committed or had attempted to commit suicide. It is a sobering reflection on our society that each health board has its own 'suicide resource officer'.

In 2000, the first ever large-scale Irish epidemiological study to examine rates of psychiatric illness among young people[75], found that one fifth of adolescents were at risk of developing psychiatric disorders. Another report, *'The male perspective - Young men's outlook on life study'* released in January 2004 by the Mid Western Health Board, and referred to earlier, found that half of those surveyed had contemplated suicide at one time, and 4% had actually planned it.

The National Suicide Research Foundation has developed a parasuicide (attempted suicide) registry, the first of its kind in the world. Parasuicide rates among teenage girls aged between 15 and 19 have outstripped all other age specific rates among men and women, making them the most vulnerable group[76]. The registry's second report, for 2002 but issued in 2004, found that the incidence had increased from 2001, but also reported that not all hospitals participated in this survey. The peak rate of parasuicide was in girls aged 15-19, at 626 per 100,000. This figure indicates that 1 in every 160 girls in this age group presented to hospital after a suicide attempt. The highest rate was at age 17, when 1 in every 140 girls presented to hospital after an attempt. The peak rate for men appeared to be in the 20-24 age group, at 407 per 100,000.

A 2003 report by the South Eastern Health Board, *An Overview of Suicide*, notes that parasuicide is a growing phenomenon among adolescents, reflecting their feeling of helplessness and hopelessness in coping with life stresses, their impulsiveness in relationship breakdown, and the vulnerability of those with poor education, low incomes or no employment. 'The increase of affluence and material well-being has been met with a parallel increase in societal pressures that some young children cannot cope with' Paul Gilligan, the chief executive of the ISPCA[77], said when commenting on the shocking statistic that 201 children aged between 10 and 14 were treated in Irish hospitals for attempted suicide in 2002. Over €4.5 million will be spent in 2004 to try to reduce the suicide and attempted suicide rates.[78] Unfortunately, these and other mental health services will tend to be concentrated in areas of highest affluence, not in areas of greatest need[79].

Male suicide increases during economic growth spurt

Suicide Deaths per 100,000 of Population
1990-2001

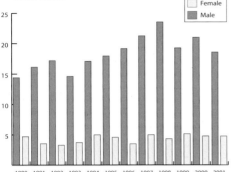

Figure 12 shows that while the number of women committing suicide stayed fairly constant during the high growth years, there was a marked rise in the number of men taking their own lives.

Alcohol and drug use

Many people deal with stress by turning to drink or drugs. And they did. 'Against the backdrop of the fastest growing economy in Europe, Ireland has had the highest increase in alcohol consumption among EU countries,' a government report[80] stated. 'Between 1989 and 1999, alcohol consumption per capita in Ireland increased by 41%, while ten of the European Union member states showed a decrease and three other countries showed a modest increase during the same period.' Ireland's consumption continued to increase in 2000 and ranked second after Luxembourg for alcohol consumption with a rate of 11 litres of pure alcohol per head of population or 14.2 litres per adult. The EU average for 2000 was 9.1 litres per head. The same report noted that while alcohol consumption per adult had been gradually rising over the previous 40 years 'since 1995, there has been a dramatic increase in consumption'. Irish alcohol consumption was below the EU average until 1996, when it began its rapid ascent[81].

Big increase in Irish alcohol consumption

Hospitals came under pressure as a result. A pilot study undertaken in the Mater Hospital in Dublin found that one in four attendances was alcohol related.[82] 'The health service is creaking and groaning and is collapsing under the weight of our new lifestyle. The nation is richer than it has

Change in alcohol consumption

Capita 1989-99 (%)

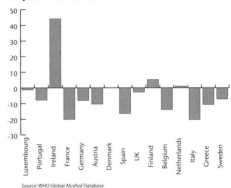

Source: WHO Global Alcohol Database

Figure 13 shows that, while almost every other EU country reduced its consumption of alcohol between 1989 and 1999, the increasingly wealthy Irish boosted their drinking by over 40%. The health service and the police were put under pressure as a result.

ever been and yet the health service is under severe pressure because of this lifestyle' an Accident and Emergency consultant in Cork University Hospital told a conference on alcohol in November 2003.

Drinking rises in step with increasing incomes

Alcohol Consumption litres pure
alcohol/capita, Ireland 1969-99

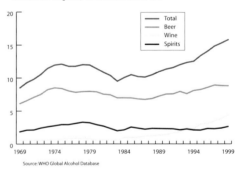

Source: WHO Global Alcohol Database

Figure 14 shows that an increase in wine consumption accounted for a large proportion of the rise in the average Irish person's alcoholic intake since the early 1980s. The rate at which consumption increased accelerated during the boom years.

Alcohol abuse is also a problem with older people. One in five Irish people are now drinking in a manner that is either harmful or hazardous to their health and Dr. Ann Hope, National

Alcohol Policy Advisor at the Department of Health and Children, has stated that suicide, cirrhosis, crisis pregnancies, and sexually-transmitted disease have risen dramatically with the increase in the consumption of alcohol.

According to a 2003 report comparing drinking patterns in Ireland with six other European countries,[83] half of all Irish men now binge-drink at least once a week, the highest in the countries surveyed, and 16% of Irish women do too, which was also higher than the other European countries studied. 12.4% of Irish men said that their alcohol consumption affected their ability to do their job, again the highest of all countries surveyed. 11.5% of men had 'got into a fight', three times the EU average, 9.6% said that friendships had been harmed and 6.3% had been in an accident as a result of drinking, both figures again the highest percentage. Alcohol is a factor in a quarter of visits to casualty in Irish hospitals, thirty percent of road accidents and forty percent of fatal accidents. It is also associated with one in three cases of marital breakdown and public order offences. The economic cost of 'alcohol harm' has been estimated at €2.3 billion[84].

Big increase in alcohol-related offences

Alcohol Related Offences 1995-2000

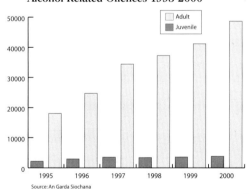

Source: An Garda Siochana

Figure 15 shows just how rapidly the number of alcohol-related offences rose during the high-growth years. Surprisingly, in view of the increase in drinking among young people, it was adults rather than juveniles who were responsible for the rise.

The *Interim Report on Alcohol*[85] highlighted the link between alcohol and street violence. 'Of particular concern is the increase in intoxication in public places among teenagers which has risen by 370% since 1996,' it said, adding that in

the five-year period between 1996-2000, assaults and public order offences by adults increased by 97%. The Garda Commissioner highlighted the link between alcohol and the rise in street violence.

Changes in the behaviour of Irish schoolchildren in the 15-16 year old age group between 1995 and 1999 were examined by ESPAD, the European School Survey Project on Alcohol and Other Drugs (See figure 16). The study covered alcohol, tobacco and drug use by schoolchildren in 26 European countries. It found that there had been a marked deterioration in behaviour patterns between the two years among Irish participants and that Ireland ranked among the highest of all participating countries in relation to alcohol and illicit drug use. The proportion of Irish participants who reported using alcohol ten or more times in the previous 30 days had increased. This was particularly true for the girls, whose rate had almost doubled. The number of Irish students of both sexes who reported having been drunk on three or more occasions in the previous 30 days rose from 15 per cent to 24 per cent, ranking Ireland joint second with the UK for this indicator.

Schoolchildren become heavy drinkers and illegal drug users

Key Health Behaviours Children under 16 years (%)

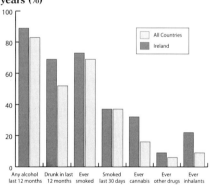

Source: ESPAD Report, 1999 (Ireland and All Participant Countries)

Figure 16 presents the results from a study in 26 European countries which showed that Irish sixteen-year-olds were among the heaviest users of drink and drugs. Moreover, their consumption increased between 1995 and 1999.

There is no sign that the situation has improved since 1999. A survey[86] of 2,297 post-primary students in 2003 found that 39% had used drugs, an increase of 10% on a 1998 study. It was also noted that the number of teenagers who had used inhalants had increased by almost 8% to 21.3% in the four years since 1998, with 6.8% having used inhalants in the previous month, compared with 2.7% in 1998. Another survey, this time of 1,200 secondary school teachers in 2003, found that a third of teachers had taught in classes where students were under the influence of alcohol or drugs[87]. Furthermore, a 2003 report from the Drug Treatment Centre Board found that rates of opiate, cannabis, benzodiazepines, cannabis and ecstasy use remained high, and cocaine abuse was increasing[88].

A survey[89] of 2,297 post primary students carried out in the Mid West region in 2002 found that rates of smoking and drinking had increased since a similar survey four years previously. It found that over a fifth of 14-year-olds reported that they had been 'binge drinking' or had consumed five consecutive drinks in the 30 days before the survey, and 44% of 16-year-olds had been drunk in the month before the survey. And the stark reality of the alcohol problem among young people was illustrated by an analysis of patients admitted for acute alcohol intoxication to Mayo General Hospital in 2000[90]. Of all admissions under the age of 16, 30% had been found in the open, comatose and alone.

Obesity and diabetes increasing

Besides alcohol and drugs, stressed, anxious people also comfort themselves by eating. This may be a contributory factor in the rise in obesity. Recent research has shown that people who are struggling socially tend to have low self-esteem which in turn is reflected in their diet and tendency to obesity'[91]. Since 1990, the prevalence of obesity in Ireland has increased by 250% in men and by 125% in women. In 2002, 14% of men were obese, up from 11% in 1998, and 12% of women were obese in 2002, up from 9% in 1998[92]. At present, one in eight Irish people is obese and every second person is overweight[93] 'There has been an alarming increase in both diabetes and obesity in the past ten years' according to Professor John Nolan of Trinity College, Dublin, a consultant endocrinologist, speaking at the launch of a new study on obesity. An international study carried out in 13 countries found that Ireland had one of the highest proportions of overweight teenagers[94]. An all-Ireland survey, undertaken in 2001 and 2002, found that of 18,000 children, one in three 4 year olds were overweight[95].

'Obesity-related type 2 diabetes is presenting at younger ages than in the past, and is now seen in young teenagers in Ireland'[96] (Type 2 diabetes is usually more common in obese people over the age of 40). Ireland was one of the first countries to report type 2 diabetes in young people[97]. In 2003 Professor Nolan[98], stated that 'Ireland will drown in diabetes' if the current trend continues, warning that obesity-related conditions such as polycystic ovary syndrome would reach epidemic proportions. He had seen a doubling of the number of patients referred to him in the previous three years.

The medical director of the VHI (Voluntary Health Insurance) is also alarmed. In 2003[99] she described childhood obesity as a time bomb and said that obesity was storing up problems for future health care provision. Indeed, the Irish environment has been called 'obesegenic' by a principal investigator in an international study on childhood obesity[100] referring to the fact that 'most families had two cars and used a remote control for their TV.'

Obesity is an important risk factor for heart disease, blood pressure, stroke, diabetes, and increases the risk of cancers of the breast, bowel, womb, ovary and prostate. Mortality as a result of cardiovascular disease is almost 50% higher in obese patients than in those of average weight, and is 90% higher in these with morbid obesity, which is defined as a Body Mass Index greater than 40. If the Body Mass Index is greater than 30, there is also an increased risk of diabetes, if it is over 40, there is a 90% chance. (The Body Mass Index takes into account an adult's weight and height to gauge total body fat, and thus whether they are obese.)

A 2003 study showed that the average Irish schoolchild eats 50% less fresh fruit and vegetables than he or she did five years ago and that they spend 15 hours a week watching television.[101] The Central Statistics Office reported that the proportion of primary school children walking to school declined from 47% in 1981 to 26% in 2002 even though most children lived near their schools. The proportion of children being driven increased from 19.7% in 1981 to 50.3% in 2002, with most of the increase occurring since 1991[102]. Obesity is causing pressure on health services and a special clinic treating children with diabetes stopped taking new referrals because it was unable to cope with the numbers attending[103].

In a nationwide survey of general practitioners[104] 68% indicated that their workload had increased due to the surge in obesity. Studies in countries where the prevalence of obesity is similar to Ireland indicate that its direct costs are between 2% and 6% of the national health care budget. Despite this drain on resources and the fact that a 2003 survey[105] showed that 44% of young people knew somebody with an eating disorder, no research has been carried out to date in Ireland on the incidence these complaints[106]. A task force has been established by the Minster for Health to examine the country's obesity problem[107].

It will be interesting to see if the task force reaches the same conclusion as Lord Haskins, food advisor to the British government, who stated at a conference on food in Dublin in 2004 that obesity [108] 'is not an ignorance issue, it is a despair issue.... If you could solve the problem of poverty, you would solve 80% of diet problems. The 20% of middle-class people who eat too much can be left to sort it out for themselves'.

H. Other signs that health deteriorated

More prescriptions issued to people on low incomes

The only data available on the number of prescriptions written in Ireland refers to people whose income is low enough for them to have been able to obtain a medical card. It is astonishing that no record is kept of prescriptions issued to non-medical card holders. However, as can be seen from Figure 17, although the number of people covered by the medical card system in the years 1985-2001 declined as incomes rose, the total number of prescriptions issued went up, as did the number of items per prescription. This could indicate that the health of those on lower incomes had declined. The recent report from the Institute of Public Health on inequalities found that people on lowest incomes were 52% less likely to be very satisfied with their health.

A report[109] in 2002 found that medical card holders had higher incidences of cardiovascular disease, stroke, hypertension, asthma, osteoarthritis, skin cancer and all other cancers,

The poor get sicker

Medical Cards, Scripts and Prescription Items ('000s), 1985-2001

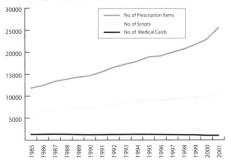

Figure 17 shows that although the numbers of people holding medical cards (the bottom line) declined somewhat between 1985 and 2001, they were issued with more prescriptions by their doctors (the middle line) and that these prescriptions had more drug requisitions on them, so that the number of items dispensed rose as shown by the top line. In fact, the number of items per prescription rose from 1.9 in 1985, to 2.05 in 1995 and 2.44 in 2001. This suggests that the health of the average medical card holder deteriorated over the period.

underactive thyroid, kidney stones, osteoporosis, gallstones, duodenal and gastric ulcers, and diabetes. A further report[110] found that 52.9% of medical card holders suffered from one or more health conditions, in contrast to 22.7% of private insurance holders. It is interesting to note that only 13.9% of medical cardholders said that their health was excellent, in contrast to 36.2% of those who had private insurance. In another study, 90% of those without medical cards reported both better health and quality of life whereas the corresponding figures for medical card holders were only 70% and 60% respectively. Professor Cecily Kelleher, one of the authors, commented that the difference was due to medical card status and was not related to whether their sample lived in an urban or a rural area.[111]

In 2002, €50 million were spent on anti-depressants and mood stabilizers, up a staggering €42 million since 1993. Department of Health figures indicated that more than one in six medical card holders was taking anti-depressants[112].

More people with longstanding illnesses

The number of people carrying a long-term illness card rose steadily between 1992-2001; from 14.2 per 1000 in 1992, to 17.7 in 1996 and to 22.9 in 2001. This card has been issued since

1991 to those with illnesses such as diabetes, epilepsy and spina bifida. (The full list comprises hydrocephalus, muscular dystrophy, parkinsonism, acute leukaemia, multiple sclerosis, diabetes insipidus, diabetes mellitus, cerebral palsy, haemophilia, cystic fibrosis, phenylketonuria, mental handicap and mental illness.)

More cancers in men

The 2003 report of the National Cancer Registry states that allowing for the effects of population change and ageing, the overall true risk of developing cancer is increasing by 0.6% per annum for men but is not increasing for women [113].

Conclusion

The only major instances of improved health I could find to set against the catalogue of decline we have just reviewed was in mortality from two great causes of death in Ireland, cancer and heart disease, but the statistical information is not adequate to allow us to say whether the gains were shared equally by all sections of society. As a result, I can definitely say as a public health doctor that the health of some sections of the Irish population deteriorated seriously during the high growth years. Moreover, I think that the deterioration is likely to accelerate in future because the full effects of prolonged stress and the recent changes in lifestyle have not yet become apparent.

I also believe that the shifts in relative income brought about by economic growth were largely responsible for the deterioration. The evidence is convincing and could become absolutely conclusive if proper statistics were kept. I will comment more widely at the end of the next section.

Part Two

A. Did growth improve the social environment?

'The concept of social capital ... couldn't be simpler. Do you trust people? How many clubs, societies or social groups are you a member of? If your child gets sick, do you have support to call on? Basically how much social contact do you have in your life? These social ties, according to research, will help you live longer and are probably worth money to the economy' a submission from Cork County Council included in a 2003 National Economic and Social Forum (NESF) report[114] states. Unfortunately, however, besides damaging physical and mental health, the increase in income inequality during the high-growth period appears to have depleted social capital by diminishing people's sense of belonging and their feelings of community and reducing the cohesiveness of society as a result.

More and more research shows that people living in unequal societies tend to have lower rates of involvement in community activities and lower levels of trust and that these reductions have inescapable psychosocial effects. Low levels of social capital have been found to be associated with relative deprivation and violent crime, including homicide (that is, murder and manslaughter), assault and robbery. In fact, Wilkinson[115] writes that the association between unequal income distribution and both homicide and violent crime is even stronger than it is for mortality.

In a US study[116] income inequality was found to be linked with decreased social capital when that was assessed according to the number of groups to which people belonged and their level of social trust as reflected by their responses to the question 'Do you think most people would take advantage of you if they got the chance?' There was also a strong correlation between income inequality, firearms offences and homicide. In another American study[117] of over 32,000 men, it was found that strong social networks (as measured by membership of church or community groups, having more than six friends), led to lower mortality by reducing deaths from cardiovascular disease, accidents and suicide. This study also found that strong social networks were associated with a reduced incidence of stroke, and were also found to possibly prolong the survival of men with established coronary heart disease. Similar results were found in a study based on data from 39 US states, where it was found that income inequality led to increased mortality via lowered social capital[118].

While researching his book 'Bowling Alone'[119], Robert Putnam found that social capital had declined in the US, due to pressures of time and money, especially in two-income families; the distance traveled to work, and the time spent watching television. His review of the research into the effects of this decline led him to state that, statistically speaking, the evidence for the health consequences of social disconnectedness was as strong today as the link between smoking and cancer was at the time of the first Surgeon

Decline in the public's confidence in Irish Institutions

	% Trusting each institution 'a great deal' to be honest and fair 2001	% Trusting each institution 'a great deal' to be honest and fair 2004	Change
The Gardai	23%	14%	-39%
The Church	18%	9%	-50%
Supermarkets	14%	7%	-50%
The Legal system	12%	5%	-58%
The health service	11%	7%	-37%
The media	9%	3%	-67%
The government	9%	3%	-67%

Table 7 shows the extent to which the public's confidence in Irish institutions deteriorated between 2001 and 2004.

General's report on smoking. He writes that more than a dozen large studies over the past twenty years have shown that people who are socially disconnected are between two and five times more likely to die from all causes compared with individuals who have close ties with family, friends and the community. The more integrated a society is, he says, the less likely people are to die prematurely or to get heart attacks, strokes, cancer, and depression. It is therefore not surprising that the Irish study by Patricia Casey[120] I mentioned earlier found that people who had difficulty in getting practical help from their neighbours were more likely to have depressive disorders. Furthermore, it has been found that people who have infrequent contact with their friends are 31% less likely to have to have excellent or very good mental health and 24% less likely to have a high general mental health score[121].

Social capital may improve our health by stimulating the immune system and buffering stress. As Robin Stott says[122] 'Health is as much a collective as an individual value, more dependent on networks than genes'.

(i) Democratic participation and social capital reduced

If one accepts the evidence that increased inequality damages social capital, the implications of the widening incomes gap in Ireland are profound. We can expect to find that, besides poorer health, violence has increased, that people have become more isolated and trust

each other less. We might also find that a change Kawachi[123] predicts has come about and that the lower levels of social trust have spilled over to create a lack of trust and confidence in government and that this has led to lower voter turnouts.

So what actually happened during the high growth years? The NESF survey did find that both interpersonal trust and levels of election turnout had declined during the 1990s and that only 25% of the survey's respondents agreed with the statement 'most people can be trusted'. Moreover, the 2004 Amarach study[124] referred to earlier reported that the number of people who trusted institutions such as the Gardai, the legal system, the church, media, government, health service and supermarkets 'a great deal' to be honest and fair had fallen between 2001 and 2004. This can be seen in table 7.

This lack of trust has an impact on health. The Institute of Public Health[125] has reported that compared to those who trust most of their neighbours, people who do not trust most of their neighbours are 24% less likely to have excellent or very good general health and 20% less likely to have a very good quality of life.

Voter turnout in presidential, local, general and European elections certainly shows a downward trend and that in 2002 was the lowest in the history of the state despite the polling stations being open for the longest time ever (15 hours) and government campaigns to encourage people register to vote. The higher turnout in the 2004 elections may have been associated with three separate votes taking place on the same day. The Institute of Public Health's report[126] 'Inequalities in perceived health – A report on the All-Ireland Social Capital and Health Survey', did not assess voting patterns; however, in the US, 90% of people in families with incomes over $75,000 tend to vote in presidential elections, but only half with incomes under $15,000. The result is that politicians become more interested in issues affecting the affluent, in turn narrowing the circle of social concern and political responsibility[127].

In 2003, social capital was reported[128] to be so low in some disadvantaged communities in Ireland that some families were unable to engage in any activities outside their homes because of low incomes, a lack of social supports and a fear of crime. The NESF study reported that half of those surveyed had not made a social visit in the previous four weeks excluding those to family members and other relatives. A startling 82.5% had not attended a public meeting, and only 5.5% had joined an action group of any kind in the previous year. Furthermore, the report added that surveys had shown that the number of people prepared to volunteer had declined from 38.2% in 1992 to 35.1% in 1994 and 33.3% in 1997/8. 'Increased work pressure, commuting and other factors are beginning to impinge on patterns of social contact and network support' it reported, echoing Putnam's US findings.

The extra traveling time to work was confirmed by the CSO's 2002 *Statistical Report*. Workers on average traveled 9.8 miles from home to work in 2001, up from 6.7 miles six years earlier while those living in rural areas travelled over twice as far as their counterparts had done twenty years before. Rural-based workers travelled over twice as far to work in 2002 as they did in 1982. The time taken by the extra travel left less for social activities. Putnam found this too and reported an inverse relationship between the two time uses.

(ii) Membership of voluntary organizations declines

The Irish have gone for a 'work hard, play hard' ethos, which leaves little place for altruism beyond the immediate family'. Amarach report 2002

When a sample of Irish people was asked in 1989 what they would do if they had more money, 48% replied that they 'would help a good cause,' followed by 'enjoy myself more'. When the same question was asked in 2001, however, the order was reversed and only 25% said they would

help a good cause while the proportion saying that they would enjoy themselves more had risen to 57%[129].

After I read in the NESF report that eighty percent of the population was not involved in local community groups or in any type of volunteering, I asked a sample of voluntary organizations if they had problems recruiting members. The results were disturbing. None reported an increase in membership in recent years.

• The Irish Girl Guides Association reported a 'dramatic drop' in membership and in the number of adult volunteers since 1990.
• The Scouting Association also reported a decline in membership since 1990.
• The Irish Red Cross said that it found it more difficult to recruit volunteers and that their numbers were down.
• Both the Lions and Rotary clubs reported a reduction in membership
• The St. Vincent de Paul society noted that the time commitment that members gave was less than in previous years.
• The Parent Teacher Association reported that both participation levels and membership numbers had decreased over the last five years.

Again, this reflects the US experience. According to Putnam, the American groups whose membership is rising most rapidly are those in which the only commitment is to pay a subscription and receive a newsletter. He notes that the bonds of loyalty in this situation are to symbols, leaders or ideals and not to other people. This also has significance for health; there is evidence[130] that those who have not been actively involved in local organizations are 37% less likely to be very satisfied with their health and 20% less likely to have a very good quality of life.

(iii) Criminal offences increase

Recorded crime, apart from murder, fell between 1995 to 2000, as can be seen in Figure 18. This could have been because it became easier for potential offenders to fulfill their economic aspirations by getting a job in the legitimate economy. A British Home Office study found[131] that when the economy grew and more jobs were created for relatively poorly-educated young men the number of offences grew at a slower pace, but when the economy slowed, the crime rate caught up with its long-term rising trend line. This might be the reason that the most recent garda reports shown that total offences in the ten 'headline offences' categories (homicide, assaults, sexual offences, arson, drug offences, theft, burglaries, robberies, fraud and 'other') went up by 18% in 2001 and by a further 22% in 2002[132], years in which the growth rate had slowed down. Certainly, homeless young men who could have obtained work at the height of the boom were finding it very difficult to do so as a result of the slowdown, Fr. Peter McVerry told a conference in Dundalk in March 2004.

While theft, drug dealing and burglary might be 'economic' offences, murder and manslaughter generally aren't and Wilkinson[133] cites a study which found that income inequality accounted for 35% of the difference in homicide rates between the 46 US states for which there was data. A similar relationship seems to hold in Ireland as Irish murder rates increased very significantly in the high growth decade. They rose from 0.69 per 100,000 in 1994 to 1.08 in 2000 and 1.43 in 2001. In the latter year, 52 murders took place, a far cry from Ireland in 1949 when just one murder was recorded[134].

Dr. Ian O'Donnell, the author of a major report on murders in Ireland, *Unlawful Killing, Past and Present* states[135] that 'contributory factors cited as possible explanations for the increase in the murder rates, include the rise in alcohol consumption, dissatisfaction among those left behind by the Celtic Tiger, demographic changes and the rise in gangland feuding'. He adds: 'An unequal society creates a context for violent crime.'

Prosecutions for public order offences increased by 161%[136] between 1996 and 2001. Intoxication in a public place and threatening, abusive or insulting words or behaviour were the most frequent charges and accounted for almost 80 per cent of proceedings taken in 2001. Between 1996 and 2001 the number of public order related referrals to the Garda Juvenile Diversion Programme grew by 162 per cent; almost identical to the growth in proceedings taken. The most striking change was in referrals for intoxication in a public place, which increased seven-fold. In a survey of 27 garda divisions undertaken in 1997[137] by the Garda Research Unit, it was found that alcohol was a factor in 88% of public order cases, 54% of criminal damages and 48% of offences against the person.

In the light of the rise in these crimes, it is not surprising that a Garda survey[138] revealed in

Murder rate up, other crime down

All Crime & Murder Rates 1990-2000

Figure 18 *shows that, while the murder rate increased in the second half of the 1990s, the incidence of other crimes declined between 1990 and 2000 when allowance is made for the rise in population. (The crime data is per thousand people and uses the scale on the left while the murder rate is per 100,000 people and uses the scale on the right.) This decline in crime could have been because the potential criminals found that they had more legitimate opportunities open to them.*

2002 that a quarter of people felt unsafe walking in their neighbourhoods after dark. 44% of the respondents said they felt less safe than six years previously and the same number also said that crime was rising in their areas. 84% of the respondents believed that crime was rising in Ireland as a whole. An Irish study found that people who feel unsafe after dark are 56% less likely to be free of longterm illness[139] compared to those who feel otherwise. This illustrates the link between social capital and health. Even young people were concerned. In a survey[140] of 1000 people aged 15-24, 77% said in 2003 that they were concerned about the level of crime and street violence. Their level of concern was marginally higher in Dublin.

(iv) More people become homeless

The rapid rise in house prices during the boom years meant that number of people who could not afford housing rose almost fourfold between 1993 and 2002. Furthermore, the number of families assessed as needing social housing increased by 70% in the past six years[141]. This figure almost certainly understates the situation. The Focus Ireland website points out that it does not necessarily include those who are involuntarily sharing with family or friends or not accessing services for the homeless. Furthermore, it states that many single people do not register for housing waiting lists as they know that will be given a low priority.

Housing lists lengthen and homelessness goes up

Homelessness & Social Housing Waiting Lists 1989-2002

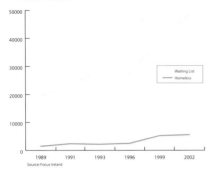

Source: Focus Ireland

Figure 19 shows that the number of people who were on a waiting list for social housing rose more rapidly than previously during the high growth years. The number of homeless people, the lower line, which had been stable, also began to increase during that period.

Speaking at the launch of Focus Ireland's annual report in 2003, Sister Stanislaus Kennedy[142] stated that despite government commitments to halve homelessness by the end of 2005, more people were homeless than was the case when the commitment was given in 1999. People were also spending longer periods homeless and those who were 'sleeping rough' were younger. The average time spent in B&B accommodation had shot up from twenty days in 1993 to an average of 18 months. She described the worsening homelessness figures in the wake of fifteen years of 'unprecedented economic growth' as 'nothing short of disgraceful'. The number of families on local authority housing lists had increased from 39,000 families in 1999 to almost 48,500, she said. In March 2004, the number of people sleeping rough in Dublin was reported[143] to be at an all-time high.

'The recent cuts in the rent allowance system, in particular, have already made it even harder than before for the most vulnerable to keep a roof over their heads,' Declan Jones, Focus Ireland's Chief Executive[144] said in 2003, adding that 85% of people on the housing list were struggling to survive on €15,000 or less a year. Every budget since 1997 had seen the better-off getting more than the less well-off, he commented.

He was right. A quarter of all houses built in 2003 were second (holiday) homes. Many of these were subsidized by tax reliefs[145] and their construction had the effect of pushing up land prices, making it harder for young people to buy their first home.

House prices soar and become less affordable

Average New House Prices, 1994-2002

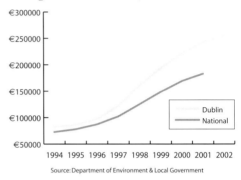

Source: Department of Environment & Local Government

Figure 20 Although average incomes increased by around 73% between 1994 and 2002, house prices rose by much more than that as the graph shows. They were up by roughly 250% nationally and by 300% in the Dublin area.

B. Did the physical environment improve?

When a country's economy doubles in size, almost everything changes in some way and many of these changes will have an effect on the population's health.

(1) Air quality

(i) Nitrogen oxide emissions.

The number of vehicles registered in Ireland increased by 68% between 1990 and 2001 and this contributed half of the 9% rise in Ireland's nitrogen oxide emissions[146] between 1995 and 2000, bringing them up to 125,000 tonnes a year. Much of the balance came from power stations. Nitrogen oxides trigger asthmatic attacks, croup in children, and in the longer term, cause reduced lung function. They also contribute to ground level ozone, a respiratory irritant. It will be necessary for Ireland to reduce nitrogen oxide emissions by 51% by 2010 to comply with EU directives. The European Environment Agency report *Environmental Signals 2002* released in 2004 finds that Ireland is not on target to achieve this goal.

(ii) Particulate emissions

Increased traffic also led to an increase in particulate emissions. When fossil fuels are burned, tiny particles are released in the fumes, especially those from diesel engines. Because they are so small, the particles can penetrate far down into the respiratory tract and cause both respiratory and cardiovascular disease. Exposure to particulate matter is now the largest threat to health from air pollution in Western cities[147]. Long-term exposure to particulate matter is associated with a reduction in life expectancy of 1-2 years and even short-term variations in particulate matter are associated with adverse health effects at low levels of exposure. Although EU legislation requires that the air should not exceed more than 50 micrograms of particulates per cubic metre more than 35 times in a calendar year, the air in some Dublin streets exceeded this level 76 times in 2000.

Vehicle numbers soar

New Vehicles Registrations 1992-2002

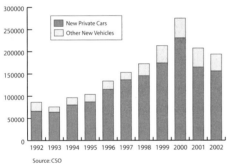

Source: CSO

Figure 21 shows that the number of motor vehicles purchased each year rose rapidly during the high-growth years and fell back as the rate of growth began to moderate. The result, of course, was a massive increase in road congestion.

(iii) Volatile organic compounds

Volatile organic compounds (VOCs) are released by road traffic, paints and organic solvents. Although emissions from vehicles are reduced by catalytic converters, the benefits of fitting them have been offset by the huge increase in vehicle numbers. VOCs interact with nitrogen oxides in the presence of sunlight to form low-level ozone, a respiratory irritant that also retards plant growth. Ireland needs to reduce its emissions of solvents and benzene by 37,000 tonnes from the 87,000 tonnes released in 2001 to comply with EU directives[148].

(iv) Sulphur dioxide

Sulphur dioxide is associated with asthma and with cardiac disease. It is produced largely from the combustion of fossil fuels, particularly in power stations. Ireland is now one of the three worst emitters of sulphur dioxide in the EU, releasing 131,489 tonnes in 2000. It will be necessary to reduce this to no more than 42,000 tonnes a year by 2010 if we are to comply with the UN Gothenburg Protocol and EU limits.

(v) Greenhouse gas emissions

On a per capita basis, Ireland's greenhouse emissions are amongst the worst in the world. As can be seen from figure 22, the energy demand from a growing economy caused our carbon dioxide emissions to begin to rise so rapidly in the mid nineties that by 2001 they were well over twice the 13% increase on its 1990 emissions level the country had been allocated by its EU partners under the Kyoto Protocol. These emissions contribute to the alarming build up of these gasses worldwide, and the warming they help produce will seriously affect the health of many people, particularly in the poorest areas of the world. Ireland will be affected too and we can expect to see an increase in heat-related deaths and in cases of food poisoning.

Carbon dioxide emissions increase

Carbon Dioxide Emissions per Capita, 1950-2000

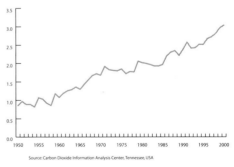

Source: Carbon Dioxide Information Analysis Center, Tennessee, USA

Figure 22 The average Irish person's emissions of carbon dioxide have tripled since 1950, rising from one tonne per person to three. It took thirty-five years to reach the two-tonne mark, and, as growth accelerated, only fifteen to add the other tonne. These emissions will have to be reduced to slow down global warming. This will require a complete restructuring of the way the economy works.

Economic growth increases oil demand

Annual Oil Consumption Per Capita

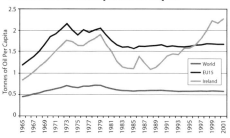

Figure 23 shows that until the mid 1990s, Irish oil consumption was below the EU average. It doubled between 1989 and 2001, while that of the EU and the world, as a whole remained unchanged. In 1996, Ireland's oil consumption per capita exceeded the EU average, and continued to rise rapidly during the high growth years. The country is now one of the most oil-dependent in the world.

Source: Amarach[149]

(vi) Industrial and agricultural chemicals

Economic growth meant the increased use of chemicals in industry and agriculture. Although chemical production is increasing in the EU, very little is known about the health and environmental effects of most of the vast numbers of chemicals being made and used. The report of the UK's Royal Commission on Environmental Pollution[150] issued in June 2003 found that only forty of the more than 30,000 synthetic chemicals currently available on the UK market have been subject to a systematic risk assessment. 'We are conducting a huge and unacceptable experiment on ourselves and the environment' Sir Tom Blundell, the Commission's chairman, said.

The Pesticide Control Service of the Department of Agriculture reported in 2004 that in 2002, 29.7% of 551 samples of food contained quantifiable residues of pesticides, and 1.3% of the total sampled had levels exceeding the regulatory limits. The investigators said they would like to increase the number of pesticides for which they were testing and to broaden the range of food products they covered.

While we may know the levels of pesticides on some fruit and vegetables, we do not know the levels of pesticides that the Irish population is carrying in its body tissues. Many pesticides and other chemicals are chlorinated chemicals and these are particularly worrying because not only

are they are not easily broken down but the body is unable to excrete them and they accumulate in our body fat. Exposure to chlorinated chemicals has been linked to depressed immune systems, reduction in sperm counts, altered fertility and some adult cancers. In children they have also been associated with low birth weight, genital abnormalities and impaired neurological development. It is difficult to get an accurate picture of the amounts of chlorinated chemicals Ireland imports as there have been frequent code changes for different chemicals and the records have only been computerized since the early 1990s. It is also difficult to estimate the impact these chemicals might be having, as Ireland does not keep a national database of congenital malformations.

Dioxins and PCBs, both chlorinated chemicals, were found in human and animal food in Belgium in 1999 and 2000. Phthalates, which have an oestrogenic effect, exceeded permitted concentrations in children's toys in Denmark in 2001 and 2002. Another class of persistent organic pollutants, flame-retardant chemicals, were found in human milk in Sweden 2000[151]. Yet Ireland has still to ratify the Stockholm Agreement on the phasing out of persistent organic pollutants. Although a survey of dioxins in human breast milk in Ireland showed low levels of dioxins and PCBs, we need to measure levels in fatty tissue as well since the level in breast milk falls in the course of each lactation as the concentration in the mother's body is reduced.

(vii) Domestic chemicals present dangers

The link between environmental estrogens and cancer is well documented. Many detergents contain alkyl phenols which mimic the female sex hormone estrogen and have been associated, along with some other chlorinated organic chemicals, with genito-urinary problems and some types of cancers. The origin of these compounds includes domestic and industrial effluents, leachate from solid waste disposal sites, agricultural leachate and urban run-off [152]. Breast cancer is the commonest cancer in women, and prostate cancer (having overtaken lung cancer) is now the commonest cancer in men, see figure 24. In other words, the commonest cancers in both sexes are hormonally related. The levels of synthetic hormone mimicking chemicals in both the water supply and in the tissues of the Irish people are unknown but some information should be available in 2005 after a study coordinated by Teagasc has been completed [153].

Commonest types of cancer increase

Crude Cancer Rates per 100,000 population 1994-2001

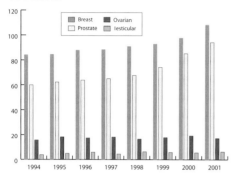

Figure 24 shows that the number of cases per 100,000 people of the two commonest types of cancer - breast and prostate – have increased steadily over the past few years. Both these cancers are hormone-related and the rise could be due to the increase in synthetic hormones in the environment as a result of increased chemical use.

THE HEALTH BENEFITS OF A MORE EGALITARIAN SOCIETY

Improvements in health

Even a modest reduction in income inequality could have an important impact on population health, including infant mortality, homicide, and deaths from cardiovascular disease and cancers. Recent research from workers at the London School of Health and Tropical Hygiene indicates that eliminating socio-economic inequalities would save almost 13,000 deaths from cancer in the U.K. every five years and almost certainly save more lives in the next decade than innovative treatments[154]. In Ireland, North and South, the Institute of Public Health estimates that there could be 6,000 fewer premature deaths every year if the overall death rate could be reduced to that of the highest socio-economic grouping, or 5,400 if it could be reduced to the EU average[155] And in Canada it is estimated that 23% of the years of life lost prematurely before the age of 75 can be attributed to income differences. The disease responsible for most of these deaths is heart disease as a result of social exclusion[156].

The Robin Hood Index [157] is sometimes used to measure the income gap between rich and poor.

A reading of 30 on the index means that the top 10% of the population enjoys 30% of national income. Researchers at Harvard have found that the index is so closely correlated with the overall age-adjusted death rate in the US that each percentage point increase in the index is associated with an increase of 21.7 deaths per 100,000 population each year. The Robin Hood index was also positively correlated with infant mortality, cancers and coronary heart disease – so much so, in fact, that the Harvard team stated that reducing inequality from 30% to 25% would cut the number of deaths from coronary heart disease by a similar amount. Strong associations were also found between the index and causes of death amenable to medical intervention.

Strangely, another measure of inequality in the distribution of income, the Gini coefficient, where 0 signifies perfect equality and 100 means that one person holds all the income, does not show any correlation with health. This could have been because the coefficient gives great weight to changes around the middle of the income distribution and little to changes at the extremes.

Inequality causes reduced life expectation for the wealthy as well as the impoverished: the more unequal the society, the worse are the life chances of everybody in that society. Researchers at the Harvard School of Public Health in the US found that moving from a state with high social capital to one with very little social capital increased one's chance of low to middling health by roughly 40-70%. Indeed, the researchers worked out that if one wanted to improve one's health, moving to a high social capital state would do almost as much good as stopping smoking.

Inequality is not an accident

I want to end as I began, with a speech by an Irish political leader to a group of visiting Americans. Five months before Mr. Ahern boasted of Ireland's transformation to President Clinton, his deputy, Mary Harney, the Tanaiste, (Deputy Prime Minister) made her famous 'Berlin or Boston' speech in Dublin to a group of American lawyers. This is part of what she said:

> Political and economic commentators sometimes pose a choice between what they see as the American way and the European way. They view the American way as being built on the rugged individualism of the original frontiersmen, an economic model that is heavily based on enterprise and incentive, on individual effort and

Table 8 *Between Berlin and Boston*

	Proportion of national income received by poorest 10% of population	Proportion of national income received by richest 10% of population (Robin Hood Index)	Proportion of children living in households with income less than 50% of median income	GDP per capita (Dollars)
United States	1.8%	30.5%	22.5%	35,935
Ireland	2.5%	27.4%	16.8%	28,662
Germany	3.3%	23.7%	10.7%	26,233

Source: www.nationmaster.com and CIA Fact Book

with limited government intervention. They view the European way as being built on a strong concern for social harmony and social inclusion, with governments being prepared to intervene strongly through the tax and regulatory systems to achieve their desired outcomes.

Both models are, of course, overly simplistic but there is an element of truth in them too. We in Ireland have tended to steer a course between the two but I think it is fair to say that we have sailed closer to the American shore than the European one. Look at what we have done over the last ten years. We have cut taxes on capital. We have cut taxes on corporate profits. We have cut taxes on personal incomes. The result has been an explosion in economic activity and Ireland is now the fastest-growing country in the developed world.

She then went on to ask the question that I have been asking in this paper 'And did we have to pay some very high price for pursuing this policy option?' she asked. 'Did we have to abandon the concept of social inclusion?' Her answer was quite different from mine: 'The answer is no: we didn't.'

The evidence assembled in this paper suggests that Ireland in fact has paid, is paying and will continue to pay a very high price for adopting American ways and moving closer to Boston. The table shows where Ireland was positioned in relation to Ms. Harney's two marker countries during the high growth period she felt so proud about.

Tax and budgetary policy

The move towards American levels of inequality was no accident but deliberate government policy. "A dynamic liberal economy like ours demands flexibility and inequality in some respects to function" the Minister for Justice, Michael McDowell, said in 2004. So, in spite of all

the international evidence of the harmful effects of allowing the distribution of income to become more unequal, the governments of which Ms. Harney was a leading member shifted income to the better-off. As the ESRI[158] stated in 2002: 'On balance, budgets over the past 10 to 20 years have been more favourable to high income groups than low income groups, but particularly so during periods of high growth. During Ireland's recent growth spurt, budgetary policy acted to reinforce income gains for the higher income groups, while involving losses for those in the lower income groups. Measured against the neutral benchmark, tax cuts raised the incomes of top income earners by more than 12 per cent over the years 1995 to 2001; but welfare increases lagged 2 percentage points behind wage growth'.

The effects of these policies are well described by Kawachi[159] even though he did not have the Irish model in mind.

The more unequal the distribution of income, the longer and harder families need to work to keep from slipping behind on the economic ladder. The greater the disparities in wealth and income, the greater the effort expended by producers of goods and services in catering to the spending habits of the rich – more space on first class seats on commercial airlines, building bigger cars, more spacious houses and so on. As the consumption pattern of the rich become more normative, the more ordinary families need to spend to keep up with the average standard of living. The harder families work to pay for lifestyles beyond their means, the less time we invest in maintaining family and community ties. The more caught up we become in competitive spending, the less regard we have for the external costs our habits impose on the social and physical environment'.

In cutting taxes, Ireland was leading an international trend. Figure 25 shows that all OECD countries except Japan cut the proportion of national income that governments spent in the past ten years but that as a proportion of its 1993 revenue share, the Irish cuts were proportionately deeper than anywhere else. The result was a big increase in poverty among welfare recipients as the following table shows.

Percentage of persons in receipt of welfare benefits/assistance living in poverty.

Welfare benefit	1994	2001
Old age benefit	5.3%	49%
Unemployment benefit/assistance	23.9%	43.1%
Illness/disability	10.4%	49.4%
Lone Parent's allowance	25.8%	39.7%
Widow's pension	5.5%	42.1%

Source: Conference of Religious In Ireland (CORI)

Governments spend less of national income

Government spending as % of GDP

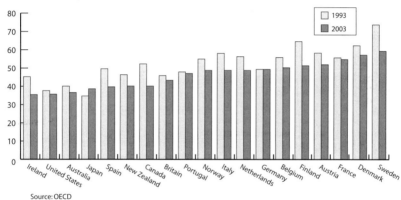

Source: OECD

Figure 25 shows that Ireland cut state spending by proportionately more than comparable nations in the period between 1993 and 2003.

Less scope for income redistribution

Gross government current expenditure as a % of GNP, 1975-2003e

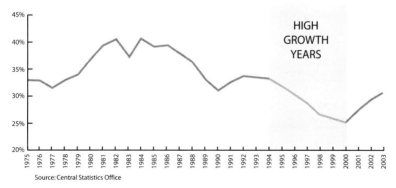

Source: Central Statistics Office

Figure 26 The share of national income taken by the Irish government fell sharply during the high-growth years. This left the better-off with more of their earnings, thus widening the gap between rich and poor, particularly as social welfare payments were not increased in step with other groups' higher earnings.

Source: John Lawlor and Colm McCarthy, "Browsing Onwards: Irish Public Spending in Perspective", *Irish Banking Review,* Autumn, 2003.

GALWAY COUNTY LIBRARIES

The tax-cutting strategy was deliberately designed to maintain the rate of economic growth by increasing the country's international competitiveness. So as to limit the wage increases sanctioned under the various national wage agreements, the government would undertake to cut income taxes, thus increasing the employees' take-home pay. However, as low-paid workers paid little tax, they could not benefit as much as the more-highly-paid from this arrangement. Moreover, as many of them, such as those in the clothing trade, were in direct competition with workers in low wage economies overseas, there was little scope for their employers to raise their wages directly. Others, such as those in the hotel and catering trade and in retailing, saw their wages kept down by the government-sanctioned importation of workers from Eastern Europe, India, China and the Philippines. The tax changes were one of the reasons the richest 10% of the population increased their share of the national income by about 1.4% during the high-growth years, while, as we saw in figure 6, the poorest 10% saw its share shrink by just under 0.4%.

In short, a system was created in which costs were kept down at the expense of the weakest people in society and, since the tax base had been cut, social welfare payments could not be increased to compensate. This led to the situation we noted in Table 2 - the growth of the number of employed people living on less than half the national median wage. That table also showed that the proportion of the unemployed, the sick and the old who lived in relative poverty rose significantly too.

Thus, if the Robin Hood Index works in Ireland in the way it does in Boston, this means that the cost Ms. Harney mentioned was something like 1,200 additional premature deaths a year, to say nothing of the extra ill-health, violence, stress, and social breakdown the income shift caused.

Conclusion

Essentially, by setting the achievement of economic growth rather than its citizens' welfare as its primary target, successive governments have run the country for the benefit of the economy rather than for the people. If this continues, as the 2004 CORI report, *Priorities for Fairness* states: 'The government's current policy focus will ensure that substantial numbers of people are condemned to live in social exclusion and substantially larger numbers of people will be forced to accept a poor quality of life for the foreseeable future'

Personally, I believe that the best way to counteract income inequality and promote the nation's health would be to introduce a basic income for all Irish residents. There could be three rates, child, adult and retired. The latter rate would also be paid to those unable to work through ill-health. The adult rate would not be

Social welfare gets smaller share of national income

Expenditure as a % of GNP Individual Headings 1975-2003e

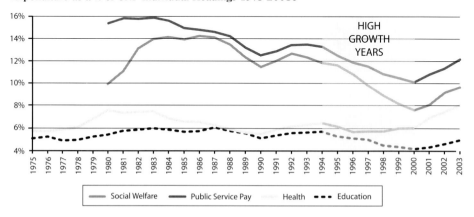

Figure 27 shows that state spending on social welfare and public service pay fell appreciably as a proportion of national income during the high growth years. The reduction in the social welfare bill was in part due to less people being unemployed but another factor was that payments were allowed to fall in relation to average incomes.

Adapted from: John Lawlor and Colm McCarthy, "Browsing Onwards: Irish Public Spending in Perspective", *Irish Banking Review,* Autumn, 2003 worth less than the current package of benefits received by people who are unemployed and the retired rate would be at least equal to the state pension. The big advantage of this sort of arrangement is that it puts everyone in society on the same side. At the moment, taxpayers see social welfare benefits as being paid out of their taxes and consequently resist higher benefit levels. Once a basic income was introduced, however, those in work would begin calling for higher basic income payments just as loudly as those who were unemployed.

It is not possible to prove the relationship between inequality and ill-health as conclusively as it is to test a relationship in the physical sciences. Nevertheless, for me, the weight of the international evidence is compelling. Accordingly, I believe the greatest public health challenge of our time is to scrap a system which puts the achievement of economic growth so far ahead of human welfare that it thinks it unimportant to keep adequate statistics to show the damage it is doing.

'We took the tough decisions and we developed a new model – the Irish model - to manage our affairs' the Taoiseach, Bertie Ahern, told the Fianna Fail ardfheis in March 2004. He continued: 'That is why Ireland today is becoming a better, fairer and more prosperous nation.'

It is hard to see how 'better' and 'fairer' could be correct. The system Mr. Ahern's government runs is depleting our true wealth - our health, our society and our environment. It must be changed. The object of our economy should be to maximize our health and quality of life. It must not be run just to generate wealth and maximize consumption purely to avert the onset of unemployment and recession.

Other people in Feasta are examining how such a change can be brought about, addressing issues such as the way money is created and the development of economic systems that are fairer to people and the planet. Meanwhile, it is to our shame that we cannot more accurately quantify the true price that we paid for allowing the Celtic Tiger the free run of our land and that our leaders can still get away with boasting about the progress they and their tiger have made.

Recommendations

Our economic system, by polarizing income distribution in the interests of economic growth, is the greatest single threat to everyone's health and wellbeing, not just that of the least well off. Income inequality is also a threat to our physical and social environments, which also affect our health The great rise in feelings of stress in the years coinciding with our economic boom, the increase in suicide, the increase in perinatal mortality in babies born into families on lower incomes, the increase in alcohol abuse, the rise in obesity, the increase in drug use, and evidence for the need to reduce our levels of pollutants in the environment, all indicate that something is going seriously wrong.

Here is what I believe needs to be done to correct the situation:

1. The effects of changes in income distribution on health and well-being need to be measured much more carefully. Irish statistics are totally inadequate at present. We need regular census data on income, income inequality, occupation, social position and health. The Hospital In-Patient Enquiry System should collect such information and disease registries should be established to do so too. "The section on income categories in the provisional census form for the 2006 census is welcome, but 60,000 euros as the top income level in a country where income is polarized is a little low.

2. We also need to measure other indicators of health such as the levels of industrial chemicals in our bodies and the prevalence of depression, asthma, diabetes and other illnesses, on a regular basis. We need to ask meaningful questions about health in the census, and we also need to encourage other countries (not all in the EU) to follow suit.

3. While the government is committed to reducing absolute poverty, it only monitors relative poverty and, as the latter has such a grave impact on health, this needs to change. The National Anti-Poverty Strategy must not only adopt the targets[160] outlined by its working group for reducing the disparities of health between rich and poor but also carry out a Health Impact Assessment for the economic system as a whole.

4. It is necessary to look again at health education, which currently tends to focus on the individual's health behaviour rather than the social determinants of health. Research has shown that health behaviour, though not unimportant, has a relatively small impact on overall health inequalities.[161]

5. The introduction of a basic income should be seriously considered as a way of reducing inequality and rewarding work that the present economic system does not appreciate. As James Robertson says in *Transforming Economic Life, A Millennial Challenge*[162], what we need is 'a vision of a people-centered society in which the amounts that people and organizations are required to pay to the public revenue are based on the value they subtract by their use or monopolization of common resources; and in which all citizens are equally entitled to share in the annual revenue so raised, partly by way of services provided at public expense and partly by way of a citizen's income. The citizens of such a society will be more equal with one another in esteem, capability and material conditions of life than now'.

6. Finally, we need to examine the reasons why our economic system needs continuous economic growth if it is not to collapse. The study should include the problems associated with creating money by lending it into circulation rather than putting it the economy in other ways.

Acknowledgements.

I am greatly indebted to Richard Douthwaite for his help with this article. I would also like to thank Andrew Butt for preparing the graphs and for his helpful comments on the data and its interpretation. I am grateful too to the Garda Press Office and the Central Statistics Office for their help and for the trouble they took in preparing figures for me.

Endnotes

1 Remarks made by Bertie Ahern to President Clinton and members of the Oireachtas, Guinness Storehouse, Dublin, 12 December, 2000
2 Central Statistics Office, Statistical Year Book, 2003
3 'Ireland ranks as the most globalized of 62 states due to exports', *Irish Times* 8-1-2003
4 'Three out of four report life is more stressful' *Irish Times* 9-10-2001
5 SLAN survey Department of Health 1999
6 'Student Futures' from the Amarach website www.amarach.com
7 'Celtic tiger did not improve quality of life, study finds' *Irish Times* 9-11-2002
8 Policy Implications of Social Capital No. 28 NESF, Dublin, Table 8.1, p.100
9 www.amarach.com
10 Urban-rural differences in the occurrence of female depressive disorder in Europe—evidence from the ODIN study. Lehtinen V. et al *Soc Psychiatry Psychiatr Epidemiol*, June 2003 vol.38(6) pp283-9
11 'One in 3 Dublin women hit by depression' *Sunday Times* 22-7- 2003.
12 Eurobarometer 57
13 Eurobarometer 47
14 'Mental illness study results 'frightening'' *Irish Times* 9-1-2004 and 'Young men face 'frightening suicide risk'' Irish Independent 9-1-2004
15 As 9
16 Monitoring Poverty trends in Ireland, Results from the Living in Ireland survey ESRI, Dublin, 2003 Policy research series No 51
17 'State's engines for tackling poverty are failing those on the margins' *Irish Times* 25-8-2000
18 CORI website 19-7-03
19 Irish Banking Review Summer 2004 page 7
20 Monitoring Poverty Trends in Ireland Results from Living in Ireland survey 2001 ESRI
21 Helen Johnson, Director Combat Poverty Agency Press Release 7-10-2003
22 '2.8 billion euros needed to help socially excluded- SVP' *Irish Times* 11-11-2003
23 'A League Table of Child Poverty in Rich Nations' UNICEF June 2000
24 'Poverty eroding quality of family life'. Combat Poverty Agency, Dublin, 2002
25 Health of our Children, report of the Chief Medical Officer, Department of Health, Dublin, 2002.
26 PHD expert says 'data observatory needed of health' *Medicine Weekly* 26-11-03
27 Adverse socioeconomic conditions in childhood and cause specific adult mortality: prospective observational study Davey-Smith G. et al, *British Medical Journal* 1998 316:1631-1635
28 Socioeconomic determinants of health: Stress and the biology of inequality Brunner E. *British Medical Journal* 1997 314:1472.
29 Implications of European Public Health 2001 page 41 Institute of Public Health in Ireland
30 Central Statistics Office Statistical Year Book 2003
31 'Harsh reminders why the Irish farmer wants a life' *Irish Times* 29-7-2003
32 'A career choice that makes no economic sense' *Irish Times* 30-7-2003
33 As 31
34 Monitoring Poverty Trends and exploring poverty dynamics in Ireland ESRI PRS41 pages 89-90
35 'A mechanism converting psychosocial stress into mononuclear cell activation' Bierhaus A. et al *Proceedings of the National Academy of Sciences* February 18, 2003 vol. 100 no. 4 |
36 Stress and peptic ulcer: life beyond helicobacter Levenstin S *British Medical Journal* 1998 316 538-541
37 'Self reported stress and risk of stroke' Truelson T. Boysen G. Stroke 2003 34 856
38 'Does stress cause cancer? There's no good evidence of a relation between stressful events and cancer. Mc Gee R. *British Medical Journal* 1999;319:1015-1016

39 Chronic stress and age-related increases in the proinflammatory cytokine IL-6 Kiecolt-Glaser J et al Proceedings of the National Academy of Sciences 22-7-2003 Vol 100 No. 15 9090-95

40 'Work stress and risk of cardiovascular mortality: prospective cohort study of industrial employees. Kivimaki M. et al *British Medical Journal* 2002 325:857-860

41 'Depressed patients have higher heart risk' *Irish Medical News* 8-3-2004

42 'Life-course exposure to job strain and ambulatory blood pressure in men' Landsbergis P. et al. *American Journal of Epidemiology* 2003 157 998-1006

43 'Interaction of workplace demands and cardiovascular reactivity in progression of carotid atherosclerosis: population based study' Everson et al *British Medical Journal* 1997 314 553 –558

44 As stated Dept. of Health Website Health Statistics Jan 2004 Section B

45 Eurostat 2003 as reported in "Irish are top of EU baby league" *Irish Times* 6-3-2003

46 'Irish look forward to longer lives' *Irish Times* 24-6-2004

47 'Martin boasts of success in fighting killer disease' *Irish Times* 24-2-2004

48 *The Ecology of Health*, Schumacher Briefing No.3 Green Books. Totnes 2000, page 10

49 Richard Wilkinson, *Unhealthy Societies*, Routledge London, 1997

50 Richard Wilkinson, 'Income distribution and mortality: A 'natural' experiment', *Sociology of Health and Illness*, vol. 12, No. 4, 1990, pp. 319-412.

51 *The Health of Nations: Why inequality is bad for your health*, Ichiro Kawachi, New Press, New York 2003

52 For a contrary view see Mackenbach 'Income inequality and population health' *British Medical Journal* 2002 324 1-2

53 R. Douthwaite, *The Growth Illusion*, Lilliput Press, Dublin 2000 page 102

54 Wilkinson R. 'Class mortality differentials, income distribution and trends in poverty', 1921-1981 *Journal of Social policy* vol 18, No. 3, pp.307-35G.D. Smith, et al, 'Socio-economic differentials in health and wealth. Widening inequalities in health - the legacy of the Thatcher years', *British Medical Journal*, 1993, Vol. 307, pp1085-6. from *The Growth Illusion* Douthwaite R. Lilliput Press 2000 page 108

55 'The height and weights of adults in Britain' Knights I. 1984 cited in *The Growth Illusion*, Douthwaite R. Lilliput Press, Dublin, 2000 page 108

56 'Two-tier system puts poor to the top of sickness list' *Irish Times* 1-12-00

57 'The Health of our children' Department of Health 2002

58 'Inequalities in Mortality 1989-1998' Institute of Public Health in Ireland

59 Personal communication 10-3-2004

60 'Inequalities in Health Hard facts' TCD Department of Community Health and General Practice 2001

61 'The child is father to the patient' *The Economist* June 14th-20th 2003 page 85-86

62 'Trend analysis and socio-economic differentials in infant mortality in the Southern Health Board, Ireland (1988-1997)'. Ryan CA et al. *Irish Medical Journal* 2000 Oct 93(7) 204-6

63 'Quality of Life in Europe An illustrative report European Foundation for the Improvement of Living and Working Conditions' page 55

64 Inequalities in Perceived Health A report on the All Ireland Social capital and health survey Dublin Institute of Public Health in Ireland 2003 Balanda K. Wilde J.

65 'Ireland's drink problem' Professor Ian Robertson Professor of Psychology TCD *Irish Times* 10-12-02.

66 'Suicide rate in adolescents trebles in just one decade' *Medicine Weekly* 1-10-03

67 'Suicide level higher than RTA deaths' *Irish Medical News* 30-9-2003

68 'Ireland has second highest suicide rate worldwide among young males' *Medicine Weekly* 26-11-03

69 1 October 2003 *Medicine Weekly*

70 'Suicides being under-reported' Irish Medical Times 16-8-02

71 'Suicide rates don't show full extent of despair' *Irish Medical News* 7-1-2

72 'Rate of suicide in young females has doubled in past ten years' *Medicine Weekly* 13-3-02

73 'Blame everything on the box' *Irish Times* 1-11-02.

74 '55% of young people know of peer suicide attempts' *Irish Times* 20-9-03

75 'One fifth of adolescents at risk of developing psychiatric disorder – Mater study' *Medicine Weekly* 19-2-2000

76 'Teenage girls top new parasuicide tables' *Medicine Weekly* 16-10-02

77 'Pre-teen depression rise alarms doctors', *Sunday Times* 16-5-04

78 '4.5 million euros allocated for suicide prevention' *Medicine Weekly* 25–2-2004

79 'Mental Wealth' *Consumer Choice* August 2003 page 319

80 Interim report of Strategic Task Force on alcohol Department of Health 2002 page 5

81 How much do we drink? *Irish Times* 21-11-03

82 'Time to ban alcohol advertising, minister' *Irish Times* 10-3-2004

83 'Irish Drinking Culture – The results of drinking and drinking related harm' – a European Comparison Department of Health 2003

84 'Conference told of increase in binge drinking' *Irish Times* 10-10-02

85 Department of Health 2002

86 'Teenage Alcohol, Smoking and Drug use in the Mid-West region' Mid Western Health Board 2003

87 'Drinking and drugs drive teachers out of the classroom' John Walshe *Irish Independent* 6-4-04

88 'Current trends in substance misuse in Ireland' *Irish Psychiatrist* Vol 5 Issue 1 Feb/Mar 2004

89 42% of 14 year olds 'consume alcohol' *Irish Times* 14-11-03

90 O'Neill M et al 'Adolescent Alcohol Misuse- searching for a solution' *Irish Medical Journal* October 2003 Vol 96 No 9279-280

91 'Study links obesity to social classes' Sophie Blakemore, *Birmingham Post* 2-3-04

92 'Obesity and cardiovascular disease' Daly S. and O'Shea D. *Irish Medical Times* 8-8-2003

93 'Reducing obesity rates by half could cut cancers by 36,000' *Medicine Weekly* 17-3-04

94 'Body Mass Index and Overweight in Adolescents in 13 European Countries, Israel, and the United States' Lissau I et al al *Arch Pediatr Adolesc Med*, Jan 2004; 158: 27 - 33.

95 'One-third of 4-year-olds overweight, study finds' *Irish Times* 25-3-2004

96 'Five year European diabetes study announced' *Irish Times* 10-1-04

97 'Child obesity is no longer just 'American problem' *Sunday Tribune* 3-3-03

98 'Warning that Ireland 'will drown in diabetes''. *Irish Medical News* 7-10-03

99 'Irish children are health 'time-bomb'' *Irish Medical News* 2-10-03

100 'Environment 'key to obesity'' *Irish Times* 6-11-03

101 'Irish children are health 'time bomb'' *Medicine Weekly* 24-9-03.

102 'Only 8.8% go to work by bus or train' *Irish Times* 16-10-03

103 'Children's diabetes clinic halts intake due to demand' *Irish Times* 23-12-2003

104 'GPs indicate obesity has increased their workload'
Medicine Weekly 7-11-03

105 '42% of females 'always tying to lose weight' *Irish Times*
20-10-03

106 Personal e-mail from BodyWhys, an organization dealing
with eating disorder, 4-11-03

107 'Task force planned to target obesity' *Irish Times*
25-12-2003

108 'Fat tax' no way to tackle obesity – expert *Irish Times*
18-6-4

109 Statistical release, Quarterly National Household Survey,
30-5-2002

110 'Medical card holders sicker than others' *Irish Times*,
6-12-2002

111 'Health level 'better' for non-medical card holders'
Irish Times, 28-3-2000

112 300,000 patients on anti-depressants *Irish Times*
18-5-2004

113 Annual report of the National Cancer Registry 2002

114 'The Policy Implications of Social Capital', National
Economic and Social Forum report No. 28 p. 30

115 As 49

116 Social capital, income inequality, and firearm violent crime
Kennedy BP et al *Soc Sci Med* 1998 Jul;47(1):7-17

117 'A prospective study of social networks in relation to total
mortality and cardiovascular disease in men in the USA'.
Journal of Epidemiology and Community Health
1996;50:245-51

118 Social capital, income inequality, and mortality Kawachi I.
et al *American Journal of Public Health* 1997 87 1491-8

119 *Bowling Alone* New York: Simon & Schuster, 2000

120 As 10

121 As 64

122 Address to AGM of Irish Doctors' Environmental
Association, Crumlin, 14-2-04

123 Socioeconomic determinants of health : Health and social
cohesion: why care about income inequality? Kawachi I. ,
Kennedy BP, *British Medical Journal* 314 5 April 1037-40
1997

124 As 9

125 As 64

126 http://www.apsanet.org/ps/dec95/putnam.cfm

127 Personal communication 17-7-2004

128 *Poverty Today*, No 2, p. 3, Summer 2003, Combat Poverty
Agency

129 See ref "The Politics of Inequality" and discussed in
'Settling for less than we wanted, but more than we had'
Fintan O'Toole *Irish Times* 20-4- 2002

130 As 64

131 Trends in crime and their interpretation Home Office
Research Study No. 119 (1990) from page 141 Field S.
Douthwaite R. *The Growth Illusion* Lilliput Press, Dublin,
2000

132 'FG describes figures as 'national emergency' *Irish Times*
4-4-03

133 As 49, page 156

134 'That was then, this is now; Change in Ireland 1949-
1999', CSO, Dublin 2000.

135 'Sharp rise in murder rate could be linked to increased
drinking' *Irish Times* 29-10-02

136 'Public order offences in Ireland' page 21 National Crime
Council 2003

137 'Think before you drink Alcohol policy A public health
perspective' August 2003 Department of Health page 88

138 '25% feel unsafe out walking at night' *Irish Times* 2-10-02.

139 As 64

140 '77% worry about crime, street violence' *Irish Times*
20-9-03

141 'Housing need' Cornerstone page 2 Issue No. 15 2003

142 'Homeless figures 'a disgrace' says Sr. Stanislaus'
Irish Times 24-7-03

143 'Figures show 237 homeless people sleep rough in Dublin'
Irish Times 25-3-2004

144 'State needs 1b for homelessness crisis, says Focus'
Irish Times 27-11-03

145 'Housing: A growing trend towards inequality' Burns M.
Working Notes Issue 48 June 2004

146 *Environment in Focus* EPA, Dublin, 2002.

147 *Europe's environment the third assessment* European
Environment Agency, Brussels, 2003

148 As above

149 'Ireland's alarming reliance on oil' Gerard O' Neill in *Before
the Wells Run Dry*, edited by Richard Douthwaite. Feasta
and Tipperary Institute, 2003

150 www.rcep.org.uk

151 National Resources Defense Council www.ndrc.org website
10-4-04

152 'The mutagenic, carcinogenic and genotoxic potential of
oestrogenic chemicals from Irish effluents' Kathryn Quinn,
Dr. Cepta Brougham, Athlone Institute of Technology

153 'Cancer and endocrine disrupting compounds' *Medicine
Weekly* 14 –1- 2004.

154 'How many deaths have been avoided through
improvements in cancer survival?' Richards M et al
British Medical Journal 2000; 320 895-898

155 'All-Ireland report highlights socioéconomic obstacles still
facing health services' *Medicine Weekly* 27-7-01.

156 www.yorku.ca/wellness/heart.pdf

157 'Income distribution and mortality: cross sectional
ecological study of the Robin Hood Index in the United
States' Kennedy BP et al *British Medical Journal*
1996;312:1004-1007

158 *The distributive impact of budgetary policy A medium term
view* Tim Callan, Mary Keeney, John Walsh, ESRI Dublin,
2002.

159 *The Health of Nations Why inequality is harmful to your
health* Kawachi I. Kennedy BP. New Press New York 2002

160 The targets are the reduction of the gaps between the
lowest and highest socio-economic groups by at least 10%
for circulatory diseases, cancers, injuries and poisoning by
2007. There are also targets for reducing the gap in life
expectancy and the gaps in birth weight.

161 *Quality of life in Europe an illustrative report*, European
Foundation for the Improvement of Living and Working
Conditions, Dublin, page 59

162 James Robertson *Transforming Economic Life A Millennial
challenge* Schumacher Briefing No. 1 Green Books, Totnes,
1998.

HomeNews

Social funding must rise to reduce poverty

Joe Humphreys

The Government will have to increase spending on social protections such as unemployment benefit and the old-age pension if it wants to reduce relative income poverty in Ireland, a new report from the ESRI suggests.

However, funding a Danish-style welfare system would require at a 10 per cent increase in income tax.

The study, published today, confirms that Ireland has the highest level of relative income poverty in Europe with 21 per cent of the population living on less than 60 per cent of median income in 2001.

Median income is the midpoint on the income scale, with equal numbers on greater incomes above and on smaller incomes below. In 2001, a single person earning less than €150 per week was said to be in relative income poverty.

Moreover, relative income poverty has increased in Ireland since 1995 in contrast to most European countries, including the UK, Portugal and Greece.

The report, *Why Is Relative Income Poverty So High In Ireland?*, found that differences in age and employment profiles, household composition and single parenthood did not explain much of the variation between member-states. Rather, the disparity was linked to contrasting tax and welfare regimes in Ireland and the EU.

PERCENTAGE OF PEOPLE EXPERIENCING RELATIVE INCOME POVERTY

Percentage of Persons below 60 percent of Median Income

	1995	1997	1999	2001
Sweden	-	8%	8%	9%
Denmark	10%	10%	10%	10%
Finland	-	8%	11%	11%
Germany	15%	12%	11%	11%
Netherlands	11%	10%	11%	11%
Austria	13%	13%	12%	12%
Luxembourg	12%	11%	13%	12%
Belgium	16%	14%	13%	13%
France	15%	15%	15%	15%
UK	20%	18%	19%	17%
Spain	19%	20%	19%	19%
Italy	20%	19%	18%	19%
Greece	22%	21%	21%	20%
Portugal	23%	22%	21%	20%
Ireland	19%	19%	19%	21%
EU average	17%	16%	15%	15%

Source: ESRI / EuroStat 2004   © IRISH TIMES STUDIO

Prof Brian Nolan, a co-author of the report, said relative income poverty was now "a key indicator at EU level", measuring "risk of poverty" rather than absolute levels of poverty in member-states. While it was up to the Government to decide whether or not to tackle relative income poverty,

he said, "we do have to decide what sort of socio-economic model, what sort of society, we want to end up as".

He said social welfare recipients had seen "real improvements" in their living standards in recent years. But this had not stopped them from lagging fur-

ther behind the rest of society in terms of relative income poverty.

The report found that the imposition of a "Danish-type" social welfare system in Ireland would have a "very substantial" impact on reducing the number of people at risk of poverty.

If no other economic indicators changed the reduction in relative income poverty would be in the order of 7 per cent, bringing Ireland to below the EU average for "poverty risk".

But funding such a welfare system would lead to an increase in income tax rates of 10-11 per cent.

The report noted that Ireland spent least in Europe in 2001 on social protection as a proportion of GDP at 14.6 per cent compared to an EU average of 27.5 per cent.

The study also highlighted differences in spending priorities with 43 per cent of social protection spending in Ireland going to healthcare compared to just 24.8 per cent to the elderly and 5.2 per cent to disabilities.

In contrast, Denmark apportioned 38 per cent of its social protection spending to the elderly and 12.5 per cent to disabilities.

Were a Danish-style welfare system to be introduced in Ireland, the report said, both the old-age non-contributory pension and the carer's allowance would rise from about €93 to €129.17 a week, and both disability benefit and unemployment benefit would rise from €89.52 to €194.13 a week.

Ireland has the highest level of relative poverty in the EU-15 according to an ERSI report *Why is Relative Poverty So High In Ireland?* which was published while this issue of the *Feasta Review* was being typeset. This summary of the report appeared in the *Irish Times* on September 16, 2004.

Lack of long-run data prevents us tracking Ireland's social health

ANA CARRIE

Just as Elizabeth Cullen found that inadequate statistics made it impossible to prove a conclusive link between Ireland's growing inequality and declining health, Ana Carrie found that the range of data required to construct an index showing the trend in the well-being of society just did not exist.

The original goal of this paper was to incorporate a variety of Irish social indicators into an aggregate index which would show the general trend in Ireland's social health. I hoped to produce an index going back at least twenty years and to publish an updated index on an annual basis. However, after reviewing the available historical data, I have concluded that it is not possible to produce a meaningful index of social health for Ireland at present. The paper therefore explains why and looks at what might be done to improve Irish social indicators in the future.

The index I had hoped to assemble would have been based on the Fordham Index of Social Health which was first produced at the Fordham Institute for Innovation in Social Policy in 1987. This index is discussed in great detail in the book *The Social Health of the Nation: How America is Really Doing* by Marc and Marque-Luisa Miringoff.

The Fordham Index is a composite of sixteen separate indicators. These are:

- Infant Mortality
- Child Abuse
- Child Poverty
- Youth Suicide
- Teenage Drug Use
- High School Dropouts
- Teenage Births
- Unemployment
- Wages
- Health Care Coverage
- Poverty, Aged 65+
- Life Expectancy, Aged 65+
- Violent Crime

Ana Carrie is currently pursuing a PhD in economics at Trinity College, Dublin. Following her brief foray into historical social indicators during the writing of this article she decided to conduct her PhD research in the area of agent-based computer simulation, where the data are plentiful, consistently generated and not covered with dust.

- Alcohol-Related Traffic Fatalities
- Affordable Housing
- Inequality

The Miringoffs emphasize that these are not necessarily the sixteen most important social indicators but that they were selected on the basis of data availability and international comparability to give a balance between social and socioeconomic concerns, and to reflect the concerns of all age groups.

To compose the Index from the sixteen indicators, each indicator is first scaled from 0 to 100, and then they are averaged to form the Index. The value of 100 is meant to indicate a practical maximum, rather than a theoretical ideal. If unemployment drops to 5% at its lowest, this value would be scaled to 100, even though 3.5% might be attainable in other years or in other countries, and even though 0% might be seen as ideal. Note that if unemployment varied between 5% and 5.5%, the 5.5% value would be scaled to 0, whereas if unemployment varied between 5% and 10%, then 5.5% would be scaled to 90. The Index would reach a value of 100 if each individual indicator were at its optimal value in the same year.

A Fordham-style index for Ireland was produced by Charles M. A. Clark and Catherine Kavanagh and published in 1996 in *Progress, Values and Public Policy*. Clark and Kavanagh used 15 indicators, adding Net Migration as an important indicator in the Irish context, and omitting inequality and elderly life expectancy. Their conclusion was that during the period 1977 to 1994, the social health of Ireland as measured by the index changed rather little, beginning and ending at a level of approximately 70. Certain indicators improved (infant mortality, school drop-out rate) while others worsened (violent crime, drug use, traffic accidents). This contrasts sharply with per capita GNP, which showed a marked improvement during the same period.

The Miringoffs bemoaned the relative lack of social data in the United States in comparison with data of the economic kind. However, when compared to the Irish situation they had, and have, a wealth of information available. They were able to assemble data for their index from 1970 (and possibly earlier) to today with breakdowns by race, age, gender and region. So what is the situation in Ireland with regard to these statistics?

Infant Mortality, Teenage Births, Unemployment, Youth Suicide, Teenage Drug Use, Life Expectancy – Aged 65+

Irish national data is readily available on infant mortality, teenage births, unemployment and net migration. Infant mortality numbers, but not rates, are available on a county/county borough basis. National data on youth suicide and youth drug use [convictions for drugs-related offences] are available, but both would warrant further research to ensure that they have been consistently gathered over the past 20 years. Elderly life expectancy can be proxied by the death rate amongst over-65s which is available regularly.

Child Abuse

Accurate data on child abuse is simply not available for any historical period, and this fact is acknowledged in a 2001 study which cites hugely varying reported rates of child abuse across the country as evidence of inconsistent data integrity and collection. For example, in 1999, one health board reported 18.4 cases per 1000 children while another reported 4.4, with a national average of 8.4. The study was part of an initiative to overhaul the Department of Health and Children's information infrastructure in the area of child care, and so we can hope that improvements will be made in the future.

Child Poverty, Poverty – Aged 65+, Inequality

Data on child poverty and elderly poverty are not produced in Ireland on an annual basis. Clark and Kavanagh used Social Welfare data to produce proxies for these indicators, however this approach is problematic in that social welfare schemes and entitlement thresholds can and do change over time. Census and Household Budget Survey/Living In Ireland data can be analyzed to produce figures, but at this time there is no consistent regular source for this information. Inequality data can be obtained from the same sources with the same difficulties.

High School Dropouts

Of those students who commenced post-primary education in 1994, 81.8% completed their secondary education, known as the adjusted Senior Cycle Retention rate. The report in which this fact was presented opens with the statement, "This is the first published analysis by the Department of Education and Science of school retention in Ireland." Prior to this, data on the percentage of students completing secondary education is available for certain years from census and survey data.

Wages

Wage data is available historically, but only for the industrial sector. Up to 1985, 'Manufacturing' wages were reported but from 1982 to the present, a separate dataset reports 'All Industrial' wages. A dataset can be produced by combining these two time series, but this is not entirely appropriate as they are not measuring the same thing. Also, it is not clear how wages in the industrial sector related to wage levels generally during the time period in question.

Health Care Coverage

It is difficult to know how to measure Health Care Coverage in Ireland. Medical Card coverage is not an appropriate indicator, nor is the number of private health insurance subscribers, as it is quite possible to have neither and still have good access to health care. This is an area where, in the absence of a readily identifiable metric, research should be undertaken to find indicators

Lack of long-run data prevents us
tracking Ireland's social health
Ana Carrie

which go beyond waiting lists and emergency room overcrowding and properly measure access to health care.

Violent Crime

Violent crime data is available in Garda annual reports. Beginning with the 2000 annual report, the PULSE system modernized and defined new categories for the reporting of crime data. For example, chemical weapons offenses were added and Larceny of Horses ceased to exist as a separate category. This change, however beneficial for the future, prevents us from easily comparing crime rates historically.

Alcohol-Related Traffic Fatalities

Traffic fatality data is available going back quite far, but unlike the US, the contribution of alcohol is not recorded. If traffic fatality data in itself were determined to be appropriate for a social index, it would need to be adjusted either for population or for car ownership.

Affordable Housing

Affordable housing can be measured in a variety of ways, one which is rather straightforward is to look at the ratio of the average house price to the average industrial wage, although this is looking at the affordability of home ownership rather than simply accommodation and does not take into account the impact of interest rates in making mortgage payments. In 2001, this figure was a multiple of 8.4, which can be contrasted with the figure of 3.5 used by banks when approving mortgages.

Conclusions

A fundamental problem with Irish historical data is its lack of continuity. Where statistics are available, they generally have not been gathered in a consistent manner over the time period in question. Ironically, improvements in the quality of official statistics will almost always come at the cost of continuity. For instance, recent redefinitions in Garda crime information mean that, while this year's data may be more relevant and accurate, it is not possible to make comparisons going back even three years as different definitions were in place at that time. As a researcher, I would urge that where a change is made to a definition, criterion or other factor which will result in a data set being discontinuous from previous values, two sets of data, one from each method, should be produced for the transition year to enable pseudo-

continuous index numbers to be produced. Then again, as a realist, I understand that any additional workload at a time of transition will not be welcomed.

In contrast to the US where data is collected for each state, in Ireland regional breakdowns are generally not possible since different government bodies break the country into different regions. For example, crime statistics follow Garda administrative boundaries while health statistics are determined by health board regions. Many statistics are only available at a national level. Government departments should report data using standardized administrative regions, or better yet, report county or sub-county level data to allow end users to construct their own regions.

The statistics which are relevant to our lives are likely to change over time. Twenty years ago, computer ownership would not have been thought of as a meaningful social indicator. Any programme to improve the quality and quantity of social indicators will need to take into account that these indicators will change over time. I do not believe that this is at odds with implementing good statistical practices to ensure that datasets are consistent over decades.

I have mentioned that several government departments are modernising and expanding their data collection systems, and in the future Irish researchers can look forward to a much broader selection of high quality data. A hopeful sign is the Strategy for Statistics, 2003-2008 published by the National Statistics Board.

This document discusses the increased demand for social and environmental statistics, brought about in part by the need to evaluate commitments made by the government in social partnership agreements, and proposed policy initiatives to identify, produce and disseminate high quality statistics.

I am also gratified that the Strategy for Statistics calls for more training in data analysis within the public sector and elsewhere. Statistics are meaningless without proper interpretation and a proper context. It is very easy to be seduced by a "hard" fact, when of course any single statistic is only a one-dimensional perspective on a complex reality, subject to a margin of error which may be quite large. A lack of numeracy and statistical training is dangerous in that it allows the unscrupulous to misrepresent statistics, and denies the uninitiated the tools to make their own judgments about the numbers which measure our world.

While the future of Irish social statistics looks reasonably bright, evidently brought about by a combination of internal modernization and external pressure to report on social and environmental issues in a consistent and systematic way, we have irrevocably lost the opportunity to use historical statistics to monitor the economic and social upheavals of the transition to modern Ireland. In view of the statistical problems, I don't feel that the Irish Fordham index constructed by Clark and Kavanagh can be held up for discussion with any greater authority than our own gut feelings of "some things have improved, others have worsened, others stayed the same". This is not tragic since, when such indexes do have a reasonable statistical validity they can of course be abused and given too much importance. It is, however, unfortunate, as the blossoming of regional and local Fordham-like indexes in the United States and elsewhere has given a valuable tool to communities, inspired by the publicity afforded to the original index, that wish to track their progress.

References

Clark, Charles M. A. and Catherine Kavanagh. "Progress, Values and Economic Indicators" in *Progress, Values and Public Policy*, edited by Brigid Reynolds and Sean Healy, (Dublin: CORI, 1996)

Miringoff, Marc and Marque-Luisa Miringoff. *The Social Health of the Nation: How America is Really Doing*, (Oxford University Press, 1999)

National Statistics Board. *Strategy for Statistics*, 2003 – 2008, (Stationery Office, Dublin, July 2003)

Social Information Systems Limited. *Child Care Management Information*. Consultant's report for Department of Health and Children, (2001-2002)

---

4   THE IRISH TIMES   Tuesday, September 21, 2004

HomeNews

Study highlights lack of data on Irish children

Insufficient information to assess whether child policies are working, report finds

FRANK MCNALLY

Irish children are generally happy and literate, a new study has concluded, but their schooling ends a year earlier than the international average, and spending on their pre-school education is "negligible".

Other findings are that infant mortality rates here continue to be among the highest in the European Union, and that while childhood poverty has fallen over the past decade, there are 50,000 children in families on housing waiting lists.

Yet one of the main conclusions of the study – compiled by former Labour TD Ms Eithne Fitzgerald for the Children's Research Centre at Trinity College, Dublin – is that there is not enough information available about childhood in Ireland to determine whether policies are working.

Noting such major recent developments as the big rise in one-parent families and the growth in the numbers of children born to immigrants, Ms Fitzgerald complains of "significant gaps" in the information available.

"We don't know how many children never make it into second-level school. We don't know how many children have an educational disability, nor whether they are getting appropriate services.

"There is no official information on the quality of childcare. There is little information on the relationships between parents and children, a key influence on children's well-being."

However, speaking at the study's publication yesterday, the Minister of State with responsibility for children said that one of the main goals of the Government's National Children's Strategy was to develop a statistical base for policy formation.

The Minister, Mr Brian Lenihan, praised the report – *Counting Our Children: an analysis of official data sources on children and childhood in Ireland* – as "the most comprehensive study in this area to date".

But he promised that a survey of 18,000 children and their families – co-funded by the National Children's Office and the Department of Social and Family Affairs – "will have a significant impact on our future understanding of children's lives in Ireland".

Ms Fitzgerald also regretted that collection of statistics had traditionally been dominated by "the adult world of economics".

She said this was at the expense of "finding out how our children are doing".

She identified the main deficits in official knowledge as those concerning "children in education, children with disabilities, and children born outside marriage".

"Almost a quarter of all children born in 2001 had a non-resident father.

"There is little information about children's contacts or relationships with non-resident parents, who are mostly fathers, as they grow up.

"Indeed, we have no official data on Irish parenting style and parental activities with children. It would be interesting to learn of our children's values and attitudes, but here again we have no information," Ms Fitzgerald added.

The director of the Children's Research Centre at Trinity College, Dr Jean White, said the report showed the need for a different approach.

"The well-being of children is a current public concern, as well as being likely to affect well-being in adult life.

"This research shows that to get a rounded picture of childhood, we need to go beyond the standard adult-centred statistics and include issues of particular interest to children."

Elizabeth Cullen and Ana Carrie are not the only researchers to complain about the inadequacy of the data on Irish social conditions, as this story from the *Irish Times* of September 21, 2004 shows.

The freedom to be frugal

Molly Scott Cato

> *Raising the incomes of the poor in relation to those of the rich would improve the health and life expectancy of the less-well-off. Unfortunately, however, if the poor are enabled to catch up by growing the economy, their gain will be at the planet's cost.*

How do you know that Adam and Eve were Russian?

Because they thought they were in paradise when they had no clothes and only one apple to share between them – Russian joke

Ever since the publication of Peter Townsend's book, *Poverty in the United Kingdom*, in 1979, liberals have generally agreed that an absolute definition of poverty is archaic and that in a modern, civilised society we should define poverty in relation to some proportion of the average income in that society rather than in terms of the absolute minimum necessary for survival. The most recent contribution to this consensus comes from a Nobel-Prize-winning economist, and darling of the liberal élite, Amartya Sen.

Sen's approach to poverty has been refined over several decades, most recently in his collection of essays, *Development as Freedom*. In this he provides a powerful case for his 'capability approach' to poverty, suggesting that the inability to function in society is the best marker of poverty, and that this can be related to different levels of actual income in different societies at different times. "Poverty" he says, "must be seen as the deprivation of basic capabilities rather than merely as lowness of incomes." He goes on: "Being relatively poor in a rich country can be a great capability handicap, even when one's absolute income is high in terms of world standards. In a generally opulent country, more income is needed to buy enough commodities to achieve the *same social functioning*". (Sen's emphasis).

This makes it clear that that the capability definition of poverty is a simply a variant of the relative-income definition. This matters to those of us striving to achieve sustainability because a relative poverty definition means that the resources required to reduce poverty are related to a country's level of economic growth and the pressure on the planet that such growth creates.

Traditional economists see the economic system as being like the peach in the Roald Dahl story *James and the Giant Peach*: it will simply expand for ever, while we sit on its ever-expanding skin, enjoying the sunshine, and munching to our hearts' content. Greens, on the other hand, are opposed to growth because they recognise that planet Earth is a closed system. Growth must face the limits imposed by that system, whether they become apparent via resource depletion or the overloading of the natural environment with waste products. And, since the resources of planet Earth are finite, if there are five peaches and I eat four, that only leaves one for you. Or if we eat five between us and then our friend Bettina comes along, she will have to do without.

From a Green perspective, then, the danger of defining poverty as relative is that it follows the growth dynamic. If, as the relative definition requires, we base our understanding of poverty on the consumption of a sample of 'ordinary people', then it will be driven by the consumerist, advertising-led society we live in. Most people consider a fridge a necessity, but what about a freezer, a tumble-dryer, or a CD-player?

Unfortunately, the assumption that the standard of living typical of one's neighbours is a given, which one can rightfully claim for oneself, is unquestioned in Sen's theory: "The need to take part in the life of a community may induce demands for modern equipment (televisions, videocassette recorders, automobiles and so on) in a country where such facilities are more or less universal (unlike what would be needed in less affluent countries), and this imposes a strain on a relatively poor person in a rich country even when that person is at a much higher level of income compared with people in less opulent countries" (Sen, 2001: 90).

Molly Scott Cato teaches at the University of Wales Institute in Cardiff. She is economics spokesperson for the Green Party in England and Wales and was one of the party's candidates for Wales in the 2004 elections to the European Parliament. She was born in Wales in 1963 but grew up in Bath before studying politics, philosophy and economics at Oxford University. After graduating she worked for the Refugee Studies Programme of Oxford University and later made a career in publishing with Oxford University Press.

After marrying and having children Molly took an MSc with the Open University in social research methods and in 2001 graduated with a PhD in economics from the University of Wales, Aberystwyth. Her doctoral research focussed on work motivations and the future of employment policy in the Rhondda-Cynon-Taff area of South Wales. She wrote *Seven Myths About Work* in 1996 and co-edited *Green Economics: Beyond Supply and Demand to Meeting People's Needs* in 1999. She also published a report about the structure of government specialist science advice committees called *I Don't Know Much About Science*, which influenced the structure of the British government's committee examining the effects of low-level radiation. Her latest book, *The Pit and the Pendulum*, was published in April 2004. It examines UK employment policy using the post-mining unemployment crisis in the Welsh Valleys as a starting point.

Molly has three children – Ralph, Joshua and Rosa – and lives near the sea in Aberystwyth. In her spare time she enjoys choral singing, opera, and reading.

In a rich society, as the rich accumulate more gadgets, the poor will be forced to follow along, always a little behind, always rather 'deprived', but always in the direction of an inexorable increase in consumption.

But what about international comparisons? It would be naïve to ignore the fact that General Motors is targeting the Chinese market with advertising that will soon suggest that another one billion are deprived unless they have a car. But can the planet possibly survive such a massive increase in CO_2 production? We are caught between the need to avert global warming and a commitment to permitting equal development of all nations. A definition of poverty that accepts the cultural norms about what citizens have a right to is an advertiser's dream but the planet's nightmare. In this context it is no accident that the Green movement has been attacked on the grounds that it is élitist because it is opposing the right of citizens of developing nations to the 'standard of living' that we in the West enjoy (see North, 1995; Furedi, 1997).

Rights and freedoms

An unexpected consequence of the relative definition of poverty and the growth dynamic that underlies it is the loss of another freedom: the freedom to be poor. In response to the realisation that the level of consumption of most citizens in the developed world is a threat to the survival of our species, some environmentalists have adopted a frugal lifestyle, yet this can result in disapproval from their neighbours. In an article called 'Poor not Different', the German economist Wolfgang Sachs tells of a visit he made to Mexico City shortly after the 1985 Earthquake. He was impressed by the restoration that had been carried out:

> "We had expected ruins and resignation, decay and squalor, but our visit had made us think again: there was a proud neighbourly spirit, vigorous activity with small building co-operatives everywhere; we saw a flourishing shadow economy. But at the end of the day, indulging in a bit of stock-taking, the remark finally slipped out: 'It's all very well, but, when it comes down to it, these people are still terribly poor.' Promptly, one of our companions stiffened: 'No somos pobres, somos Tepitanos' ('We are not poor people, we are Tepitans') ... I had to admit to myself in embarrassment that, quite involuntarily, the clichés of development philosophy had triggered my reaction. (Sachs, 1992: 161)

The insult was created by Sachs's assumption that he could impose an objective judgement of poverty, that he could decide from the outside the acceptable standard of living, that he could deprive the Tepitans of their right to be poor. As Sachs concludes, "The stereotyped talk of 'poverty' fails to distinguish, for example, between frugality, destitution and scarcity ... Frugality is the mark of cultures free from the frenzy of accumulation." His conclusion about the Mexican village where he was working was that 'Poverty here is a way of life maintained by a culture which recognizes and cultivates a state of sufficiency; sufficiency only turns into demeaning poverty when pressurized by an accumulating society.' (Sachs, 1992: 161)

Much of the suffering for those in poverty in Britain and Ireland today is caused by unsatisfied wants rather than basic needs. Of course we have no real basis from which to judge which wants are valid and which not, but it would be naïve to ignore the impact of the advertising industry on such preferences. There have been cases of mothers going to gaol because they have stolen expensive trainers to keep their children happy; can these women really use *poverty* as an excuse? Sen himself presents a quotation from Adam Smith pointing to an early awareness of the relative aspect of poverty, which he offers in terms of 'necessaries':

> By necessaries I understand not only the commodities which are indispensably necessary for the support of life, but whatever the custom of the country renders it indecent for creditable people, even the lower order, to be without … Custom has rendered shoes a necessary of life in England. The poorest creditable person of either sex would be ashamed to appear in public without them. (Smith, 1776: 351-2)

In other words, people are poor if they do not have enough money to buy shoes, not because they need the shoes to keep their feet warm, but because they would be embarrassed to be seen with bare feet. But can we extend this to the example of the child who is embarrassed to wear supermarket-brand trainers to school; and if so, where do we draw the line? Certainly, we cannot assume that wants and needs are the same, or that either is innate. Wants do not arise from human nature, or even from a social agreement, for the most part they are created by an advertising industry that has no other purpose. Following a simplistic relative definition of poverty without taking this into account will inevitably lead to ever-increasing consumption, and the economic growth that facilitates this.

The right to be socially excluded

The importance of consumption in establishing who is in poverty has advanced in recent years thanks to the redefinition of the poor as 'socially excluded': as if there were a club to which we all belonged but they were not allowed to join. Of course, within the club we all agree about what is an 'acceptable' way to live, what items we should all have, how often we should wash, how our children should be dressed and should behave. And the most serious cause of being excluded from the group is being unemployed. Those who are accidentally out of work may be considered with patronising sympathy; in the UK they may claw their way back into the club by claiming various means-tested benefits. But what about those who reject the work ethic, or the kinds of employment that are possible within a complex, developed, capitalist consumer society? What about those who choose to exclude themselves? The refusal to grant normal social rights to those who are poor, and especially those who are unemployed, is not an accident: as Beder has demonstrated (2001; see also Scott, 1996), the social inferiority of those outside the work system is an important support system for the work ethic.

There is much evidence to support the contention that the psychological results of unemployment are almost as crippling as the financial ones (as Sen discusses on pp. 94-6; see also Smith, 1997), but this is a consequence of the nature of our economic system rather than an intrinsic aspect of human nature. There is no reason why paid work should provide the only basis of our human identity, such that we claim a 'right to work' (see my further discussion in Cato, 1998 and Cato, 2004; see also the conclusions of a workshop at an OECD (1997) conference on the future of work held in Oslo in 1996, which reached similar conclusions). When stripped of its capitalist assumptions, this clarion call seems likely to fall on deaf ears. Can you imagine a Trobriand islander or a New Age Traveller marching for the right to work? If paid work is necessary for our identity within a capitalist economy then that is a problem with capitalism, not with those who choose to find their identity elsewhere. Instead of a system that assumes work as the norm, many of the 'self-excluded' have suggested an alternative view of the provision for basic needs based around a Citizens' Income as a rightful share of the national or global wealth (see van Parijs, 1995).

The freedom to destroy the planet

A debate has been underway amongst political philosophers at least since the time of Hobbes and Rousseau about competing freedoms. I may have perfect freedom of action up to the point where my actions impinge on you. At this point the argument diverges, with libertarians arguing that the disagreement should be resolved in law, with the prior or more essential right taking supremacy, while more interventionist political theorists allow a role for government in determining fair allocations. But the expansion of human activity has added an extra dimension that has yet to find its way into political philosophy. Following the recognition of the closing of the planetary frontier and the pressure on its ecology resulting from such a vast human population, the Brundtland definition of 'sustainable development' makes clear our obligation to weigh our freedoms against those of future generations.

As individuals we may claim the freedom to drive whenever we choose, and as societies we may choose the freedom to produce whatever level of carbon dioxide we choose, but how can we justify this when our actions remove the freedom of those in Bangladesh to exist, as rising sea levels overwhelm their low-lying land, or when we deprive future generations of existence on a planet whose air is no longer clean enough to breathe? The trivial freedoms to buy and sell, or to decide whether or not to engage in labour-market activity, can be considered second-order when compared with the freedom of the species as a whole to survive. This is the limitation to the concept of 'development as freedom' and it is absolute.

Hyacinth Bouquet and the trip to Mount Splashmore

The key concept of 'shame' features prominently in discussions by those who favour a relative definition of poverty, including Adam Smith and Sen. Although these definitions are almost invariably made by men, those who suffer the shame are more likely to be women. The struggles of women to maintain their social position are the stuff of dramas ranging from mam scrubbing the front step free of coal dust in *How Green Was my Valley* to Hyacinth Bouquet in the UK sitcom 'Keeping up Appearances' who is always peering through her net curtains to make sure she has successfully kept up with the Joneses next door. Yet where do these ideas about social acceptability come from? Although they are often taken as innate they are of course the result of social processes and primarily the overpowering influence of the advertising industry. If you doubt this you need only spend some time perusing the pages of the *International Journal of Advertising and Marketing to Children*. It includes articles on marketing to children via the classroom and the internet and provides helpful profiles of what might appeal. An example is reproduced as Box 1. The statements such as 'turned on by money and the prospect of making money', 'Violent TV

and Videos rule!', and 'risk takers with tobacco, alcohol, drugs (including solvent abuse) and gambling' are reproduced without comment: they are useful selling tips requiring no moral judgement.

This lack of special moral concern for children is unsurprising given that we read in another article that 'I look at children as just another group of consumers'. This director of a promotional marketing agency continues:

> I would like to introduce you to Charlotte, she is my target and my customer. What do I know about her and her friends? ... She has taken pester power to new levels. Remember her disposable income depends on it.
>
> (Bowen, 2000: 18-19).

These pressures on the consumers of the future are often mediated through their mothers. Advertisers have turned their attention to children as responsive targets of advertising, but since they are legally barred from earning for themselves, once they have been inculcated with a desire for a certain product in order to obtain it they must put pressure on their parents, so-called 'pester power'. This phenomenon is satirised in the episode of *The Simpsons* when Bart and Lisa watch the advert for the theme park Mount Splashmore and repeatedly ask Homer 'Can we go to Mount Splashmore?' all through the evening. Eventually he gives in, asking 'If I say yes, will you let me get some sleep?'

An account of the advertisers' plans for China demonstrates their endless amoral concern to create new and wider markets for their brands:

> China's population of children is the largest in the world. . . Since marketers tend to use a simple formula for determining market potential of a geography, that is People X Dollars = Markets, these facts are causing China's children to receive increasing attention from Western marketers. Brands such as Lego, Barbie, Nestle, M&M, Pepsi, Kraft, Crayola, Johnson & Johnson, Nike, and McDonalds are in head-to-head competition with many of China's major producers and retailers for a share of this market.
>
> (McNeal and Zhang, 2000: 31).

The domination of global capitalism by brands has aroused concern in recent years (Klein, 2000), and it is clear that this strategy is most successful with children. 'Brands', we are told 'are an active part of their lives, they are fundamental to their existence. The wrong trainers or T-shirt and there goes all that hard earned credibility.'

Box 1. Profile of 10-12-year-old boys for use by potential advertisers

MONEY MERCENARIES!
Boys 10-12 years

- Turned on by money and the prospect of making money.
- Prime target for financial institutions – Saving/Earnings schemes rule!
- Explosive energy – often boisterous and impulse driven.
- Bicycles, Blades and Music Accessories are status objects prized by peers.
- Sports and Computer interests intensified.
- Computer magazines avidly read.
- Violent TV and Videos rule! Combat sports are essential viewing. Schwarzenegger remains a hero. Soaps keenly watched.
- Collections are in the decline.
- Entertained by TV advertising but sceptical of hard sell.
- Club memberships reflect specialist interests (Computers, Sports, Music).
- Big Brand (global) preferences, particularly sports brands, which translate into fashion statements.
- Mothers still important as clothes suppliers, footwear excepted!
- Board games still played with other family members.
- Girls kept at some distance – tolerated.
- Risk takers with tobacco, alcohol, drugs (including solvent abuse) and gambling.

Source: Reproduced from *Advertising and Marketing to Children*, March/April 2000.

(Bowen, 2000: 19). Advertisers also attempt to persuade us that they play a useful role in 'socialising' our children, although the people that are likely to result will be shoppers rather than human beings as we are informed that: 'Socialization is the process by which "young people acquire skills, knowledge and attitudes relevant to their functioning as consumers in the marketplace"' (Mangelburg and Bristol, 1999: 28). And it is made clear why advertisers target children: 'In the short term, the hedonic value of a commercial, its emotional allure, and its ability to tap into powerful motives may be sufficient to eclipse momentarily any cognitive knowledge/defense' (Goldberg, 1999: 287). In less technical terms, advertising on children works because they are intellectually vulnerable. Their additional advantage is that they have a much longer 'consumption life expectancy' (as an adman might say) than the older person with more disposable income and hence are the ideal target for maintenance of the market cycle (see also Beder, 1998).

Conclusion

I have attempted to show how the relative definition of poverty and the growth dynamic of a capitalist society enjoy a symbiotic relationship, catalysed by the advertising industry. These major forces combine to impose consumptive pressure on people and the planet and in themselves increase perceived inequality and hence unhappiness. Such definitions actually reduce human freedom, by setting a standard of consumption that we feel pressured to achieve. The role of the advertising industry in driving the onward advance of that standard is clear: its purpose is to manipulate the market for consumer goods against the interest of both people and planet. The limits of planetary capacity must be recognised as a brake on this accelerating movement towards greater consumption.

It is important that we do not seem to be self-satisfied and neglectful of the needs of others, but what we need to keep sight of is the fact that it is inequality that is the central problem.

Studies repeatedly indicate that income disparities (although now between classes rather than genders) generate ill health in advanced societies such as the USA and UK (see Kawachi and Kennedy, 1997). A correlation of the Robin Hood Index used as a measure of inequality in societies with longevity indicates that inequality causes reduced life expectation for the wealthy as well as the impoverished: the more unequal the society the worse are the life chances of everybody in that society (Kennedy and colleagues, 1996). Research on the psychological ill-health of citizens of the United Kingdom concludes that the constant pressure to reach a level of consumption equivalent to that of our neighbours generates a significant proportion of the epidemic of mental illness (James, 1998).

We need to challenge assumptions about human happiness and well-being. If, as Sen and the comfortable liberal consensus suggest, development is about freedom, then we must not forget the Brundtland definition and must respect the freedom of future generations to meet their own needs. We must also free ourselves from the advertising industry's views of what constitutes an acceptable level of consumption and be spared its endless cycle of new market creation. This would represent a move towards development as emancipation, from oppressive economic structures and the ideologies that perpetuate them.

References

Beder, Sharon (1998), 'A Community View' from a conference Caring for Children in the Media Age' ed. John Squires and Tracy Newlands, New College Institute for Values Research, Sydney, pp. 101-111. Available online at: www.uow.edu.au/arts/sts/sbeder/children.html.

Beder, Sharon (2001), *Selling the Work Ethic: From Puritan Pulpit to Corporate PR* (London: Zed Books).

Bowen, Mike (2000), 'Kids Culture', *International Journal of Advertising and Marketing to Children*, 2/1: 19-23.

Cato, Molly S. and Kennett, Miriam (1999) (eds.), *Green Economics: Beyond Supply and Demand to Meeting People's Needs* (Aberystwyth: Green Audit).

Cato, M. S. (2004), *The Pit and the Pendulum: A Cooperative Future for work in the Welsh Valleys* (Cardiff: University of Wales Press).

Furedi, F. (1997), *Population and Development: A Critical Introduction* (Cambridge: Polity).

Goldberg, Marvin E. (1999), 'Advertising's Effects', chap. 15 in Macklin, M. Carole and Carlson, Lester (1999), *Advertising to Children: Concepts and Controversies* (Thousand Oaks, Calif.: Sage).

James, O. (1998), *Britain on the Couch Treating a Low Serotonin Society* (London: Random House).

Kawachi, Ichiro and Kennedy, Bruce P. (1997), 'Health and Social Cohesion: Why Care About Income Inequality?', *British Medical Journal*, 314: 1037-40.

Kennedy, B.P., Ichiro, K., and Prothrow-Stith, D. (1996), 'Income Distribution and Mortality: Cross Sectional Ecological Study of the Robin Hood Index in the United States',. *British Medical Journal*, 312:1004-1007

Klein, Naomi (2000), *No Logo: No Space, No Choice, No Jobs: Taking Aim at the Brand Bullies* (London: Flamingo).

Mangelburg, Tamara F. and Bristol, Terry (1999), 'Socialization and Adolescents' Scepticism toward Advertising', chap. 2 in Macklin, M. Carole and Carlson, Lester (1999), *Advertising to Children: Concepts and Controversies* (Thousand Oaks, Calif.: Sage).

McNeal, James U. and Zhang, Hongxia (2000), 'Chinese Children's Consumer Behaviour: A Review', *International Journal of Advertising and Marketing to Children*, 2/1: 31-5.

North, R. (1995), *Life on a Modern Planet: A Manifesto for Progress* (Manchester: Manchester University Press).

OECD (1997), *Creativity, Innovation and Job Creation* (Paris: OECD).

Sachs, Wolfgang (1992), 'Poor, Not Different', in Paul Ekins and Manfred Max-Neef (eds.), *Real Life Economics: Understanding Wealth Creation* (London: Routledge).

Scott, Molly (1996), *Seven Myths about Work* (Aberystwyth: Green Audit).

Sen, Amartya (1983), 'Poor, Relatively Speaking', *Oxford Economic Papers*, 35: 153-69.

Sen, Amartya (2001), *Development as Freedom*, first published 1999 (Oxford: University Press).

Smith, Adam (1776/1987), *An Inquiry into the Nature and Causes of the Wealth of Nations* (Edinburgh: Akros).

Smith, Richard (1997), *Unemployment: A Disaster and a Challenge* (Oxford: University Press).

Townsend, P. (1989), *Poverty in the United Kingdom: A Survey of Household Resources and Standards of Living* (Harmondsworth: Penguin).

van Parijs, Paul (1995), *Real Freedom for All* (Oxford: Clarendon Press).

Human Economics:
putting humanity and the
environment before profit

FRANK ROTERING

In the first half of 2003 about fifty Feasta members engaged in a vigorous internet discussion on Human Economics, Frank Rotering's proposed alternative to standard economic theory. Frank's aim was to develop an economic system that maximised human well-being and natural sustainability rather than profits and incomes growth and the paper that sparked the discussion can be found on the Feasta website together with all the e-mails exchanged during the discussion.

The version of Frank's theory we are printing here is the one that emerged as a result of the e-mail exchanges. It is followed by a commentary on whether it is possible to measure health in a way that could allow its maximisation to become the main goal of economic policy by Douglas McCullough, a health economist at the University of Ulster.

INTRODUCTION

Before offering a summary of human economics, let me provide two reasons why I believe that Feasta, and the sustainability movement generally, requires such a theory. First, some Feasta members tend to believe in a pragmatic form of activism based on immediate perceptions and intuitive strategies. For example, in the discussion, several participants strongly resisted the development of a new economic theory because the defects of the current system were obvious and could be directly addressed.

Many abuses of the current system are indeed glaring. No theory is required to reject profligate energy consumption and the resultant greenhouse gas emissions. Common sense alone refutes endless growth and rampant habitat destruction. Beneath the readily-apparent surface, however, lie subtle realities and counterintuitive solutions and an economic theory would force us to derive our policy prescriptions from first principles and systematic logic. It would enable us to confirm our correct notions and to repudiate our errors.

Second, our economic terminology is currently a mess. We frequently lack terms for ideas we cherish and use ill-conceived terms that subvert our purposes. For example, we have no term that refers to the injuries suffered by workers in production. Standard economics sees the world from the capitalist perspective and therefore ignores this. Without the excuse of ideology, so do we.

A prime example of an ill-conceived term is that ubiquitous oxymoron, "natural capital". Capital is an accumulation of monetary assets that finances capitalist production. It is the product of humanity's social relations, which are distinct from natural processes. "Natural capital" is the conflation of two separate realms and an invitation to deep confusion.

The development of a new economic theory would compel us to produce the terms we lack and to retire those that mislead us. Nothing would contribute more to the clarification of our ideas and the effectiveness of our actions.

Frank Rotering lives in British Columbia with his family, dog, and cat. He makes his living by teaching courses on computer software in Canada, the U.S., and the U.K. He studied economics at Simon Fraser University in Vancouver. He is currently developing a website and writing a book on the economic concepts presented here.

What follows is a summary of human economics. It was written after the website paper and reflects some modifications to my thinking, in part due to the group discussion. If you are new to economic thinking and find yourself struggling with marginal quantities and similar concepts below, read part 2 of my paper, a primer on economic analysis, on the Feasta website (http://www.feasta.org/documents/papers/rotering2.htm). If you want more details on the human and ecological frameworks, see parts 3 and 4.

One final point before I begin. An economic theory is an immense undertaking, far beyond the capacity of a single person. What I present here is a bare beginning, requiring extensive correction and development by numerous progressive thinkers.

A. THE STRUCTURE OF HUMAN ECONOMICS

Human economics is, first of all, a theory - that is, a set of ideas that can be applied to analysis. It is not a set of policy prescriptions. However, human economics is not a neutral theory. It is based on an objective that leads to policies favouring humanity over capital and environmental sustainability over growth and collapse.

The objective of human economics is to formulate economic concepts and analytical tools that permit the maximization of human well-being subject to ecological constraints.

This definition places humanity and the environment on a roughly even footing. We must maximize human well-being AND safeguard the environment. If we don't do the first, our economy has no rational human purpose. If we don't do the second, we undermine future human well-being and destroy non-human species. The fundamental challenge is to balance these sometimes conflicting objectives in a rational manner.

This paper will therefore discuss three things: the human objective for an economy, the constraints imposed on our economic activities by the environment, and the economy itself.

Let me start with the objective. Maximization of human well-being is a reasonable general goal, but it is clearly insufficient for economic analysis. What is meant by human well-being? How do we define the value of what we produce and the cost we incur in producing it? How much of an output is "enough"?

In all but the simplest economies, the answers to such questions are not readily apparent and can only be addressed with a set of conceptual tools. In human economics these constitute the human framework described in some detail below.

Next are constraints. From the economic perspective, the environment consists of inorganic resource stocks, organic resource flows, and waste flows. These stocks and flows cannot be analyzed with the same value and cost concepts used in the human framework. The human and natural realms, while ineluctably linked, are in separate conceptual domains, and require separate theoretical treatments. The terms and tools used to address environmental constraints constitute the ecological framework. This is also addressed in some detail below.

Last is the economy itself. The concepts required here, because they address the actual functioning of an economic system, are called the functional framework. There is an important distinction between this framework and the first two. While there is only one humanity and one environment, there are many existing and potential economic systems.

This implies that we can formulate a single human framework and a single ecological framework, but that multiple functional frameworks are required. In human economics I have addressed only capitalism, the globe's dominant economic organization in the current historical period. This topic is beyond the scope of the present summary.

In brief: human economics separately tackles the ends, constraints, and means of economic activities. Ends are addressed in the human framework, which can be used to define a humane economy. Constraints are addressed in

human economics: putting humanity and
the environment before profit
Frank Rotering

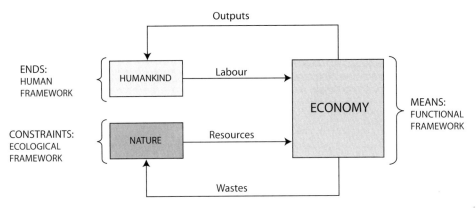

Figure 1: *Structure of human economics*

the ecological framework, which can be used to define a sustainable economy. Means are addressed in the functional frameworks, which can be used to describe actual economic systems. This structure is depicted in Figure 1.

B. GRAPHS AND RIGOUR

Except for the relationship between humanity and nature, no topic was debated more fervently in the discussion group than my attempt to inject rigour into human economics, specifically my use of graphs. The group's main objection was that the quantities I describe have never been measured, and that my graphs are therefore meaningless. This is a misconception which must be addressed before I proceed.

Graphs can be divided into two categories: those that express known quantitative relationships and those that express general conceptual relationships.

Open in front of me is a physics text, showing a graph that relates the force on an automobile as a function of time during an impact. Force is on the vertical axis, in Newtons. Time is on the horizontal axis, in seconds. The curve traces the force on a Mercedes-Benz during the 120 milliseconds of a crash. This graph is based on actual measurements and therefore expresses a known quantitative relationship.

I am now looking at the intriguing book *Rare Earth: Why Complex Life Is Uncommon in the Universe*. On page 172 the two authors, professors of geology and astronomy, show a graph that relates species diversity to mass

extinction events. Diversity is on the vertical axis, without units. Mass extinction events is on the horizontal axis, also without units. There are two curves, depicting two possible relationships between the variables. These curves are not based on any measurements because none are available. Nevertheless, they accurately express general conceptual relationships and they are useful in clarifying the authors' meaning.

So long as the underlying ideas are sound, conceptual curves can accurately depict broad relationships and permit the analyst to draw general conclusions. Such curves are frequently indispensable in the early stages of scientific development. Before we can measure we must conceptualize the quantities to be measured. Before we can construct a thermometer we must understand that there is heat and cold.

Given that human economics is in its infancy, all my graphs express general conceptual relationships. The test of these graphs is not whether the quantities have been measured, but whether I base them on sound concepts and whether the relationships between the curves are correct.

I should add that, while I'm interested in detailed quantification in the long term, my immediate objective in using graphs is to express my thoughts with the greatest possible clarity and to expose them to the sternest possible scrutiny. It's easy to hide sloppy logic in a profusion of words. Graphs enforce tight definitions and strict relationships, allowing a sharp critic to quickly expose fallacies.

C. THE HUMAN FRAMEWORK

1. THE STANDARD OF VALUE AND COST

Value is what human beings need or desire in an output, while cost is the sacrifice we must make to obtain this value. Among the most fundamental questions for any economic theory are:

a) How do we judge needs and desires? That is, what is the standard of value?

b) How do we judge sacrifices? That is, what is the standard of cost?

We might, for instance, decide that population is the appropriate standard of value. Consumption that results in a higher population would then be preferred to consumption that results in a lower population. We might decide that energy use is the appropriate standard of cost. Production that uses less energy would then be preferred to production that uses more.

This example uses separate standards for value and cost, but this is not necessary. We might decide to use self-reported happiness for both. Our aim would then be to consume so as to gain the most happiness and to produce so as to lose the least happiness.

Standard economics uses a single standard - subjective wants expressed in money - for value and cost, and a single standard is required in the human framework as well. If we try to apply separate standards we encounter insurmountable analytical hurdles.

The next question is: should this single standard be subjective or objective? I find a subjective standard, such as personal wants, to be unacceptable for the following reasons:

1. Subjective needs and wants can only be measured by something external, such as money. If money is used, then demand means "effective demand" - it must be backed by cash. A penniless person dying of thirst has, in this sense, no demand for water. If water is not free, and if a good Samaritan does not appear, this person will perish. Money - or whatever expresses subjective desires - masks our real needs and wants.

2. A subjective standard makes interpersonal comparisons impossible. The internal state of one person cannot be compared with that of another. This leads to gross economic injustices. For example, it places a poor person's desperate need for a necessity on the same plane as a rich person's frivolous desire for a luxury. It fails to differentiate between widely divergent ethical situations.

3. Subjective demand can be powerfully shaped by social influences, such as advertising, media images, peer pressure, and the like. So-called subjective demand is frequently nothing but the implanted whims of corporate marketing departments.

The human framework thus requires a single, objective standard of value and cost. Following are the key considerations to determine what this standard should be:

> Human economics seeks to maximize human well-being. The standard should therefore be intimately tied to the survival and flourishing of human beings.

> To be useful as a set of analytical tools, the human framework should be as rigorous as its subject matter permits. The standard should therefore be quantifiable and allow for at least a rough unit of measurement.

> Human beings interact with an economy in three main ways: directly through labour and consumption, and indirectly through the economy's impact on the environment. The standard must be capable of measuring all three interactions.

A standard that meets all these criteria is human health. It is objective, is intimately associated with well-being, permits quantification, and is capable of measuring all three economic interactions.

Stated more fully, the standard of value and cost in the human framework is human life and the physical, mental, and emotional health of human beings. Thus, if an output supports human life and increases health, it has value. If production destroys human life and decreases health, it incurs cost.

2. THE HEALTH UNIT

While the standard of value and cost is adequate as a general criterion, it is too broad to serve as a standard of measurement. That is, it appears impossible to define a measurement unit that embraces both life and a broad conception of health.

human economics: putting humanity and
the environment before profit
Frank Rotering

My solution here is to use physical health as an index, or indicator, of life and overall health. Physical health implies life and is directly measurable. Recent research has found it to be strongly influenced by mental and emotional factors. Stress, worry, and loneliness all have physical symptoms. Poverty has recently been linked to obesity. Even joy and laughter are expressed at the physical level. Physical health is probably the most accurate single indicator of overall human well-being available to us.

It is not difficult to see how a unit of measurement can be established on the basis of physical health (simply "health" from here on). The zero point in the measurement of health is the state where a representative person is minimally alive. From this point, any reduction in health will result in death. At the other extreme is the currently attainable peak of health. This means complete freedom from disease and injury, and the greatest possible vigour, strength, flexibility, sensory acuity, stamina, and so forth.

This continuum of health states, from minimal life to its currently achievable peak, can be divided into equal increments. The details of such a division must be left to health experts, but there is no obstacle to it in principle.

A rudimentary example of such a scale already exists for newborns - the APGAR score. When a baby is born, a doctor can assign 0-2 points for each of muscle tone, pulse, reflex, skin colour, and respiration. The total score tells the medical team if the baby is healthy, warrants some attention, or requires immediate resuscitation. Extending this scheme appears relatively straightforward.

The other essential aspect of health is time. An increment in health that lasts for 20 days is 10 times greater than the same increment lasting for two days. For example, an apple might increase health by ten increments for three days. A house might increase health by eight increments for 50 years. Although the apple has the greater short-term health effect, the house has a much greater long-term impact.

In brief, the health unit can be defined in terms of a specified increment along the physical health continuum, for a specified period of time. To continue the conceptual development, I presume below that such a unit has been operationally defined.

3. EVALUATING FINAL OUTPUTS: INTRINSIC VALUE

My use of the term **intrinsic value** derives from John Ruskin, a 19th century social theorist and critic of art and architecture. Ruskin defined intrinsic value as ".. the absolute power of anything to support life." He insisted that this power is objective and thus independent of human desire and judgment.

Based on the standard of value and cost developed above, I define intrinsic value as the capacity of a final output to support human life or to increase overall human health. If the output has the opposite effect - if it destroys life or decreases health, then its intrinsic value is a negative quantity.

The key word here is "capacity". Earlier I stated that an apple might increase health by ten health increments for three days. If we define the health unit as one health increment for one day, then an apple contains 30 health units of intrinsic value.

An apple, however, can be thrown away or allowed to spoil. The 30 units constitute only a potential, which may or may not be realized. The apple has to be eaten, while fresh, by someone who can fully assimilate its nutrients. Only then will the 30 units of potential health be transformed into 30 units of actual health.

Note that the discussion here is about final outputs - objects and services that are directly consumed, such as food, furniture, and haircuts. These outputs must be distinguished from intermediate outputs such as raw materials, buildings, tools, and machinery. While intermediate outputs are essential to production, they are not directly consumed and do not, themselves, contribute to human life and health. They therefore fall outside the definition of intrinsic value.

The intrinsic value of an output is a constant quantity. No matter how many apples are produced, it is presumably always possible for someone to consume the last one so as to extract its full health potential.

Intrinsic value refers to the potential health flowing from an output during its entire lifespan. If a house is expected to last 50 years, and if it will deliver an average of 100,000 health units per year, then the intrinsic value of the house is 5,000,000 health units. The same principle holds for effectual value and input cost, which are discussed next.

To summarize, intrinsic value can be positive or negative, and is measured in health units. It is used in the human framework to judge the quality of an economy's outputs.

4. EVALUATING CONSUMPTION: EFFECTUAL VALUE

Whereas intrinsic value is a capacity, **effectual value** is the realization of this capacity through consumption. It expresses the degree to which the conversion of potential to actual health has been successful.

If the apple mentioned above is consumed in such a manner that all its intrinsic value is realized, the outcome is 30 health units of effectual value. If half the apple is eaten and the rest discarded, the outcome is 15 units. If the apple is left to rot, the result is zero units.

Like intrinsic value, effectual value can be positive or negative, and is measured in health units. Unlike intrinsic value, it tends to decrease at the margin as more of an output is consumed.

There are several reasons why effectual value tends to decrease. An output is generally applied first to highly valued uses, and then progressively to less valued uses. Clean water, for instance, is first used to slake thirst, then to cook food, and finally to water lawns and wash cars. As the available quantity of clean water increases, the health benefits of the last increment tends to decline.

Another reason is satiation: one apple a day produces excellent health benefits, but the body can absorb only a finite quantity of an apple's nutrients. As more apples are eaten, the health gains of the last one will steadily diminish. Eating too many apples will eventually decrease health, which is why marginal effectual value becomes negative in Figure 2.

In brief, effectual value is used in the human framework to judge consumption. It answers the question: given a certain amount of intrinsic value created in production, how effectively is this converted into real health benefits?

5. THE ECONOMY AND NATURE

The standard proposed above pertains to human beings exclusively. It is inapplicable to the natural world outside our bodies. Humanity is the realm of value and cost, while nature is the realm of physical stocks and flows.

A key conceptual problem is how to bridge this divide. If production destroys an environmental asset we cannot refer to this as a cost without self-contradiction. Yet we must account for the negative impact if we are to respect ecological constraints. I have adopted the following approach.

First, I make two distinctions:

1. **Between marginal effects and threshold effects.** When a lake is initially polluted, the pollutants affect human health incrementally by contaminating fish and poisoning drinking and swimming water. These are marginal effects. Beyond a critical point, the lake's ecosystem will collapse. This is a threshold effect.

2. **Between marginal effects that impact human life and health, and those that do not.** The latter include environmental changes that some people may find aesthetically or spiritually destructive, but that do not have health consequences.

Second, based on these distinctions, I divide the natural effects of production into three categories:

1. Marginal effects that impact human life and health
2. Marginal effects that do not impact human life and health
3. Threshold effects

The first category can be addressed with the concept of natural cost, defined below. The second category falls outside the scope of the standard of value and cost, which means such effects cannot be analyzed in the human framework. The third category cannot be addressed with marginal analysis in principle because a threshold entails discontinuity. An analytical approach to threshold effects is offered in the ecological framework.

The fact that the second category falls outside the scope of the human framework is not a weakness, but reflects the intentional limits placed on the framework. As indicated in part 1 of my paper, an economic theory should not overextend itself. Many issues are not primarily economic, but rather political, ethical, or spiritual. Economics is the study of production, exchange, and consumption. It should fully address these, but if it attempts to do more it will blur its concepts and impair its analytical acuity.

human economics: putting humanity and
the environment before profit
Frank Rotering

6. EVALUATING PRODUCTION: COSTS

When inputs are used up in production, two different things are sacrificed:

1. The possibility of employing the same inputs for any other production
2. The impacts on the participants in production - the human beings who provide the labour and the natural facilities that furnish the resources and receive the wastes

Among the most blatant ideological distortions in standard economics is the reduction of both types of sacrifices to the first. The second type is ignored, thus sweeping the potential destruction of people and nature under the rug. This ethically bankrupt combination is called opportunity cost.

Despite its misuse by standard economics, opportunity cost is not a false concept, but rather a limited one. The human framework accepts the concept within its proper scope. In the human framework, the **opportunity cost** of using an input in production is the intrinsic value of the best alternative output to which that input could have been applied. By minimizing opportunity cost in production we allocate labour and natural facilities to the outputs that maximize potential health benefits.

The second type of sacrifice is called **input cost**, defined as the direct and indirect effects of production on human life and health. When these effects are direct - through labour - they are called **labour cost**. When they are indirect - through environmental changes associated with production - they are called **natural cost**. The sum of labour cost and natural cost is the input cost of production.

Labour can cause both positive and negative health effects. Labour cost is positive when labour causes excessive fatigue, debilitating stress, injuries, disease, or death. It is negative when labour increases strength, stamina, vigour, etc.

Note the potential confusion here. Cost - meaning positive cost - refers to the sacrifice human beings make in obtaining value. A positive cost is therefore a bad thing - it implies a decrease in life and health. Conversely, a negative cost is a good thing - it implies an increase in life health. Please take this inversion into account when you examine Figure 2.

Natural cost can also be positive or negative, and the same inversion applies as for labour cost.

Natural cost is positive when production fouls the environment and destroys habitat in such a manner that human health is adversely affected. It is negative when production creates a cleaner or more habitable environment, resulting in increased human health.

Both labour cost and natural cost are assumed to increase at the margin. This is consistent with our experience: as labour time increases, fatigue, stress, and injuries will all tend to rise; as pollution accumulates, its health effects will steadily worsen.

7. OPTIMUM QUANTITY FOR A FINAL OUTPUT

The four quantities discussed above can now be graphed to determine, in a general conceptual sense, the optimum quantity for a final output. This is depicted in Figure 2.

The optimization rule is that quantity should increase until the rising cost of production (input cost) exceeds the falling value of consumption (effectual value). This occurs at quantity Q^*, which is therefore the optimum quantity for the final output.

At Q^* human beings gain the maximum possible health - represented by the shaded area at left. If less is produced, this area will shrink. If more is produced, losses are incurred, as shown by the shaded area at right. These losses must be subtracted from the gains, thus reducing net gains.

It is important to note that Q^* is an optimum quantity, not just a maximum quantity. We must decrease output to Q^* if it is currently more, but we must not fail to increase output to Q^* if it is currently less. I underscore this because many outputs are underproduced, not overproduced. This is particularly true for those that address the needs of the poor.

The optimization shown here is based on the current value and cost curves, but an economy can - and frequently should - be reorganized to change these. If outputs are distributed more equally and fewer are wasted, the effectual value curve will move up. This will increase the optimum output quantity.

Similarly, if fewer workers die and suffer injuries in production, and if reduced pollution improves health, the input cost curve will move down. This will again increase the optimum output quantity.

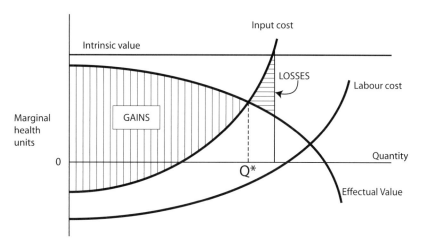

Figure 2: *Optimum quantity for a final output*

The optimum quantity of an output is therefore not fixed, but shifts according to the conditions of production and consumption. To improve an economy, we can choose to move output quantity toward the optimum, change the conditions, or both.

One more point: if input cost is equal to or greater than effectual value when quantity is zero, then this output should not be produced at all.

An apparent limitation of the above method is that it applies exclusively to final outputs. This leaves open an important question: what is the optimum quantity for an intermediate output such as a raw material, lorry (truck), or accounting service?

As stated, intermediate outputs have no intrinsic value. We can consume the food transported by a lorry, but not the lorry itself. The "value" of an intermediate output is therefore a derived quantity - it depends on the intrinsic value of the final outputs it helps produce. If a community needs 20 lorries to transport the optimum quantity of its food from farm to shop, then the optimum quantity of its food-transporting lorries is 20.

In general: The optimum quantity of an intermediate output is the minimum required to produce the optimum quantities of all the final outputs with which it is associated.

If the above is correct, we have a broad conceptual approach for determining optimum quantities of both final and intermediate outputs.

This answers two fundamental questions for any economy - what to produce and in what quantities.

However, the logic is incomplete because it ignores thresholds, which are critical factors in a world of expanding populations and rising production levels. The method must therefore be modified to account for the potential destruction of human life and health caused by threshold collapses associated with production. This modification is a central element of the ecological framework.

D. THE ECOLOGICAL FRAMEWORK

1. HUMANITY AND NATURE

The relationship between humanity and nature was a highly contentious issue in the group discussion. In the view of several participants, human beings are creatures like all others, are fully integrated with and dependent on nature, and must submit to natural realities.

I agree that human beings are integrated with and dependent on nature, but in my view our species plays a unique role which must be fully acknowledged.

Human beings are part of nature in that they are biological entities, have evolved along with the planet's other life forms, and support their existence by converting low-entropy resources into high-entropy wastes.

Our species is unique in that we possess acute self-awareness, high intelligence, advanced

human economics: putting humanity and
the environment before profit
Frank Rotering

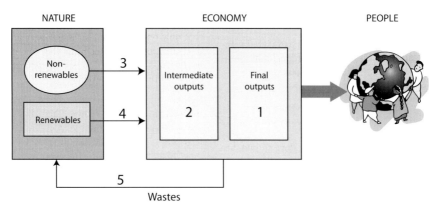

Figure 3: *The ecological abstraction*

technical capabilities, and have the resultant capacity to decisively impact the other life forms and the earth's environment. It is this potential impact that separates us ethically from the planet's non-human inhabitants.

2. THE ECOLOGICAL ABSTRACTION

To address any complex reality, a theory requires an appropriate abstraction. An abstraction is appropriate when it ignores extraneous details while highlighting the features for which the theory assumes analytical responsibility. Human economics must find an abstraction of nature that permits it to address ecological constraints in sufficient, but not excessive, detail.

Figure 3 depicts my proposed ecological abstraction.

Nature is the source of nonrenewable and renewable resources flows, and the recipient of waste flows. The economy is the consumer of resource flows, the producer of intermediate and final outputs, the source of waste flows, and the provider of outputs to human beings.

The two resource flows are separated because renewables can be exploited beyond the rate of natural regeneration, which means they are subject to thresholds. This is not true for nonrenewables, which are finite stocks that can be depleted at will. Wastes can overload natural sinks and, like renewables, are subject to thresholds.

Intermediate and final outputs are separated because they have different economic roles, and because their optimum quantities are determined in different ways.

The resource and waste flows are not further subdivided in order to restrict the scope of the ecological framework. A more detailed abstraction would encroach on the physical sciences and expand the framework beyond its analytical requirements and aims.

The numbers in the diagram indicate the five critical quantities in the nature-economy relationship. Human economics must find general conceptual approaches for determining their target values. Deriving these methods will permit us to accurately define a sustainable society.

3. ECOLOGICAL EFFICIENCY

Ecological efficiency is a relationship between a specific resource or waste flow and a final output. It is defined as the intrinsic value of the final output divided by the flow used in its production, use, and disposal. This includes the flow associated with the production, use, and disposal of all intermediate outputs in the final output's production chain.

Because final outputs usually incorporate several resource or waste flows, more than one ecological efficiency is normally associated with a final output.

Ecological efficiency is a ratio of mixed dimensions. The numerator is always in total health units, but the unit in the denominator varies with the material nature of the flow. Examples:

- Health units/board-feet of lumber (Renewable resource)
- Health units/tonne of iron (Nonrenewable resource)

- Health units/gigatonnes of greenhouse gases (Waste)

Unless ecological efficiencies are associated with the same flow, they are incommensurable and thus cannot be summed or compared.

An important objective is that human beings must strive to maximize all ecological efficiencies. This means that for any combination of final output and flow, the health gains of the output should be maximized, and the flow should be minimized.

This is an important principle because it transcends scarcity. It compels us to economize on ALL flows, not just on scarce flows. Standard economics, through prices and opportunity costs, seeks to optimally allocate only scarce inputs. It thereby neglects non-scarce resources and indirectly encourages scarcity to appear.

4. THRESHOLDS

a. Summary of the Issue

A threshold is an ecological discontinuity - the point where the flow of a renewable resource into the economy, or of a waste back to nature, triggers a sudden ecosystem collapse. In most cases, the physical sciences can determine only approximately when such a collapse will occur. Thresholds confront human economics with two distinct questions:

1. What, if any, is the ethical justification for risking a threshold collapse?
2. If such justification exists, how should the risk and consequences of collapse be analyzed?

The graph in Figure 4 will help me frame the issue:

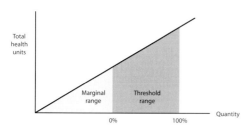

Figure 4: Marginal and threshold ranges

The upward-sloping line indicates that total health increases linearly with the quantity of a final output. As quantity and health increase, so

does the flow of a renewable resource or waste (I assume a resource here). For simplicity, assume that only one resource flow is involved, and that it is uniquely associated with this output. The flow itself is not shown - it is expressed in terms of the output that incorporates it.

Assume that the flow's ecological efficiency has been maximized, and that no alternative output can achieve the same health effect. We therefore have an unavoidable trade-off between health and threshold risk.

From the physical sciences we learn that the flow initially poses no risk of ecological collapse. This is called the marginal range, shown in Fig 4. Within this range, the marginal analysis employed thus far is valid.

Science further informs us that this flow is subject to a threshold effect, and that a threshold range therefore exists. This is the right hand zone in Fig 4, where the probability of ecological collapse increases from 0% to 100%. Marginal analysis, which assumes continuous change, cannot be used here.

As quantity increases within the threshold range, the probability of ecological collapse tends to rise more and more rapidly. That is, the probability increase from 0% to 100% is exponential, not linear. This is not shown in the diagram, but is assumed below.

Based on the diagram, the problem can be restated as follows: should the quantity of this output enter the threshold range, and if so, how far should it rationally go?

b. Ethical Considerations

A common view among environmentalists is that human beings have no right to risk any ecological collapse, under any circumstances. While this stance appears commendable, it has extreme consequences. If strictly applied, it would prevent us from incurring even the smallest chance of collapse for an extremely localized threshold effect, while sacrificing immense potential health gains.

Imagine, for example, that farming over a large area will incur a 1% probability of driving an indigenous flower to extinction, but that the farm products will significantly improve the health of millions of poor peasants.

Does a well-founded ethical principle exist that justifies the sacrifice of such a large health

GALWAY COUNTY LIBRARIES

human economics: putting humanity and
the environment before profit
Frank Rotering

benefit to humanity for such a small risk to nature? I have been unable to formulate one, and the discussion group did not offer one in response to my request.

I tentatively conclude that - as an *economic* principle - human beings should risk threshold collapse if the potential health gains from production exceed the potential health losses from collapse.

I ignore the "inherent worth" of nature in this conclusion not because it is irrelevant, but because it falls outside the scope of economic logic. The peasant society in my example might decide to forgo the health benefits from farming in order to avoid the small risk of destroying the indigenous flower. Such a decision might be based on the inherent worth of the species, or on other ethical or cultural considerations. Any of these can legitimately override economic calculations.

c. Analytical Method

Because marginal analysis does not apply to thresholds, a different logic is required - one developed specifically to handle risk and uncertainty. Statisticians have developed several decision-making criteria to deal with such cases. Among the best-known are maximin, minimax regret, and expected monetary value.

Both maximin and minimax regret have been used to address environmental issues, but neither can incorporate the fact that the probability of threshold collapse tends to increase exponentially. Only expected monetary value permits this, making it is the most useful criterion for dealing with thresholds.

My suggested method, which is described in detail in part 4 of my paper, retains the essential aspects of expected monetary value, but transforms this into expected threshold cost. This is the probable loss of human health from threshold collapse for each level of output in the threshold zone.

As might be expected, the application of expected threshold cost to the marginal analysis can dramatically reduce the optimum output quantity. For a pervasive threshold such as that associated with global warming, the method virtually forbids entry into the threshold range. For a localized threshold with negligible health impact, on the other hand, the method permits quantity to increase beyond the threshold range,

to the original optimum. This is the case in my peasant society example.

5. TARGET QUANTITIES

When I introduced the ecological abstraction I cited five sets of quantities and flows for which human economics must be find target values. These are:

1. Final output quantities
2. Intermediate output quantities
3. Nonrenewable resources flows
4. Renewable resource flows
5. Wastes flows

Final outputs are logically first because they directly support human life and health, which constitutes the economy's purpose. All the other target quantities and flows are derived from these initial targets.

To maximize human gains, the effectual value of final outputs must be maximized, and the input cost of producing these outputs must be minimized. In terms of the graph in Figure 2, this means the effectual value curve must be as close to the intrinsic value line as possible, and the input cost curve must be as low as is feasible. The optimal output quantity that results from these curves defines the maximum rational quantity for an output.

To respect ecological limits, this maximum quantity must be scaled back by the threshold logic. The optimum that results is called the **target optimum**. See Figure 5.

The target optimum is the quantity of a final output that achieves the maximum possible gains in human life and health when thresholds are taken into account. It is the starting point for deriving all the target quantities and flows. Referring to each individual quantity and flow, these are:

1. FINAL OUTPUT QUANTITY: the target optimum established above.
2. INTERMEDIATE OUTPUT QUANTITY: the minimum quantity required to produce the target optimums of all associated final outputs.
3. NONRENEWABLE RESOURCE FLOW: the quantity required to produce the optimum quantities of all associated final and intermediate outputs, at peak ecological efficiencies.

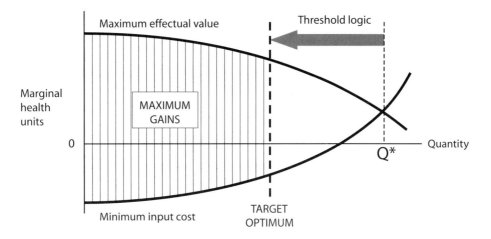

Figure 5: *The target optimum*

4. RENEWABLE RESOURCE FLOW: same as for #3. Threshold effects have already been considered in establishing the optimum quantities for the associated final outputs.

5. WASTE FLOW: also the same as for #3. Again, threshold effects have already been considered.

To summarize, the target quantity of a final output is derived by maximizing its associated health gains and applying threshold logic. We then work backwards through the production chain to find the target quantities of its associated intermediate outputs and flows.

Applied to the economy as a whole, this logic maximizes human well-being while respecting ecological constraints. In other words, it achieves the objective of human economics.

E. A HUMANE AND SUSTAINABLE ECONOMY

I am now in a position to define sustainability. For clarity, I limit the scope of the term to an economy's ecological soundness. If an economy adequately meets human needs it is referred to as "humane".

I reject two common notions:

1. Sustainability is not the same as stability, or lack of change. An economy can be extraordinarily dynamic and still be ecologically sound.

2. Sustainability does not mean living off self-regenerating renewables. Nonrenewable resources can sharply increase human well-being. To leave such resources untapped is not a triumph of environmental integrity, but a collapse of human reason.

In my view, sustainability refers to the maximum justifiable rates at which an economy can consume the earth's resources. As an ethical principle, I suggest that there is no better use for any resource or waste flow than meeting the vital needs of the present generation. Since future generations issue from our bodies, our health is the basis for their health. Fully meeting our vital needs is thus more than justified, it is a moral imperative.

Using the concepts introduced above, an economy is sustainable if its resource and waste flows do not exceed their target quantities. It is humane to the extent that each of its final outputs approaches its target optimum.

If all five target quantities are achieved, the result is a humane and sustainable economy.

A Response to Frank Rotering's "Human Economics: A Theory for Humanity and the Environment"

Douglas McCulloch

Introduction

I would like to start by thanking Frank for his paper, which I found very interesting. This response follows the structure of Frank's main paper; I have tried to be as objective as possible, and to respect the views of someone who has obviously taken the issues very seriously.

I do not agree that "those who hold conventional views are bolstered by a set of sophisticated economic concepts". There is no inequality, as such, between us and our political opponents. Also, economics does not represent the viewpoint of the class of capitalists, if such a class exists. Everyone who has a pension plan is a capitalist; for the rest of us, in the words of an old trade unionist, "you compromise with capitalism in every breath you take". In any case, do we really need a theory of economics with which to meet the theory of "the establishment"? There are many ideas in economics which can be used by Greens (externalities, public goods, competition). The present situation has come about because of the interests of people, and what they do, not what they believe about economics.

Human Economics: A theory for humanity and the environment

"An economic theory would force us to derive our policy prescriptions from first principles and systematic logic. It would enable us to confirm our correct notions and repudiate our errors." Would this help us make our economy more sustainable? If the theory is incomplete, presumably we should put off doing anything until it is right - when would we know, and how long will it take?

What does it mean to say "our economic terminology is currently a mess"? Do we really "lack terms for ideas we cherish and use ill-conceived terms that subvert our purposes"? These are quite serious charges, for which I do not see any evidence. I do not agree either that capitalists have an ideology, nor do I share Frank's optimism that a new theory would clarify our ideas and the effectiveness of our actions. Conventional economics does not do this for business people, who rely on cunning and wit, and not on economics; why should our own do it for us?

The world is not a debating chamber; "winning the argument" does not mean getting a motion passed in some kind of forum of world opinion, to the eternal betterment of mankind. "Winning the argument" within the Green movement could mean silencing those who feel unable to criticise analysis, or it could mean helping to develop a common view of the way the world works, with which to inform wider debates, in the knowledge that there is some agreement among those of us who understand that we cannot stand by and continue to watch the destruction of the planet. .

The structure of Human Economics

"To formulate economic concepts and analytical tools that permit the maximisation of human well-being, subject to ecological constraints" is not a soluble problem. The failure of the theory of markets to solve it should make us beware similar attempts.

Graphs and rigour

I spend a lot of time trying to get people to see the value of functional relationships presented in graphical terms. If people are to consider graphs useful and illuminating, they must first recognise the variables described; in this case, it seems that some at least did not find the variables meaningful. This is a flaw in the theory, not in the recipients. The objective of argument is to persuade; a theory will not persuade unless it ties in, somehow, with the experience of the intended recipients

Also, is it really easy "to hide sloppy logic in a profusion of words"? We may be surrounded by sloppy logic and poor writing, in words, but words themselves do not conceal bad reasoning. Anything expressed using mathematics, if worthwhile, should be capable of expression in words.

The human framework

The use of single standards on which to base resource allocation is perhaps the single greatest curse afflicting public policy in the UK. As Andre

Douglas McCulloch has been a lecturer in economics at the University of Ulster since its creation in 1984, and at the Ulster Polytechnic since 1975; his PhD was awarded in 1998. In that time, he has also worked in the Northern Ireland Government service, and at the Irish Centre of Pharmacoeconomics in Dublin, as a health economist. Publications include numerous articles, a textbook on health valuation, and the Irish Health Technology Assessment Guidelines. He is Chairman of the Health Economics Association of Ireland.

Gide put it, "Tyranny is the absence of complexity", and the UK government is abdicating from its democratic responsibilities by using budget limits and crude measures of output to determine resource allocation. Together, these are slowly strangling the education and health sectors of the UK. It might be that some single standard is possible, but the political problems of a single standard, in that it focuses power with those who determine and measure such a standard, have to be reckoned with.

It is surprising that Frank considers health to be objective and measurable, because most Greens have a degree of scepticism about the claims of science to objectivity. Certainly, an appreciation of randomised controlled trials, and the application of their results to medical practice, should make us pause before crediting physicians with objectivity.

Also, it turns out that health is actually quite hard to measure. There is a whole literature on valuing health [see references below], which has attempted to provide a metric with which to compare health states. None of the measures has been put forward, far less accepted, as objective; they are part of the health economists' (fairly laudable) attempt to help determine which drugs or interventions are better value for money. In the absence of such an objective metric, regrettably, Frank's rather satisfying theoretical construction cannot work.

Thresholds

The distinction between threshold effects and marginal effects is a valuable contribution to our thinking. However, it may be a mistake to suggest that Greens should not be concerned about habitat degradation in principle. We simply may not be aware of it when the biosphere has passed the point where its destruction cannot be prevented. Until we know, it seems better to err on the side of maintaining biodiversity, at least, or anything else which might prevent the ultimate disaster.

"Such a decision might be based on the inherent worth of the species, or on other ethical or cultural considerations. Any of these can legitimately override economic calculations." Why are we going to all the trouble of developing this new economics, and putting so much resources into collecting the necessary information, if all our complex analysis can be dumped because someone goes dewy-eyed over a rare orchid? Frank is trying to be hard-headed, but he still gives precedence to non-materialist ideals, unlike the reductionist economists who have so impressed him.

Does economic analysis as such make a difference? I doubt it. I teach people to think using economics; they do not seem to become indoctrinated with materialist values, not more than other people, anyway. In my view, Frank has too high an opinion of the importance of economic ideas. Other people (non-Greens) are more like us than unlike, and they are often open to reason. They have their own reasonable beliefs. They will have interests which will affect the arguments they are willing to listen to, or even affect the meaning they ascribe to the words they hear, but the facts will speak to them if their interests are affected. We have to find the right arguments, based on the facts, case by case, and we should share our experiences as we go. That's about it.

Conclusion

The objective we share is progress towards a clearer view of how the sustainable economy might work, and the Rotering papers have made a large contribution to that. The main problem I have with Human Economics is that it relies on the measurement of health. My feeling is that if health could be measured objectively, the pharmaceutical multinationals would have found a way. Most developed countries have guidelines for the acceptance of new compounds which require the companies to demonstrate cost-effectiveness using a measure of health outcome. Any objective measure which enabled the companies to provide this would have been developed and in use by now.

Health economists have done little better than the drugs firms. As health economics developed, it appeared that the measurement of a procedure's impact on the quality of the patient's life and on his or her survival, amalgamated into a single measure, the "quality-adjusted life year" or QALY, might help prioritise the allocation of resources. Over the past thirty or so years, although several QALY measures have been developed, none of these is objective since all rely on patient or carer evaluation of health states. Thus, despite a generation's work, no QALY measure has achieved the status of an accepted objective measure of health which permits the comparison of all interventions in cost per QALY terms.

Deciding what was to be produced in an economy on the basis of the cost per QALY would require large assumptions about what was known (or could be known) about costs and outcomes, especially the relationship between each and the level of production, across the whole range of possible outputs. The amount of information, and the cost of assembling it, would be immense.

What is produced in an economy depends on the consumer wants. Consequently, in determining the mix of production technologies the economy should use, we have to know what wants we are meeting. This presents difficulties because the division between consumption and production may be an ideologically unsound carry-over from conventional economics if one is aiming to build a sustainable economy. For example, the taking of holidays (consumption) would not be so necessary if people's working lives (production) were adequately healthy and congenial; and the production of health services would be much less if many individuals' consumption patterns (diet, drugs, alcohol) were different. There are many other possible examples. The division in our thinking between consumption and production may conceal important possibilities for re-structuring our economies towards sustainability.

Finally, while I am not sure that the global approach of Human Economics will be as productive as the development of policy frameworks and strategies for particular sectors, I am convinced of the value of the Rotering papers. They constitute a substantial contribution to the working out and the eventual development of the sustainable economy, whatever form it takes, and however we get there.

References

Barer ML, Getzen TE, and Stoddart GL *Health, Health Care, and Health Economics* Wiley 1998 [See Uwe Reinhardt in this]

Drummond M and McGuire A *Economic Evaluation in Health Care* Oxford University Press 2001 [Conventional economist's approach to producing cost-effectiveness analysis]

McCulloch D *Valuing Health In Practice* Ashgate 2003 [Assumptions examined]

Nord E *Cost Value Analysis in Health Care* Cambridge University Press 1999 [Probably the most important criticism of the idea of a health metric]

Sloan F *Valuing Health Care* Cambridge University Press 1995 [Conventional scientific approach]

The Third Annual Feasta Lecture, Trinity College, Dublin, 30 October 2001

THE LEAN ECONOMY

A Vision of Civility for a World in Trouble

David Fleming

The depletion of oil and gas, the degradation of the environment and the decline of social capital all threaten to collapse the market economy. Fleming believes that such a collapse cannot be averted and that public policy should concentrate on laying the foundations for the transformed political economy that could rise from the ashes. In his lecture he explored the social and cultural qualities that will be indispensable for surviving the crash and moving on to recovery, renewal and stability.

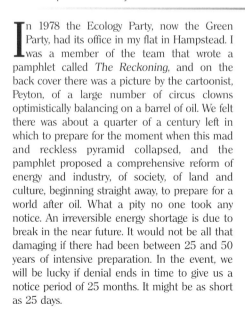

David Fleming studied history at Oxford (1963), business management at Cranfield (1968) and economics at Birkbeck College, London, completing a PhD in 1988. After working in industry he became an independent consultant and writer. He was elected to the Council of the Ecology (Green) Party in 1977 and served as economics spokesman and press secretary; the party office was his flat in Hampstead. He later worked on the Council of the Soil Association, which he chaired 1988-91. He has recently completed two books: *The Lean Economy: The Book of Sustainable Civility*, and *Lean Logic: A Dictionary for Our Time*, which are due to be published shortly.

In 1978 the Ecology Party, now the Green Party, had its office in my flat in Hampstead. I was a member of the team that wrote a pamphlet called *The Reckoning*, and on the back cover there was a picture by the cartoonist, Peyton, of a large number of circus clowns optimistically balancing on a barrel of oil. We felt there was about a quarter of a century left in which to prepare for the moment when this mad and reckless pyramid collapsed, and the pamphlet proposed a comprehensive reform of energy and industry, of society, of land and culture, beginning straight away, to prepare for a world after oil. What a pity no one took any notice. An irreversible energy shortage is due to break in the near future. It would not be all that damaging if there had been between 25 and 50 years of intensive preparation. In the event, we will be lucky if denial ends in time to give us a notice period of 25 months. It might be as short as 25 days.

When it does hit, and when oil famine is joined with the other problems on the way, we will need to respond to it as to an avalanche. There is no point in trying to stop it; instead: survive; think; start again on safer ground and on totally different principles.

1. OIL AND GAS

We begin with conventional crude oil, the stuff that can be pumped from oilwells in reasonably accessible places on land and on the sea-bed, and source of almost all the petroleum in use today – and there is one main thing to remember about it: in order to produce it you must, first, discover it. That is obvious enough, but there is an important corollary. Production follows discovery by something of the order of 20-40 years, so that, if you draw a graph of the rate in which oil is discovered in any particular place (the curve on the left in figure 1), you can draw another graph of the rate at which it will be produced (the curve on the right).

And in figure 2 we have those two pictures drawn with real numbers for the world as a whole. Discovery of conventional oil peaked in 1965; this means that the production of conventional oil peaks some forty years later.

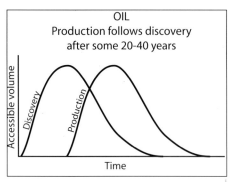

Figure 1. *The production of oil follows discovery.*

Conventional crude oil is by far the most convenient form of oil; it is accessible, easy to pump, transport and refine. But there are alternatives. "Unconventional" sources of oil include tar sands, present in abundance in Canada, and heavy oil from a variety of places, notably the Orinoco oil deposits in Venezuela. The difficulty with these deposits is that they are very energy-intensive to produce; in the case of the tar sands, for example, opencast mines have to be dug; the product then has to be heated and compressed, and the waste material must then be disposed of in unstable mountains of spoil. You cannot always be sure that the energy actually derived from this process is more than the energy put into it; this is not the massive rich

flow of energy which comes from conventional oil. Then there is deep-water oil (more than 500m); and ways are also being investigated of extracting that little bit more ("enhanced oil recovery") from conventional oil wells. And there are "natural gas liquids" from gas fields, which have been making a useful contribution to the supply of oil since the early 1970s, and will continue to do so.

The main alternative to oil is gas. The world as a whole has used about 35 percent of its original endowment. Most of the remainder is in Russia (at the end of a very long pipeline from the Western Europeans that will depend on it) and in the Middle East. It is far from certain that the stability of either of these sources can be sustained in a global political economy devastated by the depletion of oil.

This is summarised in figure 3. The best estimate is that the peak production of oil, worldwide, is due around the middle of the decade 2001-2010. The story could be elaborated by adding in the peak and depletion of gas, to give a picture of "all hydrocarbons", but the effect of the oil peak on demand for gas is highly uncertain: better to stay with oil for the moment. Oil drives the world's transport; transport drives the world's economy, and it is the necessary condition for practically every material need of urban life. The global economy relies on an ever-growing production of

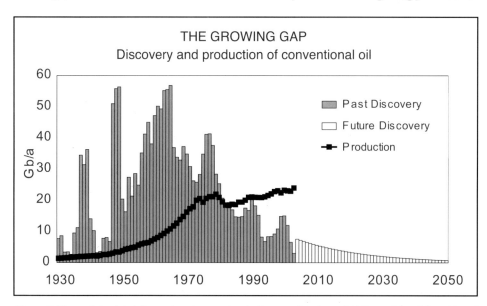

Figure 2. *The peak in global discoveries of conventional oil occurred in the mid 1960s, and was followed by a long decline. Production's peak follows about forty years later.[1] Source: Colin Campbell: ASPO Newsletter.*

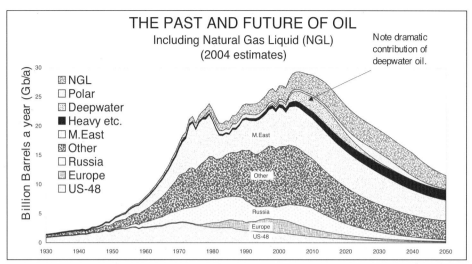

Figure 3. *The past and future of oil worldwide. (Production is measured in gigabarrels of oil equivalent; 1 gigabarrel = 1 billion barrels.). Source: Colin Campbell: ASPO Newsletter.*

oil, but oil production is about to go into decline.

You may also be thinking that if all this is true, then the experts would have been forecasting it long ago - in the 1960s, perhaps. Well, they were. The petroleum geologist King Hubbert established the science in the 1950s. And after that, forecasts that oil production would peak around the turn of the century followed fast - from the UK's Department of Energy, from President Carter's *Global 2000 Report to the President*, and from geologists in every oil province of the world who have pooled their hard evidence and have been consistently disbelieved.

We could, you know, had we taken these forecasts seriously, have built a solar economy by now. "We" - if someone had taken the lead - could have meant the whole global economy; the cost of energy - given the technical sophistication and the economies of scale which would by now have developed for the world economy - would be low. Global warming would be under control. There would be very much larger oil reserves still in the ground. And we would not be becoming increasingly dependent on oil provinces already half a century old and showing their age in five countries in the Middle East: Iran, Iraq, Saudi Arabia and the United Arab Emirates.

Now, if the path ahead of us were really one of gentle decline at some 2 percent a year, even this would land us in deep trouble, with global growth abruptly stopped, and the energy that underpins our way of life, including food production, declining more quickly than the rate at which there is any real prospect of developing alternatives on the needed scale. But the transition is unlikely to be so smooth. Rivalry over access to oil, combined with near-monopoly powers in the hands of a few producers, will set the scene for the start of disruptions in supply.

And, in North America, reserves of gas have reached a level of depletion at which production will go into steep decline in the middle years of this decade. Gas, the fuel which heats American homes, drives much of its industry, provides much of its electricity, and is the feedstock for its fertiliser, will have to be imported from Russia. Gas will suddenly become scarce, and America will become very vulnerable, being dependent on increasingly unstable import supply lines for the two hydrocarbons on which its political economy depends. When breakdowns in supply and increases in price occur, this will be to everyone's surprise and dismay - which is an odd thing, considering that the essential nature of the problem has been understood for decades.

New technologies – renewables, conservation systems, ways of substituting between oil, gas and coal – will be ready to be developed. They will not, however, be ready to take over. The market economy will be in shock. Like an army caught napping, it will not have time even to reach for its trusted, new, high-tech equipment.

2. OTHER THREATS TO THE MARKET ECONOMY

The coming oil shock is not the only reason why the prospects for the global market economy and for civilisation as a whole look poor. A complex system, such as a car or a human body, tends at the end of its life to fail in many different ways at about the same time. A second sign of systems failure is climate change. Thirdly, there is the complex and still poorly-understood issue of how a mature market economy can, even under ideal conditions, sustain the perpetual economic growth which is an essential condition for its stability: along with Richard Douthwaite and others I argue that it simply cannot do so. Fourthly, there is the increasingly intense phenomenon of disengagement – a failure of participation, consent, shared values, social cohesion – in short, a failure of social capital which ultimately matures into insurgency, both from dissidents on the outside of modern society and from within it. The system is failing in many other ways: soil fertility, water, hormone disruptors, the collapse of fisheries – but that is enough for now.

If we put all these together, then we find ourselves looking at the climax of the market economy, followed by its comprehensive failure, very high unemployment and an atrophy of government revenues, leading towards what could be called hyperunemployment - that is, unemployment so high that government cannot fund subsistence payments and pensions. Unemployment on this scale means no income. No income means no food. No food means the collapse of urban populations on the scale experienced by former civic societies – the Romans and some two dozen other accomplished civilisations – in the closing phase of their life-cycles. I hope I am wrong or, rather, that it doesn't come to this. But it does seem obvious to me that the opportunity is rapidly passing in which it will be possible to avoid the high levels of mortality that have been associated with the collapse of other civic societies.

With the Romans, there was a long period of troubles, some 250 years, before the empire finally collapsed. Our period of troubles is likely to be condensed (figure 4) because the four problems I have mentioned are converging *so fast*. My suggested period of 25 years is indicative only. From the climax of the market economy - when the downturn comes, and employment

(solid line) falls decisively - to the point of hyperunemployment, could be some 25 years. Perhaps the turning point is 2010. According to these very arbitrary time intervals I am giving you, that makes 2035 the point at which hyperunemployment and its consequences occur. By that time, the Lean Economy (dashed line) must have been built up to a scale at which it can provide a working alternative: a new economic and social order.

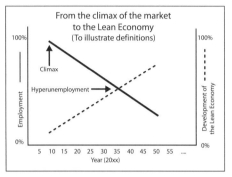

Figure 4. *After the climax of the market economy, it will go into steep decline. The damage will be immediate, and the task will be to build the essential structures of the Lean Economy before the crisis of hyperunemployment – when the government can no longer maintain subsistence payments to the unemployed.*

3. THE NEW DOMESTICATION

Now, I want to draw attention to an advantage and asset that our civilisation can bring to solving its problem: industry.

In the world of hyperunemployment and market breakdown, industry will be substantially bankrupt, of course. And yet, it *has* developed some stunning assets in the course of the last century or so. It has developed a technology capable, for instance, of working on a very small scale; it is learning how to capture energy and store it, using very little of it to get results.

Industry has also successfully developed methods of creating effective human groups and keeping them working constructively together. It has been creative. It has some understanding of the way in which systems function, and how to audit a proposal for its unintended consequences, how to avoid denial. It has worked out how to manage itself with the decisive effectiveness of "lean thinking". Not every company we can think of is a shining example of these properties in practice, and companies' ultimate values and culture do tend to be thin and trivial. But, on the fundamentals of how to make things happen neatly, with minimum waste and on a small scale, companies have something important to offer – just, in fact, what households will need very badly indeed.

After the failure of the market economy, households will lack jobs, they will lack state handouts; above all, they will lack primary goods - food, water, energy and materials. Those are the things that really matter; they provide the basis for coping with life – and they are the things that urban populations cannot easily provide for themselves. Primaries will fall within the range of assets open to households if and only if there is a revolution in their effectiveness as producers. Households will need to become as competent in the future as industry is now; they will need to use many of industry's technologies and practices. The name of this revolution is "the new domestication".

There is an inspiration for this. 8000 years ago there was an evolution in human society when many human groups gradually began to turn away from being hunter-gatherers. Instead of going out, foraging and taking what they found, they began instead to bring animals and plants within the perimeter fence - domesticating them, taking *direct* responsibility for the fulfilment of their own primary needs. It was the start of something big. It was the first domestication. What I suggest lies ahead now is the second domestication when, instead of relying on industry to do the work and then foraging in the market, households and local economies bring industrial insights and technologies within, so to speak, the perimeter fence - bringing it under their direct control. The *new* domestication, then, can be seen for local economies as a process of growing-up, of evolution - not just a means of survival in the midst of global economic catastrophe, but a vision of civility.

Now, at the heart of the market economy is the idea of the specialisation of labour. Adam Smith explained the story, as I am sure you will remember. If you want to make a lot of pins, you can get ten men to turn them out - each individual completing as many pins as he can, or you can divide the job up into ten parts and get each man to do just one of the parts, and the output of pins will go up by (as Smith calculated), 4,800 times.

And the Romans made the same discovery. And so did every other civic society in history. But specialisation triggers off an astonishing spiral of elaboration. The sequence goes from *specialisation* to *productivity* to a *concentration* of the specialists in *towns*. And then we have long distances, transport, police forces, money, bureaucrats. Then there is the need for lots of equipment, for more productivity, for more specialisation. There is a *capture* and *concentration* of particular functions in particular places. The sequence has a dynamic of its own; it is virtually impossible to stop. It is a very expensive business. It is very *complicated*. It takes lot of swapping around just to get anything to work at all. And eventually it crashes under its own weight.

All civilisations crash. In the end, the political economy flips into a quite different, lightweight, decentralised order requiring a drastically reduced quantity of goods and services, minimal transport and much less specialisation. In response, people and localities start to provide most of what they need for themselves. This is the inevitable sequel to the closing stages of a civic society.

> *All civilisations crash. In the end, <<< the political economy flips into a quite different, lightweight, decentralised order*

In the past, those closing stages have led to a collapse into dark ages, with the population, as the Venerable Bede put it, being "cut down, like ripe corn". I would argue that the sooner we start to build distributed, decentralised, broadly competent local economies, the more realistic they become: the less the pain; the less the grief; the greater the prospects of evolution beyond the market economy - making something of what we have inherited, and building on it.

That is to say, there is a logical sequence which goes something like this (figure 5). We start with Capture and Concentration (left hand panel) with big, concentrated producers, far from home; the sequence moves through greater local complexity (centre panel) with smaller producers and many more of them. And then onwards - towards the

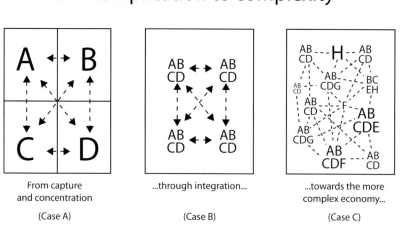

From complication to complexity

From capture
and concentration

(Case A)

...through integration...

(Case B)

...towards the more
complex economy...

(Case C)

Figure 5. Rethinking land-use: The market economy's pattern of "capture and concentration" with large centres linked by routine transport is inappropriate for the stabilised Lean Economy of the future, which will require a more sophisticated, complex organisation.

more complex economy (right-hand panel). The integration of functions on a small, local scale creates complex economic and social orders – communities – which, while having substantial qualities of self-sufficiency, are also dependent on the wider ecosystem; they integrate the two complementary properties of belonging and independence. What we have here is diversity, robustness to shocks, the ability to learn from experience, to make good use of available niches and opportunities, to innovate.

And, you will notice, there is no *routine* transport, no churning around from A to B to C to D. There are journeys to H, but every place is adapted to its own circumstance, develops its own personality. There is a sense of place. The presumption is that every place has learned how to hang on to its own material assets - how to use and re-use materials, using today's waste as tomorrow's resources, in the perpetual cycle of renewal known as a closed system.

Closed systems. It is here that the solution lies. And closed systems will take the form of local organisation, local economies. There will be no alternative. They will not be able to buy-in their needs, to import their way out of trouble. Local lean economies will not simply be a good idea; they will be the only option. And they will be organised on principles of lean thinking.

4. CLOSED SYSTEMS

Lean thinking, adapted to this context, is about establishing and sustaining a closed system which provides food, water, energy and materials from local resources and, as far as possible, conserves and renews these primary assets in the local economy. A closed system means no material imports, no material waste, and dependence on solar energy. Well, you cannot get completely closed systems in human affairs, except on the scale of the planet as a whole, but, on a local scale, you can get very much closer than we are at present.

A closed system in the case of food requires fertility to be retained locally – that is, not only nitrogen, phosphates and potash – but the micronutrients too. If conserved as capital, composted and used again and again, fertility – including human waste – can be more than simply sustained; it can be built up towards the extraordinarily high local yields achieved by such virtuosos of food production as Alan Chadwick and John Jeavons.

You don't have to do this, quite, with water, because it rains, of course, though we will have to get used to droughts as global warming intensifies, but even in a rainy climate, a local economy needs to maintain, shall we say, a conservation system in its use of water. Among the reasons for this – first, lean production will use aquaculture, which is a more productive food system than the soil; secondly, permaculture, which loves closed, circular systems, typically has a central place for water – for instance, the pond is habitat for water weeds, that fertilise the land, that grows the food, which is attacked by slugs, that are eaten by the ducks, that live in the pond, and fertilise the water weeds. Water has a way of connecting things up. One immensely effective form of it is the Japanese Aigamo method for rice production. It can be many times more productive, for a given area of land, than the most high-tech agriculture.

In the case of energy, closed systems do not really apply since they are defined in terms of materials, and energy takes a one-way ticket from the sun to dissipation in the form of low-level heat. But the principle is similar, because the Lean Economy is built on "solar string" technologies – that is, various forms of renewable energy derived ultimately from the sun, and strung out in a minigrid in which every member of the grid is generator, user or storage depot as opportunity offers.

A minigrid uses the full range of technologies including solar, wind, water and biomass, conserving energy through the use of the benign army of emerging energy technologies that is on the way. It stores energy with the use of media such as hydrogen, biomass, supercapacitors, fly-wheels, ceramics and pumped storage. It uses information technology to manage demand. And the giant users of energy – transport and industry, and houses that leak energy – are not, and cannot be, part of that world.

The stabilised Lean Economy gives a sharp and very ambitious meaning to energy efficiency. Changes in behaviour, including (for example) a drastically reduced dependency on transport, could reduce the demand for energy-services by two thirds (a factor of 3); and energy efficiency – the energy services provided by a kilowatt of energy - could be improved by as much. That multiplies up to a 90 percent improvement – or a demand for just 10 percent of the energy we use now – and that is well within the capability of renewables.

The transition will require energy rationing. There is an electronic rationing system for energy called Domestic Tradable Quotas (DTQs) which uses information technology to distribute fair access to fossil fuels, allocating an equal ration, measured in "carbon units" to all individuals, auctioning them

to industry, and sustaining an electronic market in which everyone can buy and sell the units they need within the overall budget. The DTQ budget looks like this (figure 6). It is the basis for a step-by-step decline in emissions of carbon dioxide from all fossil fuels. This is, I would argue, the only way of achieving equitable allocation of the declining access to fuel that we will face in the near future. It will need to be a national scheme, firmly based on a strong sense of national solidarity. And its significance extends beyond energy. A decisive and persistent reduction in energy use could provide the pathway by which our present day economy can achieve the transition - a massive achievement it would be, if it happened - to the stabilised Lean Economy.

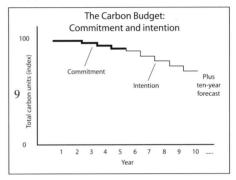

Figure 6. The Carbon Budget for Domestic Tradable Quotas is defined over ten years: the first five years (the Commitment) cannot be changed; the second five years is set in advance but can be revised. There is then a ten year "forecast" which gives guidance on the scale of the reduction that can be expected in the future. The budget represents a guarantee that reduction targets are met and it enables people to make informed preparation for it.

5. THE GREENING OF WASTE

And then, there is the material economy itself. I am going to skip that - it is rather a matter of dirty detail. But there is one thing to say as we come to the end of this review of practical matters of food, water, energy and materials. We, in our consumer-driven economy, have a sense of guilt about material goods. It is understandable, but strange, in a sense, because previous societies, those that existed in sustainable coexistence with their environment, were quite comfortable not only with goods, but also with *waste*. Certainly, they were doing it all on a vastly smaller scale than our own society, so that, in that sense, there is no comparison. But in another sense there is a comparison.

It is quite a complex argument, and I will just trail it past you. The argument goes that primitive societies were in fact incredibly productive. Their environments were so fertile that they could produce in abundance all too easily. In fact, they produced too much, and the problem was to get rid of the excess. Ecosystems develop ways of getting rid of the excess, not least by evolving a vast array of charismatic predators.

Early human societies, faced with excess, regarded this excess as a curse: *la part maudite*, in Claude Bataille's words. The accursed share. They then set about *wasting it*: potlatches; sacrifices; parties. Tibetan monks, in our own day, make immensely complex sand mandalas, months of painstaking work and a huge quantity of embodied human capital; a magnificent investment - and then they chuck it all in the river for the delectation of the river god. Problem solved.

By contrast, when we - that is, we in the market economy - create a vast investment, we use it to create an even more vast investment. We accumulate it. Bataille suggested that the bigger the accumulated capital the bigger the eventual crash. Primitive societies knew better; they kept the stakes low. They had fun. They had something to tell us. I call it the Greening of Waste.

Now, the next part of the Lean Economy is lean society, which we will come back to. The third part, lean consumption, considers what, amongst the vast quantity of goods and services consumed by households and by government, we could in fact do without. And the first thing to recognise is that, in the Lean Economy, there is no burning question about *reducing* consumption at all. On the contrary, the aim is to *increase* consumption.

The deep economic meltdown that will occur after the failure of the market economy will make a fine job of reducing consumption down indeed to catastrophic levels. But try as we might to increase consumption, we will not be able to increase it very far. The only sort of economic and social order that will then be possible will be one that travels light. We may be forced to travel very light indeed.

Why? Because the great support systems, the transport, the waste disposal systems, the infrastructure of bureaucracy, security and large-scale state services, will no longer be there. All those regrettable necessities of a large scale society will have been brought down to size, localised, internalised, reintegrated back into the community − in fact, substantially eliminated. In an inverse of the usual green interpretation of the matter, our needs will have been dramatically reduced by circumstances outside our control; if we are lucky, we will be able to indulge some of our wants. And this will require a radically different way of using land, with a new conception of industry, integrated into localities, domesticated.

6. IS CULTURE REALLY NEEDED?

And then there is lean culture. Now, we need to think about this for a moment, because it is a reasonable question to ask - whether a society actually needs to have any culture at all. After all, if we have jobs, and we have income, and we have a body of law, and a police-force to enforce it, why do we need the sense of solidarity conferred by a culture?

Well, to a substantial degree, we don't. This was explained, somewhat ambiguously, by Adam Smith: so long as we have a functioning market we do not need to feel towards each other any particular sense of benevolence. All that is really needed is that the butcher and baker, and the others who have useful services to offer, should themselves be hungry for an income. And Karl Polanyi, in his celebrated book *The Great Transformation*, published in 1944, thought that, in the presence of the market economy, that amazing mechanism for automatically regulating society and keeping order, none of the great loyalties, obligations and traditions of a previous age are really needed at all.

However, as Polanyi points out, there is a fatal flaw in the idea of the self-regulating market economy: the lack of a safety-net. If the market economy should, for any reason, break down, we would be left *without any* of the loyalties, obligations and traditions by which society in a previous age was held together. And this would be a serious problem. Indeed, it would mean that society would simply disintegrate down to the level of a crowd, a riot. And the loyalties, obligations and traditions which go to form a culture, once broken up, are very hard to put together again.

Polanyi was even more right than he knew, because, since he wrote, we have not only diligently been dismantling all trace of the loyalties, obligations and traditions which we once had, but, taking what traces are left, we have mixed them up with the remains of other cultures so that it has become divisive to refer in terms of loyally to any particular culture, and the remnants of social cohesion that we are left with have become instruments of disorder.

A double-bind. A mess. As if we didn't have enough to contend with. You know, it is impossible to look at any aspect of our economy and society in the context of what lies ahead, at the prospects for energy, food, climate change, land-use, skills, social order, international order and culture, to name but a few – without reflecting that, if we had been governed by a hundred thousand malevolent devils they could not have made more of a mess of it.

>>> *there is a fatal flaw in the idea of the self-regulating market*

But we have to start from where we are. We have to rebuild a culture, a multiple culture, making a celebratory virtue out of diversity. And we need to have an idea of the job that a strong culture has to do. You see, there is a great deal more to local economies than renewable energy and local currencies; material need is not, and never has been, a sufficient incentive for wholehearted cooperation in anything. What we are talking about here, what we are looking for, is a society which is capable of lasting for a very long time, picking up from the defunct market economy, containing and channelling ambitions, providing a social and cognitive setting for the greatest minds, being fun, tolerating dissidence, moving beyond sustainable development and environmental policy, and joining together to build a political economy for a new era. What local economies have to achieve in the future is survival, permanence and civility.

7. THE THREE VITAL FUNCTIONS OF CULTURE IN THE LEAN ECONOMY

That was the easy part. Now for culture. We shall leave the environment far behind and talk now about a human culture that has permanence - or, at least, one that can bounce back. In a society without a culture, two things happen, both of which are horrible: it falls apart, and it develops simplistic cultures on the hoof - fundamentalisms, which we are beginning to find out about.

Lean culture is just as important as each of the other three parts of the Lean Economy. They need each other. And lean culture has to do three things.

7.1 Cohesion
First, it is the foundation for social cohesion. It allows a society to recognise itself as having something in common beyond simply a sense that people may from time to time be instrumentally useful to each other. Social cohesion implies that there is some willingness to recognise that society exists, that it contains institutions which are to be valued, and that cooperative behaviour is justified and to be encouraged.

Now, the key to understanding this is the idea of "consent", a willing acceptance by a person that in his association with his society there is a sense of obligation: this is not a matter of making a choice, but of recognising a covenant. The great Irish political philosopher, Edmund Burke (brought up in Ballyduff, in County Cork), explains: "Men without their choice derive *benefits* from that association; *without their choice* they are subjected to *duties* in consequence of these benefits; and without their choice they enter into a *virtual obligation* as binding as any that is actual."

There is a powerful bonding implied here: not an arrangement, but a destiny, and Burke adds, "Much the strongest moral obligations are such as were never the results of our option." Lean culture turns social cohesion into a deeply held obligation.

7.2 The Public Sphere
Secondly, lean culture has to develop the public sphere. The public sphere? The distinction between private and public is not immediately obvious nor easy to explain. I think the best way to explain it is by placing it immediately in the context of the local economy. There you are, building a local economy, against the odds, in a troubled world. You have the food and water systems, the currency, the schools. You have community – and you have claustrophobia. You know each other all too well. You have no secrets. No courtesies.

There is a danger of it becoming sheer hell, and in truth the record of communities staying together is poor. Those with a well-defined purpose, having more in common with firms than communities, like Machynlleth, have stayed together for a long time. Very loose local economies that depend basically on the formal economy but find ways of cooperating when they feel like it have also got a reasonable record of longevity. But close-knit communities, particularly those with high ambitions of sharing and cooperation, tend not to survive. On some definitions in the literature, none of them have survived.

>>> *the record of communities staying together is poor*

Now, there are many reasons for this, but the particular reason we are talking about now is that there can be, in communities, a cloying sense of invasion of privacy. It is not just that you know each other to the point of being desperate for a change of scenery, but that there is a sense of invasion of privacy, a sense that you cannot get away, a sense that you want to talk about something else for a change, and that you wouldn't half mind, if your neighbours wanted to express themselves *again*, that they would go and do it somewhere else.

The solution is to develop a public culture. That makes it sound simple, but it is not. Here are three properties of a public culture: (1) it has "self-distance"; (2) it is a form of play; and (3) it is a skill – I prefer the word accomplishment.

First, self-distance.. There is an impersonal quality, here, a sense of a lack of spontaneity. The discourse tends not to be about one's own life and problems. There is a reserve. But perhaps clothes get to this point better. Comfortable grunge signals, "Hey, this guy's unpretentious, he presents himself as he really is". Whereas, a guy who's kitted out in, oh, all this - the tie, for instance - invites the question, "What's his game?" Well, there is a game, in a sense, but the real meaning of the question is, "What has he got to hide?" Well, I must admit, I've got a lot to hide. If I told you about my irritating sense of humour, my anxiety neurosis, my workaholism - my obsession with detail, the erotic feelings I have about seagulls – enough – I shan't tell you, because if I did, it would bore you sick and you might put up with it for an evening, but it would very quickly pall, and the prospect of a lifetime of Fleming's self-revelation is simply horrible.

Better to be a bit impersonal. Better to sustain a bit of reserve, or of what that great writer on the public sphere, Richard Sennett, describes as "self-distance". This is the starting-point of a culture. It is not an exercise in self-revelation, but a public expression. You might get a better lecture, too, if I sustain a certain detachment. You have no reason to be interested in what I think. But if I am a bit impersonal about it, and try, instead to follow where the logic of the argument may lead and, crucially, if I don't mind very much if I get my hands dirty when the argument leads to some very strange and uncomfortable places, then there might be a story here worth reflecting on.

That sense of reserve and self-distance may begin to capture the meaning of the public sphere.

The second property of public culture turns on the idea of play. Play is one of the core themes of the Lean Economy, and one of the defining conditions of it is that there are rules: it is arbitrary. So, if you are defeated, or insulted, it does not matter. Victory in a game does not make you into a real-life tyrant. No offence is taken.

Play lowers the temperature. It therefore relishes – *in the play context* – the extremes of self-expression, without spilling over into the extremes of self-revelation. And this, in turn, opens the way to inclusiveness. In a play context you can interact with people who are different from you in a way which you could not, or at least not so easily, do out of that context.

Young children can join in an older children's game though they would be left out of the older children's conversation.

It is inclusive, therefore; and in the process, it is fun. No *fun* means low serotonin levels. Serotonin is a neurotransmitter and when levels in the brain run low, the result is liable to take the form of anger attacks, addiction, violence, of behaviour which is antisocial or withdrawn - all characteristics of a community breaking up. Serotonin levels in the brain are raised, however, by excitement, confidence, success, particularly success when you thought that all was lost. These are the things that are provided by play.

And the third approach to the public sphere takes us into thinking about accomplishment. Another great Irish philosopher, Alasdair MacIntyre, tells us something about this – well, he calls it "practice", but it is the same thing. It means being very good at something – at an objective skill which is not satisfied by mere good intentions; it has to be done right if it is to be done at all. And he points out the ways in which this accomplishment affirms, and needs, the inheritance of the community's own past accomplishments and traditions. There may, indeed, be personal expressiveness here but it is expressed on the community's own terms; it belongs to – that is to say, its medium is – the community's own public life.

It is for these three reasons then, which I have labelled as three properties, self-distance, play and accomplishment that the public sphere is central. It is the place where a community's culture *happens*. Without it, forget the solar panels and local food. If the local economy, the community, can produce accomplished music, dance, celebration, it will have a chance.

Now, all that about the public sphere was just the second argument in support of my claim that lean culture is exceedingly important. The third one is about "judgment".

7.3 Judgment

The argument goes like this. There is a tendency, particularly in the case of people with substantial authority, for their judgment to be poor. This is for various reasons, but mainly because they reduce their thinking down to simplified categories, universal principles which they apply to all circumstances. They stand for a position. They are defined by it. They represent a certain view, a certain set of good intentions, a rigid, plausible, catastrophic mind-set.

Now, it doesn't have to be like this. The alternative is to get down to the dirty detail, to find out about the particular circumstances and let them and their logic speak for themselves.

There was - there were some ambiguities and massive exceptions, here - but there was a mediaeval way of thinking, known as casuistry which made a point of avoiding generalisations – idiot simplifications, as Bernard Crick calls them. Instead, casuistry prefers to get to grips with the specific, local, case-by-case detail, and it has had its powerful advocates, notably (again) Edmund Burke, and Aristotle, who wrote "Decisions about which practical theory will best allow us to resolve any particular problem can only be made in the context of, and with an eye to, the *detailed* circumstances of that particular problem."

Now comes the crunch of the argument. What does "particular" mean? Well, it means, among other things, "particular *place*". And in the Lean Economy, we are not just building local economies; we are making particular places, with their particular associations, and bringing particular places to life.

Play is one of the core themes of <<<
the Lean Economy.
No fun means low serotonin levels.

That is to say, *the Lean Economy is located.* Its culture is a culture of place. Art that celebrates a particular place has a quality of ritual to it. It validates a place, gives it its own values; it gives people, not just the courage of their convictions, but the courage of their locations.

8. LEAN SOCIETY

And that brings us to lean society. When the market economy, with its nice, regulating price mechanism, has broken down, it will be necessary to rediscover social order and social structure from first principles - not to build a Utopia but to recognise the absolutely undisputable fact that there has to *be* a social order in the future. The market won't be there to do the job. And the first principle of society is that, while it can be imposed, or be led, or guided, from the top down, it has to be constructed from the bottom up.

I see four layers of lean society. First, there is the primary group, essentially the extended household on a scale of around six adults. It can consist of several families, next door to each other, or round a "turning" as they used to call it in the East End of London. This is the essential building block of social order.

Secondly, households are located within what I describe as the precinct, the size of which is around 150 active adults, a scale which is one of the most persistent features of social order in the anthropological record. It is possible, within the precinct, to sustain cooperation without exchange systems such as local currency. It may not be possible to do so now, because we are not used to it, and we do not have the necessary structure of social order. But it is a skill which is embedded in our human personality and it is there to be developed.

And above that layer, there is the parish, and above that, the nation. I want to finish this lecture by taking a closer look at issues arising with respect to one of these scales of social organisation: the parish.

Local currencies are absolutely fundamental

The parish is a strange sort of size in terms of sociology. For small groups (that is, the primary groups) and for the very large group in the form of the nation, there is a characteristic form of "reciprocity", that is, a particular way in which people exchange things amongst each other and cooperate. For households, it is "generalised" reciprocity – that is, unconditional obligation. You cooperate with people in your household unconditionally. At the other extreme, with people who are not local, and whom you are unlikely ever to see again, it is "negative" reciprocity – that is, the exchange is based on the principle of going out for what you can get.

For parishes, reciprocity is "balanced", a sort of half-way house between the two. Local currencies are absolutely fundamental to this. And the right scale for the local currency is the parish. The parish is an easier, less competitive regime than that of the tough exchange systems that exist outside, but that is not enough to keep parish economies in order; neither local currencies nor anything else can carry it off on their own. Remember, we are in a state of economic disorder here – hyperunemployment, no incomes, crashed markets. It is all too likely that it will also be a case of crashed local communities.

The task of getting this local parish economy off the ground, and protecting it, is very tough indeed. And the technique which I would like to suggest is based on the absolutely standard fully accepted and uncontroversial principles of economics: that is, on the criteria which have to exist in an economy which enjoys the benefits of *perfect competition*. The modification I would suggest in this case is that every one of them should be stood completely on its head.

In other words, if you want to know the way forward in the future, listen to what standard neoclassical economics has to say, and do the opposite. The criteria for perfect competition are:

1. there should be a LARGE NUMBER OF SELLERS AND BUYERS – so that none can influence prices;
2. PRODUCTS SHOULD COMPETE ON PRICE, and on no other criteria;
3. FREE ENTRY AND EXIT – sellers and buyers can come and go as they wish;
4. PROFIT MAXIMISATION – sellers are simply out to make money;
5. NO LOCAL STANDARDS can be imposed, and there is no discrimination except on grounds of price against another producer;
6. PERFECT MOBILITY of the factors of production - labour, capital and land follow the money, with no strings attached;
7. PERFECT KNOWLEDGE – so that buyers can compare the quality of all products on the market.

For parishes in the Lean Economy, just the opposite will need to be the case.

1. There will be a *small* number of buyers and seller, with a lot of influence over the local market.
2. There will be immense product diversity, every product will be bundled-in with other things, such as neighbourly services, and the process of building a local community.
3. There will be barriers to entry and exit. Loyalty to local suppliers will be essential. Bargain hunting for the best price is essentially the cause of the collapse.
4. Clear objectives? Forget it. The nature of the Lean Economy will be one of improvising, invention and muddling through.
5. Local standards – that is to say, standards of lean production, not be confused with the destructive regulatory regime of the World Trade Organisation and the EU, will be essential.
6. There will indeed be barriers to the mobility of factors of production. There will be precisely that tissue of loyalties, obligations and traditions which keeps labour and capital at home.
7. Imperfect knowledge will be absolutely vital. If local economies really knew how hard their future would be, and how long it will

take to stabilise, they would be dispirited, and might not try it at all. Whenever you are starting something big, it is best not to be too realistic about it, to look no further than the next step.

Put all these together, and we begin at last to have a blending of people and economics, mending the broken world left by the market economy. Civil disobedience may be part of the road that lies ahead. Economic disobedience will certainly be part of it. The rule is: break the rules of economics, reintegrate society; join together, make a future.

And now, finally, all this has to be located. Remember, *place* is one of the core concepts of the Lean Economy. And place, in turn, has to be placed in … well, what? The sequence, remember, goes from primary group, through precinct and parish up to the nation. And what about the region? What about the EU?

Well, I have drawn your attention to a number of tragedies this evening, and I don't want to end on another one, and yet, there is the Tragedy of the Regions. Regions can be an effective scale. Britain fought the last war governed as a federation of regions with a very high degree of local autonomy in implementing the war effort. They did what Britain expected of them. In the future, I fear, they will do what the European Union expects of them.

The volume of thinking which is beginning to face up to the consequences of EU regulation in ruling out the possibility of local invention is becoming persuasive. It takes the argument far beyond the old categories of Euroscepticism, and into the serious political analysis of thinkers like David Miller and Larry Siedentop. They are recognising that creative, robust, inventive local autonomy needs the setting of a strong nation which helps them, protects them, but does not feel compelled to interfere in local detail. In a regime of authoritarian superstate regulation, implemented by the regions, the Lean Economy would have no chance: no chance of achieving its ambitious tasks of inventing and managing a political economy, of sustaining order and civility. Regional government is not a way of taking politics to the people; it is a way of taking it away from the people who already have practical, located governance in a variety of forms, including counties, which are in line to be abolished when regional units become firmly established. Counties' accessibility, their right of local government, their local knowledge and competence – indeed, their existence – need to be defended with courage.

The Lean Economy will need both courage and independence. And it will have a heart. There is a tradition of affection to draw on in our civilisation. There is a resource of feeling, responsibility and sheer affection, in Europe, in Britain, in Inishbofin. Despite the turbulence of our history, our society has been kept going by real concern for one another; much of this network of obligation has been shredded by the impersonal relationships of the market economy, but the essence of it is still at the heart of our culture. Here, for example, is the sixteenth century Briton Miles Coverdale commenting on the German Martin Luther's commentary on the ancient Jewish Psalm 23. The subject of his commentary is sheep. The emotional energy he celebrates will be recruited by the Lean Economy as, in part at least, a substitute for oil:

If any go astray, he runneth after it, seeketh it, and fetcheth it again. As for such as be young, feeble and sick, he dealeth gently with them, keepeth them, and holdeth them up, and carrieth them, till they be old, strong, and whole.

GALWAY COUNTY LIBRARIES

The story of the boy who cried wolf

One of Aesop's Fables is the story of the boy whose job was to look after the sheep but, having a nervous disposition, he was forever crying "wolf" when no wolf was there. One day the wolf really did come, and he cried "wolf" again, but nobody believed him, and the wolf was able to dine off the sheep and the boy at leisure.

There are two morals to the story. The first is: avoid giving false alarms. The second is: in the end, the wolf came, so do not be misled by previous false alarms into thinking that the latest alarm is false, too. Of these two morals, the second one is more significant. Believing false alarms wastes time, but can lead to some helpful advice for apprentice shepherds; disbelieving all alarms can lead to a local lad being eaten, for starters.

We have an example of the fallacy of the wolf in the case of supplies of oil. A century or so ago, there were some false alarms about how little oil remained; the art of forecasting oil supplies earned a bad reputation. However, estimates of the quantity remaining in the world, and of the turning-point (the "peak") at which oil production would start to decline, steadily improved and, in the 1970s estimates of the accessible and liquid oil which had been in place at the start of the industrial era settled at, or around, around 2000 billion barrels, and that estimate has held. The expected peak was estimated to be around the year 2000 – later extended to a few years into the new century thanks to the slower growth in demand following the oil shocks of 1973-1979. The "2000:2000" warning, starting with a report by Esso in 1970, has since been independently confirmed and published by official sources, such as the UK's Department of Energy, *Energy Research and Development in the United Kingdom* (1976), the *Global 2000* Report to the President (1980), the World Bank, *Global Energy Prospects* (1981), and by numerous independent studies such as M. King Hubbert (1977), Petroconsultants (1995), L.F. Ivanhoe (1997), Colin Campbell (1999), Roger Bentley (2002)...; it has been established and confirmed for three decades. Analysts have also pointed to the devastating consequences of a breakdown in oil supplies on a global market which has neglected to make any serious preparation. Here was a wolf that gave thirty years notice of its arrival, and has been thoughtfully issuing reminders ever since.

It is, however, the sceptics that tend to carry the day. "There is always a series of geologists who are concerned about imminent depletion of world supplies", an energy economist, Peter Davis, reassured a House of Lords Select Committee on Energy Supply in 2001. "They have been wrong for 100 years and I would be confident they will be wrong in the future". So that's all right then: the anguished warnings are nothing more than that new kid trying to draw attention to himself. Aesop might be tempted to revise his fable slightly. Here we have the apprentice shepherd growing mature and experienced in the job. He has been giving precise fixes of the wolf's advance for as long as anyone can remember. He is specific and credible about the action that must be taken to save the village. And still he is disbelieved.

David Fleming

Biotechnology Briefing: A *Lean Economy* Paper

Genetic manipulation
An unnecessary technology
David Fleming

Fundamental biological barriers mean that genetically-engineered crops are more likely to reduce yields than to increase them. They launch us into a sea of troubles. Their use will rack up industrial agriculture another notch and make it much more difficult to revert to a sustainable, low energy systems of cultivation. So how has this technology developed such momentum?

Biotechnology seems to have a lot to offer. It can extract genes from the plants and animals in which they evolved, and insert them in other species. It can design altered species with useful qualities such as better resistance to pests, drought and toxic chemicals. It can produce crops with more vitamins and the ability to use sunlight more efficiently. This is a technology that comes bearing gifts.

Agriculture, on the other hand, is in trouble. Its long record of rising productivity is faltering; the resistance of crops to pests and diseases is declining; weeds are becoming harder to manage. The natural resources on which it depends are at risk: gas, the main raw material for fertilizer and pesticides, and oil, the fuel for all other tasks and transport, are close to peak and decline; water is approaching critical scarcity in the main food-producing regions of the world; soil fertility itself is being depleted as industrial agriculture neglects the rotations and care needed by a living soil. And along with the fertility, freedom is in retreat – the freedom of farmers to make their own decisions, to keep their own seed, to apply intelligence, experience and local knowledge, to make at least some of the food they produce informally available in the community. Locally-skilled farming is being eliminated. Farmers are losing their right to think.

But those are not problems which the new technology can cure. On the contrary, biotechnology reinforces all that is wrong with industrial agriculture, postponing the needed reform, and enabling agriculture's problems to mature to the point at which reform itself ceases to be an option. The gifts being borne by this technology are not benign.

To some extent, those gifts have already been accepted: the agricultural industries of Canada, the US, Argentina and China have in varying degrees done so, but other countries are debating it. Two conditions should be present in a public debate: (a) the public should be reasonably well informed in the subject, and (b) both (or all) of the options under discussion should in fact be feasible and reasonable ways forward, so that the choice is a matter of preference rather than a discussion about whether or not to make a catastrophic error. In the case of biotechnology and the use of genetically-modified organisms (GMOs), neither of these conditions apply – or not yet: the first of them, at least, should not be impossible to meet, for (as the first part of this paper explains) there are just seven central but simple points to note:

1. GMOs do not, in general, produce more food.

2. GMOs do not improve crops' resistance to pests and diseases except for short periods.

3. GMOs increase weeds' resistance to herbicides.

4. GMOs are unmanageable: they cannot be controlled or contained.

5. GMOs are unpredictable: the full effects of transplanting a gene between species are unknown.

6. GMOs increase the risk to food security arising from depletion of oil, gas, water and fertility.

7. GMOs are unnecessary.

The second part considers a single question: Why is the case for GMOs so strongly pressed?

Part One: Notes on a flawed technology

1. GMOs do not, in general, produce more food

For most of its history, the productivity of agriculture has been growing. One of the periods of most rapid advance was the twentieth century, when yields rose dramatically, keeping roughly in step with the rising population – although the actual benefits of this have been mixed (see box).

Now the hope is that GMOs will be able to pick up on the record of growth and take it yet further, but this is unlikely. Not only is the harvest index already close to its best, but the genetic engineering of plants to improve their resistance to pests and herbicides has generally tended to *reduce* yields: a

study of recent experience in North America shows that the yield of soya fell by between 1 percent and 19 percent, with a typical reduction of about 10 percent; the yield from some maize, engineered for pest resistance, rose very slightly, but in the case of oilseed rape, the study found a 7.5 percent reduction. There is as yet little experience of using GMOs explicitly to improve yields as distinct from protecting crops from pests and weeds, and GM traits were initially introduced only into a few varieties, so that some yield problems may have been due to unsuitable varieties being used for local conditions. Now a greater range of varieties is available, and yet the reductions in yield (e.g. the 7.5 percent fall in the case of rape) and the unpredictability of yields indicates a problem which may be expected to persist.[4]

Yield

Agriculture is producing much more grain now, but is that all we want it to produce?

Higher yields. The transformation in the productivity of cereals in recent times began with the Japanese dwarf strains of rice. Until the late nineteenth century, a mere 20% of the photosynthate (the production of plant material by photosynthesis) was turned into seed; the rest went into the straw, the roots and the leaves. Selective plant breeding since then has progressively raised this "harvest index" to not far short of the theoretical maximum of 60%; it produces massive heads of seed, but it cannot be taken very much further without reducing the stalk, the leaves and the roots to the point at which there is no viable plant there at all. Breeding also developed plants' ability to survive high densities – for instance by selecting for plants with leaves that point upwards to catch the sun in a field of densely-packed grain. And these hyper-productive cereals, in turn, allow much greater applications of fertiliser and water than before; when the old thin-strawed varieties were heavily fertilised, they promptly collapsed under the weight of their seed-heads. It is this interaction between breeding, fertiliser and water which drove the "Green Revolution", and which has taken the productivity of plants about as far as it will go.[1]

There is more to "yield" than just grain. Productivity is not just a matter of the amount of grain a crop produces. Industrial agriculture, which is committed to the principle of uniformity, concentrates on a narrow range of crops, and it is concerned only with the primary product (the grain) without regard to any of the other resources that the crop can provide. These vital secondary products include fibre, fuel, fodder and medicines; and they include water conservation, organic matter for soil conditioning, and the broader role of the crop as a resource for a stable local ecology which keeps pests in balance. They also include useful plants growing in association with the primary crop. For example, the green leafy vegetable, bathua (fat hen, or Good King Henry) which normally grows as an associate of wheat, has very high nutritive value, rich in vitamin A and iron, and a is remedy for intestinal worms. Together with the wheat, it contributes to a high *combined* yield – but, dismissed by industrial agriculture merely as a competitor of wheat, it is declared a "weed", and is efficiently killed with herbicides.[2]

Industrial agriculture does not allow these essential secondary products to intrude on the simply-defined and simply-measured goal of yield. And yet, it is the total yield of all parts of the plant that really matters to local people, particularly in the third world. The combined yield of a traditional harvest may well be, in terms of value to local people, greater than the simple yield of grain provided by the Green Revolution and its GM sequel; high commercial productivity is obtained at the cost to local communities of profoundly reduced useful yield.[3]

2. GMOs do not improve crops' resistance to pests and diseases except for very short periods

The pesticide which is chiefly used by GMOs is *Bacillus thuringiensis (Bt)*. This is the latest in a sequence of pesticides, each used for a decade or so before losing its potency (see box).

Bt is a bacterium originally found in 1911 as a pathogen of flour moths in Thuringia in Germany, whose cells contain a powerful insecticide protein which is of exceptional value. It is safe for humans and for all other higher animals, and the most widely-used strain (kurstaki) is safe also for insects,

lethal. Newly-developed strains of *Bt* are effective against the larva of other pests, including mosquitoes, some flies and gnats, Colorado beetles and elm leaf beetles. These properties – the combination of effectiveness where it is needed, coupled with harmlessness at all other times – may be unique; should *Bt* become ineffective, there are no close substitutes.[8]

The use of *Bt* in the form of a spray requires skilled planning. It degrades quickly in sunlight, it must be applied at the right stage in the development of the larva, at the correct temperature and before the pest has bored into

---

The pesticides arms-race

Pesticides have a useful life of about ten years before the pests become immune to them

Pesticides of various kinds have been doing a useful job in the protection of crops for centuries, but the practice of relying almost exclusively on them for the control of pests did not come until the arrival of neurotoxins with the lethal persistence required to defend a crop from predators throughout the growing season. First to arrive were the organochlorates, including DDT, deildrin and chlorane, whose effects on the natural environment were described by Rachel Carson in Silent *Spring*. By the end of the 1960s, however, the pests which they were designed to control had built up an immunity, and it became necessary to turn to something stronger. The solution was provided in part by the organophosphates – parathion, malathion, chlorpyrifos and others – and Rachel Carson describes one experiment to assess the toxicity of parathion:

A chemist, thinking to learn by the most direct possible means the dose acutely toxic to human beings, swallowed a minute amount, equivalent to about 0.00424 oz. Paralysis followed so instantaneously that he could not reach the antidotes he had prepared at hand, and so he died.[5]

The organophosphates were used alongside an even more powerful group of neurotoxins, but less persistent – the carbamates, which included insecticides such as aldicarb, carbofuran, carbaryl and oxamyl. Together, the organophosphates and carbamates provided protection from insect predators through the 1980s until their effectiveness, too, started to decline. By the 1980s, farmers would have run short of defences had it not been for yet another group of chemicals, the pyrethroids. They were derived originally from chrysanthemums but, in their synthetic form (permethrin, cypermethrin, esfenvalerate), they were the most potent of all: applied at the rate of just one tenth of the carbamates, they provided protection through the 1990s.[6] The agricultural industry was able, for a little longer, to remain defended, not just against pests and diseases, but against any real incentive to think again about its methods.[7]

Then, in the mid 1990s, a new technical fix became necessary, and the sequence moved on towards *Bacillus thuringiensis (Bt)*.

---

but *Bt* is lethal for the lepidoptera larva (caterpillars) that are the primary predators of crops. The reason for this is clever: the toxin itself, *delta endotoxin*, is contained in a protein which is insoluble in normal conditions; it is only in the highly reducing conditions (with a pH of 9.5 or more) which exist in the gut of lepidoptera larva that it becomes soluble – and when it dissolves, it releases the very powerful toxin which is rapidly

the crop plant where it will be protected – and it must be actually eaten by the larva.[9] For all these reasons it has in the past been applied strategically to deal with particular problems. The only way in which it can be effective as a routine defence is by integrating it into the tissue of the crop itself, which becomes possible with the use of GM technology: the gene which produces *Bt* is inserted into the DNA of the crop.

However, it has no more chance than any other routinely-used pesticide of preventing pests from building up their resistance. *Bt* is claimed by the agronomists to be a miracle; for the pests with predatory designs on the crops, it is at first a tricky problem in chemistry; but then, all too soon, it is lunch. As the environmentalist Jonathon Porritt writes,

> It is astonishing that serious scientists can be so childishly enthusiastic at the prospect of swapping today's chemical treadmill for tomorrow's genetic treadmill, all in pursuit of the unattainable dream of pest-eradication.[10]

The pattern is now established: as pests develop a resistance to the toxins that are designed to destroy them, the toxins have to be made more powerful, and the technologies become more cunning, so the pests adapt, and the technologies raise their game yet further… GMOs, in the end, make little difference to this arms-race other than to speed it up: when the genetically-engineered insecticide is present permanently in several different crops and at constant concentrations, it provides ideal conditions for the pests to develop immunity at their leisure. For pest control in agriculture to be effective, there has to be flexibility; whereas sprays can at least be switched around, forcing the pests to deal with a variety of different chemicals, GMOs are limited to a narrow range of chemicals – and for the early years *Bt* has been doing the job virtually on its own. It is unlikely that genetic engineering has other insecticides on the way with an effectiveness anything like as great as *Bt*, and the risk of finding that there is no effective replacement for it is real. Global harvests depend on the biotechnology of the future finding another way of achieving the exceptional effectiveness of *Bt* – and then continuing to achieve it every ten years indefinitely.

In response to this problem, industrial agriculture is starting to turn to the development of completely new toxins: just moving genes around is no longer enough; it is necessary to start from scratch. Nanotechnology is likely to be used to build toxins, behaviours and properties that have never previously existed, and to produce new creations – a combination of genetics, robotics, information technology and nanotechnology (GRINs). There may be some consumer-resistance to GRINs becoming integrated into the daily diet. They can also be expected to escape into the wild ecology, and it is likely that, in due course, it will be possible to hack into GRINs and maliciously insert or develop a virus intended to cause trouble.

3. GMOs increase weeds' resistance to herbicides

The other main use of GMOs is to enable industrial agriculture to rely exclusively on herbicides for the control of weeds. Intensive applications of herbicides have become necessary as the only way of dealing with weeds which have become viciously persistent after years of selection for their ability to survive them; the problem is that the quantity now needed to kill the weeds is enough to kill the crops too. The solution offered by GMOs is to insert a gene into the crop to confer resistance to the most widely-used weed-killers – glyphosate, or "Round-Up" (Monsanto), glufosinate (Aventis), and imidazolinone (Cynamid).[11]

This is, however, only a short-term solution for, as the herbicide doses increase, so does the immunity of the weeds (see box). "Inevitably", writes the agronomist Charles Benbrook, "the use rates of herbicides will trend upwards" – that is, until the trend reaches its limit. That limit is set when the quantity of herbicide used makes the crop unfit for consumption, or when the soil becomes so degraded that it is unable to support crops, or when farmers can no longer afford to buy the quantity of herbicide that is needed.

Tough Weeds I

Weeds that rise to the challenge of GMOs

Horseweed, a prolific weed in the soya crops of Mississippi, quickly developed an immunity which required a six- to thirteen-fold increase in the amount of glyphosate to achieve the same level of control as normal horseweed. Velvet leaf developed a tolerance for quantities of glufosinate larger than many farmers could afford; water hemp's response to glyphosate application was simply to delay germination until after it had been applied. In Iowa, after a few years of GM use, the 10 percent most heavily-treated fields required at least 34 times more herbicide than fields in which GM varieties were not used.[13]

Limits could also be set by the build-up of herbicide in the local drinking water, or by the presence of weeds which are so resistant to herbicides that cultivation of a tolerably clean crop is no longer possible.[12]

Here, too, the response in the long term might be expected to take the form of GRIN technology. It will, of course, call for exhaustive testing, requiring many years to reach any measure of assurance that the newly-invented herbicides can be used safely – but the incentive to develop the new technology more speedily than that will be hard to resist.

same crop for years on end without a break.[14]

That is, if the previous years' crops cannot be eradicated from this year's crop, then the only solution available within the reach of GM agriculture is to abandon rotations altogether, raising the same crop in the same place for year after year. This affront to the most elementary principle of husbandry is a guarantee that pests and weeds, and the ineradicable remains of previous crops (which do not breed true), will become firmly established. Agricultural ecology in this condition is unmanageable. The application of yet stronger chemicals reaches its

Tough Weeds II

When last-year's crop comes back, and back, and back

In 1997, Tony Huether, who farms in northern Alberta, planted three different kinds of GM oilseed rape resistant to, respectively, Monsanto's glyphosate, Aventis's glufosinate, and Cynamid's imidazolinones. The following year, he found his fields invaded by strains of oilseed rape which had acquired genes giving them resistance to all three herbicides: in order to clear his land, he had to use 2,4-D. In Manitoba, Monsanto has been reduced to sending out teams of students to weed out indestructible volunteer rape plants by hand.[15]

4. GMOs are unmanageable: they cannot be controlled or contained

GM crops are unmanageable in three ways. First, persistence: GM varieties have a persistence which can – and, with increasing frequency, does – place them beyond the control of standard agricultural practice. Secondly, contamination: they cannot be prevented from invading agricultural and natural ecosystems extending far beyond those for which they were intended. Thirdly, uniformity: if a new disease becomes established anywhere in the world, the use of genetically uniform crops will ensure that nothing impedes its march.

1. Persistence

When a farmer plants a new crop, he has to be confident that the crop which grew in the previous year will not try to come back in force; at the very least, he needs to have the option of using herbicide to eradicate newly-germinated plants from the previous crop (farmers call them "volunteers"). However, if the volunteers happen to be genetically engineered to survive applications of the normal herbicides (glyphosate, etc), the remaining options are to turn to intensely toxic chemicals such as 2,4-D and paraquat, or to weed the fields by hand, or to abandon any pretence of variety and to grow the

intrinsic limit when the land becomes unable to support any crops fit for human consumption. The changes to the composition of the soil due to the presence of GMOs include alterations to microorganisms, seeds and other genetic material which, through reproduction, persist indefinitely, so that there could be effects which cannot be eradicated. The degree to which reconversion or "decommissioning" can subsequently restore the land for conventional or sustainable agriculture is not known.

2. Contamination

The genes that have been inserted into the crop do not stay put; they spread themselves around in three ways:

Pollen and seeds: Pollen spreads GM genes fast and far. Tree pollen can travel 600 kilometres on the wind; pollen from all plants is industriously spread through the locality by birds, bees, insects, fungi, bacteria and rain. When this year's pollen has gone as far as it can, it fertilises the plant which will be the starting-point for next year's journey. And, not far behind the pollen come the seeds, spread by the wind, by birds, by the transport of grain, the contamination of grain elevators and combine harvesters. There is no effective way of containing genetic pollution. The cultivation of GM-free crops of maize, oilseed rape and soya, is for practical purposes no longer possible anywhere in Canada.[16]

Competition: GM plants do not necessarily have a competitive advantage with non-GM plants, but in some cases their advantage could be decisive. GM trees containing insecticide-producing genes, for instance, will be able to invade wild ecosystems with ease, disrupting the system as they go.[17]

The wandering gene: When a gene is inserted in the DNA of an organism, it is bundled together in a "construct" with genes needed for various functions such as inserting the gene, activating it and identifying it. The constructs are designed to be mobile – and that mobility persists so that, when the gene has moved in, it is reasonable to suspect that it could all too easily move out again, in a process known as "horizontal transfer".[18] There is growing evidence that the mobile properties conferred on a gene are indeed likely to work in both directions. Among the accessible organisms into which the wandering gene can migrate are the gut bacteria of the animals (insects, bees, cattle and humans) that eat the GM food, although it is not known to what extent the gene can continue to function after the transfer. There is also evidence that the transfer can occur among fungi and bacteria in the soil, spreading among the microorganisms and fungi that sustain the soil and the natural environment.[19]

3. Uniformity: crops without boundaries

All hybrid crops produce uniformity, which helps in harvesting, in processing and in the identification of particular varieties and their breeders; it also helps sales of seed, since hybrids cannot themselves be successfully used for the following year's seed, so that farmers have to buy seed from the breeders every year. Naturally, the case for hybrids has been pressed by the seed industry rather than by farmers, and the dominance of hybrids in American agriculture was established in the 1930s following a vigorous campaign by the industry. The danger of this uniformity showed up in 1970: corn leaf blight swept through the southern states of America; it encountered no genetic resistance for thousands of miles.

GMOs make the evolution of a virus even more likely than it is in the case of uniform non-GM hybrids. Conditions for the rapid evolution of viruses and pests are provided, for instance, by

the permanent presence of a GM substance in every tissue of the crop, and as an example of that, we have the practice of engineering plants such as papaya and plum with genes instructing them to make viral proteins (which provide protection against the virus with which they are associated). If a different virus now invades the plant, it will have a ready-made supply of alien virus protein with which it can, in a process of viral recombination, evolve into a new form against which the plant has no defences. Another way in which a new virus, or a predator with new characteristics, could come into existence is simply by evolution in response to the constant presence of an engineered toxin. A third route, as explained below, is a direct but unintended consequence of importing alien genes into a cell: it is not known in detail what those consequences will be: it is likely, however, that some of the unexpected effects will survive and multiply.

5. GMOs are unpredictable: the full effects of transplanting a gene between species are unknown

Almost all commercial operations in the late market economy involve some degree of asset-stripping of the natural environment. Biotechnology takes this down to the detail of DNA; it claims that what it is doing is science, and that criticism of GM technology is criticism of science. However, this is as accurate as the idea that opponents of logging are anti-forest, or opponents of industrial fishing are anti-fish.

The principle on which GM technology is based – so simple that it should immediately arouse suspicions – is that, when a gene is extracted from the DNA of its own species and implanted in another, it will carry on doing the same job as before. On this assumption, useful characteristics can be fitted together almost at will to produce a designer-organism, so that the range of new plants and creatures that can be created and brought to life is limited only by the imagination: "...furniture that is grown rather than made; clothing that eats the dead skin its wearer sheds; miniature pet dragons (fire-breathing optional) as household pets".[20] It is, perhaps, fortunate that this vision of the future from *The Economist* magazine is an extreme case of the banal, kitsch and dispiriting, since this tempers the disappointment of discovering that, actually, the function of DNA is not as easy as that: it is not a self-service counter at which biotechnologists can simply pile up their plates with whatever combination of goodies they wish. What the science actually tells us is that the gene's activity depends on its interactions with the proteins and other constituents of the cell and that, when a gene finds itself in a new biological environment, this collaboration is disrupted. The biologist Barry Commoner explains:

> The living cell is a unique network of interacting components, dynamic yet sufficiently stable to survive. [It] is made fit to survive by evolution; the marvellously intricate behaviour of the nucleoprotein site of DNA synthesis is as much a product of natural selection as the bee and the buttercup.[21]

It is, therefore, only to be expected that the organisms into which genes have been implanted usually die, and that most of the survivors are damaged. Those with obvious damage are weeded out; the less obvious failures are those that survive but have a defect which becomes apparent later, in subtle ways. Some curious effects are being observed by farmers in the form of unexplained interactions between crops and the animals that eat them (or refuse to eat them). There are the pigs that do not farrow (conceive) when they are fed on GM grain, the cows, elk and rats that refuse to eat it, the soya plants whose stems split open before the harvest, that fall victim to pests that the farmers have never seen before, that refuse to germinate, that prove to be highly unstable in successive generations.[22] The studies which could show for certain whether such effects are due to GMOs or to some other cause, and which could explain why they occur, have not yet been done; all that can be said for the time being is that these effects are linked by experienced observers to the presence of GM crops, and that they are indications that the technology has unintended consequences.

Such practical experience by GMO growers is commonly dismissed as the effect of the weather, as anecdotal, or as evidence of poor husbandry. What we have here, however, is a technology built on unknowns. This is not the first time the application of a new technology has developed far beyond the understanding of the science on which it is based; there is an honourable, if painful, tradition of trial and error in every field from flight to medicine, but in the case of biotechnology, there are three differences. The first is that the error tends to be suppressed and denied because the flaws that are revealed are so fundamental that they threaten the existence of the entire technology. The second is that GMOs seem to be so very innocuous: a GM plant looks so like a non-GM plant that any concern about the GM process can be maliciously derided as paranoia. Thirdly, many of the errors which can be expected to occur in the case of GMOs do not become apparent until after they are already established as unwanted mutations in living and reproducing organisms in the environment. They can then reveal their true characteristics at leisure.

6. GMOs increase the risk to food supplies arising from depletion of oil, gas, water and fertility

Industrial agriculture depends on a steady flow of cheap oil and gas, on abundant supplies of water, and on its inherited capital of fertile land. All of these, to varying degrees, are at risk, and it is here that we see the chief threat to the security of supply of food. GM technology, far from offering a solution, actually intensifies the problem.

Oil: GMOs are designed for large-scale production of single, uniform crops, using giant labour-saving equipment, and backed by long distance transport with central processing and distribution. Industrial agriculture is already vulnerable to any interruption in the event of a breakdown in the flow of oil but it would, in principle, be possible to convert to an energy-efficient, localised form; eventually the chemical residues in the soil would decompose, and fertility would rebuild. In the case of GMOs, however, changes they cause to the soil and problems with their volunteers could make decommissioning and returning to conventional crops a very lengthy process, or impractical. The heavy energy-dependency of agriculture could become irreversible.

Gas: GM systems are dependent on gas as the raw material for chemicals and fertiliser.[23] GMOs reduce yet further or eliminate the use of good fertility-building practices such as mixed farming, the composting and re-use of organic material, and rotations – the practice of switching crops around in successive years and using fallow periods to prevent the build-up of pests and diseases and to build fertility. Dependence on artificial fertiliser becomes even more deeply entrenched.

Water: The effect of GMOs is more ambiguous. Crops which are engineered for herbicide resistance make it possible for farmers to prepare the land for next year's crop by spraying their fields with a powerful herbicide, instead of ploughing. This "no-till" cultivation has the advantages that it does not disturb the soil, and leaves a covering of dead plants (a kind of mulch) on the land which protects it from erosion and helps it to conserve water. It may well be, therefore, that in the short term, biotechnology is consistent with water conservation. The disadvantage is that, with the heavy application of herbicide and the lack of rotations, the fertility of the soil can be expected to deteriorate, ruling out any savings in water. An adequate analysis is still lacking; current knowledge of fertile soils, however, indicates that the water-retention properties of an impoverished soil are poor. Moreover, crops which are engineered to be drought-resistant would be no compensation for the loss of a water-retaining fertile soil.

Fertility is directly eroded by GMOs. Genetic modification is intended, amongst other things, to eliminate the need for crop rotations. In fact, soil that has been repeatedly treated with herbicides which only a GM crop can withstand will not be able to support any other crop, and it may even be poisoned by *Bt* toxin exuded through the roots of the GM crop. Cropland which lacks rotations, drenched with toxic chemicals and drained of much of its organic content cannot be regarded as fertile.

7. GMOs are unnecessary

There might conceivably be a case for putting up with the array of problems and dangers presented by GMOs if there were no alternative. However, genetic engineering is an unnecessary technology. Much better results – higher yields and more jobs – can be delivered in other ways, at much lower cost, and with a protected environment. GMOs are an extended – or overextended – development of industrial agriculture, and the alternative to them lies in an alternative to industrial agriculture itself. This is a practical, down-to-earth way forward, and it has two central defining features: it builds and conserves fertility by using rotations and recycling nutrients, and it controls pests and diseases effectively by intelligent local management of plants and predators. From those two starting-points, it is possible to develop other opportunities which include conserving water both in the soil and as a productive resource in aquaculture, conserving and using the farm's endowment of renewable energy, and sustaining cooperative relationships with consumers and other farmers in the locality.[24]

Sustainable agriculture, freed from the paralysis of chemical-dependent technology, is capable of being extremely productive: it produces a lot of food. In developing countries, for example, the yields achieved by farmers using sustainable agriculture – though variable, depending on the crop and the particular circumstances – have been shown to average almost twice the yield obtained from the conventional combination of fertilisers and pesticides. As reported in a recent survey by Jules Pretty and Rachel Hine[25], soil erosion can actually be reversed, with the soil increasing in depth and recovering its ability to retain water and nutrients; water needed for irrigation can be reduced by as much as 80 percent; pesticides can be cut by two thirds, or eliminated entirely. And secondary benefits follow, such as the opportunity to produce fish in the pesticide-free water of paddy-fields and freedom to experiment in ways which combine modern science and local knowledge. Examples of this kind of local innovation include the newly developed "System of Rice Intensification" in Madagascar which improves productivity by between three- and six-fold, and the design of cultivation systems for salt water in Vietnam.

In comparison with advances in husbandry such as these, GMOs are an irrelevance. The technology is simply *unnecessary* for sustained or expanded food production – and not just in the third world. In the industrialised countries, yield is not at the moment the major issue; farmers already produce too much. What matters here is, first of all, the high cost of industrial agriculture which is mainly paid (and obscured) by subsidies; the other three problems are the acute vulnerability to an interruption in the supply of oil and gas, the damaging impact of agriculture on the environment, and the increasing resistance of weeds, pests and diseases to industrial biocides. GMOs are, at best, neutral with respect to the first of these (cost), and the next two problems are intensified rather than relieved by GMOs. Only in the case of overcoming resistance could GMOs have, in theory, a useful part to play – but here, too, we have seen how the brief mitigation of crops' vulnerability to pests and weeds quickly breaks down. The only coherent response to all these four issues confronting modern agriculture is to approach them in a completely different way:

sustainable agriculture consists of working *with* the local ecology, using the enduringly effective services it provides for free.

GMOs, then, are a technology we do not need. Even the special services it is claimed to supply turn out to have doubtful value. One example of this is the case of Golden Rice, that famous source of vitamin A: it turns out that a person would have to consume some nine kilograms of cooked rice, twelve times the normal intake, to get the necessary vitamins. The rational way of supplying vitamin A, and a lot of other nutrients at the same time would be to eat green vegetables.[26] Even drought-resistant GM grain is at best an imitation of the many drought resistant varieties now being revived in India after becoming temporarily obsolete during fifty years of profligate irrigation in the twentieth century.[27]

And – beyond food production itself – there is the matter of the production of industrial materials which, as is now beginning to be recognised, can be provided in immense and unexplored variety by the application of good science to materials derived from plants, animals and microorganisms. Do we need biotechnology to make this happen? The materials scientist, Paul Geiser, thinks not:

> ... the technological possibilities for new industrial materials based on natural processes are rich and varied enough that it appears unnecessary to leap to gene-altering technologies that raise unexplored risks. A rush to invest in genetically modified industrial materials or materials development processes appears cavalier when so many natural processes remain unexplored and untapped.[28]

In medical research, too, it is now recognised that GMOs are not simply unnecessary; as the medical scientist David Horrobin, explains, the technology has become a handicap:

> From the 1930s to the 1960s, biomedical science bore some resemblance to an integrated whole. There were researchers working at every level of biological organisation – from subcellular biochemistry, to whole cells, to organs, to animals, to humans. This was a golden age.

> But, starting in the 1960s, molecular biologists and genomics specialists took over biomedical science. Everything was to be understood completely at the molecular genomic level. Everything was to be reduced to the genome. Now we have an almost wholly reductionist biomedical community, which repeatedly makes exaggerated claims about how it is going to

revolutionise medical treatment – and which repeatedly fails to achieve anything. The idea that genomics is going to make a major contribution to human health in the near future is laughable. But the tragedy is that the whole-organism biologists and clinicians who might have helped to unravel the complexity have almost all gone, destroyed by the reductionists.[29]

Unnecessary: we do not *need* to launch ourselves onto this sea of troubles.

Part Two: Why is the case for GMOs pressed so strongly?

In view of what we have seen, why have GMOs developed so much momentum? Why does this technology seem to be unstoppable? Four reasons are particularly relevant.

1. The technology: Technology has advanced faster than our understanding of how to handle it. We are still at the naive, even primitive, stage at which we regard technology with awe and reverence, sacrificing to it whatever it demands. What we get back is a host of problems – but they turn out to be rather useful, for they call for another technical fix, so that the need for technical advance becomes greater than ever. The result is an endless series of technical fixes, each one more remote from the husbandry at the start of it all; each fix demands greater sacrifices and prepares the ground for a sequence which, for some key industrial and academic interests, is a source of income.[30]

The problem is that GMOs are embedded in a debased scientific culture which sees it as desirable to *avoid* the application of critical judgment. This is a "hands-off" approach to science: there is an ostensible commitment to intellectual rigour, which is sought by allowing the evidence to "speak for itself", without contamination by the application of critical judgment, or by any interpretation of how it fits into a wider picture. The price of this rigour is simplification and reductionism, substituting a neat model for the turbulence of the real thing; the prize is certainty, an escape from the systems-literate, scientific reality that it is the *connections* that matter and that a degree of uncertainty and unexpectedness is intrinsic to any grounded understanding. We see the effect of this parody of science in the brilliant, yet socially and culturally empty mathematical modelling which has been so influential in the development of academic economics;[31] we see it in statistics, where the ideal of allowing the numbers for speak for themselves, explicitly avoiding the error of thinking about the issue itself, has led to improbable but influential conclusions about the environment.[32] It is there in the reduction of biology to genomics, as David Horrobin (above) explains. And we see it, as Larry Siedentop notes, in the narrowing and fragmentation of intellectual life as a whole:

> At first glance the separation of philosophy, economics and political science into distinct "subjects" has brought to them far greater precision and sophistication, and nowhere more so than in the development of economic theory. [But it] has fostered a widespread fear about straying outside one's subject, outside the discourse of any profession. ... Those concerned with the nature and operation of political systems – 'political scientists' as they are now called – have by and large ceased to operate with any conception of human well-being or flourishing. They shun passion.[33]

There is no reason why agriculture should be exempt from the curse of reductionism. This means that, in a sense, the debate about GMOs is vetoed before it has started: the technologists are self-appointed guardians of the thin and infantile specialisms they misrepresent as "science"; any attempt to apply judgment which challenges or even attempts to understand the direction of technology can in this way be simply ruled out of order on the grounds that it is anti-science or – as one leading representative of this view, John Maddox, puts it – "so partial and deliberately biased as to be misinformation".[34]

2. The logic: The case that is made for GMOs typically employs a logical fallacy of a particular kind: "begging the question" – *petitio principii*. An argument begs the question when it uses the *assumption* that a proposition is true as the basis on which to *argue* that it is true. For example, the statement, "We have to use GMOs in order to feed the world" contains within it the assumption that GMOs *can* (safely and sustainably) feed the world, but the question as to whether GMOs can actually do so is precisely what the debate is about – and it follows that a statement which takes this as a given begs the question: it is a pointless but misleading statement, and it should be as unacceptable for a politician as the related misdemeanours of telling lies or taking bribes. The standard of logic-literacy at present is poor, so the error is almost never recognised or picked up; even the term "begging the question" is used mainly in the different sense of "raising a new question". In fact, the use of the fallacy is often

merely a warm-up act for a restatement of it in a yet more logically-collapsed form, e.g.: "By opposing GMOs, you are condemning millions to starvation".[35]

Corrupt argument, once established, tends to pollute the entire debate: "After a pointless experiment that involved feeding rats with potatoes modified to produce a poison," writes *The Economist*, "parts of Europe developed mass hysteria."[36] This hyperbole refers to a careful experiment by Dr Arpad Pusztai which compared the effect of the non-toxic snowdrop lectin (*Galanthus nivalis* – GNA) administered to rats in identical quantities by (a) engineering the gene into the potatoes, and (b) adding lectin itself to the potatoes. The rats fed GM potatoes showed significant changes, notably increases in the mucosal thickness of the stomach and the crypt length of the intestines, indicating that the GM process itself has consequences which we know nothing about. Dr Pusztai notes, "it is therefore imperative that the effects on the gut structure and metabolism of all other GM crops developed using similar techniques and genetic vectors should be thoroughly investigated before their release into the food chain."[37]

This issue of safety is assumed away by advocates of GMOs: the neglect of the safety of GMOs in a culture of paranoia about the safety of long-standing assets such as local abattoirs, small-scale cheese production, homoeopathic remedies and children's swings seems to be an indication not just of logical error but of a pathology of public debate which has deteriorated to the point of derangement. In a debate without logic, there are no links, no "therefores"; instead, as Pusztai calmly reflects, "most of the adverse comments on this Lancet paper were personal, non-peer reviewed opinions and, as such, of limited scientific value".[38]

3. The economics: The obvious alternative to using GMOs would be simply to stop using them. However, this would be resisted for two reasons. First, the seed and chemical providers like Monsanto, which have not been making the large profits from GMOs that they expected, and are already faced with mounting litigation, would quickly be bankrupted. Monsanto's patent on the world's leading weed-killer, glyphosate, ran out in 2000, and the genetic engineering of crops which were resistant exclusively to glyphosate was at first sight a clever response. The industry now has the motivation, resources, politics and persuasive skills to mount a formidable defence.[39]

Secondly, industrial agriculture already has difficulties of its own – notably the increasing persistence of pests, diseases and weeds. The solution to this is to reform agriculture as a whole, rebuilding it on the principle of sustainable husbandry and moving away, substantially or completely, from dependence on agricultural chemicals. Although the economic benefits of this would be immense, there is inertia: changes not just in the use of GMOs but in the nature and fundamental principles of the whole agricultural industry worldwide would be a massive undertaking, involving loss of face, loss of revenue, and unbearable changes to life-long, industry-defining mindsets.

One of the powerful advantages which the agricultural chemicals industry has in its defence is that the alternative – sustainable agriculture – is so *detailed*, so diverse, so local. But details are the content of the discipline of husbandry; they are its reality, as distinct from the quick fixes of industrial agriculture, which are its drug. Sustainable agriculture would restore to farmers the power to make decisions in the light of their own needs and experience; it would lift the burden of regulation and distrust from the food producers of the world. Simple, global rules are easy to devise and administer, but complex local detail is impervious to central administration; local sustainable agriculture would therefore spell redundancy not only for the agricultural chemical industry, but also for regulators and bureaucrats. However, control is addictive; naturally, the controllers, too, will use every means they can to defend themselves.

4. The soil: Once GMOs have been used in an area, it will not be easy to go back to GM-free husbandry. A changed soil and resistant weeds are to be expected; uncontaminated seed has become hard to get in areas where GMOs are widely used; conventional *Bt* spray is becoming less effective as a result of over-use by GM crops, eliminating one of the main lines of defence open to sustainable agriculture; habitats for the predators of crop pests are altered, particularly as GM crops spread to forestry; the produce of farms can no longer be guaranteed to be free of GMOs, and will remain suspect for many years. The technology is unforgiving; there is a sense that, once it has started, it will never go away, and that there is no choice but to develop constant new fixes to try to control it. Governments and companies, having started down that path, and

having produced something which threatens to be unstoppable, are likely to be driven by fear.

Now for the positive feedback: the most effective way of allaying fear of something which is suspected to be unstoppable is to *join* it, to maintain the pretence that actually you are using its powers for your own ends, that you are in control. With each rise in the level of fear, the industry's standing as the only body with the power and the expertise to solve the problem is advanced; the incentive for an alliance between the industry and the authorities gets stronger. All regimes built on fear are extremely stable; after a long delay, they are eventually destroyed – rather suddenly.

Conclusion

Can genetic engineering be stopped? It can. However, there are difficulties. First, in the countries where it has already become established, the many technical problems we have noted in this paper would not end immediately upon a decision to stop using GMOs; and yet, the presumption has to be that these difficulties are not insuperable. In the many countries where GM crops have not yet been grown commercially, the technical difficulties are of course much less, though some contamination from testing sites has occurred. Secondly, there are the borderline cases between medicine and agriculture – the breeding of pigs for spare parts surgery, for example. The arguments for and against this are not the same as those relating to agriculture, but the two uses of biotechnology are similar enough to complicate the debate: Where exactly is the borderline to be drawn between the engineering of pigs to be used for agriculture, and pigs to be used for spare parts? Where do you stop? This "slippery slope" objection, though logically trivial, is effective in sabotaging sensible debate and decisive action. Thirdly, there are weighty political and commercial interests in favour of continuing with the technology.

The fourth difficulty is that, our society has a poor record in the field of science policy: there are instances, such as human cloning, where an informed public choice has been insisted-upon, but the usual presumption is that where technology leads, society should follow.

There is a real prospect of the technology being prevented in the countries where it has not yet become established, but it is far from certain that it will be stopped throughout the large areas of the primary bread-baskets of the world, where it is already used. But it should be ended, everywhere, unequivocally. The way forward is to reform agriculture, root and branch, starting now – to focus policy on a farmer-centred, localised, deregulated, scientifically-coherent, sustainable agriculture. Ultimate aim: to feed the world, sustainably.

Research for this paper was made possible by Sanders Research Associates and was first published on the SRA website www.sandersresearch.com The support of Elm Farm Research Centre for *The Lean Economy* project is acknowledged with thanks.

Endnotes

1 For a review of changes in grain yields see Lester Brown and Hal Kane (1995), *Full House: Reassessing the Earth's Population Carrying Capacity,* London: Earthscan, chapter 10.

2 Vandana Shiva (1993), *Monocultures of the Mind,* London: Zed Books, p 113.

3 Shiva (1993), p 50.

4 Hugh Warwick and Gundula Meziani (2003), Seeds of Doubt: North American Farmers' Experience of GM Crops, Bristol: The Soil Association, chapter 4. (Available on Soil Association website).

5 Rachel Carson (1962), *Silent Spring,* New York: Houghton Mifflin (Penguin 1965), p 43.

6 Pyrethroids: http://ace.ace.orst.edu/info/extoxnet/pips/pyrethri.htm

7 Charles Benbrook (2001), "Do GM Crops Mean Less Pesticide Use?", *Pesticide Outlook,* in www.mindfully.org/Pesticide/More-GMOs-Less-Pesticide.htm

8 For details on *Bt* see, for instance, http://helios.bto.ed.ac.uk/bto/microbes/bt.htm and http://www.colostate.edu/Depts/IPM/ento/j556.html

9 Most formulations last for up to a week; some of the newer formulations decay within 24 hours.

10 Jonathon Porritt (2000), *Playing Safe: Science and the Environment,* London: Thames & Hudson, p 85

11 "In 2002 ... the dominant traits continued to be herbicide tolerance (75%), insect resistance (17%) and both traits (8%)" Genewatch UK (2003), Genetic Technologies: A review of Developments in 2002, http://www.genewatch.org/publications/Briefs/brief22.pdf

12 See Warwick and Meziani (2003), chapter 4.

13 Ibid.

14 Warwick and Meziani (2003), chapter 6.

15 Ibid.

16 See Viola Sampson and Larry Lohmann (2000), "Genetic Dialectic: The Biological Politics of Genetically Modified Trees", *The Corner House Briefing,* Sturminster Newton: The Corner House. Warwick and Meziani (2003), chapter 7.

17 See Sampson and Lohmann (2000).

18 Mae-Wan Ho (2003), Institute of Science in Society Recent Evidence Confirms Risks of Horizontal Gene Transfer. For full reference see http://www.greens.org/s-r/30/30-14.html

19 For non technical background to this, see Nathan Batalion, "Biotechnology is a Vital Issue that Impacts All of Us", at www.mercola.com/2002/pct/30.biotechnology.htm

20 Geoffrey Carr (2003), "Planting a Seed", in Climbing the Helical Staircase, survey in *The Economist,* 29 March, p 18.

21 Barry Commoner (2003), "How Well Can Science Predict GM Impacts?", paper presented at the Gene Futures Conference, 11 February, (abridged), at http://www.genewatch.org/Debate/GeneFutures/GeneFutures_Speeches.htm

22 Warwick and Meziani (2003), chapter 8.

23 It is probable that crops could be engineered to develop the ability to fix nitrogen, theoretically eliminating the need to use artificial nitrogen fertiliser, but this is not a solution: GM crops are more dependent than non-GM crops on fertiliser, because they are essentially inconsistent with normally fertility-building rotations. The release of newly-evolved nitrogen fixing varieties into the environment would be a major intervention without knowledge of the consequences.

24 Jules Pretty (2002), *Agri-Culture:* Reconnecting People, Land an Nature, London: Earthscan, chapter 4.

25 Jules Pretty and Rachel Hine (2001), Reducing Food Poverty with Sustainable Agriculture: A Summary of New Evidence, Final Report from the SAFE-World Research Project, Colchester: University of Essex. Main points summarised in Pretty (2002), chapter 4.

26 Bran Halweil (2002), "Farming in the Public Interest", in Christopher Flavin et al, *State of the World 2002,* Washington: Worldwatch Institute / London: Earthscan, chapter 3, p 58.

27 Rahul Nellithanam, Jacob Nellithanam and Sarvodaya Shikshan Saiti (1998), "Return of the Native Seeds", *The Ecologist,* vol 28, 1, Jan/Feb, pp 29-33.

28 Kenneth Geiser (2001), *Materials Matter: Towards a Sustainable Materials Policy,* Cambridge, Mass: MIT, p 304.

29 David Horrobin (2003), "Not in the Genes", *The Guardian,* 12 February, at http://www.guardian.co.uk/genes/article/0,2763,893869,00.html

30 For a discussion of the "continuous cascade of ingenuity absorbing technical fixes", see Sampson and Lohmann (2000), p 10.

31 See, for instance, Herman Daly and John Cobb (1990), *For the Common Good: Redirecting the Economy Towards the Community, the Environment and a Sustainable Future,* London: Green Print, Part One.

32 See Bjørn Lomborg (2001), *The Skeptical Environmentalist,* Cambridge University Press, especially Part 3, section 11, "Energy", pp 118-136. See also the critique by Stephen Schneider, John P. Holdren, John Bongaarts and Thomas Lovejoy. Introduction by John Rennie; "Misleading Math about the Earth", *Scientific American,* January 2002.

33 Larry Siedentop (2000), *Democracy in Europe,* London: Allen Lane; (Penguin, 2000), p 57.

34 John Maddox (2003), "We should be told", *Times Literary Supplement,* 25 April, p 3.

35 See, for instance, Frans H. van Eemeren and Rob Grootendorst (1992), *Argumentation, Communication and Fallacies,* Hillsdale, New Jersey: Lawrence Erlbaum, pp 153-154, 214.

36 Carr (2003), p 11.

37 Arpad Pusztai (2001), "Genetically Modified Foods: Are they a Risk to Human Health?" in Actionbioscience.org: http://www.actionbioscience.org/biotech/pusztai.html

38 Ibid.

39 Warwick and Meziani (2003), p 59

Big biotech's plans for domination run into difficulties

The giant transnational biotech companies have set their sights on controlling the world's food supply by owning and licensing the genes used to produce it. Jeffrey M. Smith's excellent book *Seeds of Deception: exposing corporate and government lies about the safety of genetically engineered food* (Green Books, 2004) reports that a representative of the Arthur Andersen Consulting Group told a biotech industry conference in January 1999 that his company had asked Monsanto what their ideal future looked like. Monsanto replied that they wanted a world in which 100 percent of all commercial seeds were genetically modified and patented. Andersen Consulting then worked backward from that goal and developed a strategy to achieve it.

Part of the plan was to get GM foods into the marketplace quickly before resistance could build up. According to a biotech consultant, "The hope of the industry is that over time, the market is so flooded [with GM] that there's nothing you can do about it. You just sort of surrender".

The companies have already gained the right to sell animal feed containing GM material without the resulting human food having to be labeled as such. They are now trying to get the World Trade Organisation (WTO) to force the world's governments to accept their patented and proprietary GM seeds, crops, livestock, and related foods. If they succeed, the consequences will be irreversible, since GMOs cannot be recalled after their release. GM contamination of crops and livestock reduces farm incomes, makes organic farming impossible, threatens biodiversity and human health, and robs consumers of their right to choose whether to buy GM food or not.

The companies insist that foods containing GM ingredients are safe because they are "substantially equivalent" to conventional foods. The WTO has accepted this and is using its rules prohibiting countries restricting trade because of differences in production methods to try to stop governments banning imports of GM goods.

With corporate encouragement, the governments of the USA, Canada and Argentina have filed a joint complaint against the EU with the WTO, claiming that European resistance to GM food and crops is illegal and costs GM companies and GM farmers billions of dollars in lost revenues. If the WTO rules in favour of the complainants, EU governments may face massive punitive sanctions and other governments will probably abandon their resistance to the global GMO invasion.

World-wide resistance to GM food and farming is growing rapidly. In 1998, the European Commission imposed a *de facto* moratorium on GMOs because 70% of EU citizens opposed GM food. This was lifted in 2004 subject to the proviso that (a) human food containing more than 0.9% GM ingredients be fully labeled and traceable, and (b) member states set up legislation and liability régimes prior to allowing any "co-existence" of GM with conventional and organic crops. But the official EC report on "co-existence" found that the process would be extremely difficult to manage, and *New Scientist* magazine reported in September 2004 that GM pollen can contaminate crops 21km away. As a result, European "co-existence" of GM with conventional crops is unlikely to be accepted.

In 2001, EC directive 2001/18/EC recognised the right of local areas to be GM-free and allowed for GM-free buffer zones to protect organic farms and other special places. The Assembly of European Regions is now campaigning to strengthen the legal recognition of GM-free zones and regions. These have already been established in 22 of the 25 EU member states (www.gmofree-europe.org).

In 2003 major food brands removed GM ingredients, and the Cartagena Protocol on Biosafety recognised the right of any government to ban or restrict GMOs on the basis of the Precautionary Principle. In August 2004, the EU won the first round in the legal struggle with the US, Canada and Argentina when the WTO Dispute Panel accepted the EU's demand for scientific opinion on GM risks. This will delay the resolution of the dispute until 2005 or 2006.

But perhaps the best news of all is that the demand for GM-free food and animal feed will soon outstrip supply. This will make GM-free farming much more profitable than the alternative and remove any commercial incentive that farmers might have had to make Monsanto's dreams come true. - **Michael O'Callaghan.**

Michael O'Callaghan is chairman of Global Vision Consulting Ltd – www.global-vision-consulting.com and co-ordinator of the GM-free Ireland Network – www.gmfreeireland.org

The Fourth Annual Feasta Lecture,
Galway, Trinity College, Dublin and Cork 8th-10th December 2002

PEOPLE FIRST

Justice in a Global Economy

Stan Thekaekara

> *The rules about what one can and cannot own are fundamental to the way an economy operates and determines the kind of society that results. The economies of indegenous people are based on a concept of no ownership. How can you 'own' the land, the water, the forests, the birds, the animals?*

Stan Thekaekara was born on his family's farm outside Bangalore and has a degree in English Literature from Bangalore University. He first became involved with tribal groups through AICUF, an all-India student organisation, and between 1974 and 1977 lived in a tribal village in Bihar. Between 1979 and 1983 he started a rehabilitation centre for people with alcohol and drug problems on the family farm and founded the Bangalore Disaster Relief and Rehabilitation Centre. In 1984 he became Community Development Officer with the Nilgiri Adivasi Welfare Association, a small NGO in the Nilgiri Hills of South India. In 1986 Stan and his wife Mari set up ACCORD to help tribal people reclaim their land. He is a Trustee of Oxfam GB and has worked as an adviser to Oxfam on its UK Poverty Programme.

I was lying in a hospital bed in Chennai when the invitation to deliver the Feasta Annual Lecture arrived. A very sudden and totally unexpected illness had left me fighting for my life. When my wife Mari told me of the invitation, my first thought was 'Why me – what have I got to say?' But when I started wondering about this I found that there was actually quite a lot. I don't know how important or valid it is but, yes, years and years of working to protect the rights of indigenous people in different parts of India had taught me a great deal.

And so my second reaction was 'Well, why not?' And suddenly I began looking forward to it so much that I am sure it made a significant contribution to my recovery. So you see this opportunity to stand here before all of you and deliver the 2002 Annual Feasta lecture is much more than just an honour, it is something I have looked forward to with, I must admit, quite a bit of trepidation as well. I thank all of you assembled here for making this possible.

On the 28th of February, 1984, my wife Mari and I along with our one-year-old daughter got on a bus in Bangalore to begin a 7-hour journey to the Nilgiri Hills in Tamil Nadu to throw in our lot with the adivasi or indigenous people of the area. We never imagined for a moment that this journey would one day lead here to Ireland.

Let me warn those of you who expect me to present a cutting edge analysis of the global economy and its impact, you may be disappointed. I am not an economist, much less a theorist. I don't pretend to understand all the shenanigans of the WTO, the World Bank and the IMF any more than most ordinary people. But from the little that I have read and understood, I know one thing – these global economic institutions and the many treaties and agreements they have engineered have *not* added one cubit in value to the social and economic well-being of the people I work with. If anything they have drastically taken away from it. They have not contributed in any way to the eradication of the poverty and deprivation of the adivasis and similar disadvantaged communities across the globe – they have aggravated it.

So what I intend to present today is a view from the ground. A view rooted in the everyday reality of scores of people trying to find enough to feed their children for the day. The reality of people to whom economic well-being is not measured by graphs and curves and indices but by whether there is enough rice for the night meal.

I would like to present this is in three parts. The first part is a brief history of our work with the adivasi people of the Nilgiri Hills of Southern India. The second part is the lessons we have learnt from this experience, which I believe can contribute to finding solutions to the problems of a globalised economy. And the third part will put forward a proposal of what can be done.

Part I – The Journey into Tribal India

This journey actually began in 1974 when I, fresh out of university and quite wet behind the ears, marched into a tribal village in rural Bihar armed with little else than a mix of Marxian analysis and liberation theology. Unjust economic structures had to be changed, wealth re-distributed, poverty eradicated. The revolution seemed to be lurking around the corner.

In the 28 years since then, this struggle against poverty and its root causes has continued. And though there has been no revolution, differences have been made to peoples' lives. Especially in the last 16 years after we set up ACCORD, a voluntary organization to work with the adivasis in the Gudalur Valley of the Nilgiri Hills. When we arrived in Gudalur in 1984, the majority of adivasis were working as daily wage earners inextricably trapped in a web of deprivation and poverty. It quickly became evident that the root cause of their poverty and exploitation was the loss of control over the land and forests their ancestors had held sacred since time immemorial. British India nationalised their forests. Colonial economic interests then took them over and converted huge areas of centuries-old forests into tea plantations. Post independence India continued the trend with land-hungry colonisers from the neighbouring state, Kerala, flooding the area in large numbers. They grabbed, through fair means and foul, whatever land they could and in the process enslaved the adivasis, luring them with alcohol and trapping them in debt.

And so we started the Tribal Land Rights Movement through which we grabbed – no, we prefer to call it 'reclaimed' – hundreds of acres of land that had once been in adivasi hands. And we helped them to plant tea on those lands. While tea did wonders for the tribal economy and radically changed some of the local power equations, it also meant that we had catapulted the adivasis from a local daily wage economy into a global market economy over which they had absolutely no control. At least in the wage economy if they did not get a decent wage we could mobilise hundreds of people to challenge the landlord and demand a fair wage. But when the price of tea crashes as it has done over the last few years, whose collar do we catch? We are told it is market forces – faceless, conveniently anonymous forces which we cannot control. And suddenly our years of empowering one of the weakest communities in India is rendered futile as powerlessness in the market economy overwhelms us all.

the root cause of their poverty and exploitation was the loss of control over the land <<<

At least so we were told. But chose not to accept. We decided we would fight back and seek to gain power even in this new market economy. And so we dug deep into the history and culture of the adivasi people in an effort to find insights and signposts that would lead us to discover new and untrodden paths. In the process we have discovered that for centuries these people have had social, political and economic systems that would serve us well.

So in the next part I would like to share with you some of the concepts, which lie at the heart of adivasi society.

Part II: Ancient Concepts for a Modern World:

Ownership

The capitalist economy is rooted in the concept of individual ownership and enterprise. In the socialist economy, state ownership and collective enterprise is supreme, even if it means coercing people into working in the collective mode. The collapse of the socialist economy seems to have vindicated the American view that the capitalist economy is the only viable one. And because of a warped media bias, the focus of attention has always been only on the socialist and capitalist economies. An either/or scenario. But both these economies are still founded on a concept of 'ownership' – where the individual in one and the state in the other has the fundamental right to 'own' and use the earth's resources as they will. What no one has talked about are the economies of indigenous people, which are based on a concept of NO ownership! How can you 'own' the land, the water, the forests, the birds, the animals. If I were to walk around the streets of Dublin with a plastic tent around me and sign that says 'this air is private property – trespassing not allowed' and was surrounded by armed guards that ensured my private airspace was protected from encroachment by others, I am sure you would all laugh at this crazy Indian and his strange foreign customs!! To the adivasi the air is no different from the land, or the water, or the forests – we did not create them, we cannot own them. To them these are common property resources to be used by all – you can have usufruct rights, which are collectively regulated but not ownership rights. So what happens when these two differing notions of the right to ownership come in contact with each other?

Let me tell you the story of Subramanian - a young Moolakurumba tribal who started ACCORD with Mari and I. His father, Kappala Thambi, was revered as a hard-working and skilled farmer. One day when Subramanian was still a child, a young pioneering family from the neighbouring state of Kerala came in search of land in the Nilgiri hills. Thambi welcomed this young family, sheltered them, fed them and offered land that he had cleared the previous year saying 'It is too difficult for you to begin with clearing land – use this land this year and grow your food.' But George, the young Syrian Christian from Kerala, quickly put up a fence around this land and when questioned said it was to protect his crops from cattle and wild animals.

>>> *the air is no different from the land, or the water, or the forests – we did not create them, we cannot own them*

The next year he started tilling the land again and when Thambi questioned him and said 'You must not cultivate the same patch of land, you must let it rest otherwise it will not yield,' George said 'Don't worry, there are new chemicals and fertilisers that will feed the earth and it will yield year after year'. A year passed and another and another and the fence kept getting moved as George brought more and more land under cultivation and finally when ten years had gone and Subramanian was a young boy, his father asked George for the land. And George produced a paper with official-looking stamps and signatures and said 'This land is mine – I have title to it.' This story was repeated to us in village

after village and many were less fortunate than Thambi and his people. Because in many villages the colonisers took over the entire land and the adivasis, in order to survive, were forced to accept wage labour on land that once was their own. So, finally, not only does the coloniser own the land, he also owns the labour of the adivasi.

This concept of the right to own is fundamental to how an economy operates and will determine the kind of society that we have. The pioneers of the American Wild West epitomised the right of the individual to own whatever he was physically able to take, protect and control. Over the years this right to take and own is no longer based on individual effort – but on the ability to pay for what we desire to own. So I can take as much of the earth and the oil and minerals below it, the water and forests on it, the birds and the air above it as long as I can pay for it.

In what is common wisdom to them, bewildered indigenous people have asked over the centuries 'How can you pay for the earth? How can you own the earth?' But we have been too busy in our quest for economic growth and ownership to pause and try and answer their questions. We are only now beginning to wake up to the fact that there is a limit to what one can take from the earth, what one can own of the earth. But we do not know how to stop this cannonball we have set in motion.

Distribution of Economic Benefit

Another very different concept is one that has to do with how the fruits or benefits of economic activity are to be distributed. In 1997, an adivasi group was invited to Germany to be a part of the Protestant church's Kirchentag, a celebration that takes place every alternate year. At one service, there was a gospel reading, the parable of the labourers who worked different hours but were all paid the same wage. As kids we had debated the justice behind it.

The adivasis however, had no problem with this biblical concept at all. They couldn't figure out what there was to debate. They told us how at the end of the hunt, a share of meat was sent to every family in the village, regardless of whether they had participated in the hunt or not, even adding a portion for guests who were visiting at the time. There was no question of calculating any individual's labour or input! But this was not all. Even stray passers-by were given a share to take home, and apparently knowing this, many opportunistic non adivasi neighbours would ensure that they 'happened' to pass by when the spoils were being divided. The adivasis just laughed. They bore no ill will towards the uninvited guests.

Yet another story comes from the Boran tribe in Kenya and Ethiopia. The Borans are basically pastoralists. Cattle – camel, cows and goats - are the backbone of their economy. They have a system called *buusa gonofa* that ensures no one ever falls below a collectively-defined poverty line. There is a committee whose task it is to keep track of the cattle population of each and every family of the tribe. If for any reason the number of someone's cattle falls below the minimum required, the committee orders someone who has more to hand some over to this person. 'What happens if everybody in the village is below or close to this minimum?', I asked. 'Then we go to the committee at the next level which is of the region and they will call on some other village to give their cattle and there is finally a still higher level of the entire tribe or nation'. I am told that this system still continues in many of the villages of the Boran tribe.

What is the purpose of economic activity – to acquire and hoard more wealth? If the creation and acquisition of wealth is the primary purpose of the economy, then the distribution of wealth becomes secondary. Distribution ceases to be the concern of the economic system and becomes the responsibility of the political system. And if we fail to achieve an equitable distribution of wealth, we believe the fault lies not in the way we conduct our economy but in the way we conduct our politics. So we continue to battle with the political system, bringing in new schemes, new programmes, new deals for the poor while we allow the economic system to continue unbridled and roaming free, seeking new pastures in faraway lands.

Whereas if the well-being of all people is the primary purpose of the economy, then distribution of wealth becomes an integral part of the economic system – like the *buusa gonofa* of the Boran. Our politics, our beliefs and our values should direct and control the economy and not the other way around.

The Meaning of Wealth

In 1995, after ten years of work with the adivasi people of the Nilgiri Hills, we undertook a massive exercise to evaluate what had happened over the last few years in order to determine the future course of our work. A crucial part of this exercise

was to understand whether we had succeeded in bringing about a redistribution of wealth. This led to inevitable questions about the meaning of wealth. Hundreds of meetings were held in hundreds of villages. And in every one of them wealth was defined as the earth, forests, water, our culture, our unity, our songs, our children. But not one village – not one single one – mentioned money!! When we heard this in the first few villages, steeped in our superiority we thought what simple, naive and adorable people. And we gently prodded them to understand that the world had changed, the economy around them had changed – and that today wealth did mean money. But in village after village people said, No! money was not wealth but a means to create wealth. Nobody denied the importance or the need for money – how could they since it was their daily earning of money that put rice in the pot? – they simply challenged the role of money in society.

These differing notions were put to an interesting test when the group of adivasis visited Germany. We wondered about plunging them from what we considered their abject poverty into the overflowing wealth of the West and the impact it would have on them. All our fears were put to rest and one incident clearly showed us that their notion of wealth remained with them even in Germany.

Nobody denied the importance or <<< the need for money – they simply challenged the role of money in society

Let me share that story. We were in Hamburg and our hosts, who took great pains to show us different aspects of German society, arranged for a visit to an old people's home. A very well-to-do one. And when they were told that there were many such homes, the adivasis were truly amazed – what a wonderful society that cared for its lonely old people so well. But they were surprised that there were so many old people without families, without children and grandchildren to look after them and who were so poor that they had to have special homes for them. Our German friends were quick to correct them – these old people were in fact quite wealthy. They did have children and grandchildren but these were sometimes too far away or too busy to look after their old people. And so they paid from their life's savings to be looked after in these homes. The adivasis were silenced – they could not comprehend. And one of the adivasis, Chathi, finally expressed everyone's feelings when he said, 'What poor people – in spite of all their money, they have to live their old age away from their children and grandchildren'.

But sadly, living in the hills of South India, I see this notion of wealth being steadily eroded as it slowly becomes more and more synonymous with money. When our economy is divorced from our culture, our politics, our social relationships, wealth simply means money, money and more money.

The Concept of Money

One of the things that has never ceased to intrigue me is how money in one person's hand becomes capital – a means for investment and the generation of more money - while in another person's hand it is only cash to be spent. One person's money grows and grows while the other person's is lost and gone forever and he or she has to begin another day struggling to ensure that they have earned enough to meet that day's expenses. How and why does money change its nature so? When a labourer is paid why do we call it a wage, but when a shareholder or investor is paid why do we call it a dividend or returns on the investment? Why is a wage fixed irrespective of the profits made on the labour while the dividend or returns on investment is directly related to the profits made on the investment? Why does money have the capacity to be an investment and earn more money while labour is only a commodity that can be purchased with money? Why does money mean different things in different circumstances? Why is ownership determined not by the amount of participation in the economy either in terms of time or human effort but by the investment of money in these special situations called capital? Why do we know the same thing by two different names?

Wasn't money created as a counting mechanism invented to keep track of complex economic exchanges? As a symbol of value? Why have we over time allowed the symbol to become the real thing?

A few days ago I overhead my two teenage sons arguing with each other. Tarshish, the older one, said 'You owe me three shirts' and Tariq, the younger one, replied 'No way. I owe you only two because you owed me five and then you won three yesterday and four today.' Intrigued, I enquired what was going on. Apparently over the

last month they had started challenging each other on various things and whoever was proved wrong would have to iron a predetermined number of shirts for the other. What a nice idea I thought – their cupboard would be tidy at last. 'So are all your shirts ironed now', I asked and they said not one. Though they started off thinking this was a good way to get through a chore they both hated doing, they were no better off than when they started. Because the promise of ironed shirts became a value in itself. And their game continues but the shirts remain unironed!

Another thing that I find intriguing, especially when I travel, is the differing values of money. Why is an English pound worth 70 rupees or an American dollar worth 50 rupees? And worse why was a pound worth 60 rupees only a few months ago and even less a year ago and was only worth somewhere around 40 rupees a couple of years ago? Who is counting, who is keeping track, who is making these decisions?

Before 1991, when India still had a fully protected economy, it was very clear – it was the government of India through its Reserve Bank that made these decisions. These were political decisions, taken under economic pressure no doubt, but political decisions nonetheless. After structural adjustment and the liberalisation of the Indian economy under blatant arm twisting by the IMF and World Bank, today these decisions are made by 'market forces' I am told.

If all this isn't madness, tell me what is? I won't even go down the route of stock markets and share prices, where something like an Enron share could be worth hundreds of dollars one day and nothing the next day. Where a shareholder is a millionaire one day and nothing the next. We are dealing with shadows. Imagined or notional wealth. Quite like the unironed shirts.

Co-operation or Competition?

The capitalist market economy reveres competition and upholds it as the cornerstone, the driving force of growth and development. So strong is the economy's hold on our values and beliefs that the spirit of competition has seeped into every part of our lives. But I suspect that deep down in our hearts we know that this is not right - that's why we invariably find that we qualify it by saying 'healthy competition'. Thereby giving competition a sense of goodness. But I have been privileged to be part of a society where the notion of competition is very highly undeveloped. Competition does not dominate or control the way society functions. Co-operation does.

Take for instance, *pannthi uratal* or the rolling wild boar, a favourite sport and pastime of the Moolakurumba tribe during the hunting season. Young men and boys stand in a row girded in the fashion of hunters in the forest, bows cocked and arrows ready to fly. Somebody rolls a small wooden disc along the ground and everyone shoots at it. And it is rolled again and again till it disintegrates. Then coconuts are hurled along the ground and shot at and when everyone has their fill of shooting, the broken coconuts are all collected and someone shoots an arrow high into the air. The coconuts are placed where the arrow lands and every one dances around and ends with a feast of coconut. The result? Winners: all. Losers: none.

In a competitive society, winners and losers are inevitable. And each win gives you an advantage, placing you that much more ahead in the next round of competition and then the next and the next – year after year, generation after generation. Advantage and privilege heaped upon advantage and privilege. While those who lose begin each round that much farther back and recede further and further. We applaud the winners and pity the losers – and, by making the winners the great of the earth and the losers the pitiable failures, we once again skilfully place the blame, not on the system of competition, but on the participants themselves. We delude ourselves that everybody can win if only they try hard enough.

There is yet another element to competition – especially what we all like to call healthy competition – there can be no end to it. If religion is no longer the opium of people, competitive success surely is. It dominates every aspect of life but nowhere does it cause as much harm and damage as in the economy. Where giant faceless transnational companies compete with another in a no-holds-barred fight for profits. Bribing, lying, cheating their way to an imagined pinnacle of success. By declaring Enron and its like bankrupt, have we cleaned the stables or is it only a whiff of a dung heap we are yet to uncover?

Part III: Is There Any Hope At All?

The vast majority of human rights activists who have worked at the grassroots for the last few decades are plunged into gloom as economic globalisation becomes the order of the day. The Bill Gateses of the world wield far more political clout than rallies of millions of poor people demanding justice and human rights. Is this mindless, profit-driven, market economy inevitable? Are justice and human dignity no longer relevant? Will we remain helpless pawns moved about on an economic chess board in a game played by speculative gamblers and wheeler-dealers in the so-called market economy? Are there no other choices and options?

I believe there are – but we have to create them. We have to reclaim the political space that has been steadily encroached upon and is in danger of being completely usurped by economic interests.

If religion is no longer the opium <<<
of people, competitive success
surely is

Our search for options has led us to develop an idea, which for the present we will call 'Just Change'. It is a concept intended to challenge the traditional notions of ownership in both the capitalist and socialist models.

Just Change is proposed as an alternative economic structure that will allow people to express solidarity in far more effective ways than has been done in the past. It is rooted in the concept of creating direct links right across the economic chain - from labourers and producers all the way through to consumers and investors. Thus enabling them to participate in the economy in a co-operative manner rather than a competitive one.

Basically, the concept is to create a new marketing chain where the traditional links between investors, labourers and consumers can be redefined. In the present market economy, persons with capital are the ones who are seen as 'investors' and therefore gain ownership and control over the economic chain. Persons with labour are not 'investors' – labour is purely a commodity that can be purchased. Consumers are not investors either. Merely a 'market' that should be encouraged to buy whatever the economy can produce. Even with ethical investments, with Fair Trade, with aid, this basic relationship between capital, labour and consumers is not changed.

Hence we propose creating a structure where all three participants in the economic chain will be seen as 'investors'. A invests in the economic process by providing capital. B invests by providing labour. C invests by consuming the product of A's capital and B's labour. If we have a structure that will enable all three to participate in the economy as equal partners then perhaps we have a possibility of a more equitable distribution of the fruits of economic activity.

How Can This Work?

Again going back to our experiences with adivasis as very marginal producers of tea, let us say that our 1000 families together produce one thousand kilograms of made tea every day. Each family requires Rs.100 a day – approximately €2 - to meet their basic needs including the cost of producing the tea. We would therefore need a 100,000 rupees (€2000) a day for these 1000 families to survive. Traditionally they therefore would 'sell' their tea at the 'market price' to whoever provided them this money and their involvement in the economic chain would stop at that point. The amount they receive would bear no relationship to their cost of living. The person who invested the capital to buy this tea then puts in more money to deliver the tea in a marketable form to 1000 more people. The investor therefore recovers his investment and profits, if any, from these 1000 consumers.

But let us say there are 1000 'investors' – persons who have money left over after meeting their basic needs and would therefore like to invest it. Let us say that these 1000 investors together can put up the €2000 required by the producers and also another €2000 to deliver this tea to the consumer.

Now let us say, there are 1000 consumers who are each willing to buy this tea at €6 a kilogram. That means a surplus of €2 per kilogram or €2000 for the whole lot.

The important point here is that these 1000 investors have not 'bought' the tea and the 1000 producers have not 'sold' the tea. Ownership has not changed hands – ownership is spread to include the persons who put a product – tea in this case – and the persons who put money into the economic chain.

In the present capital economy, ownership over this 'profit' of €2000 legitimately lies with the person whose capital was used to intervene and act as a link between the producer and the consumers. This single aspect in an entire economic chain gives an unfair advantage to the person whose participation in the economy is the provision of capital.

So if we can create a structure where this 'profit' of €2000 is equally owned by all the three participants then we have an entirely new relationship between producers, investors and consumers. They can determine the terms on which this 'profit' will be divided (or loss shared!). The terms could be based more on equity rather than on traditional concepts of ownership.

This concept of Just Change was born not from a vague theoretical blueprint but from a critical reflection of the experiences of the last two decades. The challenge before us now is whether we can create a structure, which allows people to participate collectively? A structure, which is driven by values and not by mere profit? Where a just distribution of wealth is more important than the creation of wealth? The task before us is to see if we can link people with capital who care with poor people who produce and with concerned consumers.

Our many years of experience have led us to believe, as an article of faith, that there are millions of people who *are* more interested in a fair and equitable distribution of wealth than the market would like us to believe.

In conclusion, I would like to place before each and everyone of you a challenge – will we remain in our little boxes, separated by nationality, colour, religion, class and geographical distance or will we reach out and find people with similar values, people who believe justice and equality should be an integral part of society and not just words to adorn constitutions and declarations.

If globalisation is here to stay then let us together reach out and create a global village of our own making!

I thank Feasta for making it possible for a little voice from a remote hill in South India to be heard here in Ireland. For me today has been a privilege and an honour and I go away even more firmly convinced that it is possible to create a new world order where the desire for justice and the well-being of all people will triumph over greed, over the market economy and over the forces of a capitalist rather than a people's globalisation.

JUST CHANGE
Humanising globalisation
Stan Thekaekara

> *Why is it that all the profits from a business go to those who put up the capital? A new form of producer-consumer-investor co-operative gives all the participants a share.*

For nearly three decades now, my wife Mari and I have struggled for the poor. We have fought human rights abuses, land alienation, untouchability, feudalism and violence against women. We have won major victories and changed the lives of the poor we worked for. But, finally, we have been forced to conclude that fighting poverty and fighting for the economic rights of our people seems to have moved beyond our control.

Many people I know feel the same way. The vast majority of human rights activists who have worked at the grassroots for the past few decades are plunged into gloom. Whether we are working with adivasis[1] in the Nilgiris or dalits[2] in Orissa; or with unemployed people living in run-down council estates in London; or with the homeless on the streets of Dublin, the forces defeating us are faceless and frighteningly anonymous.

So what is going wrong? Are we fighting the wrong fight? Are we too fainthearted in battle, surrendering to more powerful adversaries too easily? Or is it simply that our strategies are deeply flawed? Different people give different answers. The most common one is that young people have been de-politicised and are single-mindedly pursuing careers in the hope of finding an imaginary pot of consumerist gold at the end of an imaginary yuppy rainbow.

But at events like the 2004 World Social Forum in Mumbai, a more likely explanation has been rolled out in high decibel sloganeering to the accompaniment of deafening dalit drums – "down down globalisation"; "down down liberalisation". Yet when you stop anyone of those whose throats have gone dry with the shouting and ask "what is globalisation?", "why has it caused you so much pain?" – they are not quite sure. They can describe the pain in vivid and heart-rending detail but they cannot articulate or analyse why it happens.

While many of these campaigners may not understand how or why globalisation has created poverty, they do know that the vulnerability of the poor is steadily increasing and that this was aggravated when the government of India decided to toe the World Bank/IMF line and liberalise the Indian economy. This moved the country away, surprisingly quickly, from its socialist underpinning. The concept of a mixed economy as envisaged in the Indian constitution gave way to a modern free market economy. As a result, the ground gained over the previous two decades in the fight against poverty began to slide out from under them. Accordingly, they are not taken in when they are told again and again that globalisation is good for all of us but that we must go through the belt-tightening phase even if eating less means malnutrition or death for the poorest women and children. At the same time, there are bigger houses, faster cars, and more partying opportunities for the rich who can afford them.

Like the campaigners, ordinary people feel helpless against the globalisation juggernaut that ruthlessly mows down anything that smacks of protectionism even if it is directly protecting the weakest and most vulnerable. Sure, it promises heaven on earth but there is a rider in micro-fine print – 'Heaven, yes, but only for those who can afford it.'

But let us cut through the emotion and anger and try to analyse what is actually happening, and why is it that at a time when nations like India can declare "India Shining" with record-breaking 8% economic growth and foreign exchange reserves ballooning to an all-time high of over a billion dollars; those of us who work with the world's poorest are not able to share the euphoria.

Changed Rules

The first thing we need to recognise is that the rules have changed. Not just the rules of trade, not even the rules of governance, but the fundamental rules on which economies are based. And this impacts on poor people in new ways that are not fully understood.

Trade dominates the economy. Not production. And we now have an economy where trade extends far beyond just goods and services! You can trade in notional wealth like stocks and shares, or even in non-existent things like a banana crop expected in the future, or even the very thing that was meant to keep track of trade and exchange – money itself.

Twenty years ago, when we started working with the adivasis here in the Nilgiris[3], the analysis was Marxian clear. Poverty was caused by a loss of control over the means of production.

>>> *The end result: a once proud and self-reliant community reduced to being unskilled landless labourers*

In the Nilgiris, a rural agricultural economy, land lay at the heart of production. And once upon a time the adivasis had complete control over the land and its forests. It was obvious that the root cause of the adivasi's poverty and exploitation was their loss of control over the land and forests their ancestors had held sacred since time immemorial. British India nationalised their forests, colonial economic interests then took over the land and converted huge areas of centuries-old forests into tea plantations. After independence, India continued the trend with land-hungry colonisers from the neighbouring state, Kerala, flooding the area in large numbers. They grabbed, through fair means and foul, whatever land they could and in the process enslaved the adivasis, luring them with alcohol and trapping them in debt. The end result: a once proud and self-reliant community reduced to being unskilled landless labourers, the bottom of the economic heap, in a land that was once their own. Their life, a daily struggle of ensuring that there would be enough food for the evening meal.

An analysis of the forces that trapped them in poverty threw up the obvious solution - reclaim control of the land. So we began a Tribal Land Rights Campaign in 1988 which, 15 years down the line, has seen the majority of adivasis gain control of small pieces of land ranging from half an acre to three acres.

Further analysis led us to the conclusion that, in addition to reclaiming their ancestral land and organising the community against further exploitation, it was imperative that the land should start to yield. After much debate, we decided that it was best to plunge into the mainstream economic activity - the cultivation of tea. There were several reasons for this. It was a permanent crop which once planted would establish possession rights over the land. A tea bush properly planted and tended would provide a steady income for the next one hundred years! The local infrastructure for the tea trade was already present and we would not have to invest in developing it. The people already had the requisite skills and we were not introducing something alien and new here. But most importantly, it would make a strong political statement if supposedly unskilled labourers became tea planters. It would radically change their social and economic status.

So the adivasis of Gudalur have moved from being part of the faceless masses that provided labour to the local plantation and agricultural economy to being key players in the local tea industry. However, with this transition has come a host of new problems. The most relevant one was pointed out by a colleague, Ramdas, who asked why we were moving the community out of the local economy into a global economy over which it had no control.

As India hurtles down the path of structural adjustment and liberalisation, tea prices have crashed plunging adivasis into dangerous levels of debt. Cotton farmers in Andhra Pradesh are committing suicide by the hundreds[4] as they find it impossible to cope with their ever-increasing poverty, and all over the country, people who depended on land for their livelihood are being plunged into unimaginable poverty. Before Mari and I arrived in the area, the adivasi population worked for local farmers. They could negotiate, protest. What would their weapons be if the adversary became a faceless multinational company?

Gaining control over small pieces of land, once the solution to poverty, is now no longer enough. And it is not just the marginal farmer who is feeling the pinch - even small and medium farmers are struggling to cope. For that matter, so are large corporations! We were recently approached by a large tea company which owns thousands of acres of tea plantations. They were very reticent on the 'phone about the purpose of the proposed meeting and when we found out we were stunned! They were prepared to hand over their entire land holdings to their workers! Just give it away! Why? A conversion on the road to Damascus? A newly-discovered social conscience? It was straightforward market sense. The money was no longer in the production of tea but in the trading of it.

What we are seeing today is capitalism in its purest form. Wealth is no longer created through the control over the means of production. It is created through the trading of the fruit of production. And trading requires one single resource – capital. Not land, not labour. And so it is not the feudal owner of land who is today the powerful controller of a rural economy like ours in Gudalur. It is corporations like Unilever who control the trade in products like tea among a host of others.

So if history was to describe our civilisation, I think we could be called a civilisation of traders. Not just traders of goods. But traders of money, traders of capital. The market dominates every aspect of our economic life and, more importantly, our social life as well. Which is why it is rightly called a market economy. The obvious beneficiaries of any market are the traders and in today's market economy – which is a far cry from the local farmers' or village market – capital is of the essence. Power in no longer defined by natural assets like land or property, but by the control and ownership of capital.

Is it surprising then that the Bill Gateses and George Soroses of the world wield far more political clout than millions of poor people demanding justice and human rights? Is it surprising that Dick Cheney and his ilk with their interests in the trading of oil are more influential than the millions who marched against the war in Iraq in London, Rome, Washington and all over the world? Is it surprising then that profits come before people?

Is this profit-driven market economy inevitable? Are justice and human dignity no longer relevant? Are there no other choices and options? We like to believe there are. And so over the past few years we have been pursuing one such option, Just Change.

Just Change

Several strands linked together to shape it. In 1993 we sent tea to a group of women handloom weavers and received beautiful saris in return. Both groups were ecstatic. Our women who got beautiful saris at half the local market price and the women weavers who received our garden-fresh tea at one-third their local market price. This made us think. Why not use the strength of mass mobilisation and the infrastructure that we had built up to help poor producers' communities trade with each other?

The next strand was the advent into our lives of GEPA, a German fair trade organisation. The "fair trade not aid" concept intrigued and appealed to us. We started selling tea to GEPA and used the premium earned to assist more adivasis to get control over their land. The experience reinforced our belief that there were many people all over the world who were willing to work for ideals of justice and equity.

Is this profit-driven market economy <<<
inevitable? Are justice and human
dignity no longer relevant?

But the visit of an adivasi group to Germany in 1997 raised some questions about the concept of fair trade. Bomman, one of the adivasi leaders, was thoroughly upset to hear that his new-found German friends paid three times more for our tea than it cost in Gudalur. "That's ridiculous and unfair," he protested. "How can our friends who work to support our struggle for self-reliance pay more for our tea? They should pay less, not more." Bomman's perspective led us to look at new ways of working which would incorporate his concept of what was fair.

In May 1994, sponsored by Hilary Blume of the Charities' Advisory Trust and Michael Norton from the Directory of Social Change, Mari and I visited Britain to look at development work there. In Easterhouse, Scotland, we looked at the endless cups of tea consumed and thought why don't we send them our tea? We could cut out some fat cat middleman and start a small marketing and distributing business for the local people. Or ginger? Michael Norton was delighted at the thought of our ginger coming to Scotland and being made into chocolate ginger in

Easterhouse. Value addition, income generation and a wonderful solidarity between two groups an entire continent apart. He even gave it a name "Direct Links".

In 1998, through Oxfam, we came in contact with the Matson Neighbourhood Project working with the residents of a council estate in Gloucester. The high level of unemployment in the estate made the idea of Direct Links between the adivasis of Gudalur and the residents of Matson very attractive. Impractical, maybe even impossible, but the coordinator of the project, Mark Gale, was convinced it was worth giving it a shot. The local press picked it up and BBC Radio 4 followed with a four-part serial called 'Trading Places'.

>>> *traditional aid diminishes the justice aspect of the poverty divide*

An article in the *New Internationalist* outlining the idea brought a tremendous response from readers and convinced us that the concept was far bigger than tea, adivasis, Matson or Easterhouse. It convinced us that there *is* a global community which cares. All we need is a means to link them. The traditional means of linking these groups has been through aid and donor agencies. But traditional aid somehow diminishes the justice aspect of the poverty divide. Here, the Fair Trade groups have gone a step ahead and played a tremendously important role in bringing the question of justice to the forefront. They have created an awareness among ordinary people about the unfairness of the trade game and appealed to them to give a better deal to poor producers by paying more for their products. But the Fair Traders have not tackled the inherent injustice of the blatantly unfair structure of the entire trade economy.

These strands, then, were the germs of the Just Change concept, an attempt to link producers, consumers and investors in a cooperative chain which allows the three factors of production and wealth creation to work together for mutual benefit. It is now slowly developing into a fully-fledged system through which community groups have begun to trade directly with each other. From being helpless victims in a marauding global market economy over which they had no control, these communities are now beginning to hope that by working together they can strengthen their local economies by restructuring the way they trade.

Where we are now

Just Change is now a registered trust both in India and the UK. For strategic reasons we are developing and strengthening the model in India before moving into other countries. Pioneered by the Adivasi Munnetra Sangam[5] (AMS) from Gudalur, three more people's organisations – Bhoodhan Vikas Mandal (BVM), SAWARD and Sahabagyi Vikas Abhiyan (SVA) have joined the network here in India. BVM and SAWARD are both women's organisations in Kerala while SVA is a federation of dalit and adivasi organisations in Western Orissa. A number of other organisations will be joining soon.

These organisations will become shareholders in Just Change by providing a common pot of working capital. They will take out of the pot whatever it costs them to participate in the chain either as producers, value-adders or retailers to their consumer-members. The final value of the tea (or other products) when consumed goes back into the common pot and when books are closed, the surplus will be divided between all the shareholders. It will be left to the organisations to decide how to pass on this surplus to their members. While all of us are agreed that we will not touch the surplus for the next three years, the AMS has already decided that any surplus will be collectively used to contribute to the health care and education costs of their community while BVM is considering distributing the surplus among its members on the basis of how much of the tea each member has consumed.

At the heart of this system is the fact that everyone who joins the network, irrespective of their role in the network, are all seen as investors and therefore are entitled to share in the surplus.

In the much-touted free market economy, only one participant in the economic chain is seen as an investor, the person who provides the capital, and it is accepted that this person owns the entire surplus - or profit. All other participants - the producer, the consumer – get nothing although their actions contributed to the creation of that profit. This is the reason that the rich are those with capital and the poor are those without. This applies to countries too. It does not matter whether a country is rich in natural resources or in labour as these commodities can be purchased with capital. It is the capital that counts. And if a country decides to protect its natural resources or its labour by regulations that restrict foreign capital, then in come the unholy trinity of the WTO, IMF and World Bank to force it to open up its economy to allow the unfettered flow of foreign direct investment.

Because we know in our hearts that the very nature of a capital economy with its narrow notion of the meaning of investment must result in some people being rich and some people being poor, those of us concerned with poverty seem almost reconciled to accepting that the poor must always be with us. And so our language has changed – we no longer seek to eradicate poverty, we seek to alleviate it. Poverty is no longer an injustice, a blot on our civilisation and society- it is an inevitable part of it.

Yes, as long as we accept the capital economy as it is, poverty is inevitable and the best we can do is to cry ourselves hoarse demanding the redistribution of wealth. But if we really want to eradicate poverty, it is not enough to talk about the redistribution of wealth. Even in the best-case scenario, redistribution will amount to a small fraction of the wealth generated.[6] We need to challenge the structures that create wealth. Redistribution should not be an afterthought, an action to be taken after the creation of wealth. It has to be an inherent and integral part of the creation of wealth.

Just Change challenges the notion that investment is just a matter of the capital employed, that one can scoop up the entire surplus of any economic activity simply by putting up the necessary capital. Instead, Just Change offers a structure where it is possible for any participant in any economic activity to be seen as an investor as long as they are willing and prepared to work as part of this structure. Just Change ensures that the generation of surplus is not for the benefit of any one participant but for all. The purpose of economic activity then changes from the creation of wealth (profit) to the creation of well-being for all.

Tea was the first product to be traded through the Just Change network but at the time of writing, August 2004, rice was about to be introduced. Our hope is that, over time, the network will trade in a range of products among communities both in India and across the globe.

In Britain, we have developed links with community groups in Newcastle, Manchester, Gloucester and Cheltenham. We need to make these more robust.

as long as we accept the capital economy as it is, poverty is inevitable <<<

Frequently Asked Questions

Let me end by raising some of the most frequently-asked questions and attempting to answer them.

Is Just Change compatible with the goal of strengthening local economies?

It has become obvious to anyone concerned about the negative impact of the free market global economy that the only way to challenge it is by strengthening local economies. But we need to be clear about what we mean by global and what we mean by local.

To me, local is not geographical. Local is not a small community, tucked away in some tiny village, struggling to produce all its requirements within a five kilometre radius. I think we live in a far too sophisticated, complex world for that to happen. And so I would redefine what we mean by local. To me local means linking up communities who believe in certain fundamental principles. It means linking up people who subscribe to a similar kind of thinking. To a similar set of values. It does not matter where we live. What matters is whether we are willing to work together for mutual benefit. Irrespective of our role within the economy – irrespective of whether we function as producers, consumers, or investors.

Years of "thinking globally and acting locally" has led us now to think locally and act globally as well! And so Just Change seeks to link these producers, consumers and investors in a cooperative chain where they can work for the mutual benefit of all within the chain, irrespective of where they might reside.

How is this different from Fair Trade? Is it different? Are you in competition?

In terms of values it is not different and we are not in competition. In fact, Just Change builds on the concept of fair trade – that trade is *not* fair and we need to do something about it. The Fair Trade movement has worked wonders in terms of creating awareness of the unfairness of the trade structures, in increasing the demand by consumers for fairly-traded products and forcing the likes of Sainsburys and Starbucks to stock and make fair trade goods available.

But Fair Trade does not change the fundamental relationship between labour and capital. Capital still has the power to "buy" labour and the fruits of labour. Paying a higher price will definitely alleviate the suffering of the producer but Just Change argues that we need to go further. We need to change the structure under which we conduct our trade and our economy in a way that will change the power relationship between labour and capital. We need a structure that recognises that labour and capital have a role to play in the economy but in a way that ensures they are not in competition with each other but work in tandem for mutual benefit.

>>> *I do not believe that we are fundamentally or naturally selfish*

Just Change is not about fair prices alone - it is about the relation between capital and labour, between "investors", producers and consumers. It is about creating a true market chain where all the forces of the market work collectively. So that one person is not the controller of market forces and another the victim of it! Just Change is tackling a centuries-old way of managing our economies. We are taking on powerful vested interests. We are Davids against a Goliath and we need as many stones as possible in our slingshot.

But is this practical? Isn't this too idealistic? Aren't people basically so selfish that you are asking for the moon when you expect them to work together in such a positive manner?

Of course it is idealistic. But isn't our society built on precisely that – ideals? I do not see being idealistic and being practical as opposing or contradictory concepts. Ideals are what we seek or hope to achieve; being practical is how we will go about achieving it! The concept is idealistic - the way we go about it is not!

Whether human beings are basically selfish is not an economic question but a philosophical one. How much of our own behaviour is due to conditioning and how much of it is natural? What gives us most satisfaction, contentment and well being? How many of our most joyous activities are individual and how many are based on group or collective action?

Let me simply say I do not believe that we are fundamentally or naturally selfish. I have lived for too long with too many communities and have many friends – none of whom are selfish. They may commit selfish acts but they are not selfish by nature and they are too numerous for me to believe that we as human beings are basically selfish and individualistic.

The first consignment of Just Change tea went to Gujarat to the " dalit" community, which is treated as the lowest of the low in the Indian caste system. A community condemned by custom to perform only the most menial and "polluting" tasks like cleaning toilets and handling carcasses. Toilets in many parts of India mean an open ground enclosed by a wall and the members of this community are forced to go in and gather the shit, put it into baskets and head load it out of the village, a practice banned by law but still alive and well in many parts of the country. Mari has been campaigning for years against this practice and our adivasis in Gudalur were familiar with the plight of this community.

When the tea was about to be despatched we had a meeting with all the adivasi tea growers in Gudalur and asked them how they thought the profits if any, should be divided. One old man spoke, "Are we mad? Don't we know these people are much much worse off than us? Surely they should keep all the profits that are generated!!". Everyone was vehemently in agreement. And this from a community that itself struggles to make enough each day to ensure their children do not go to bed hungry.

Selfish? Think again!

But surely it is a very small minority that thinks like this?

The Adivasi Munnetra Sangam has 3,000 families as its members. The people who were at the meeting were representatives of these families and spoke for them, an entire community. At a recent meeting, representatives from various organisations committed to become part of the Just Change network. We added up the number of people these organisations represented and shocked ourselves when we discovered we were talking of nearly two million people. And this is only the beginning.

But yes, perhaps we are a minority. Yet, all change begins with a minority and, given the right conditions and opportunities, I cannot help believing that it will become a majority.

People will have many more questions and we do not pretend to have the answers to them all. Let us just encourage everyone to be idealistic, to redefine the purpose of economic activity and then to be practical and create the climate, the opportunity, and the structures that are needed to achieve their ideals. Step by step, brick by brick, community by community. And then perhaps, just perhaps, one day we will have a society where we can proudly say the poor are no longer with us. Because poverty has been eradicated and not just alleviated, because justice has been done.

Endnotes:

1   Adivasis – literally translates as the "first inhabitants" – India's indigenous or aboriginal people.

2   Refers to the communities in India that are condemned by the caste system to be "untouchable" or "outcaste".

3   Nilgiris – or the Blue Mountains in Tamilnadu, South India

4   The issue first hit the headlines in 1987 when 20 cotton growers committed suicide. The problem assumed alarming proportions in 1997. In the last seven years, about 200 farmers have ended their lives each year. And these are conservative estimates.

5   A "sangam" is a mass organisation based on direct membership and is very common phenomenon in the Indian voluntary sector where NGOs have mobilised thousands and thousands of people into sangams

6   The UN target for aid from rich countries is just 0.7% of their GNI and even this not honoured by the majority of countries. America gives just 0.19% even though its wealth per person doubled between 1961 and 2000. Source; Never richer, never meaner by Tony German and Ruth Randel

GLOBALISATION:

Who Benefits?

Stan Thekaekara

> *Globalisation will not bring about a redistribution of wealth from the rich to the poor. But it is taking more and more money out of local economies and putting it into an ill-defined global one*

She turned 18 just two months ago. Her birthday horoscope said that her "prospects" were bright. And when she landed her well-paid call-centre job a few days later, you could hardly blame her for believing in astrology.

Shantha by day and Susan by night. Every evening at 7 pm she dons her headphones, clicks a mental switch and transforms herself from a middle-class South Indian Brahmin girl into a friendly, almost flirtatious 20-something American woman.

She, with the rest of middle-class India, is rubbing her hands in unadulterated glee. Everyday the newspaper headlines scream of yet another multinational shifting its operations to India. British Airways, HSBC, and even Britain's National Rail Enquiries. More jobs, more money and the promise of enjoying all the good things of life right at the start of her career. Quite unlike her father, whose entire working life was one long continuous struggle of saving, saving and more saving till, clubbed with all his retirement benefits, he could finally afford to build himself a modest house. Prudent to the core, loathe to spend money on anything but the essentials, borrowing money was something he wouldn't dream of doing – he could not think of a worse stigma being attached to his stolid, middle class upbringing. No wonder he shakes his head in bewilderment at the way his daughter and her ilk spend money – mostly money they do not have.

But, nevertheless, he reluctantly admits that globalisation and liberalisation are indeed good things. Look at the all the goodies available in India. The cars, the clothes, the televisions, the computers, the cell phones, the food – you name it and you can buy it. It wasn't long ago that these were the wares flaunted by his richer, more fortunate, older cousin who by a stroke of good luck had emigrated to America – things that he couldn't have dreamt of buying in his lifetime. And now his daughter not yet twenty was beginning to have them all!! Why go to America?

Globalisation and the accompanying privatisation has sent India's GDP soaring, interest rates and inflation plunging, all at a pace that has Marxists and other anti-capitalist ideologues running for cover. The economy appears to be on overdrive, jobs seem to multiply faster than the population. Perhaps we will soon be the land of milk and honey. America in India. The middle-class dream seems to be finally coming true.

Of all the perceived benefits of the new liberal, structurally-adjusted, globalised economy, the flight of jobs from the North to the South seems to be the one that has even the most die-hard anti-capitalist, anti-globalisation campaigner caught on the defensive. The steady flow of jobs from the North to the South seems to be poetic justice for the 200 years of colonial rule when wealth flowed unimpeded from the South to the North. Here finally we have a modern reversal of the raj – a global redistribution of wealth. Surely a reason to celebrate?

Certainly. But who are the ones who will be clinking glasses and raising toasts to the new economic order? Pub-crawling teenagers, laptop-toting, mobile phone-hugging software geeks, helmeted young salesmen zipping around on the latest trendy Japanese motorcycle, fat-cat corporate executives commuting to work in air-conditioned Mercedes Benz luxury – these are the people who have every reason to celebrate and they do with a vengeance!

Bangalore, Chennai, Hyderabad, Mumbai, Delhi and other cities are falling over each other trying to transform themselves into the cities of the new global order, a fitting place to carry out the celebrations.

But what of rural India? Where almost 70% of India's people live? No champagne and caviar for them. In fact they struggle to get even their rice and dal – their daily staple. They along with the millions of India's urban poor are not the ones who will be celebrating.

I suspect that India's poorest along with the poorest from Britain, Germany, France, Ireland , yes, even the US of A, will be the ones who will pay for the costs of all the celebration.

I know Shantha and her family well. But I also happen to know Janet, a single mum, raising two children in a council estate in working-class Britain. Two years ago, Janet re-trained through one of the New Deal programmes introduced by the Labour government. I happened to be in England and was able to join her and her friends at the local pub to celebrate her landing a job at a call centre that had opened nearby. After being on welfare for nearly five years!! When I visited Janet again last year, that celebration was a painful memory because the company had closed down and moved to India.

Last month I was invited to join Shantha and her family at a US pizza chain in Bangalore to celebrate her landing her highly-paid call-centre job. I declined. Thinking of Janet.

I cannot but feel that Janet's loss was Shantha's gain. But knowing both women and their families, I do not for a moment believe that this transfer from a rich Northern country to a relatively poorer Southern country was actually a redistribution of wealth from the rich to the poor. While Janet, living in the rich North could easily be classified as being among the poorest of British society, Shantha and her family could by no stretch of imagination be called poor or even near-poor in India. They are good, solid, middle-class folk heading determinedly on their path to upper-class India. The loss of jobs for the poor of rich nations is NOT the gain of poorer people in a poorer country. It is dangerous to presume that a movement to poorer countries is a movement to poorer people!

No, we do not have a redistribution of wealth. We are not seeing a correction of a historical wrong. What we are seeing is a further concentration of wealth. Globalisation at best has redefined the geography of this concentration. What we are seeing is the continuing movement of wealth upwards making what is now seen as a cliché more true than ever before – the poor are getting poorer and the rich are getting richer.

In the Nilgiri Hills of South India, where I live and work with adivasis or indigenous people, this statement is challenged even by close colleagues. When we began our work in the mid 80's, the majority of adivasis lived on a meagre four to five hundred rupees a month. Today their monthly income is closer to Rs. 2500. How can you say they are poorer? Even allowing for inflation and increased cost of living this is surely an improvement? Yes, if you compare the adivasis with themselves 17 years ago they are definitely not poorer.

comparing them against themselves <<< is to confuse development with justice.

To compare them with themselves gives us a distorted understanding of their development. They are part of a larger society, a larger economy. *And comparing them against themselves is to confuse development with justice.* Of course they have developed, more children are going to school, almost no women are dying of childbirth, malnutrition is rare. Yes indeed, all the indicators are proof of very significant development. But has there been justice? Has there been redressal of a historical wrong that left a yawning gap between them and the rest of dominant Indian society? We have indicators for development. What are the indicators for justice – especially economic justice?

If we are to understand whether their economic growth has been coupled with justice, we should measure their share of the total wealth of the region. We should compare their share of the total wealth of the region today with their share 17 years ago. Without going into abstract theoretical figures, let me just say that looking at all the goods and services available in the region now – the adivasis' share has definitely come down when compared to 1986. Development yes, justice no!

Poverty has two faces. One – underdevelopment. Which is very visible and epitomised by the starving pot bellied beggar child. The other – injustice – is almost invisible. You see it only if you look for the causes of poverty. Development or the attempt to reduce underdevelopment will find it difficult to argue against globalisation.

Especially in a capitalist economy. Investment must result in wealth creation. Developing nations, lured by the seductive nature of foreign direct investment and its tantalising fruits, are straining at the leash to liberalise their economies and not be left out in the cold as the world hurtles into an era of globalisation. There are falling over themselves to restructure their economies to ensure increased creation of wealth.

>>> *they are dismantling the very instruments that were created to ensure an equitable distribution of wealth*

Ironically, almost correspondingly, they are dismantling the very instruments that were created to ensure an equitable distribution of wealth. While allowing multinationals to import rice from America into India on the one hand, the government is dismantling its public distribution system that ensured subsidised rice for the poorest. Both arguably contribute to wealth creation. And are therefore seen to be in sync with the mantra of development. Even granting the argument of the proponents of globalisation and free trade, that liberalisation will result in a flow of wealth from the North to the South, this flow cannot be at the expense of poor and disadvantaged people of the North; it cannot stop in the bank accounts of the affluent in the South. Having fought and campaigned for justice for nearly thirty years, it would seem to me that the least the government can do, if they must allow the import of cheaper American rice, (which is of course debatable) would be to increase the subsidy given through the public distribution system. Thus ensuring that the benefit of this new, liberal, global economy does go to the people who need it the most. It is only then that we can rightly say we have development with justice. Only then that people like us who are concerned about justice and the redistribution of wealth can begin to consider accepting globalisation.

To the adivasis however, globalisation is not something new. They encountered it and paid dearly for this encounter at the turn of the last century when British India discovered two things - that the Nilgiri forests were ideal for growing the much needed hardwoods for their shipbuilding

and railway industry, and the hills were ideal for growing plantation crops like tea. In the blink of a generational eye, the adivasi saw their local subsistence economy, shattered by a global market economy. Up until then, wealth and well being generated from the forests and the soil around their homesteads was equitably distributed among all their people. These same forests and land now generated wealth that sped on ships across the ocean. Wealth from the remote corners of the then malaria-infested Nilgiri hills flowed unfettered to faraway England. And there was hardly anyone to cry foul – at least not loud enough to be heard.

Until Gandhi and the movement for independence. August 15, 1947 when the whole of India celebrated freedom from the yoke of foreign rule, the adivasis and millions of Indians like them had little reason to celebrate. The impediment to the flow of wealth from India to Britain brought about by independence did not mean a redistribution of that wealth to the adivasis and other impoverished people like them. The flow of wealth from these areas continued unabated – only the destination of this wealth had changed. From flowing away into the global economy it now flowed into the national economy. The local economy continued to be stripped bare and impoverished.

Since 1991 when India decided to turn its back on its rather weak socialist roots and embark on the path of a liberalised capital economy we have removed barriers to the free flow of wealth from the local and national economy into a global one. Proponents of liberalisation would argue that this is also a removal of the barriers to the flow of wealth from richer countries into India. And the last few years would seem to vindicate their stand. The call-centre jobs, the back-office jobs, the rocketing growth of the ICT industry, the automobile industry are all cited as examples of this reversed flow of wealth.

Indisputable. No one can argue that globalisation can result as easily in a flow of wealth from the North to the South as from the South to the North. What I am disputing is that globalisation will bring about a redistribution of wealth from the rich to the poor. Of this I see no evidence. What I do see is that more and more money and wealth flows out of local economies into an ill-defined global one. Globalisation does not ensure that wealth will flow where it is needed most. On the contrary, it seeks to suppress the political imperative of the nation-state - of ensuring a fair and equitable distribution of wealth among its citizens and attempts instead to supplant an economic imperative of a global market economy – the imperative of profit – which, translated, means nothing more than an accumulation and concentration of wealth.

The failure of the nation-state, especially the poorer ones, to fulfil its responsibility of ensuring equity has resulted in a near total loss of credibility, leaving it vulnerable against the forces of globalisation. The market would like to argue that it can do better what the nation-state has failed to do.

Is it then any wonder that even though we consider ourselves enlightened modern democracies, increasingly we put our faith more and more in the market than in our governments?

Globalisation of the WTO kind is definitely about the creation of more wealth, just as colonisation was. It is all about economic growth just as colonisation was. But globalisation is not about equity just as colonisation was not. It is not about

we have removed barriers to the <<< free flow of wealth from the local and national economy into a global one

justice just as colonisation was not.

And the only hope for the future lies in the likes of Janet and our adivasi people uniting and working together to ensure that whatever little wealth is generated in their local economies does not flow vertically upwards to line the pockets of the affluent; that as much as possible stays within their economy and what must flow out flows laterally to other communities like them. If we accept that today we live in a global economy, then let those of us who are concerned with the economics of justice form new alliances and strive to create a global economic order of our choosing.

This then is our task. Our challenge.

Why localisation is essential for sustainability

Richard Douthwaite

The global economy has an in-built tendency to increase inequality. It is also inherently unreliable and the monoculture it creates puts excessive pressures on the environment. We should therefore attempt both to change the way it works and to build local alternatives to it.

W hy should anyone want to swim against what appears to be the tide of history by attempting to rebuild local economic systems which, over the past century, have been almost entirely swept away? Don't small countries and the regions within larger ones really have no option but to participate in the global economy in a whole-hearted way? This paper will explore the answers to these questions. Certainly, rebuilding a local economy is not an easy option, but I hope to show that it is one that is definitely worth making the effort to achieve.

Few of us would worry about the regions in which we live being entirely absorbed into the global economy if that system was equitable, sustainable, and worked reliably and well. But it is none of these, which is why we need both to develop local alternatives to it and also to attempt its reform. Let's look at each of these three areas in turn to see the extent to which the global economy fails. First, is it equitable?

1. Equity

A few years ago, Westport, the town where I live, decided that it would attempt to lengthen its tourist season by advertising golfing-holiday packages in Sweden in the spring and autumn. Why Sweden? Well, the Swedes were regarded as rich and therefore a potentially lucrative market. For a few years, the plan worked and more visitors came. Quite soon, however, as one golfing holiday is much like another, Westport found itself competing for business with Scottish and Portuguese golf resorts. Everyone's prices came down in the ensuing promotional battle, lowering the return to the holiday providers and effectively raising the incomes of the Swedes as they could now buy the same vacations for less money. In other words, the rich got richer and the (relatively) poor, poorer.

Richard Douthwaite was one of Feasta's founders and is the co-editor of the *Feasta Review*. He is a writer and speaker and lives in Westport, Co. Mayo.

That is the way the global system almost always works. Indeed, selling anything outside your area in competition with other communities is likely to increase the relative wealth of your target customers. Your goods and services don't have to cross international borders to have this effect. For example, I once stayed for several days in a very poor village in Tamil Nadu in India and I inevitably began to think about what the villagers could do to ease their poverty. The only assets they seemed to have were their labour and their land - could they grow extra vegetables and set up a co-op to sell them in Bangalore, the nearest big city? Well, they obviously could, but if other villages did the same thing too, the extra supply of tomatoes, okra and eggplant would bring the prices down, making the Bangalore people slightly better off while giving the farmers quite a lot less for their labour. The most obvious strategy for the village might not therefore be the best in the longer term.

Rich countries and rich people always call for freer trade and better transport links because this heightens competition, brings down prices and thus makes them better off. As India's roads improve, more and more villages will find it possible to send perishable produce to distant cities. This will destroy the partially-protected niches within which existing producers have been making modest incomes. The natural reaction of the producers to this will be to attempt to maintain their own families' livelihoods by reducing their costs. They will cut their wages bills (thus eliminating other families' incomes) by buying more industrial inputs such as pesticide sprays and machinery. This will reduce the proportion of the money from the sale of the goods sold to the outside world that is available to their village as a whole to live on. In other words, unless the total income from selling the vegetables increases by more than the cost of the inputs, freer trade and the extra competition it brings will make the village worse off.

This process has been one of the factors widening the gap between the rich and the poor, both within countries and between them. An UNCTAD report[1] shows that in nine out of a sample of ten Latin American countries, the differential between the earnings of more highly skilled workers and their less skilled colleagues increased markedly between 1984 and 1995 as a result of freer trade. Indeed, in most cases, the real purchasing power of the least skilled workers actually declined, in several cases by over 20%. Similarly, an International Labour Office (ILO) study of 30 countries in Africa, Asia and Latin America found that in two thirds of the countries, the real wages of all workers fell between the late 1970s and the late 1980s, with the least skilled falling by the greatest percentage[2]. And a 1999 World Bank paper[3] reported that data from a sample of 38 countries between 1965 and 1992 had shown that greater openness to trade had reduced the incomes of the poorest 40 percent of the population, but strongly increased those of the remaining groups. "The costs of adjusting to greater openness are borne *exclusively* by the poor" the Bank said in a commentary. The italics are in the original.

This widening of the gap between the least well paid and all other income earners in their societies is, in fact, exactly what standard economic theory predicts. In the 1930s Eli Heckscher and Bertil Ohlin developed the theorum which is now named after them and which states that each country tends to export goods that use the highest proportion of its most abundant, and hence relatively cheapest resource. For most 'developing' countries this resource is its unskilled labour and, as competition in international markets between such countries will tend to force the prices of their exports down, the earnings of the unskilled

will be reduced by more than those of more highly skilled workers less exposed to foreign competition. All workers in sectors exposed to international competition may therefore see their wages fall as markets open up, but those most exposed will fare the worst.

According to UNDP the difference in per capita income between the wealthiest 20% and the poorest 20% of the world's population was 30 to 1 in 1960; jumped to 78 to 1 in 1994, and decreased a bit to 74 to 1 in 1999. The poorest 20 per cent saw their share of global consumption decline from 2.3 per cent to 1.4 per cent in the same period.

"We live in a world that has become more polarised economically, both between countries and within them. If current trends are not quickly corrected, economic disparities will move from inequitable to inhuman. In more than a hundred countries per capita income is lower than it was fifteen years ago, and, as a result, more than a quarter of humanity - 1.6 billion people - are worse off." James Speth, then the administrator of the UNDP, said in 1996. Nothing has improved significantly since then. Indeed, Professor Robert Hunter Wade of the London School of Economics and many other commentators think the inequality has become worse[4].

Besides freer trade, another reason for the growing gulf between rich countries and poorer ones is that the rich countries issue the reserve currencies - the dollar, the euro, the pound, the Swiss franc and the yen - which the rest of the world uses to trade and to save. When gold was the world currency, wealth was created wherever the gold was found. Today, wealth is created in the reserve currency countries − the US, Britain, the Eurozone, Switzerland and Japan - when their banks approve loans. The total gain from having a reserve currency (the technical term is seignorage) is the cumulative balance of payments deficit on the import-export account that the issuing country is able to run up. At present most of these gains are going to the US, which except for 1991 has imported more than it has exported every year in the past twenty. In those two decades it has amassed a cost-free debt to the rest of the world of $2,500bn. This amounts to half the other countries' total savings and, as I write in 2004, US indebtedness is increasing at $1.5bn a day because it is importing half as much again as it exports. Britain's gains from having a reserve currency are tiny in comparison and none of the other issuers is currently exploiting its ability to borrow cost-free at all.

> >> *Having the world's main reserve currency has brought quite remarkable benefits to the US*

The US is able to finance its trade deficit cost-free mainly by selling government bonds and shares in US companies. Interest and dividends are paid on these securities of course, so it is not correct to say that the borrowing is interest-free. However it is cost free because the payments are made in dollars that are merely added to the total amount the US owes. The payments will only cost America anything if the dollars are ever used by the foreigners to whom they belong to purchase goods and services from the United States.

Having the world's main reserve currency has brought quite remarkable benefits to the US because the more dollars that the US creates and spends in the rest of the world, the more dollars the rest of the world will wish to invest in the US. These extra dollars push up the price of shares on Wall Street giving the foreigners who have already invested there an attractive capital gain – on paper. These gains encourage the investment of even more foreign-owned dollars, allowing the US to increase its current account deficit even more.

We can get a good idea of how big a benefit this $2,500bn has been by recalling that in 1998, the United Nations Development Programme estimated that the expenditure of a sixth of that sum - $40bn a year for ten years - would enable everyone in the world to be given access to an adequate diet, safe water, basic education and health care, adequate sanitation and pre- and post- natal attention. The world-wide acceptability of the dollar is, in fact, the reason why the US, with a population of 281 million, is the world's sole superpower, able to spend as much on armaments as the next twenty biggest arms-buying nations put together, countries with a total population of 3.5 billion.

Even if the US were not misusing its position as the main provider of the world's money, the reserve currency system would be undesirable. What it means is that if one poor country wants to buy from another, it has either to sell something to a reserve currency country or borrow the funds from one in order to get the money to do so. The situation is exactly the same in the Indian village – if two neighbours wish to

trade, one of them has to get the money first, directly or indirectly, from an urban centre to which somebody in the rural area once supplied something or went into debt. In both cases there is another powerful positive feedback mechanism. The poorer area sells to the richer one because that's where the money is. Then, as we saw, competition builds up between the producers of the relatively standardised goods – minerals, foodstuffs, clothing and footwear - made in poorer areas, reducing the price each receives and thus widening the gap between them and their customers. Despite this, however, the poor have no option but to continue to sell to the rich because while other poor people might desperately want the things they are making, they don't have the money to buy. In both the international and the internal case there is an inherently unequal relationship in which the richer party always wins. The system is fundamentally unfair and is made more so by breaking down trade barriers and improving transportation to increase competition.

2. Sustainability

As a result of globalisation, a high proportion of the world's population now eats the same foods, is housed in buildings constructed of the same materials, drives the same cars and lives and works in much the same way. This uniformity means that much of humankind competes on world markets for the same raw materials – cotton, steel, cement, oil - and thus puts their sources under a high - and in many cases unsustainable - degree of pressure.

Worse still, globalisation creates a positive feedback that rewards those countries and companies that consume the Earth's resources most rapidly with incomes that enable them to purchase and destroy even more. It also destroys the negative feedback mechanisms that once warned communities to mend their ways when they started behaving unsustainably. Now that goods can be transported from anywhere for those with the money to pay, the better-off know that once the fertility of a district's soil declines, its forests are felled, its mines exhausted, its seas fished out, they can always import their requirements or, if necessary, move somewhere else.

There is therefore a close link between restoring local economic self-reliance and achieving sustainability. Theoretically it might be possible to develop a world-wide industrial culture that enables all humanity to live sustainably within the limits of the world, but the scale and the complexity of the task are immense. An easier, more feasible alternative is to create a system that would encourage a greater diversity of diet, clothing, building materials and life-styles. This would take the pressure off over-used resources just as it does in the natural world where each species has its own ecological niche and avoids competing directly with the others.

Diversity is desirable for other reasons too. For everyone who grows up in an area to find an occupation there in which they can feel fulfilled, a wide variety of jobs and other activities is necessary because people differ widely in their interests and aptitudes. A wide range of jobs creates a richness of life. It is important economically too because if a community or a country imports a lot of its requirements and relies on exporting a limited range of goods and services to pay for them, it risks getting caught out if something goes wrong or the market changes. For example, Ireland is the world's second-largest producer of computer software. It also earns a lot from exporting milk products and beef and from selling itself as a tourist destination. Suppose that there is an airline strike, so the tourists can't come. Or that the software companies find they can get equally good programmes written much more cheaply in Bangalore. Or that an outbreak of foot-and-mouth disease spreads to hundreds of farms and makes Irish beef, cheese and butter unexportable. The economic and social costs of any of these would be immense.

Diversity is therefore essential to achieving sustainability. Unfortunately, though, a highly competitive world trading system which deliberately sets out to remove every possible barrier - including those of distance and, as with genetically-modified foods, consumer preference - to the free movement of goods and services leaves very few niches in which diversity can persist. Part of the problem is that a diverse economy almost inevitably produces at higher cost than one which specialises in a very few products. This is because many products exhibit what economists call 'increasing returns to scale'. In other words, the more of them you produce, the cheaper they become. The first model of a new car to come off the production line will have cost many millions to create. In comparison, the one immediately behind it will be very cheap and the ones that follow that will become cheaper still as the company, its suppliers and its workers move along learning curves. Consequently, anyone producing relatively small numbers of cars will be at a price disadvantage because they will have to spread the development costs of their first car over a more limited production run and be unable to move as far as their bigger rivals along the learning curve.

Exactly the same can be said of almost every product. Take something basic like, say, shoes. To produce them using modern methods needs an extensive infrastructure including specialist suppliers (or, better still, producers) of leather, soling materials, adhesives, clicking presses, press knives, sewing machines, thread and much more. It also needs people who know how to design shoes, others who can use the specialist equipment required to make them, and still others with the skills to keep delicate machines in working order. It therefore takes a considerable investment in people, equipment and facilities to produce the first shoe. This is the reason why every industrial economy in the world developed behind tariff barriers.

Tariff barriers are necessary if a country is to develop or maintain a diverse, more sustainable economy.

The German government knows this well. The main aim of its programme to get photovoltaic (PV) panels fitted on 100,000 roofs between 1999 and 2004 is not primarily to generate electricity. It is to give German PV manufacturers a chance to build up production volumes and get their prices down sufficiently to undercut all other producers in the world.

The problem with increasing returns to scale is that, other things being equal, the biggest producers (like Microsoft, for example) will to be the cheapest and most profitable and will drive almost all their rivals out of business. This leads to activities that could in theory be carried out equally well in many places in the world being concentrated in very few. Tariff barriers or some other sort of protection are therefore necessary if a region or a country is to develop or maintain a diverse, and thus more sustainable economy.

The globalised economy is becoming increasingly unsustainable for another reason too. As we've seen, cheap transport is one the pillars on which it stands – take that away and a re-localisation would automatically come about. And, in turn, cheap transportation depends on having cheap oil to fuel ships, planes and road vehicles. So how long will cheap oil last? The answer is that while oil itself will never run out, cheap oil will because many countries' fields are becoming depleted. As a result, world production will peak within the next four or five years and then begin a steady decline so that by 2050, output will be no more than half the current level. Natural gas, which some vehicles burn, will also be becoming scarce by then. Its output is expected to peak in 2040 and then decline rapidly. Although alternatives to both fuels could be found – hydrogen from wind-generated electricity, perhaps, or oil substitutes produced from coal – a massive amount of capital and resources would be required to build the new systems required to take their place. In other words, the substitutes cannot be cheap, which in turn means that the movement of low-value commodities and any time-sensitive goods that have to be flown will decline. This will open new opportunities to local producers.

>>> *the fundamental problem with the world economic system is that it is constantly poised on the brink of depression*

In conclusion, then, while the global economy will always exist, it is not sustainable at its present size because it is destroying both the diversity required for its stability and the energy resources on which it relies. Local production for local use will therefore become very much more important.

3. Reliability

Is it safe to rely on the world economy to deliver the essentials of life year after year? And can it provide us with a reliable income with which to buy those essentials? The answers are, clearly, 'No', for, although in mid-2004, the industrialised economies seemed to have recovered reasonably well from the slow-down two years earlier, the system has been failing to provide people in much of the rest of the world with adequate livelihoods for many years. All of sub-Saharan Africa is depressed. Lesotho apparently[5] has the highest rate of unemployment in the world at 39.3%, South Africa (23.3%) comes fourth and Botswana (21.5%) sixth but there may be worse places where government has broken down and doesn't keep statistics. In Asia, employment levels

have not recovered since the tiger economies crashed in 1997 and the fierceness of the competition between them means that deflation has set in. Japanese prices, for example, fell by an average of 2% in 2002. In Latin America, the currency crisis in Argentina pushed joblessness up to around 24% at the peak. Even oil-rich Venezuela has the 17th highest rate of unemployment in the world.

However, the fundamental problem with the world economic system is not that it leads to high levels of unemployment. It is that it is unreliable because it constantly poised on the brink of depression. And this, in turn, is because of the way that the money it uses is created. This money typically begins its life when someone writes a cheque on a loan facility they have been granted by their bank or runs up a debt on their credit card. It disappears when that debt is repaid. Consequently, if someone has no mortgage or debts of any sort and a positive balance in the bank, he or she only has that money because someone, somewhere, has borrowed it and is paying interest on it.

The snag with creating money this way is that it depends on confidence and if optimism about the future shrinks, so will the money supply and, as a result, the volume of trading it is possible to carry on. So if enough people say to themselves something like "Perhaps I'd better not take out that car loan just at the moment. My firm isn't doing too well and there might be redundancies. I'll wait to see how things work out", their fears for the future might well be realised. With fewer people like themselves borrowing, less money will be spent, and this will mean less work for their employers. Their collective caution could put them out of work.

On the other hand, when lots of people borrow, it creates plenty of work and encourages further borrowing. The extra borrowing is needed because higher property prices require people to take out bigger mortgages and firms find they need extra capacity to keep up with demand. A virtuous circle is created with each round of loans creating the necessity for another. A boom develops which will carry on until either an external event cools things down or the central bank gets worried about inflation and increases interest rates to discourage everyone from borrowing quite so much. The danger is that the bank will over-correct, gloom will set in, and the level of lending contract far too much, throwing the economy into recession. Our national economic systems are therefore fundamentally unstable. They swing violently between boom and bust and it is almost impossible to keep them moving steadily along.

Until recently, the world economy was more stable than the national economies that make it up because, as some economies were slowing down, others were speeding up. Now, however, globalisation has synchronised them all. No longer does a depressed economy have a bouyant one to take in its exports and thus give it a hand up.

It's going to be very hard to correct this situation. In the protectionist world of the 1930s, the great British economist Maynard Keynes showed how national governments could lift their economies out of depression by making up for the fall in company and consumer borrowing by borrowing more money themselves and putting it into circulation by spending it. The extra state spending – priming the pump it was called - created jobs, which in turn increased consumer spending and thus more jobs, re-establishing the virtuous circle.

Unfortunately national governments can't use Keynesian methods this time. Supposing one of them borrowed so that it could employ a lot of people on public works projects. When the workers spent their wages a very high proportion of the money would leak away to create jobs abroad and very little of the resulting extra spending by the overseas workers would ever find its way back to create a second batch of new jobs in the country concerned. Consequently, to reflate a depressed national economy in today's globalised world, you either have to restore protection by re-introducing trade barriers and foreign exchange controls, or you have to reflate the whole world.

Reflating the world would require every country to adopt Keynesian policies simultaneously. That would be hard enough to achieve by itself but counties must also agree to run budget deficits of the right amount. This is because if a country spends too much, its increased imports will outweigh its extra exports and its trade deficit will increase. On the other hand, if it spends too little, it will earn more from its increased exports than leaks out to pay for its greater imports and its currency reserves will rise. The latter is a favourable outcome, the first not, so every country will be tempted to spend too little in the hope of improving its trade balance.

> *Local and global economies are complementary. Our aim has to be to get a better balance between the two.*

Huge amounts of public borrowing would be required to reflate the world. Couple this with the natural tendency for states to wish to limit their public spending to keep their imports and their deficits under control and the likely result is that the total increase in world demand would be insufficient to get the corporate sector's idle capacity into production again. In that case, firms would not resume borrowing to invest unless there were new products to make. In Britain in the 1930s, when the traditional export industries – coal, cotton and shipbuilding – declined, the only significant new investments were in products based on new technologies or to meet new needs, like the Hoover vacuum cleaner factory in West London or the Ford car plant at Dagenham which employed 15,000 workers from the start. The depression was only ended by the outbreak of war with its demand for a vast range of new products like aircraft and tanks. Without a crisis of equivalent severity and urgency, it seems unlikely that governments would have the guts to spend the necessary amounts. High levels of unemployment therefore could drag on and on.

To sum up, then, the global economic system is prone to break down and, once broken, is very difficult to restore. It cannot therefore be relied upon to provide everyone with the goods and services that they need if they are to live at a satisfactory level.

Bringing re-localisation about

There are two possible responses to the inequity, unsustainability and unreliability of the global economy. One is to seek to change the way it works, the other is to build local alternatives to it. Both responses need to be pursued simultaneously because while it is impossible to imagine a global system without some of the problems we have discussed, it is equally impossible to imagine a world without complex products - like computers and aircraft – unless people are prepared to live very simply indeed. And, as we saw, such products are best produced by a few companies operating at a global level because of increasing returns to scale. Local and global economies are therefore complementary. Our aim has to be to get a better balance between the two. At the moment, the global is dominant, so the scales need to be weighted to make them tilt the local way.

>>> *A local culture is simply a way to live reliably, enjoyably and well on the resources of an area.*

Some of the reforms required to make the world economy work better were set out in the 2004 Feasta paper *Curing Global Crises*[6]. Here are some ideas about how local cultures (rather than just the local economy component of them) might be rebuilt. A local culture is simply a way that the people living in a place have found by trial and error over many generations to enable them to live reliably, enjoyably and well on the resources of their area. They developed a distinctive cuisine, style of dress and architecture so that they needed to import surprisingly little. "So little trade went on with neighbouring towns that one carrier with a donkey cart was able to do it all, and even he, it was understood, went to town weekly only if he had orders enough to make the journey worthwhile" writes Walter Rose in his book *Good Neighbours*[7] an account of life in the village some thirty miles from London in which he was born in 1871. George Bourne, who is best known for *The Wheelwright's Shop*, his classic description of the business his father ran in Farnham in Surrey until 1884, also stresses how little was brought from outside in *Change in the Village*, a fascinating account of the decline of rural self-reliance first published in 1912:

It is really surprising how few were the materials, or even the finished goods, imported at that time [the 1850s]. Clothing stuffs and metals were the chief of them. Of course the grocers (not "provision merchants" then) did their small trade in sugar and coffee, and tea and spices; there was a tinware shop, an ironmonger's, a wine-merchant's; and all these were necessarily supplied from outside. But, on the other hand, no foreign meat or flour, or hay or straw or timber, found their way into the town, and comparatively few manufactured products from other parts of England. Carpenters still used the oak and ash and elm of the neighbourhood, sawn out for them by the local sawyers: the wheelwright, because iron was costly, mounted his cartwheels on huge axles fashioned by himself out of the hardest beech; the smith, shoeing horses or putting tyres on wheels, first made the necessary nails for himself, hammering them out on his own anvil. So, too, with many other things. Boots, brushes, earthenware, butter and lard, candles, bricks - they were all of local make; cheese was brought back from Weyhill Fair in the waggons which had carried down the hops; in short, to an extent now hard to realise, the town was independent of commerce as we know it now, and looked to the farms and the forests and the claypits and the coppices of the neighbourhood for its supplies. A leisurely yet steady traffic in rural produce therefore passed along its streets, because it was the life-centre, the heart, of its own countryside[8].

Each area of the world has a unique combination of natural and human resources and, as a result, in the absence of outside competition, the relative costs of the things it makes will be unique too. Those products that draw on its most abundant resources will tend to be cheaper than those that require scarcer ones. Unfortunately, the global economy creates a single all-world price structure reflecting global abundance and scarcity rather than that at the local level. Consequently, if an area is forced to adopt world price relativities rather than evolving its own, a lot of the products it could have made using its scarcer resources will go unused because it cannot make them at competitive prices because it lacks the necessary economies of scale. The effect of this will be that small acreages with, say, the ideal conditions for producing plums, will be used to grow something else for which they are less suited but which is more profitable at the world price. The plums sold in the local markets will be imported instead.

Each local economy and the culture that goes with it therefore needs to be able to protect itself from external competition. If this protection is absent, its diversity and hence its sustainability will disappear and for as long as the protection is lacking, it will be impossible to bring them back. Of course, as we've already mentioned, it would be quite ridiculous for a region to try to make everything it needs from whatever set of resources it happens to possess as a result of chance and history. A balance has to be struck between those of its needs it meets for itself out of its own resources and those it meets indirectly by exporting its abundance and then bringing in the products of other regions' different abundances. Each area should decide for itself where this balance lies but, in my view, they should all try to meet their basic food, energy and housing needs completely from their own resources so that they can be never be exploited and forced to behave in an unsustainable way to obtain the necessities of life. Needing to trade rather than choosing to do so is often a sign that the economy concerned is unsustainable and could certainly lead to its becoming so. The best motive for trading in any economic system that aims to be sustainable is to increase the population's range of choice by swapping, say, apples for oranges.

The optional nature of such trade would leave those regional economies that adopted it free to ban technologies suspected of having undesirable side effects regardless of whether or not other regions did so too. This would speed the rate at which the world could react to unsustainability crises. In the present system, the need to be competitive means that it is often impossible for individual nations to act unilaterally to deal with pressing problems. Moreover, every time a country or region gives in to the constant competitive pressure to reduce environmental and social standards for the sake of profits and employment, global unsustainability is increased.

The fact that a regional economy was not compelled to trade would not make it problem-free, of course, and if it wished to maintain its sustainability it would have to be able to protect itself militarily and economically from territories that had destroyed their own resources and wanted access to resources that had been managed well. The problem of providing military protection - which would include the policing of borders to stop sustainability being destroyed by an influx of environmental refugees - is not something we can deal with here. All we can do is note that if an arms race developed between a sustainable part of the world and an unsustainable one, the need to use resources for the purchase or manufacture of weapons could destroy the sustainability of the former.

For its economic protection, a sustainable territory would need its own independent currency and banking system. One reason for this is that the moment a territory gets its own currency, its people no longer have to trade with the outside world to assemble the means of exchange to trade with each other. In other words, the volume of business they are able to do amongst themselves becomes independent of inflows and outflows of national or international currencies. If a region has to ensure that enough outside money is always available for local trade to be carried on at the optimal level it is very difficult for it to become sustainable. Moreover, if it issues its own currency it can avoid making it

debt-based. Its own money could be issued by being spent into circulation by its government. Provided the government behaved responsibly, this would make its level of economic activity very stable and predictable and remove the dependence on continual economic growth.

Needing to trade rather than choosing to do so is often a sign that the economy concerned is unsustainable.

Similarly, if a territory had its own banking system, it could ensure that interest rates were related to the rate of profit possible on projects within the territory rather than to the highest rate of return that could be found anywhere in the world. This would mean that there would be very much less pressure for the territory's resources to be used unsustainably in order to generate the financial returns required for investment funds to be committed and projects go ahead.

A sustainable region also needs to be able to prevent net capital flows across its borders either by enacting laws against them or by creating a social climate which makes investing elsewhere a matter for shame. Why? Consider what happens when a sustainable economy becomes mature, by which I mean that although its buildings are repaired and its capital equipment is replaced as it wears out, no new buildings are erected and no extra equipment is installed because the benefits from doing so are so small it's not considered worth while. In other words, all the sustainable projects which give a reasonable rate of return have been carried through and the territory's economy has ceased to grow significantly except when, from time to time, new technologies come along which make additional production possible without upsetting the area's sustainability by using more resources and releasing more waste, or by damaging its social fabric.

The low rate of return in a mature sustainable economy means that the owners of capital there will always be tempted to remove their funds to unsustainable or immature sustainable economies to get a higher rates of return. If these capital movements take place, the mature economy runs down because funds that would have been used to repair buildings or replace worn-out equipment get invested elsewhere. The resulting shortage of equipment causes unemployment to appear, increasing competition for jobs and pushing down wage levels. Moreover, less goods and services are produced, pushing prices up. Both these changes enable businesses to make additional profits and thus pay higher interest rates and when these rates match those available elsewhere, the capital outflow will cease.

>>> *people investing outside the areas in which they live can only be interested in one thing - the rate of return they get on their money.*

Capital movements out of sustainable economies therefore reduce the territory's total output and shift a larger share of this smaller output to the owners of capital, who also benefit from the interest payments they receive from their investments outside. Put another way, allowing capital movements maximises the return per unit of capital but not per citizen. It therefore means that no territory can become sustainably mature until everywhere else in the world does too.

It might be thought that allowing outside investors to put funds into sustainable projects in immature sustainable economies would allow those economies to reach maturity faster. This, however, is wrong because if the interest on this capital has to be paid in an external currency earned by selling goods and services on external markets in competition with output from places that subsidise their prices by using unsustainable systems, the need to trade to earn this external currency would undermine the territory's sustainability.

Even if the interest were to be paid in a currency that could only be earned by trading in sustainably-produced goods, there are two reasons why capital transfers between territories, or even parts of the same territory, are undesirable. One is that capital creates work in the place it is spent. In Ireland after independence, the banking system collected savings from the rural areas and lent them in urban ones, enabling factories, shopping parades, cinemas and houses to be built. This work attracted young men from the rural areas who needed housing, shops, pubs and recreational facilities in the towns, especially if they married a girl who came from the country herself. These needs created a further demand for loans and

more work for the building trade. Meanwhile, back at home, businesses went into decline because the young people had left, and it became very difficult to find new projects that would support the rate of interest being asked by the banks in view of the declining population. So with fewer opportunities there, the emigration from the countryside went on and whole villages were completely abandoned. Capital transfers are therefore destabilising and undesirable even within the same territory if more than, say, twenty miles is involved.

The second reason for rejecting external investment is even more powerful. It is that people investing outside the areas in which they live can only be interested in one thing - the rate of return they get on their money. All the other income streams their investment starts - payments to workers and suppliers, for example - are seen as reducing their profits and every effort is therefore made to minimise them. If someone invests in a project in their own community, however, there are many ways in which they can get a return on their money quite apart from the interest they receive. Indeed, these non-interest returns might be so important that those financing the project might be prepared to charge no interest at all and even contribute to an annual loss in order to be sure it goes ahead. This might be because the project will provide employment for themselves or their children. Or because it will increase incomes in the area and help their existing business do better. Or because it will cut unemployment, thus reducing family breakdown and crime.

Community investment projects are therefore very different animals from those run for the benefit of outside investors. For one thing, they seek to maximise the total incomes the project generates in the community, not just the profit element. So, far from seeing the wage bill as a cost to be minimised, they regard it as one of the project's major gains. Attitudes to work are different too. Whereas outside investors seek to de-skill work within the factory so that they can hire the cheapest possible labour, a community company, particularly a workers' co-op, would want the work to be organised so that those doing it found it interesting and fulfilling.

Outside investors also have very short time-horizons for their projects, wanting to earn their capital back in three or four years. After that, if necessary, they can close the plant and move on. Communities, on the other hand, need long-term incomes for long-term projects like raising children, and a community-owned factory would want to produce for a safe, stable markets, most probably in its own area, rather than the market with the highest immediate rate of return. Similarly, while outside investors merely ensure that a plant's emission levels stay within the law because anything better would cost them money, a community company is likely to work to much higher standards to avoid fouling its own nest.

A world economy that was sustainable would therefore be almost the exact opposite of the present unsustainable one. It would be localised rather than globalised. It would have no net capital flows. Its external trade would be confined to unimportant luxuries rather than essentials. Each self-reliant region would develop to a certain point and then stop, rather than growing continuously. Investment decisions would be made close to home. And assets would be owned by the people of the area in which they were located.

There is no space here to discuss how such a sustainable, self-reliant regional economy might be initiated and built or how it would have to be organised so that one section of its population did not take advantage of another. I attempted this task in my 1996 book *Short Circuit* which is now available on the web at www.feasta.org. All I can do here is to summarise the essential features of a sustainable territory:

- It has a stable population
- It provides the basic necessities of life for its population from renewable resources under its control and expects to be able to continue to do so without over-using or degrading those resources for at least the next thousand years. It is therefore able to trade with the outside world out of choice rather than necessity. This frees it from the need to do unpalatable or unsustainable things in order to compete with other regions such as adopting potentially dangerous technologies or curtailing social protection provisions.
- It is able to protect its renewable resources and its population both militarily and economically. Its collection of economic protection weapons includes an independent currency and banking system. It has no debts to lenders outside and there are no net flows of capital across its borders, thus allowing its interest rate to fall to close to zero as it moves towards maturity.

- It does not depend on continual economic growth to stave off collapse. Its economy grows very slowly if at all.

Communities need long-term <<< *incomes for long-term projects like raising children*

Making one's own region sustainable along these lines might seem to involve turning it into a grim, restrictive place but I think that's wrong and that it will become a liberating and joyous one instead. Certainly, the only way for an area to escape from a system that continually impoverishes the periphery by taking resources to the centre, wherever that centre might be, is to build a protective niche within which its local economy can develop diversity and become more sustainable. At present, because all our ideas about what constitutes development boil down to finding ways in which some of the money circulating in the remaining islands of prosperity can be captured by communities outside, we are destroying diversity and helping centralisation along. The World Bank, ILO and UNCTAD studies we discussed demonstrated clearly that whenever a poorer country or region attempts to satisfy the needs of a wealthier one rather than attending to its own, its dependency and weakness are increased. Once we recognise this, we will begin to think in a radically different way about how our communities can be made more sustainable.

Endnotes

1   UNCTAD, *Trade and Development Report*, 1997, Part Two, chap. IV, sect. B.1.
2   *World Employment Report 1996/97*. International Labour Office, Geneva, 1996, table 5.9 and related text.
3   Lundberg, M. and L. Squire, "The simultaneous evolution of growth and inequality", World Bank Research Paper, December 1999.
4   'The Rising Inequality of World Income Distribution', *Finance & Development*, IMF, Washington, Vol. 38, No. 4, December 2001
5   The Economist, *Pocket World in Figures*, London, 2003.
6   Can be downloaded from http://www.feasta.org/events/debtconf/sleepwalking.pdf
7   Cambridge University Press, 1942.
8   Quoted from the edition published by Augustus M. Kelley, New York, in 1969. p. 103.

China's rise in wealth brings fall in health

Economic reforms lead to growth in stress-related illnesses

Jonathan Watts in Beijing

China's economic transformation is damaging the health of many of its people, with millions of urban professionals suffering from stress and the outbreak of more fatty western diets.

A study by the Red Cross Society of China found that more than 70% of the residents of the three wealthiest conurbations, Beijing, Shanghai and Guangzhou, were ill, unfit or short of energy.

The research has increased concerns about the costs of the country's economic growth.

It has also been fuelled the debate in the Communist party between the marketers who want to privatise more of the medical system and state interventionists who believe standards of public health have been neglected in the rush for profits over the past 25 years.

Surprisingly, the research suggested that the most highly-educated sectors of society appeared to be the worst affected.

The Xinhua news agency

said that white-collar workers, particularly senior and mid-level managers, complained the most about ill-health.

This followed separate studies earlier this year by the Chinese Academy of Sciences, which found that the average lifespan of "intellectuals" was 58 years, 10 years lower than the national average. IT professionals were among the highest-risk groups.

According to the academy, programmers and managers working in Beijing's hi-tech district of Zhongguancun, known as China's Silicon Valley, had an average lifespan of 53 years and four months, five years less than a decade ago.

Journalists fared even worse. A study by 50 news organisations in Shanghai revealed that the average lifespan of a reporter was 45 years. Less than one in five of the city's journalists were said to live beyond retirement age.

There are many reasons for the poor state of city dwellers' health. The political explanation is that the current gener-

ation of 40- and 50-somethings has been worn down by the famines of the great leap forward, the cultural revolution and the changes wrought by the opening-up

Links

www.chineseredcross.org.cn/english
Chinese Red Cross
lyw.sh.gov.cn/en/intro/people.aspx
Shanghai government: quality of life
guardian.co.uk/china

policy of the past 25 years. A more prosaic line of reasoning is that China is becoming vulnerable to the consumer culture ailments associated with stress, a contaminated environment and an increasingly fatty and salty diet.

As the economy grows, competition increases, and global fast food franchises become more popular, medical experts say that cases of

diabetes and coronary disease are on the rise.

"There is a contradiction in China that as the country becomes wealthier it faces a whole new set of health problems, related to diet, pollution, smoking and stress," said a spokesman for the World Health Organisation in Beijing. "The pattern of their diseases is becoming more like that of the west."

Most controversial is the assertion that the government has allowed the health sector – once one of the country's proudest achievements – to deteriorate since the start of market reforms in 1978.

Yang Xiaodiao, a medical and welfare expert, said the latest statistics showed that public health had been sacrificed for private wealth. "Bad working habits, poor disease prevention, inadequate government funding and lack of health education are the main

Richer but sicker

● **Budget** In most countries the government pays for more than 70% of health costs. But in China the proportion spent on health by the government has fallen from 36% in 1978 to 15% in 2000. Chinese people pay 60% of their own health costs, a threefold increase in two decades

● **Life expectancy** Between 1949 and 1980 life expectancy rose from 35 to 68 years. The increase since then is less than three years – a much slower improvement than in 1978.

● **Tuberculosis** Twenty years ago China said it had the disease under control. This year the health ministry acknowledged that the country had 4.5m TB patients – the second highest in the

world. The disease kills 130,000 Chinese a year

● **Aids** After a decade of cover-ups China made a U-turn in the past year with the introduction of free tests and treatment. No one knows the true scale of the epidemic, but new cases are estimated to be rising at a rate of 30% a year. The HIV-positive population is estimated at 840,000

● **World ranking** China's health sector was ranked 144th overall out of the 191 countries on the WHO's ranking of state health services. The survey in 2000 said China was fourth from bottom in terms of equality of access to medical care. Only Brazil, Burma and Sierra Leone fared worse

reasons," he told the Shanghai Daily.

The timing of the latest study may be no accident. Since the outbreak of the Sars epidemic last year the government's record on healthcare has been a battleground between the conflicting factions of the Communist party's leadership.

Jiang Zemin, the former president who lost his last senior post as head of the military commission on Sunday, advocated private hospitals and profit-motivated health bureaus.

His successor, Hu Jintao, has appointed a health minister who has criticised the lack of public funding for hospitals and quadrupled spending on Aids, cases of which are rising at a rate of 30% a year, and tuberculosis, which has made a comeback in recent years.

In the countryside the crisis is far worse than in the cities.

Following the abolition of rural cooperatives in the early 80s, less than a fifth of the country's 800 million peasants are covered by health insurance.

As a result, gains made in life expectancy and infant mortality in the three decades after the communists took power in 1949 have flattened off and in some areas gone into reverse.

The majority of China's population are now expected to pay hospital costs entirely out of their own pockets.

For most people, getting sick means going broke.

Western fast food on offer in Shanghai. Above: a seven-year-old exercises at a party for overweight people in Shenyang Man photograph: Sam Morgan Moore

---

The quest for economic growth via the global market has damaged the health of the Chinese people, according to this report from *The Guardian* dated September 21, 2004. Increased stress, a contaminated environment and a saltier, fattier diet are blamed together with poor disease prevention and inadequate government funding for health services.

Petrodollar or Petroeuro?
A new source of global conflict
Cóilín Nunan

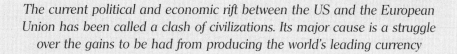

The current political and economic rift between the US and the European Union has been called a clash of civilizations. Its major cause is a struggle over the gains to be had from producing the world's leading currency

Cóilín Nunan studied mathematics at the universities of Brussels, Cambridge and Oxford. He now lives in Scotland and works for the Soil Association, the UK organic farming charity. His work focuses on the use and abuse of antibiotics in intensive farming and he has co-authored several reports examining the many ways in which this can impact upon human health. He is a Trustee of Feasta and editor of its website.

No observer of the lead-up to the war in Iraq and its aftermath could have failed to notice that the level of cooperation between Europe and America was extremely low. France and Germany were very strong opponents of the US/UK invasion and even after the war was declared over, disagreements persisted over the lifting of sanctions and how Iraq should be run. So was this just a one-off tiff or was it a symptom of deeper flaws in the relationship? I believe that the war on Iraq illustrated for the first time that continental Europe, led by France and Germany, no longer wishes to follow the Americans politically, although what has been termed a 'clash of civilisations'[1] is probably better viewed as a 'clash of economies'.

While disagreements over the US trade barriers on steel imports or the European restrictions on imports of American genetically modified crops have attracted widespread comment, the most intense economic rivalry of all has received far less media attention than it perhaps should: this is the rivalry between the dollar and the euro for the position of world reserve currency, a privileged status that has been held by the dollar ever since the Bretton Woods agreement nearly 60 years ago.

At present, approximately two thirds of world trade is conducted in dollars and two thirds of central banks' currency reserves are held in the American currency which remains the sole currency used by international institutions such as the IMF. This confers on the US a major economic advantage: the ability to run a trade deficit year after year. It can do this because foreign countries need dollars to repay their debts to the IMF, to conduct international trade and to build up their currency reserves. The US provides the world with these dollars by buying goods and services produced by foreign countries, but since it does not have a corresponding need for foreign currency, it sells far fewer goods and services in return, i.e. the US always spends more than it earns, whereas the rest of the world always earns more than it spends. This US trade deficit has now reached extraordinary levels, with the US importing 50% more goods and services than it exports. So long as the dollar remains the dominant international currency the US can continue consuming more than it produces and, for example, build up its military strength while simultaneously affording tax cuts.

Getting a share of this economic free lunch has been one of the motivations, and perhaps the main motivation, behind setting up the euro[2]. Were the euro to become a reserve currency equal to, or perhaps even instead of, the dollar, countries would reduce their dollar holdings while building up their euro savings. Another way of putting this would be to say that Eurozone countries would be able to reduce their subsidy to American consumption and would find that other countries were now subsidising Eurozone consumption instead.

A move away from the dollar towards the euro could, on the other hand, have a disastrous effect on the US economy as the US would no longer be able to spend beyond its means. Worse still, the US would have to become a net currency importer as foreigners would probably seek to spend back in the US a large proportion of the estimated three trillion dollars which they currently own. In other words, the US would have to run a trade surplus, providing the rest of the world with more goods and services than it was receiving in return. A rapid and wholesale move to the euro might even lead to a dollar crash as everyone sought to get rid of some, or all, of their dollars at the same time. But that is an outcome that no-one, not even France or Germany, is seeking because of the huge effect it would have on the world economy. Europe would much prefer to see a gradual move to a euro-dollar world, or even a euro-dominated one.

>>> *A move away from the dollar towards the euro could have a disastrous effect on the US economy*

It turns out that there is a small group of countries which is playing the arbiter in this global contest. These are the world's oil exporters, in particular OPEC and Russia. Ever since the days when the US dominated world oil production, sales of oil and natural gas on international markets have been exclusively denominated in dollars. This was partly a natural state of affairs since, up until the early 1950s, the US accounted for half or more of the world's annual oil production. The tendency to price in dollars was additionally reinforced by the Bretton Woods agreement which established the IMF and World Bank and adopted the dollar as the currency for international loans.

The vast majority of the world's countries are oil importers and, since oil is such a crucial commodity, the need to pay for it in dollars encourages these countries keep the majority of their foreign currency reserves in dollars not only to be able to buy oil directly but also to protect the value of their own currencies from falling against the dollar. Because a sudden devaluation of a country's currency against the dollar would lead to a jump in oil prices and a possible economic crisis, every country's central bank needs dollar reserves so as to be able to buy its own currency on the foreign exchange markets when its value needs to be supported.

The fact that oil sales and loans from the IMF are dollar-denominated also encourages poorer countries to denominate their exports in dollars as this minimises the risk of losses through any

fluctuations in the value of the dollar. The knock-on effect of this is that, since many of these exports are essential raw materials which richer countries need to import, their denomination in dollars reinforces the need for rich countries to keep their own currency reserves in dollars.

While the denomination of oil sales is not a subject which is frequently discussed in the media, its importance is certainly well understood by governments. For example, when in 1971 President Nixon took the US off the gold standard, OPEC did consider moving away from dollar oil pricing, as dollars no longer had the guaranteed value they once did. The US response was to do various secret deals with Saudi Arabia in the 1970s to ensure that the world's most important oil exporter stuck with the dollar[3]. What the Saudis did, OPEC followed. More recently, in June 2003, the Prime Minister of Malaysia publicly encouraged his country's oil and gas exporters to move from the dollar to the euro. The European and American reactions were polar opposites: the EU's Energy Commissioner, Loyola de Palacio, welcomed the suggestion, saying that 'in the future the euro is [going to be] taking a place in the international markets in general as the money of exchange' and that this was 'a matter of realism'[4]. Her counterpart in the US, the director of the Energy Information Administration, Guy Caruso, said that he couldn't see 'any particular merit' in the move and that over the long run 'the dollar's always won out'[5]. Either way, Malaysia is only a relatively minor oil exporter, so what it does can only have a very limited effect. A switch by a major oil exporter would be of far greater significance.

The first country to actually make the switch was a very important oil exporter indeed: Iraq, in November 2000[6,7]. Before the war in Iraq began, some observers, myself included, argued that this might well be a major reason for the US desire to invade and the strong Franco-German opposition to the invasion[8,9]. Corroborating evidence included the apparent influence which loyalty (or lack thereof) to the dollar seemed to have on the US attitude towards other OPEC members. Iran had been talking of selling its own oil for euros[6,10] and was subsequently included in George Bush's 'axis of evil'. Venezuela, another important oil exporter, had started bartering some of its oil, thus avoiding the use of the dollar, and was encouraging OPEC to do likewise[11] - and the US was widely suspected in having played a part in the attempted coup against the Venezuelan president, Hugo Chavez.

Semi-official confirmation that petro-currency rivalry was at the heart of the split between France and Germany, on the one hand, and the US, on the other, was provided by Howard Fineman, the chief political correspondent for Newsweek, in an article he wrote in April 2003, in the aftermath of the war. The Europeans and Americans were then arguing over whether the UN's oil-for-food programme in Iraq should remain in place or not. Using the term 'clash of civilisations' to describe the divide which was developing, Fineman explained that the disagreement had little to do with the French calls for the search for weapons of mass destruction to resume and for sanctions to remain in place until the search was complete. Instead, Fineman said, it was mainly about the dollar vs the euro. Citing White House officials and a presidential aide, he explained that the dispute between the two continents was really about 'who gets to sell - and buy - Iraqi oil, and what form of currency will be used to denominate the value of the sales. That decision, in turn, will help decide who controls Iraq, which, in turn, will represent yet another skirmish in a growing global economic conflict. We want a secular, American-influenced pan-ethnic entity of some kind to control the massive oil fields (Iraq's vast but only real source of wealth). We want that entity to be permitted to sell the oil to whomever it wants, denominated in dollars.' Fineman concluded his article by confidently predicting that future Iraqi oil sales would be switched back to dollars[1].

Fineman's White House sources would appear to have been reliable as that is precisely what has happened: when Iraqi oil exports resumed in June of last year, it was announced that payment would be in dollars only[12,13]. It was also decided that the billions of Iraqi euros which were being held in a euro account, controlled by the UN under the oil-for-food programme, were to be transferred into the Development Fund for Iraq, a dollar account controlled by the US[13,14,15].

Furthermore, Youssef Ibrahim, a former senior Middle East correspondent for the *New York Times* and energy editor on the *Wall Street Journal*, who is a member of the influential Council on Foreign Relations, has called Iraq's switch to the euro 'another reason' for the war, saying that a general move by oil producers to the euro would be a 'catastrophe' for the US[16].

America's willingness to use violence to defend its economic interests does not seem to have reduced the number of oil exporters considering switching to the euro as they recognise that their use of the dollar enables the US to build up its military strength. In addition to Malaysia, Indonesia has the switch under consideration[17] while Iran has been shifting its currency reserves into euros. Moreover, according to the Vice-President of the Iranian central bank, it has actually sold some of its oil to Europe for euros and is encouraging members of an Asian trade organisation, the Asian Clearing Union, to pay for Iranian oil in the European currency[18]. Along with Malaysia, it is also at the forefront of efforts to establish a new gold-backed currency, the Islamic Gold Dinar, to be used in international trade amongst Muslim countries instead of both the dollar and the euro[19]. In a further development, in June 2004, Iran announced that it had plans to establish an oil-trading market for Middle Eastern and OPEC producers which could threaten the dominance of London's International Petroleum Exchange and New York's Nymex[20]. Such a move could help remove some of the technical difficulties that exist with a switch away from dollar-denomination of oil sales.

the US has refused to get <<< involved in direct talks with the Iranian government which it views as 'evil'.

It is therefore not surprising to find that, just as with Iraq, the European Union and the US are dealing with Iran in very different ways. While the EU has been holding trade negotiations with Iran[21] and involved in dialogue about its nuclear programme, the US has refused to get involved in direct talks with the Iranian government which it views as 'evil'. The American Enterprise Institute, a highly influential American 'think tank', has in fact been actively calling for 'regime change'[22] and, although this policy has yet to be officially endorsed by the Bush administration, in July 2004 it was claimed in the British press that a senior official of the Bush administration had indicated that, if re-elected, Bush would intervene in the internal affairs of Iran in an attempt to overturn the Iranian government[23,24].

European enthusiasm for the 'petroeuro' also appears undampened by the US takeover of Iraq. Since the war, the European Union has been

The battle to become the world's key currency

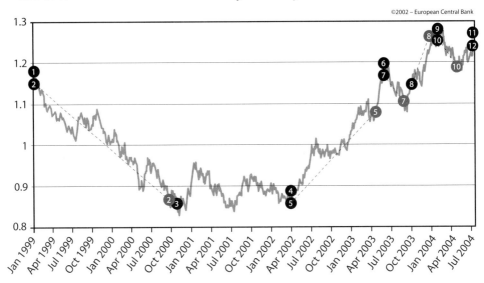

©2002 – European Central Bank

Min=0.8252 (26 Oct 2000) – Max=1.2858 (17 Feb 2004)

Source for numeric data: http://www.ecb.int/stats/exchange/eurofxref/html/eurofxref-graph-usd.en.html#1999

1) **January 1999:** launch of the euro.

2) **January 1999 – Oct 2000:** euro in "bear market" versus the dollar.

3) **November 2000:** Iraq switches oil sales to euro. Euro's fall versus the dollar is halted.

4) **April 2002:** senior OPEC representative gives speech in which he states that OPEC would consider possibility of selling oil in euros.

5) **April 2002 to May 2003:** euro in "bull market" versus the dollar.

6) **June 2003:** US switches Iraqi oil sales back to dollar.

7) **June 2003 to September 2003:** euro falls versus dollar.

8) **October 2003 to early February 2004:** statements by Russian and OPEC politicians/officials that switch to euro for oil sales is being considered. Euro's value versus the dollar increases.

9) **10 February 2004:** OPEC meets and no decision to switch to euro is taken.

10) **February 2004 to May 2004:** euro falls versus the dollar.

11) **June 2004:** Iran announces intention to establish oil-trading market to rival those of London and New York.

12) **June 2004:** euro's value versus the dollar begins to increase again.

actively encouraging Russia, another opponent of the US invasion, to move to euro oil and gas sales. In October 2003, during a joint press conference with Germany's Prime Minister Gerhard Schroeder, the Russian President Vladimir Putin declared that Russia was thinking about selling its oil for euros. A few days later, the European Commission President, Romano Prodi, said, after a summit between Russia and the European Union, that Russia was now drawn to having its imports and exports denominated in euros[25,26].

In December 2003, speculation about the future

roles of the dollar and the euro increased when OPEC Secretary General Alvaro Silva, a former Venezuelan oil minister, said that the organisation was now considering trading in euros or in a basket of currencies other than the dollar, as the US currency was declining in value[27]. Although a few days later the Saudi oil minister Ali al-Naimi said that OPEC would not be discussing a switch to the euro at its next meeting (comments reinforced by the Qatari President of OPEC and the Algerian oil minister[28]), articles discussing a possible move continued to appear in the media[29,30] and the euro's value against the dollar soared. Despite the speculation, no decision to move to the euro was taken at OPEC's meeting in early February 2004 and thereafter the euro's value fell back again.

In fact, close inspection of the dollar-euro exchange rate shows that since the euro's introduction in January 1999, petro-currency rivalry appears to have played an important part in swinging the rate one way or the other (see Graph). The markets, it seems, have noticed the importance of what is happening. On the other hand, the lack of an open discussion of the issues suggests that politicians and bankers are keen to move ahead with their plans with little or no explanation to the general public.

Should we not, however, be debating more openly what kind (or kinds) of international financial structure(s) we want to adopt, since the question has potentially huge implications for the stability of the world economy and for peace and stability in oil-exporting countries? A good starting point for such a debate would be the recognition that no country or countries should be allowed to dominate the system by controlling the issuance of the currency or currencies used. Similarly fundamental would be to prevent any country from running a persistent trade surplus or deficit so as to avoid the build up of unjust subsidies, unpayable debts and economic instability. At Bretton Woods, John Maynard Keynes, who understood how important these two conditions were, proposed a system which would have met them, but his proposal was rejected in favour of the dollar[31].

The dollar, though, is no longer a stable, reliable currency: the IMF has warned that the US trade deficit is so bad that its currency could collapse at any time[32]. Will we really have to wait for a full-blown dollar crisis before a public debate about creating a just and sustainable trading system can begin?

References

1   Howard Fineman, 'In Round 2, it's the dollar vs. euro', April 23 2003, *Newsweek*, http://www.msnbc.com/news/904353.asp?0sl=-22&newguid=FD367EA32A81424DB1136AF1FD3221F4&cp1=1

2   Anon., 'Will the euro rule the roost?', January 1 1999, BBC News, http://news.bbc.co.uk/1/hi/events/the_launch_of_emu/inside_emu/225434.stm

3   David E. Spiro, *The Hidden Hand of American Hegemony: Petrodollar Recycling and International Markets*, Cornell University Press, 1999

4   Anon., 'EU says oil could one day be priced in euros', 16 June 2003, Reuters

5   Irene Kwek, 'EIA Says Oil Price Switch To Euro From Dollar Unlikely', 16 June 2003, Dow Jones Newswires

6   Recknagel, Charles, 'Iraq: Baghdad Moves to Euro', November 1 2000, Radio Free Europe, http://www.rferl.org/nca/features/2000/11/01112000160846.asp

7   Faisal Islam, 'When will we buy oil in euros?', February 23 2003, *The Observer*, http://www.observer.co.uk/business/story/0,6903,900867,00.html

8   William Clark, 'The Real Reasons for the Upcoming War With Iraq: A Macroeconomic and Geostrategic Analysis of the Unspoken Truth', January 2003, http://www.ratical.org/ratville/CAH/RRiraqWar.html

9   Cóilín Nunan, 'Oil, currency and the war on Iraq', January 2003, http://www.feasta.org/documents/papers/oil1.htm

10 Anon., 'Iran may switch to euro for crude sale payments', *Alexander Oil and Gas*, September 5 2002, http://www.gasandoil.com/goc/news/ntm23638.htm

11 Hazel Henderson, 'Globocop v. Venezuela's Chavez: Oil, Globalization and Competing Visions of Development', April 2002, InterPress Service, http://www.hazelhenderson.com/Globocop%20v.%20Chavez.htm

12 Carola Hoyos and Kevin Morrison, 'Iraq returns to international oil market', June 5 2003, *Financial Times*

13 Coalition Provisional Authority Regulation Number 2, http://www.cpa-iraq.org/regulations/index.html#Regulations

14 UN Security Council Resolution 1483, http://www.un.org/Docs/sc/unsc_resolutions03.html

15 Judy Aita, 'U.N. Transfers Oil-for-Food Program to CPA, Iraqi Officials Nov 22', November 2003, Washington File, http://www.cpa-iraq.org/audio/20031122_Nov22-UN_Transfers_Oil_for_Food_Program-post.htm

16 Catherine Belton, 'Why not price oil in euros?', October 10 2003, *Moscow Times*

17 Kazi Mahmood, 'Economic Shift Could Hurt U.S.-British Interests In Asia', March 30 2003, IslamOnline.net

18 C. Shivkumar, 'Iran offers oil to Asian union on easier terms', June 16 2003, http://www.blonnet.com/2003/06/17/stories/2003061702380500.htm

19 Anon, 'Malaysia, Iran discuss the use of gold dinar', July 3 2003, *Asia Times*, http://www.atimes.com/atimes/Southeast_Asia/EG03Ae01.html

20 Terry Macalister, 'Iran takes on west's control of oil trading', June 16 2004, *The Guardian*, http://www.guardian.co.uk/business/story/0,3604,1239644,00.html

21 Hooman Peimani, 'EU and Iran talk trade, not war', June 7 2003, *Asia Times*, http://www.atimes.com/atimes/Middle_East/EF07AK02.html

22 Guy Dinmore, 'US lobbyists tune in for regime change in Iran', December 5 2003, *Financial Times*

23 Michael Binyon and Bronwen Maddox, 'US sets sights on toppling Iran regime', July 17 2004, *The Times*

24 Jennifer Johnston, 'Regime change in Iran now in Bush's sights', July 18 2004, *The Sunday Herald*, http://www.sundayherald.com/43461

25 Lisa Jucca and Melissa Akin, 'Europe Presses Russia on Euro', October 20 2003, *Moscow Times*

26 Simon Nixon, 'What's that in euros?', October 18 2003, *The Spectator*, http://www.spectator.co.uk/article.php3?table=old&section=current&issue=2003-10-18&id=3619

27 Anon., 'OPEC may trade oil in euros to compensate for dollar decline', December 9 2003, Associated Press, http://www.hindustantimes.com/news/181_490084,00020008.htm

28 Anon., 'Saudi Arabia: Dollars only please', December 13 2003, Reuters, http://money.cnn.com/2003/12/13/news/international/bc.energy.saudi.reut/

29 Patrick Brethour, 'OPEC mulls move to euro for pricing crude oil', January 12 2004, Globe and Mail, http://www.globeandmail.com/servlet/story/RTGAM.20040112.wopec0112/BNStory/Business/

30 Anon., 'To euro or not: should oil pricing ditch the dollar?', February 9 2004, AFP

31 Michael Rowbottom, *Goodbye America! Globalisation, Debt and the Dollar Empire*, Jon Carpenter Publishing, 2000

32 Charlotte Denny and Larry Elliott, 'IMF warns trade gap could bring down dollar', September 19 2003, *The Guardian*, http://www.guardian.co.uk/business/story/0,3604,1045193,00.html

The Irish Government has abandoned its plan to reduce the country's greenhouse gas emissions with an ecotax on the carbon content of fossil fuels which was to have been introduced in 2005. In Germany, similar taxes created over 60,000 new jobs but reduced CO_2 emissions by less than 1% in the first two years. This indicates that Irish carbon tax rates would have needed to be very steep for the country to avoid paying hefty fines to the EU because it failed to keep within its Kyoto target.

How have ecotaxes worked in Germany?

Hans Diefenbacher   Volker Teichert   Stefan Wilhelmy

Dr. Hans Diefenbacher (economics), **Dr. Volker Teichert** (economics), and **Stefan Wilhelmy, M.A.** (political science) are senior researchers at the Protestant Institute for Interdisciplinary Research (FEST) in Heidelberg, Germany. Hans Diefenbacher, a member of Feasta, also teaches economics at the University of Kassel.

In 2000, Germany released 858 million tonnes of carbon dioxide into the global atmosphere, equivalent to 9.6 tonnes per head of the population[1] This made the Germans slightly less serious polluters than the citizens of most other industrial countries as the OECD average is 10.9 tonnes a head. The British figure was the same as the German one while the Irish one was rather worse, at 11.1 tonnes. But all three countries' per capita emissions were very much higher than those from the developing world which range from 0.1 tonnes in Nepal and Tanzania, through 0.2 tonnes in Bangladesh and 0.7 tonnes in Pakistan to 1.1 tonnes in India and 2.3 tonnes in China.

Humanity's total carbon dioxide emissions currently exceed the absorptive capacity of global eco-systems ('sinks') by at least 50% - and the

amount of the excess is rising. If we take the present world population as being around 6.1 billion, the climate-neutral release of CO_2 would therefore be less than 2.3 tonnes per head per year. Per capita emissions in Germany and in the rest of the industrialised world are thus more than four times the estimated climate-neutral amount. This figure not only underlines the need for urgent decisive action but also shows that it is the industrialised countries that must take it.

Ecotaxes are one of the most effective measures to speed the crucial transition from finite, climate-changing fuels like oil and coal to renewable, climate-neutral ones. Since their introduction in Germany in 1999, petrol consumption has fallen for the first time in the country's post-war history. Purchases of three- to five-litre cars increased, for example, an illustration of the way that ecotaxes provide incentives for investment in more environmentally-friendly technologies and, in the long run, create competitive advantages.

Nonetheless, many members of the public still have reservations about ecotaxes. Some even reject them. An ideologically-flavoured party-political debate about them is going on in Germany and we have found that the only way to get the participants to change their positions is to provide them with information about the way ecotaxes work and what they are intended to do.

The EU is slowly adopting ecotaxes. Finland introduced the first CO_2-tax in the world in 1990, the Netherlands, Norway and Sweden have had ecotaxes since 1991, Denmark began in 1992 and the United Kingdom in 1993. Austria and Belgium have also incorporated ecological elements into their tax systems. What we can learn from the German experience?

1. Ecotaxes: the basics

People have paid taxes and dues to kings and emperors who promised protection from enemy attacks since ancient times. There have been cases of rulers greedy for power squeezing their subjects to such an extent that eventually both prince and people were faced with financial ruin; but also wise governments using their tax systems to finance pioneering social security measures. Eventually, thanks to attempts to develop a 'rational' theory of state finances, the following criteria for an optimal system of taxes and rates have emerged from the search for the royal road between economic efficiency and social justice:[4]

- The purpose of taxes is to finance the activities of the state. The range and scale of these activities should be freely decided by the parliament and not the other way round: In other words, the duties the state should take on must not be made primarily dependent on the volume of the overall tax intake. Consequently, taxes have to be plentiful and the tax system reasonably flexible and adaptable.
- The tax system must not put arbitrary burdens on the individual citizen. It must therefore be possible to assess someone's liability to tax on an objective basis; tax law must be transparent and drafted in commonly understandable language; and, finally, the assessment base, the tax rate and

the payment dates must be known to the taxpayer.

- The tax burden should be spread among individual citizens according to ethical criteria. As ideas on what is 'fair' often change quite rapidly in a given society,[5] tax theory has developed three very general principles in recent decades:
  1. The principle of *Generality* implies that everyone should pay taxes.
  2. The principle of *Equivalency* demands that the 'price' paid for the state's activities (i.e. the overall volume of taxes) should correspond to the benefits the citizens derive from them.
  3. Finally, the principle of *Ability* means that all citizens are asked to sacrifice, as far as possible, a fair proportion of their opportunities for private consumption, a principle often used to justify progressive income tax rates.

- A fourth criterion is that taxes should be used to steer the economy in a desirable direction. The choice of *what* is to be taxed and by *how much* should be made so that economic structures and activities and the distribution of incomes and assets develop in accordance with the government's underlying economic and social policies.[6] A number of approaches have been developed for use in socially-oriented market economies. They include:

  1. policies aimed at redistributing wealth via property taxes, estate duties and through progressive income taxation;
  2. the promotion of asset accumulation through tax rebates for certain types of income such as capital gains;
  3. policies designed to alter the geographical structure of the economy by influencing the choice of investment locations through differential rates of company taxation and local property tax rates;
  4. increasing or decreasing the production of certain products through the levying of special excise taxes;
  5. policies intended to make the economic system more stable by giving tax rebates for investments, taxing speculative share profits or by imposing anti-cyclical levies;
  6. policies to alter the exchange rate of the domestic currency through differential

taxes on foreign and domestic capital gains or through import and export taxes.

These six criteria are non-controversial – it is over their interpretation and practical application in particular circumstances that people fall out.

Ecotaxes: The most important principles

Ecotaxes are nothing special: they are simply taxes intended to achieve an environmental steering effect, just as other taxes are designed to have effects in other areas. They are intended to influence our use of the environment by changing the price that we have to pay for doing so. A great many types of ecotaxes have been designed in the past twenty years but three central features stand out[7]:

- Ecotaxes aim to make the consumption of environmental goods more expensive. Through these taxes, the relative structure of prices gets changed and, it is hoped, behaviour detrimental to the environment becomes less attractive. People frequently argue that raising the price of environmental commodities could lead to 'environmental price truth'. However, whether prices including an ecotax really express the 'true' cost is irrelevant for the steering function to have an effect. Even if it is not possible to determine the exact monetary value of a specific environmental commodity such as an endangered species, the *direction* of the price change is primarily the thing that matters, not the exact amount.

- A tax aimed at raising the price paid to use the environment should be implemented step by step and should lend itself to long-term calculation. This is so that economic agents such as firms can act to reduce or avoid shortages of environmental commodities arising in future as a result of their too rapid consumption now. The changes in economic behaviour that result from the tax will, as a rule, create employment as well as benefitting the environment.

- Revenue derived from ecotaxes should not become part of the general budget but should be reserved for specific tasks. Various approaches are under debate here: most ecotax advocates prefer strict 'revenue neutrality' which means that the revenue raised by the ecotax is fully compensated for by tax reductions elsewhere. For example, social security contributions could be lowered

or income and corporate tax rates cut by the amount the ecotax brings in.[8] The original designs of a lot of ecotax concepts included this feature. A minority of ecotax advocates believe that the environment has already been damaged to such an extent that at least part of ecotax yield should be used for ecological investment and the promotion of nature protection measures.

2. The main characteristics of the German ecotaxes

Drawing on ideas discussed since the late seventies and early eighties,[9] Germany's red-green coalition government introduced a set of ecotaxes on 1 April 1999 designed to make energy and resource consumption more expensive while lowering the cost of labour. The taxes were introduced in five steps: the initial one raised the tax on electricity by 2 Pfennigs/kWh, the tax on mineral oil by 6 Pfennig/litre, the tax on heating oil by 4 Pfennig/litre and the tax on gas by 0.32 Pfennig/litre. (2 Pfennigs is roughly the equivalent of one euro cent.) Then, in three further steps, the tax on mineral oil was raised by 6 Pfennig/litre on 1 January 2000 and again on 1 January 2001 and the tax on electricity went up by 0.5 Pfennig/kWh on the same dates. On 1 January 2002 and again on 1 January 2003, the tax on mineral oil was raised by 3.1 Cent/litre and the tax on electricity by 0.26 Cent/kWh. That is as far as the process had got by Autumn 2003.

Labour costs were cut by reducing pension contributions. By the end of 2002, the new taxes had brought in an extra €39.3 billion, most of which was used to lower the pension contributions from their level of 20.3% of gross wages in March 1999 to 19.1% in January 2002. Employers and employees have shared the 1.2% saving equally. It was not possible to make further reductions in 2002, but without the introduction of the ecotaxes, the contributions rate would by now have reached 21%.

In addition, some of the ecotax revenue, up to €150 million a year, is used to promote renewable energy. This is roughly equivalent to the ecotax taken from renewable energy sources.

One element of the German ecotaxes that comes in for consistent criticism is the exemptions and reductions given to particular sectors. Manufacturing industries and agriculture receive an 80% reduction of their taxes on heating oil, natural gas and electricity. Manufacturing firms are only charged the standard rate for the first €500 of their oil, gas and electricity taxes; once payments of ecotaxes rise above 120% of the amount saved by the reduction of ancillary labour costs, companies can apply for a full refund from the customs offices. Public rail transport (trains, trams, trolley buses, urban and suspension railways, metros) receives a 50% reduction of the electricity tax, i.e. it pays only 0.5 Cent per kWh. This amounts to an annual loss of ecotax revenue of around €65 million.

Since January 2000, buses, taxis and other forms of short-distance public transport have only paid the mineral oil ecotax at 1.5 Cent/litre for their fuel. Storage heating systems installed before April 1st, 1999 which are only taxed at half the increased rate. Further exemptions to promote efficient technologies and renewable energy sources are also being given – for example, electricity from combined heat and power generation with an efficiency rate of more than 70% is exempt from mineral oil and electricity taxes. Electricity from renewable sources used for on-site production is also exempt.

3. The ecotaxes' effects

The positive effects of the ecological tax reform were highlighted by the Federal Environmental Bureau (Umweltbundesamt) in early 2002[10] when it stated that by the end of that year, its projections showed that ecotaxes would have reduced CO_2 emissions by more than 7 million tonnes while at the same time creating almost 60,000 new jobs. Other researchers [11] were even more positive, saying that between 176,000 and 250,000 new jobs would be created. These figures were based on the assumption that the trade unions would moderate their wage demands by linking any increases in gross pay to changes in prices and productivity.

These widely-differing estimates shows how much macro-economic models depend on political decisions, which, as a rule, do not lend themselves to adequate modelling. Calculations on the employment effects of ecotaxes consequently need to be treated with caution but our own investigations have led us to take a predominantly positive view of the ecotaxes' income-distribution effects.

There is even disagreement over the reduction in CO_2 emissions the taxes will bring about. The ecological tax reform movement expects

reductions of around 15 million tonnes, twice the official Umweltbundesamt figure. But if we compare this to the target the Federal Government announced in 1992, which envisaged a 25% reduction (250,000 tonne) by 2005 (see figure 3), ecotaxes can only be a first step along the way.

German reunification and the resulting changes in East Germany have substantially helped to cut the country's CO_2 emissions since 1990, especially in the early years. During the first half of the 1990s, CO_2 emissions fell by 11%; during the following years, the reductions fell at a much slower rate. The overall reduction for the period between 1990 and 2000 was 15%.

4. Suggestions for extending ecotaxes

The environmental movement reserved its strongest criticism of the ecotax programme for the concessions given to energy use in industry and agriculture. This indirect subsidy saved these sectors around €4.6 billion in 2002 and the European Commission has also objected to it. If these concessions are to be kept any longer, they should be reserved for companies that have implemented environmental management according to EMAS and/or DIN EN ISO 14001 improving the somewhat hesitant up-take of these schemes.

We suggest that from 2004 onwards, ecotax revenue should no longer be reserved for stabilising pension fund contributions. Only a third of ecotax-take should be used that way while a further third (around €12 billion) should be used to lower social insurance rates in view of current labour market conditions. The remaining third should be used to promote renewable energy production and energy saving measures. If energy saving was encouraged, taxes on gas and heating oil, which have not been raised since April 1999, could be increased.

Our suggested changes to the ecotax regime would dissolve its revenue neutrality to some extent but the public has not, so far, noticed the positive effects of the tax reform and subsidies for heat insulation measures could increase the taxes' popular acceptance. Friends of the Earth Germany (BUND) has been thinking on similar lines and has suggested that there should be an extra line on all pay slips showing how much money from ecotaxes is refunded to citizens through reduced pension funds contributions.[12]

It is also necessary to consider how low-income people, especially pensioners and those receiving unemployment benefit, social welfare or educational grants can be compensated for the losses that ecotaxes have caused them.[13] This could be arranged through the annual assessment and pay-off procedures.

As we have already noted, ecotaxes would have to be considerably increased to achieve the Federal Government's climate protection target – minus 25% CO_2 emissions by 2005 as compared to 1990. As a result, an intense debate is going on about whether and to what extent flexible economic instruments, like emissions trading, should complement ecotaxes.[14]

The European Union intends to open up opportunities for emissions trading from 2005, starting with an initial 5,000 companies in five sectors - energy, steel, paper, ceramics and building materials.[15] Chemical industries and the transport sector are excluded from this regulation. These companies will be obliged to apply to the environmental agencies of their countries for environmental certificates for their CO_2 emissions. From 2008 emissions trading will be opened to further companies.

Many German industries are not in favour of emissions trading. It is the view of the Federal Association of German Industry (Bundesverband der Deutschen Industrie - BDI) that setting an upper limit for CO_2 emissions would mean an "entry into the European planned economy".[16] Nine of Germany's biggest companies – including RWE and Eon, BASF and Bayer and also Dyckerhoff and Thyssen-Krupp – have criticised the European Commission's plans and declared them to be intolerable. The Chemical Industry Association (Verband der Chemischen Industrie - VCI) even threatened to relocate energy-intensive production abroad. Their opposition is in contrast to the positive experiences which oil companies like Shell and BP have had with emissions trading.[17]

Any price increases for heating oil, gas, electricity and petrol due to increased ecotaxes in future must be signalled well ahead – at least up to 2010 - so that citizens and industry can take account of them when making their plans. It would also be good to arrange for price increases only every second year.

5. How sustainable are ecotaxes?

Whenever the effects of an ecotax are discussed, its promoters and detractors operate with widely differing figures especially where the economic benefits such as the effect on the labour market are concerned. Here, the claims run from "jeopardizing thousands of jobs" to "creating several hundred thousand sustainable positions". On top of this, we have the ecological and social aspects of sustainability to consider.

The way in which a particular ecotax affects these three dimensions of sustainability can neither be measured nor calculated accurately even if complex computer models are used. This is because there is a whole host of factors – wage policies, global economic developments, exchange rates, the price of crude oil etc. – which can boost or reduce the effects that are being assessed. It is, however, possible to deduce certain trends, which can subsequently be related to the relevant targets of sustainable development.

In the environmental sector, the targets most improved by ecotaxes are closely linked: *"environmentally and socially compatible mobility"*, *"sparing use of non-renewable resources"* and *"low energy input"*: According to data released by the Federal Ministry for the Environment, fuel sales in the first half of 2001 were 5% lower than in the first half of 1999, petrol consumption went down by as much as 12% in this period, while the consumption of diesel fell by just 2%.

German railways registered a passenger increase of 2% in 2000 while rail freight grew by 7.9%. The popularity of agencies organising lifts in private cars (Mitfahrzentralen) was significantly higher – they saw a plus of 25% in the first half of 2000. Overall, the effects of ecotaxes in the environmental area must be regarded as positive and in some sub-sectors even as very positive.

The discussion of the effects of ecotaxes on the economy concentrates on two things: growth and the labour market. Different economic models agree that the taxes have only had a marginal influence on economic growth[18] and earlier fears that ecotaxes might turn out to be 'job killers' can now be taken as having been refuted. There are, however, no concrete figures yet to show whether ecotaxes in their present form actually function as a 'job booster'.

The third dimension, the social one, is concerned with a *"just distribution of incomes and assets"*. Using a micro-simulation model, the German Institute for Economic Research (Deutsches Institut für Wirtschaftsforschung, DIW) arrived at the view that the ecotaxes had meant that the net income of most households had been reduced. While these losses were small as a proportion of overall household income, low- and medium-income households fared worst. However, since the ecotaxes were only part of a far-reaching package of tax reforms, the DIW was able to conclude that most households' finances had improved.[19]

Ecotaxes can therefore be judged to have made a positive contribution to all three aspects of sustainability and they would have become much more effective if their design had been more influenced by ecological imperatives than by political and economic ones. Ecotaxes will only have a decisive impact on sustainable development in Germany if they are combined with further instruments like the Eco-Audit and greater support for renewable energy production. Moreover, all players need to realise that the taxes are an essential part of a long-term strategy. We strongly believe that ecotaxes should be continued over the coming years and that they should continue to contribute to a planned, progressive increase in the price of fossil fuel.

Links to further information about ecotaxes in Germany are available with the online version of the article on the Feasta website.

Ecotaxes currently in use in Ireland

Economic Instruments	Details	Comments
Charges/fines:		
Derelict sites levy	3 per cent annually of an urban property's market value.	Low coverage. Revenue in 1994 was £21 000, on property worth £0.7 million.
Litter fines	Not applied very thoroughly.	No information on revenue.
Plastic bag levy	Introduced in 2002. 15 cent per plastic bag, revenue used for environmental functions.	Seemingly the most popular tax. Over 70% reduction in plastic bag use.
User charges:		
Domestic water and sewerage charges	Abolished in 1997.	High leakage rates, addressed by investment programme.
Domestic refuse charges	Mainly fixed charge. Some volume-based refuse charges. Costs partially covered.	Very small but strong resistance to bin charges. Local Authorities and Combat Poverty want Departmental guidance on waiver schemes.
Non-domestic water, solid waste and waste water:	Volume-based charges widespread for water and solid waste, less so for waste water.	
Urban parking	Meters and fines (but much free business parking).	Meters and fines revenue was £9.28 million in 1995.
Product charges:		
	High hydrocarbon taxes. CO_2 tax studied since 1991.	Mainly to raise revenue. Carbon taxes and permit trading due in 2004/5
Admin./monitoring fees:		
Trade effluent	Fee, increasing to cover costs.	
Integrated Pollution	Licence fee to firms.	To recover EPA costs.

Economic Instruments	Details	Comments
Tax differentiation:		
Leaded/unleaded petrol	Tax difference.	Unleaded sales rose from 7% in 1989, to over 60% by 1996.
Vehicle Registration Tax	% of vehicle value, higher for vehicles > 2500 cc.	VRT revenue was £271 million in 1994.
Annual road tax	Graded by engine cc.	Revenue was £249 million in 1994.
Tax relief if scrapping 10-year-old car (now ended)	£1000 Vehicle Registration Tax relief.	Ran from 1.7.1995 to 31.12.1996. Cost is 20 % of VRT revenue.
Exemption of VAT on public transport	Ticket sales are not charged VAT.	To reduce the price of public transport, possibly discourages adoption of new technology.
Excise tax on diesel used by public transport is rebated	To reduce costs of public transport providers.	Discourages fuel efficiency and switching to cleaner fuels in public transport.
Exemption from excise duty: waste oil	On processors of waste oil.	To encourage recycling.
Urban renewal special tax rates:	10 year Rates relief, double rent allowance and other reliefs.	Effective relief is high.
Allowance for insurance bonds	Payments of insurance bonds for rehabilitation of mines is allowable against tax.	Cost to Exchequer is £1 million per year (1997)
Subsidies:		
Food industry	Pollution control grants from EAGGF.	8 to 10% of investment.
Industry and commerce energy audit grant and efficiency grant	40% up to £3000 for audit. Up to 40% to a value of £156 000 for investment (1997).	£2 million expenditure in first year, 1995.
Rural Environment Protection Scheme REPS	Premium to farmers of £122/ha up to max 40 ha. Extra for Natural Heritage Areas (NHAs), Environmentally Sensitive Areas (ESAs) and organic farming.	Part of CAP reform: budget of £230 m over several years. To influence farming practice on small farms in its totality.
Control of Farmyard Pollution Scheme (suspended)	Grants up to 60% to a value of £22 500 to small farms for slurry storage etc.	Under Operational Programme (OP) for Agriculture, Rural Development & Forestry.
Afforestation grant	£1300 to £3000 per ha plus 20 year premium of £130 to £300 per ha (1997).	Part of CAP reform. Also OP grants for forestry improvement and amenity, of £500 to £3000.
Explicit subsidy to public transport	Mainly to rail transport.	To reduce the price of public transport.
Deposit refund schemes:		
	Cans.	Isolated (e.g. Aran Islands) and very smallscale.
Market creation:		
	Government departments and agencies use recycled paper.	

Adapted by Sue Scott of the ESRI from an appendix to Chapter 2 in A. Barrett, J. Lawlor and S. Scott, *The fiscal system and the polluter pays principle - a case study of Ireland.* Ashgate, Aldershot, 1997

Quotas as an alternative to carbon taxation

In October 2003, Feasta responded to a call from the Irish Department of Finance for submissions on a proposal to introduce carbon taxes. Feasta's submission can be found on the Feasta website at http://www.feasta.org/documents/energy/dtqsoct2003.htm. It is also with all the other submissions on the Department's website at http://www.finance.gov.ie/viewdoc.asp?DocID=1831

We gave two reasons for disliking carbon taxes and preferring tradable carbon quotas such as the Domestic Tradable Quotas (DTQs) advocated by David Fleming and described in *Feasta Review* No. 1. These were:

1. A carbon tax, however structured, cannot guarantee that any particular level of emissions will be achieved at any given date in the future whereas a quota can. A carbon tax rate which would bring about the required emissions reduction in a booming economy would be too high and thus have a depressing effect on a depressed one. As a result, for a carbon tax to work well, its rate would need to be adjusted regularly to conform with the stages of the business cycle. This would make setting the rate a perennial source of conflict between the government, the consumer and business interests. With a quota, however, the market automatically sets the price to be paid for permits giving the right to burn extra fossil fuel and leaves no scope for argument.

2. A quota system is much more compatible with international emissions trading arrangements, particularly if long-run ones like Contraction and Convergence (also described in *Feasta Review* No. 1) involving very deep cuts in emissions are introduced in the post-Kyoto period.

Feasta would like to see Ireland reducing its CO_2 emissions by introducing a system under which whatever level of CO_2 emissions was set for the country in a particular year was shared out equally amongst all residents. Under the simplest version of this arrangement, everyone would receive a permit entitling them to burn whatever quantity of fossil fuels contained their year's allocation of carbon. The recipients would take their permits to their bank and sell them for cash. The banks would then sell the permits on to importers of fossil fuels who would be required to surrender them to Customs to cover the carbon content of whatever coal, oil or gas they were bringing in. Similar arrangements would be worked out for Irish fossil fuel producers such as the commercial peat firms.

The advantage of this system is that the proceeds from the permit sales would provide everyone with enough extra purchasing power to cover the higher costs of the fuels and (because of the higher energy prices) the other goods and services they bought in the year, provided that their purchases were consistent with their emissions share. If some individuals could cut their direct and indirect fuel use below their entitlement, they would be better off. But if they continued to drive around a lot in their SUV, they would have to pay more frugal people for the privilege. Overall, of course, fossil fuels themselves and goods made with significant amounts of fossil energy would cost more but this would encourage people to find lower-fossil-energy alternatives and enable the transition to renewable energy sources to gather pace.

David Fleming's proposal for DTQs is rather more sophisticated. He would like to see emissions permits covering about 55% of a country's allowable level of emissions being auctioned off to industry and transport companies because that percentage is roughly the proportion of a country's total fossil energy use taken up by these sectors. The income from these permit sales would go to the government, which could pass some of it on to the less-well-off to compensate them for the higher prices they would have to pay for almost everything they bought. Part of the remaining permit sales income could be spent on developing renewable energy sources.

The remaining 45% of emissions would be shared equally amongst the country's residents. Each person might receive their carbon emissions allocation in units on a chip-card which they would use, along with cash, whenever they were buying electricity, petrol or some other fuel. The required

Continued...>>

number of carbon units would be deducted electronically from the amount on the card, which would act as a purse. They would also be able to sell units from the card for cash, or buy additional ones in exactly the same way that you can top up the call units on a pre-paid mobile phone.

However, there would only be any point in issuing emissions permits on chip cards, with all the expense and trouble involved, if it caused people to behave differently from the way they would if they simply got their allocation as a voucher which they then sold to their bank. Fleming expects that many chip card recipients would set out to live within their allocation and make it a matter of pride not to have to buy extra units during the course of the year. If so, they would become very fossil-energy-use conscious, which ought to accelerate the transition away from such fuels, thus justifying the expense of setting up the system and running it. Feasta member and sociologist Mark Garavan is hoping to conduct an attitudinal study to see whether this might be the case.

It seems unlikely that it was Feasta's advice that led the Irish government to abandon its plans to put a carbon tax into effect. Concerns had already been expressed about the effect that the tax would have on the poor, who spend a higher proportion of their income on fuels than do the better-off. For example, in a report[2] published by the Environmental Protection Agency in July 2004, Sue Scott and John Eakins, both of the ESRI, found that the average low-income household would need to receive compensation of €246 a year through the Social Welfare system or in reduced income tax if it was not to be worse off as a result of a carbon tax set at €20 per tonne. The €246 estimate covers just the first-round price increases – that is, the immediate effects of the carbon tax. When the knock-on effects of the first round price increases had been reflected in a second round of price rises, and those in turn had been used to justify a third, and so on, the compensation would have to be higher still.

Now that the tax has been dropped, the only emissions control system in operation in Ireland will be a rudimentary emissions quota system imposed on the country by the EU. A more deeply-flawed system is hard to imagine. Under it, major industrial emitters such as the ESB and the cement companies are to be given permits for 5.8 % more emissions than they are currently releasing - presumably to allow them to grow. It is therefore hard to see how Ireland will get its emissions down.

The EU insisted that 95% of the emissions permits be given to the companies rather than auctioned, but the Irish government is doing better than that and is giving over 96%, leaving it with less to give away to start-up companies or to auction itself to bring in revenue. Quite why the EU insisted on the permits being given away is unclear as no economist, conventional or otherwise, would recommend that course. Presumably, naïve politicians were persuaded by corporate lobbyists to believe that, if the permits were given out rather than sold, it would enable electricity and cement to be cheaper. Not so. The fact is that the permits will acquire a market value if the industries covered by the scheme increase their output faster than they restrict their greenhouse emissions. And once the permits can be sold, firms will factor in the price they could have obtained by selling them as the cost of using them in their production process. In other words, even though the necessary permits came free, the price of electricity and cement will still go up by just as much as would have been the case if the permits had been sold to them by the state. The only difference is that the companies receiving the permits make a big windfall gain, while the state will not have the revenue it will need to compensate the less-well-off for the higher prices they will have to pay. Fortunately, this scheme runs for only three years and there is some chance – not a big one because it has already been announced that 90% of the permits will be given away in the next three-year period – of changing it after that.

The free permits constitute a massive subsidy to the industries concerned. John Fitz Gerald of the ESRI, in a strong attack[3] on the arrangement, estimates that they would be worth €1, 350 million if the price being put on the right to emit a tonne of CO_2 rises to €20. This is money lost to Irish residents. Moreover, the fact that it has been announced that the permits will be given away next time encourages the owners of polluting plants to keep them open so that they can benefit from the subsidy again. If the plants had had to buy the permits, however, the dirtiest ones would have had to close.

Continued...>>

The permits will also encourage the construction of more fossil-fuel power plants rather than the development of renewable energy sources. This is because, although wind farms will benefit from the higher electricity prices that will result from the permit scheme, so will the promoters of, say, new gas-fired power stations, because they will be given the permits they require to buy their fuel. This will, effectively, reduce the costs of constructing their new power station. "For a new combined cycle gas turbine electricity generator, the subsidy in the period 2005-2012 could amount to at least 50% of the capital cost of the new plant" Fitz Gerald says.

Eco-taxes can be useful in reducing demand for such things as road space, plastic bags, chewing gum and non-returnable bottles. However, whenever it is critical that the pressure being put on a resource stays below a particular limit, quotas have to be used instead because of the greater certainty they provide that the limit will not be breached. The proposed carbon tax was not even a suitable tool to use to reliably keep the Ireland's emissions of carbon dioxide below the level needed to avoid paying €100 per tonne fines to the EU because the country has overshot its emissions target. The fine is explained in the caption to the bar chart below. − **The Editors**

Europe's Progress on Meeting its Kyoto Greenhouse Gas Emissions Targets

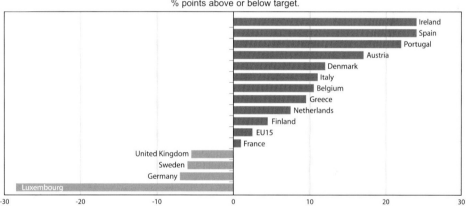

% points above or below target.

Source: European Environment Agency 2003

Ireland agreed with its EU partners to allow its greenhouse gas emissions to rise by no more than 13% above their 1990 level so that the EU-15 as a whole could honour its commitment under the Kyoto Protocol and reduce its total emissions by 7%. If Ireland fails to keep its emissions below the target, it will be able to cover some of the over-run by buying emissions permits from Britain, Sweden, Luxembourg and Germany which, as the chart shows, have some to spare because they have cut back more than they promised. However, these permits are likely to be expensive given that other EU countries are having problems meeting their commitments too. Moreover, European Commission restrictions mean that permits can only be bought to cover emissions up to 10 per cent above the target After that, the country will be fined €40 per tonne for every tonne of carbon dioxide in excess of the limit between 2005 and 2008, and €100 a tonne from then until 2012.

A €100 per tonne fine would increase the cost of a kilowatt-hour of electricity from Ireland's two new peat stations by 14.3 cents, from Moneypoint, a coal-burning station by 9.2 cents, and by 4.6 cents from a typical gas-fired station.

The above chart is based on 2001 data. Irish economic growth will have worsened the situation since then.

Endnotes:

1   These emissions figures are all taken from the UNDP's 2004 Human Development Report. They differ slightly from the federal government's data.

2   *Carbon Taxes: Which Households Gain or Lose?* Environmental Protection Agency, PO Box 3000, Johnstown Castle, Co. Wexford, Ireland.

3   'An Expensive Way to Combat Global Warming: Reform Needed in the EU Emissions Trading Regime', special article in the ESRI's *Quarterly Economic Commentary*, April, 2004. Can be downloaded from http://www.esri.ie/pdf/QEC0404_FitzGerald.pdf

4   Cf. Neumark, Fritz (1970): Grundsätze gerechter und ökonomisch rationaler Steuerpolitik. Tübingen: J.C.B. Mohr; Haller, Heinrich (1971): Die Steuern. Tübingen, J.C.B. Mohr, 2. Aufl.

5   Cf. Diefenbacher, Hans (2001): Gerechtigkeit und Nachhaltigkeit. Darmstadt: WBG, Kap. 4.

6   Cf. Streit, Manfred/Umbach, Dieter (1976): –Besteuerungsgrundsätze", in: diess. (Hrsg.): Die Wirtschaft heute. Mannheim: Bibliographisches Institut, 316ff.

7   Cf. Priewe, Jan (1998): Die Öko-Steuer-Diskussion. Positionen und Kontroversen einer Bilanz. Berlin: edition sigma; Deutsches Institut für Wirtschaftsforschung Berlin/Finanzwissenschaftliches Forschungsinstitut an der Universität zu Köln (1999): Anforderungen an und Anknüpfungspunkte für eine Reform des Steuersystems unter ökologischen Aspekten. Berlin: Erich Schmidt Verlag; zum folgenden vgl. Reiche, Danyel /Krebs, Carsten (1999): Der Einstieg in die ökologische Steuerreform. Frankfurt u.a.: Peter Lang, 25ff.

8   On this see: Binswanger, Hans Christoph/Nutzinger, Hans G./Frisch, Heinz et al. (1983): Arbeit ohne Umweltzerstörung. Frankfurt: S. Fischer.

9   For overviews of the discussion of eco taxes so far see Reiche/Krebs (1999).

10   Cf. –Positive Effekte der ökologischen Steuerreform, in: Umwelt, Heft 2, 2002, 94 – 97.

11   Cf. Bach, Stefan u.a. (2001a): Die ökologische Steuerreform in Deutschland. Eine modellgestützte Analyse ihrer Wirkungen auf Wirtschaft und Umwelt. Heidelberg: Physica Verlag; Bach, Stefan u.a. (2001b): Wirkungen der ökologischen Steuerreform in Deutschland, in: Wochenbericht des DIW, Heft 14, 220-225; Lutz, Christian/Meyer, Bernd (2001): Wirkungen der ökologischen Steuerreform auf Wirtschaft und Umwelt in Deutschland – Ergebnisse von Simulationsrechnungen mit dem umweltökonomischen Modell PANTA RHEI. GWS Discussion Paper 2001/1. Osnabrück: Gesellschaft für Wirtschaftliche Strukturforschung.

12   Cf. BUND (o.J.; 2002): Eckpunkte zur Weiterentwicklung der ökologischen Steuerreform. o.O.: hekt. Manuskript.

13   Meyer, Bettina (1998): –Sozialer Ausgleich erforderlich", in: Politische Ökologie, Heft 56, 62-65.

14   See: Ministerium für Umwelt und Verkehr Baden-Württemberg (Hrsg.) (2001): Flexible Instrumente im Klimaschutz. Eine Anleitung für Unternehmen. Guidelines on CD-ROM or on the web at: http://www.isi.fhg.de.

15   See http://www.foes-ev.de/GBNnews3/2artikel4.html.

16   Quote from: Wille, Joachim (2002): Der Streit über die Lizenz zum Klima-Vergiften, in: Frankfurter Rundschau, 26. January 2002, 9.

17   Interview mit BP-Vorstand Peter Knoedel über den Emissionshandel in dem Ölkonzern, in: Frankfurter Rundschau vom 26. January 2002, 9.

18   See the calculation in the models PANTA RHEI und LEAN in Bach u.a. (2001b).

19   Cf. Bach u.a. (2001b), 222.

Using common resources to solve common problems

James Robertson

There is such a thing as a free lunch – and many established institutions are busy eating them. Society would work more efficiently if the rules were changed to allow everyone a fair share.

James Robertson became an independent writer and speaker in 1974 after an early career as a British civil servant. He and his wife, Alison Pritchard, helped to set up The Other Economic Summit (TOES) and the New Economics Foundation in 1984. He is a member of Feasta and a patron of SANE (South Africa New Economics Foundation),which was set up following his visit there in 1996. His website is at http://www.jamesrobertson.com

His recent books include *Creating New Money: A Monetary Reform for the Information Age* (New Economics Foundation, 2000) co-written with Professor Joseph Huber, *Beyond The Dependency Culture* (Adamantine/Praeger, 1998), *The Transformation of Economic Life* (Schumacher Briefing No 1, Green Books, 1998) and *A New Economics of Sustainable Development*, a 'Briefing for Policymakers' written for the European Commission in 1997 (Kogan Page, 1999). He lives in Oxfordshire. This paper is based on a lecture he gave in Italy in October 2003 at the 29th Annual Conference of the Pio Manzu International Research Centre at which he was awarded the Centre's gold medal for being a "reasonable revolutionary" and "an outstanding example of a modern thinker at the service of society". The conference was dedicated to the "essential figures of Ernst Schumacher and Ivan Illich".

1. INTRODUCTION

Ivan Illich's insights into the systematically disabling nature of today's institutions and professions and E.F Schumacher's ideas have hardly begun to influence mainstream agendas. The course of world development is still based on what Illich saw as the erosion of "the conditions necessary for a convivial life"[1] and what Schumacher called the "onward stampede".[2] Why is this? Was their thinking lacking in some important respect? Or have we failed to act on it?

Both Illich and Schumacher were criticised for not dealing with political and institutional aspects of change. I remember Illich responding that his task was to explain what was wrong; it was for others to take the necessary action. For him the ideas were pre-eminent. Schumacher's view that "the task of our generation is one of metaphysical reconstruction" underlined that his priority too was to redefine the meaning of central ideas - like work. It is true – and important – that he set up the Intermediate Technology Development Group, and personally supported the Scott Bader "common ownership" company and the Soil Association. He saw these as "lifeboat institutions" – examples of reconstructed ideas in action in the spheres of technology, business and farming. But for him, like Illich, systematic *institutional reconstruction* to support metaphysical reconstruction was not a personal priority.[3]

It doesn't make much sense to criticise Illich and Schumacher for this. Nobody can do everything. Both men knew themselves well enough to know how best to use their time and energies. We need to ask *ourselves*:

- why have *we*, who share their vision of a more people-centred and ecological world, failed to adapt the institutions of society to it? and

- what should we do about that now?

In this paper, taking government and the money system as a case study, I shall try to outline a possible answer to that question.

Using common resources to
solve common problems
James Robertson

2. THE INSTITUTIONS OF GOVERNMENT AND MONEY[4]

Established institutions embody dominant ideas, and transmit them as norms of desired behaviour. For example, today's economic institutions embody the idea that work means a job with an employer and that normal people should work that way. But, as pioneer systems thinkers in the 1970s like Stafford Beer pointed out, institutions are dynamic systems programmed for survival.[5] So they act as barriers to change, obstructing the conversion of new ideas from thinkers like Illich and Schumacher into new norms of behaviour for most people. In that respect established institutions in society correspond to what business consultants used to call the "soggy middle layer" – conservative middle managements obstructing communication between forward-looking leaders who recognise the need for change and bright younger people eager to bring it in.

>>> *Money is the scoring system for the game of economic life*

The money system has a particular significance. The way it works rewards some activities and penalises others - at personal, local, national and global levels, in every sector of economy and society. In a monetised world this is the principal way of allocating resources. Money is *the scoring system* for the game of economic life, alongside *the rules* provided by laws and other legal instruments. The nature of any game and how it is played reflects what the scoring system rewards and penalises.

The reconstruction of today's money system is now urgent. More and more people are experiencing it as perverse - in terms of economic efficiency, social justice, environmental sustainability, and physical and spiritual health. They see it as responsible:

- for the systematic transfer of wealth from poor people and countries to rich ones,
- for the money-must-grow imperative that compels people to make money in socially and environmentally damaging ways,
- for the diversion of economic effort and enterprise *towards* making money out of money, and *away from* providing useful goods and services,

- for its systematic bias in favour of the people, organisations and nations who should be managing it on behalf of us all, and
- for eroding the credibility of political democracy after 200 years of progress. [6]

All this fuels opposition to globalisation in its present form.

One constructive response has been the spread of "alternative" and "complementary" monetary and financial innovations.[7] These unofficial initiatives will become more important, as people and businesses look for new ways of using their money. But today I shall concentrate on mainstream money -

- the existing ways in which states handle it on behalf of their peoples,
- the perverse outcomes of those, and
- the changes that are needed.

Some Background Points and Principles

1) The 20th century showed that a centralised socialist economy cannot work efficiently, justly or ecologically. On the other hand, the idea of a free market economy based on objective prices is a fantasy. In developed countries today taxation takes a third of the total value of the economy (GDP) out of some activities, and public spending puts it back into others. The taxes add to the cost of what is taxed and the public spending reduces the cost of what it supports. This affects relative prices all through the economy. So the price structure of any economy is bound to be skewed in favour of some things and against others. The proverbial 'level playing field' is a mirage.

2) So the framework provided by the state institutions that deal with money must be designed to encourage ways of using money that serve, not damage, the interests of citizens now and in the future. Within such a framework:

a) the *market economy*, freely responding to money values, would tend to deliver outcomes which combine economic efficiency with social justice and environmental care;

b) the *government* would be able to let the market economy operate more freely, with less intervention than most economies today; and

c) *citizens*, who wished to do so, would find it easier than now to reduce their need for goods and services bought from the market economy, and also therefore to reduce the amount of money they need to earn by working as employees.

3) The state's new role towards the market and the citizen should thus be to decolonise and empower. Whether to call this a basically capitalist or basically socialist approach is a matter of personal choice. It will aim to integrate economic efficiency with economic justice. So you could call it *both* capitalist and socialist or *neither*, whichever you prefer.

4) Milton Friedman's teaching that "there ain't no such thing as a free lunch" (TANSTAAFL) is false. Starting with the enclosure of the common land, modern economies have given massive free lunches to powerful individuals, organisations - and also nations. I shall say more about this and list some of today's common resources shortly. Their value should be shared as a source of public revenue, in place of the economically, socially and environmentally damaging taxes we have now.

5) This will involve a shift from the idea of *redistribution* to the idea of *predistribution*.[8] Whereas redistributive taxes aim to correct the *outcomes* of economic activity, predistributive taxes and charges will share the value of essential *inputs* to economic activity. Whereas redistribution is dependency-reinforcing, predistribution will be empowering. It will correct an underlying cause of economic injustice, inequality, exclusion and poverty.

6) In a globalised world economy, we need to evolve institutions of governance embodying those five principles at supranational and subnational levels, as well as national level.

What changes do these background points and principles imply - first nationally, and then internationally?

3. PRACTICAL CONSEQUENCES –

for the Financial and Monetary Functions of the State

The essential financial and monetary functions of the state are:

1) collecting *public revenue*;
2) organising *public spending programmes*; and
3) ensuring that the *money supply* (i.e. the supply of official currency - euros, dollars, pounds, etc) is put into circulation, and works fairly and efficiently. [9,10] How these functions are carried out heavily influences the economic activities and outcomes that characterise a society.

Collecting National Public Revenue

(a) Problems and Perversities of the Present Tax System

Pressures to reduce existing taxes are growing stronger.

- In a *competitive global economy*, the mobility of capital and highly qualified people will continue to press governments to reduce taxes on incomes, profits and capital.

- In *ageing societies*, opposition will grow to taxing fewer people of working age on the fruits of their efforts in order to support growing numbers of what economists call "economically inactive" people.

- *Internet trading* will make it more difficult for governments to collect customs duties, value added tax and other taxes and levies on sales. The internet will also make it easier to shift earnings and profits to low-tax regimes.

- *Tax havens* were estimated to hold $6 trillion worldwide as long ago as 1998, resulting in massive tax losses to national governments, criminal money laundering and economic distortion.[11] The way to deal with this will probably be to shift taxation *away* from things like incomes, profits, capital, and value added that can migrate to tax havens and *on to* things like land which cannot migrate.

These growing pressures on the existing tax base reinforce the economic, social and environmental arguments for taxing "bads", not "goods".

Existing tax structures all round the world are, in fact, absurdly perverse.

- They fall heavily on employment and rewards for work and enterprise, and lightly on the use of common resources. So they encourage all-round inefficiency of resource use - over-use of natural resources (including energy and the environment's capacity to absorb pollution), and under-employment and under-development of human resources.

- Today's taxes are also unfair and illogical. They penalise value added - the positive contributions people make to society. They fail to penalise value subtracted; they don't

Using common resources to
solve common problems
James Robertson

make people and businesses pay for the value of the common resources they use or monopolise, thereby preventing other people from using them.

- The present tax system makes it easy for rich people and businesses to escape, or at least minimise, their tax obligations, because they can afford to use tax havens, family trusts, and a range of other devices set up by expensive bankers, lawyers and accountants.

>>> *The value of a particular site is almost wholly determined by the activities and plans of society around it.*

(b) Sharing the Value of Common Resources

A new approach is clearly needed, based on collecting the value of common resources as public revenue for the benefit of all citizens.

Common resources are resources whose value is due to Nature and to the activities and demands of society as a whole, and not to the efforts or skill of individual people or organisations. Land is an obvious example.[12] The value of a particular land-site, excluding the value of what has been built on it, is almost wholly determined by the activities and plans of society around it. For example, when the route of the London Underground Jubilee line was published, properties along the route jumped in value. Access to them was going to be much improved. So, as a result of a public policy decision, the owners of the properties received a £13bn windfall financial gain. They had done nothing for it; they had paid nothing for it; they had been given a very large free lunch.[13] In 1994, based on 1990 values, I calculated that the absence of a site-value tax on land was costing UK taxpayers £50bn to £90bn a year in lost public revenue.[14]

By contrast, the auction three years ago of twenty-year licences to use the radio spectrum for the third generation of mobile phones raised £22.5bn for the UK government. The governments of Germany, France and Italy also raised very significant sums from that common resource. [15]

Important common resources include:

- land (its site value)
- energy (its unextracted value)
- the environment's capacity to absorb pollution and waste[16]
- the use of limited space (e.g for road traffic, airport landing slots)
- water - for extraction and use, and for waterborne traffic
- the electro-magnetic (including radio) spectrum
- the value created by issuing new money - on which I shall say more.

The annual value of these is very great. Collecting it as public revenue would remove the need for many damaging existing taxes.

(c) Creating New Money[17]

Those who create and put money into circulation profit by the value of the money minus the cost of producing it.[18]

In a democratic age one would expect money, created in offical currencies as part of a national or supranational money supply backed by governments, to be created by professionally independent central monetary authorities (like the European Central Bank) and given to governments or international government agencies to spend into circulation on public purposes.

But that is far from what happens now. In the UK, for example, less than 5% of today's national money supply is created debt-free by the Bank of England and the Royal Mint as banknotes and coins. Over 95% is created by commercial banks out of thin air as profit-making loans to their customers. J.K. Galbraith commented, "The process by which banks create money is so simple that the mind is repelled. Where something so important is involved, a deeper mystery seems only decent." UK commercial banks make over £20 billion a year in interest from this arrangement, while UK taxpayers benefit from less than £3 billion a year in public revenue from the issue of banknotes and coins.[19]

Estimated additional public revenue of about £45bn a year could be collected in the UK,

- if the commercial banks were prohibited from creating new money,
- and if the Bank of England took on responsibility for creating it,

- and if the Bank of England gave the money debt-free to the government to spend into circulation. (Corresponding estimates of potential extra public revenue are: Eurozone €160bn; USA $114bn; Japan ¥17trillion.)

This reform would improve the sharing of resources in many ways. To take one example, a debt-free money supply would help to reduce the costs of economic transactions and the levels of public and private debt. These are now at least partly due to the fact that almost all the money we use has been created as interest-bearing debt which has to be repaid.[20]

Some opponents of reform claim that money in current bank accounts isn't really money, it's only credit. But official monetary statistics and monetary policy-makers recognise that it constitutes the main part of the money supply. In fact, recognising it as money exactly reflects what happened in the 19th century when paper banknotes, and not just gold coins, were recognised to be money and commercial banks were no longer allowed to create money by issuing them. The Bank of England's banknotes may still say "I promise to pay... ". But that is just a historical survival. Everyone knows that banknotes now are not just credit notes. They are cash.

Today electronic money in current bank accounts is money immediately available to be spent, just as banknotes are. The continuing creation of this state-backed money for private-sector profit is a glaring anachronism.

National Public Spending

So much for national public revenue. Reconstruction of public spending is also necessary. The following points are important.

First, $1.5 to $2 trillion a year is estimated to be spent worldwide on perverse subsidies which encourage economically, socially and environmentally damaging activities.[21] These include the subsidies from rich-country governments to their food and agricultural sectors. Combined with tariffs against imported food, these devastate those sectors in poorer countries - and expose the hypocrisy of rich-country support for free trade. This led to the recent breakdown of the world trade talks at Cancun. But there are many other examples of perverse subsidies. Systematic national and international measures are needed to identify them and cut them out.

Second, support for a *basic income* (or Citizen's Income) continues to grow, especially in Europe but in other countries too.[22] It would be paid to all citizens as of right, out of public revenue. It would include state pensions and child allowances, it would replace many other existing social benefits, and it would eliminate almost all tax allowances, tax reliefs and tax credits. It would recognise that, in a society of responsible citizens, some of the public revenue arising from the value of common resources should be shared directly among them. Politicians and government officials now pay huge sums in contracts and subsidies to private-sector business and finance to provide public services. Much of that public money could be distributed directly to citizens to spend for themselves in a market economy responsive to their needs – and also to make it easier for them to develop paid or unpaid work of their own, if they wished to reduce their dependence on earnings as employees.[23]

4. THE GLOBAL DIMENSION

The development of international institutions for dealing with world public revenue, public spending, and monetary management should be based similarly on sharing the value of common resources.

In 1995 the Commission on Global Governance recognised the need for global taxation "to service the needs of the global neighbourhood".[24] It proposed making nations pay for use of global commons, including:

- ocean fishing, sea-bed mining, sea lanes, flight lanes, outer space, and the electro-magnetic spectrum; and for
- activities that pollute and damage the global environment, or cause hazards beyond national boundaries, such as emissions of CO_2 and CFCs, oil spills, and dumping wastes at sea.

The Commission also recognised the urgent need for international monetary reform in a globalised world economy. [25]

Since then there has been growing criticism of the present international monetary system based on the 'dollar hegemony' of the United States. Here are two examples from recent reports, one from Asia and one from Ireland.

1) "The dollar is a global monetary instrument that the United States, and only the United States, can produce. .... World trade is now a

Using common resources to
solve common problems
James Robertson

game in which the US produces dollars and the rest of the world produces things that dollars can buy.[26]

2) The rest of the world pays a total annual subsidy (or 'tribute'!) to the US of at least $400bn a year for using the dollar as the main global currency. A Pentagon analyst has justified this as payment to the US for keeping world order. Others see it as a means by which the richest country in the world compels poorer ones to pay for its unsustainable consumption of global resources. [27] [28]

A genuine international currency, issued by a world monetary authority, is clearly needed as an alternative to the US dollar (and other 'reserve currencies' like the yen, the euro and the pound). Issuing it would give a source of revenue to the world community, just as national monetary reform would do for national communities. It would also help to prevent national governments manipulating the value of their currencies in order to distort the terms of international trade in their own favour.

>>> *A genuine international currency, issued by a world monetary authority, is clearly needed as an alternative to the US dollar*

Revenue from global taxes and global money creation would then provide stable sources of finance for global expenditures, including international peace-keeping programmes. Some of the revenue could also be distributed to all nations according to population size, reflecting the right of every person in the world to a global "citizen's income" based on fair shares of the value of global resources.

This approach:

• would encourage environmentally sustainable development worldwide;

• it would generate a much needed source of revenue for the United Nations;

• it would provide substantial financial transfers to developing countries by right and without strings, as payments for the rich countries' disproportionate use of world resources;

• it would help to liberate developing countries from dependence on grants and loans from institutions like the World Bank and the International Monetary Fund which the rich countries now dominate;

• it would help to solve the problem of Third World debt;

• it would recognise the shared status of all people as citizens of the world; and

• by helping to reduce the spreading sense of injustice in a globalised world, it would contribute to global security.

5. IN CONCLUSION

Support for all the reforms I have mentioned has been growing. But up to now it has been fragmented. Different people have promoted each on its own merits, and different interests have opposed each because, by itself, it would disadvantage them. These reform proposals now need to be developed as integrated parts of a bigger project, to reconstruct the role of money in world society.

I hope that this suggests the nature and the scale of the challenge for all our institutions. The ancient Greek poet Archilochus said: "The fox knows many things, but the hedgehog knows one big thing".[29] Our institutionalised society today has too much of the fox. It splits our ways of life and thought into separate specialisms, careers, academic disciplines, professions, and departments of government.[30] Above all, it doesn't know how to reintegrate politics and economics and science with ethics.

That is why, in these critical breakthrough years, the initial drive for worldwide institutional reconstruction is coming from active citizens and citizen groups. But, if we are to change course successfully to what Schumacher called "the one and only direction of development that would give sense and meaning to our life on Earth",[31] a bolder and more constructive response must come from leading people in all the established institutions and professions.

Endnotes

1   *The Right to Useful Unemployment*, page 8.

2   I am grateful to Diana Schumacher for confirming that Schumacher used this phrase, and the variant "forward stampede", in a number of lectures and talks.

3   It has been pointed out - by Peter Etherden in "The Schumacher Enigma", *Fourth World Review*, 1999:93 - that the institutions dealing with money are a conspicuous example of this. Working with John Maynard Keynes and J.K. Galbraith after the second World War, Schumacher was seen as an up-and-coming authority on international finance and currency reform. So why in later life, in *Small Is Beautiful* and other books, did he say so little about how the present money system ties most people to unreconstructed ways of living and working and thinking?

4   For fuller background see:
    - James Robertson, *The New Economics of Sustainable Development: A briefing for policy-makers* (written for the European Commission), published 1999 by: Kogan Page, London, Editions Apogée, Paris (as *Changer d'Economie: ou la Nouvelle Economie du Developpement Durable*), and Office for Official Publications of the European Communities, Luxembourg.
    - James Robertson, *Transforming Economic Life: A Millennial Challenge*, Schumacher Briefing No1, Green Books, 1998 - www.greenbooks.co.uk (Publication of the Russian edition was organised by Dr Tanya Roskoshnaya, Land and Public Welfare Foundation, St Petersburg, now with UN Habitat in Nairobi; and publication of the Japanese edition was organised by Dr Takashi Iwami, Japan Renaissance Institute .)

5   Stafford Beer, *Designing Freedom*, John Wiley, 1974, p.2.

6   The following two books provide good background.
    - David Korten, *When Corporations Rule the World* (second edition), Kumarian Press and Berrett-Koehler publishers, 2001. Part IV is on "A Rogue Financial System".
    - Frances Hutchinson, Mary Mellor and Wendy Olsen in *The Politics of Money: Towards Sustainability and Economic Democracy*, Pluto Press, 2002, provide a constructive response.

7   These include:
    - "complementary", "parallel" and "community" *currencies* like LETSystems and time banks;
    - the development of "*digital*" payment systems in support of those and other currencies, using the internet, mobile phones etc;
    - local *community financial enterprises* like community development funds, community banks, credit unions and microcredit banks (eg Grameen Bank); and
    - the socially responsible and *ethical use of private money*, such as fair trading, and ethical and green consumption and investment.

8   I owe this thought to Joseph Huber, co-author of "Creating New Money" (see Note 20).

9   In technical terms, functions 1) and 2) comprise the *fiscal* functions of the state, and function 3) is the *monetary* function.

10 The state is also responsible for regulating private financial enterprises. Scandals in recent years (e.g. Enron, Arthur Andersen, WorldCom, Merrill Lynch) have underlined the importance of this task. But it is not a topic that this paper is discussing.

11 See Tax Justice Network (www.taxjustice.net).

12 Sources of information on Land Value Taxation include:
    - Fred Harrison, Centre for Land Policy Studies, 7 Kings Road, Teddington, TW11 0QB, England.
    - Peter Gibb, Henry George Foundation, 58 Haymarket Terrace, Edinburgh EH12 5LA, UK, www.HenryGeorgeFoundation.org

    - Alanna Hartzok, Earth Rights Institute, Box 328, Scotland, PA, 17254, USA. www.earthrights.net
    - Jeffery Smith, Geonomy Society, www.progress.org/geonomy

13 Don Riley, *Taken for a Ride: Trains, Taxpayers and the Treasury*, Centre for Land Policy Studies, 2001(see note 12).

14 James Robertson, *Benefits and Taxes: A Radical Strategy*, New Economics Foundation, 1994.

15 In "Manna from Heaven: Radio Rent Windfalls and the Tax Conversion Fund" in *Geophilos* 03(1), Spring 2003, from Centre for Land Policy Studies (see note 13), Fred Harrison celebrates the thinking of Nobel prize-winning economist William Vickrey as the origin of this auction, and points out that the socialisation of community-created rental values combined with the full privatisation of untaxed earned wages and savings could remove the ceiling artificially imposed on the capitalist economy by deadweight taxes.

16 A great deal of work has been done in recent years on energy and environmental taxation. Much of it points towards shifting the burden of taxes away from useful enterprise and employment on to the use of energy and the capacity of the environment to absorb pollution. For example, the EU carbon/energy tax proposal of the 1990s would have used revenue from taxes on fossil fuels to reduce taxes on employment. Valuable sources of information include:
    - Paul Ekins, Head of Environment Group, Policy Studies Institute, 100 Park Village East, London NW1 3SR. www.psi.org.uk
    - Green Budget News: European Newsletter on Environmental Fiscal Reform www.foes-ev.de
    - Timothy O'Riordan (ed), *Ecotaxation*, Earthscan, 1997.
    - Durning A. and Bauman Y, *Tax Shift*, Northwest Environment Watch, Seattle, 1998.
    - Hamond, M.J. et al, *Tax Waste, Not Work: How Changing What We Tax Can Lead To A Stronger Economy And A Cleaner Environment*, Redefining Progress, San Francisco, 1997.

17 Useful sources include:
    - Michael Rowbotham, *The Grip of Death: A study of modern money, debt slavery and destructive economics*, Jon Carpenter Publishing, Oxfordshire, 1998,
    - David Boyle, *The Money Changers: currency reform from Aristotle to e-cash*, Earthscan, 2002, and
    - Bernard Lietaer, *The Future of Money*, Random House, 2000.

18 The creators of money can *spend* this profit into circulation, as medieval monarchs and local rulers spent the "seigniorage" from minting and issuing coins. Or they can *give it away*, as the Bank of England and the Royal Mint now give the UK government a proportion of the value of new banknotes and new coin. Or they can *lend it at interest*, as today's commercial banks lend their customers money they have created for that purpose. Or they can *lend it interest-free* to finance public investment, as recent UK parliamentary motions have proposed the Bank of England should do.

19 For this and the following paragraphs see Joseph Huber and James Robertson, *Creating New Money: A monetary reform for the information age*, New Economics Foundation, London, 2000 - www.neweconomics.org. (Prof. Dr. Joseph Huber is at the Institut für Soziologie, Martin-Luther-Universität, D - 06099 Halle, Germany.)

20 A fuller list of the benefits of monetary reform would include the following:
    1) Existing taxation and government debt could be reduced, or public spending could be increased.
    2) The value of a common resource - the national money supply - would become a source of public revenue rather than private profit. That would remove an economic injustice.

Using common resources to
solve common problems
James Robertson

3) Withdrawing this hidden subsidy to the commercial banks would result in a freer market for money, a more competitive banking industry, and a more efficient economy.

4) A debt-free money supply would help to reduce the costs of economic transactions and the levels of public and private debt. These are now at least partly due to the fact that almost all the money we use has been created as interest-bearing debt which has to be repaid.

5) The economy would become more stable. Banks want to lend more and bank customers want to borrow more at the peaks of the business cycle and less in the troughs. When, as now, the money in circulation depends on how much the banks lend, the results are "pro-cyclical". Booms and busts are automatically amplified.

6) Central banks would be better able to exert "anti-cyclical" monetary control if they themselves created the new money entering the economy. Controlling inflation indirectly, as now, by raising the costs of borrowing from banks, is itself inflationary - as well as damaging to many people and businesses.

21 Norman Myers, *Perverse Subsidies: Tax $s Undercutting Our Economies and Environments Alike*, IISD, Winnipeg, Canada, 1998.

22 Sources of information about basic income include:

- Basic Income European Network (BIEN), Prof. Philippe Van Parijs, Chaire Hoover d'éthique économique et sociale, Université catholique de Louvain, Place Montesquieu 3, B-1348 Louvain-la-Neuve, Belgium. e-mail: bien@basicincome.org

- South African New Economics Foundation (SANE), Aart Roukens de Lange and Margaret Legum, web: www.sane.org.za, e-mail: sane@sane.org.za

- CORI Justice Commission, Fr Sean Healy, Bloomfield Avenue, Dublin 4, Ireland, www.cori.ie/justice

- Citizen's Income Trust, Malcolm Torry, P.O. Box 26586, London SE3 7WY web: www.citizensincome.org, e-mail: info@citizensincome.org

23 A connected point is about spending the revenue from particular sources on specified purposes. The technical term for this is "hypothecation".

- An example was the EU proposal to spend revenue from fossil fuel energy taxes on reducing employment taxes.

- Road traffic congestion charges are expected to be more acceptable if the revenue is spent on improving public transport.

- An energy tax hits poor people relatively harder than rich people. That regressive effect can be reversed by distributing the revenue as "ecobonuses" to everyone in the area covered by the tax. (For examples see *Ecological Tax Reform Even If Germany Has To Go It Alone*, German Institute for Economic Research, Economic Bulletin, Vol.37, Gower, Aldershot, 1994; and E.U. von Weizsacker, *Earth Politics*, Zed Books,1994.) Such ecobonuses could contribute to a Citizen's Income.

24 Commission on Global Governance, *Our Global Neighbourhood*, Oxford University Press, 1995.

25 Another important contribution is Hazel Henderson, *Beyond Globalization: Shaping a Sustainable Global Economy*, Kumarian Press (for the New Economics Foundation), 1999.

26 Henry C K Liu, *US Dollar Hegemony Has Got To Go*, Asia Times Online Co Ltd, 2002.

27 Richard Douthwaite, *Defense and the Dollar*, 2002 and Feasta, *Climate and Currency: Proposals for Global Monetary Reform*, 2002, prepared for the Johannesburg World Summit on Sustainable Development. Details of both from Feasta.

28 Two further quotations in similar vein are:

- "To build up reserves, poor countries have to borrow dollars from the US at interest rates as high as 18% and lend it back to the US in the form of Treasury Bonds at 3% interest." Romilly Greenhill and Ann Pettifor, *The United States as a HIPC (heavily indebted prosperous country) - how the poor are financing the rich*, New Economics Foundation, London, 2002; www.neweconomics.org

- "At the root of this new form of imperialism is the exploitation of governments by a single government, that of the United States via the central banks and multilateral control institutions of intergovernmental capital... [This] has turned the older form of imperialism into a super imperialism". Michael Hudson, *Super Imperialism: The Origin and Fundamentals of World Domination*, Pluto Press, 2003, pp23-24.

29 In a celebrated essay on "The Hedgehog and the Fox" in *Russian Thinkers*, 1978, the political philosopher Isaiah Berlin discussed Tolstoy as an example of the tension between the monist and pluralist visions of the world.

30 The British Prime Minister, Tony Blair, has found it difficult to achieve his proclaimed aim of "joined-up government".

31 E.F. Schumacher, *A guide for the perplexed*, Jonathan Cape, London, 1977, p. 147.

How interest-free banking works
The case of JAK
by Ana Carrie

In 2001, Feasta's money group investigated the feasibility of establishing an interest-free bank in Ireland. The most promising way seemed to be to persuade the Swedish JAK Bank to establish an Irish branch. However, since JAK had no experience of running branches in Sweden, its directors turned the idea down. This is a report from a money group member who went to Sweden to study the bank.

Can a bank operate successfully if it does not charge interest on its loans? The Swedish JAK Medlemsbank (Members' Bank) certainly does – it has been called the safest bank in Sweden. This account of how it does so is based on two visits to its headquarters in Skövde and numerous conversations with JAK's enthusiastic staff and members, both in Sweden and in Ireland. I am indebted to the staff of JAK for their hospitality and assistance, and to Feasta for its financial support.

Savings Points

JAK's primary objective is to provide its members with interest-free loans. In order to accomplish this, it must attract interest-free savings. JAK uses a system of "Savings Points" in order to balance saving and borrowing.

Given the choice of borrowing without interest or saving without interest, most of us would gladly choose borrowing. While people are generally willing to save temporary surpluses of money in current accounts that don't pay interest, few are willing or able to save more significant amounts over a long period of time with no compensation. JAK cannot, of course, lend money without having savings on deposit and so, using an imaginative system of Savings Points, each member who wishes to take out a loan must save money first and, over a lifetime with JAK, every member will have saved roughly as much money and for the same period of time as they will have borrowed. You could almost imagine JAK as allowing its members to borrow (interest-free) from their future selves.

For a new JAK member, the first step towards an interest-free loan is to save and thereby earn Savings Points. These are calculated as the amount saved, multiplied by the number of months for which it is saved, multiplied by a Savings Factor. This factor varies according to the type of savings account the member has selected and is lower (about 0.7) for a demand account from which savings can be withdrawn at any time. For example, assuming a Savings Factor of 0.9, we have[1]:

€100 × 1 Month × 0.9 = 90 Savings Points

The Savings Factor varies with the type of deposit account and is lowest for demand accounts where savings can be withdrawn at any time (about 0.7).

Example 1: Either of these scenarios would earn identical Savings Points.

Term Savings

Instalment Savings

---

[1]   As a Swedish bank, JAK's business is denominated in Swedish Crowns but for convenience Euro will be used in this section.

After saving for a minimum of six months, a member may apply for a loan. In order to borrow €1 for one month, one Savings Point must be redeemed. The amount borrowed and the time taken to repay are entirely up to the member, provided that the appropriate Savings Points are available. For example, borrowing €90 (or €9,000) over 1 year uses as many savings points as borrowing €45 (or €4,500) with repayments spread over 2 years.

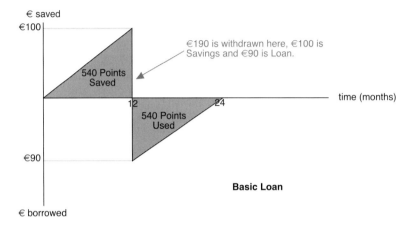

Basic Loan

Example 2: A Basic Loan.

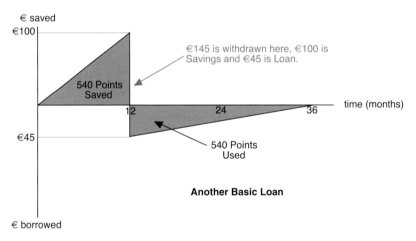

Another Basic Loan

Example 3: An alternative basic loan, borrowing half as much but repaying it over a longer period.

In addition to a Basic Loan that uses Savings Points already earned, members may apply for an Additional Loan using Savings Points that will be earned in the future. An "Allocation Factor" (currently 14) is multiplied by the member's current Savings Points to determine the number of points available for an Additional Loan.

Each loan repayment includes a savings instalment, and the payments are structured so that when the loan is fully repaid, all necessary Savings Points have been earned. A consequence of this is that upon full repayment of an Additional Loan, the member has built up significant savings. Savings made during the course of repaying a loan are known as Post-Savings, while those that precede the loan are Pre-Savings. Once the loan has been repaid, the balance of the post-savings is available to the member to be withdrawn or, as frequently happens, to be used as the start of saving for a new loan.

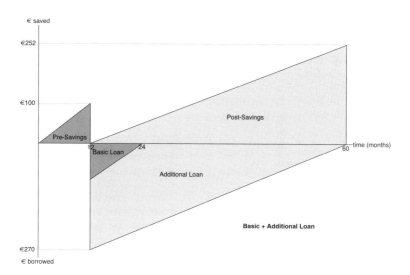

Example 4: A Basic Loan with an Additional Loan

There is no interest charged on a loan, of course, but members must place 6% of the value of the loan on deposit for the duration of the loan, and additionally pay a loan fee to cover administration costs. Members also pay 200 SEK (about €22) when they first join JAK and 200 SEK per year as a membership fee.

JAK is a virtual bank in the sense that it has no branches and business cannot be transacted in person. A necessary and prudent decision since the membership of JAK is quite spread out over a large country, and also resulting in no bias against rural members who would have to travel much farther to their nearest branch. A result of this "virtual" status is that JAK members must have an account with another bank with which to conduct their day-to-day financial affairs. Members transfer money into or out of their JAK basic account via post giro, bank giro or Internet into their other accounts. With improvements in technology and the changing financial infrastructure, JAK hopes in the near future to offer direct deposit of paycheques and credit/debit card facilities to its members. For some members, this might negate the need to bank elsewhere.

Credit control

Like any bank, JAK must ensure that loans can and will be repaid. Unlike most banks, however, JAK's system of saving and borrowing has several unique features that combine to give it an enviably low default rate.

A member applying for a loan is given a range of options for the loan size and duration based upon their desired loan amount, desired repayments and available savings points. When they have made their selection, the loan department within JAK must assess the member's ability to repay the desired loan. The member's income and expenses are evaluated with the assistance of computer software that calculates average living expenses for individuals and families based upon age and gender.

Between 20 and 25 applications are processed per week, and 95% are approved. Most loans are secured, either against property or with a personal guarantor. Loans for up to 37,000 SEK (about €4,000) with 2-5 years' duration can be unsecured, but these are limited to 5% of JAK's turnover and so surplus applications must be held in a queue until funds are available. The most common reason for borrowing is to refinance a conventional bank loan obtained to buy a house followed by purchasing a car and making home improvements.

In general, people who can save regularly are good performers when it comes to loan repayments. The JAK system where saving must precede borrowing is therefore ideally suited to attracting these regular savers. In addition, around half-way through repayment of a loan there is a break-even point where the Post-Savings on deposit are equal to the balance outstanding on the loan, and from this point forward the loan is fully secured by the member's savings.

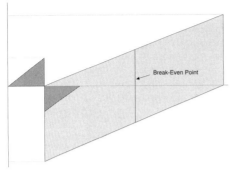

Break-Even Point

Very few JAK loans end in default. Borrowers are decidedly involved "members" as opposed to disinterested "customers". Many feel quite strongly about the idea of interest-free banking and this common bond goes a long way towards encouraging good behaviour. Personal guarantors rarely need to be asked to make good on their guarantee.

Liquidity

At the simplest level, a bank takes one person's savings and lends them to someone else. Ideological arguments aside, this presents some practical difficulties. Firstly, what if a saver wants their money back before the borrower has finished with it? Secondly, what if there are not enough or too many borrowers relative to savers?

The first point is generally dealt with in the banking system by having a reasonably large number of savers and making sure that enough money is set aside to cope with those who, on any given day, want some of their money back. While individuals might withdraw their savings in a random manner, a large group of savers will tend to be stable and predictable.

It is JAK's policy to keep a minimum of 20% of pre-savings available in either a bank account or in government bonds, either of which can be made available almost immediately. Too much liquidity means that money is lying idle rather than being lent out to members, so it is not seen as desirable to have much more than 20% on reserve. Post-savings do not need to have a component on reserve since these can only be withdrawn at specified times.

JAK also encourages stability from its savers by offering a higher Savings Factor in long-term deposit accounts. JAK members can choose from 6, 12 and 24-month deposit accounts which represent the advance notice required to make a withdrawal.

With regard to the second point, JAK has a more difficult balancing act between saving and borrowing than other banks, due to the fact that the two are intimately linked by Savings Points. Most people save with the intention of borrowing in the future. An excess of saving today could indicate too much demand for borrowing next year.

The Allocation Factor has a central role in the relationship between supply of savings and demand for loans. In general, the JAK board sets the Allocation Factor to reflect the current level of liquidity within the bank. The greater the pool of excess savings, the higher the Allocation Factor to encourage members to take out loans and reduce the excess. Unfortunately for JAK, the relationship between the Allocation Factor and the demand for loans is not as simple as this. In the short term, increasing the Allocation Factor can actually make things worse, as members decide to increase their Savings Points with a view to taking out a larger loan in the future. Excess demand for loans would be particularly problematic for JAK. Reducing the Allocation Factor would likely lead to an outcry from members who had made financial plans based on a higher factor. The alternatives, however, would be to refuse more loans or to introduce a waiting list. The dynamics of this saving/borrowing relationship are likely to be a constant challenge to JAK's management as the membership grows and the range of banking services offered by JAK expands.

JAK culture

A significant amount of JAK's energy is devoted to communicating with its 21,000-strong membership. JAK is a co-operative, fully owned by its members. In addition to a quarterly newsletter, 24 regional offices staffed by trained volunteers keep in touch with members through study groups and exhibitions. While JAK's primary function is to provide interest-free banking, it is also viewed by the membership as a vehicle for economic reform.

A recent innovation in support of economic reform is the Local Enterprise Bank. Community members save in a special JAK account and, rather than earning points themselves, their savings are used to provide an interest-free loan for a local enterprise. Savings are fully guaranteed, so members are not exposed to any financial risk. The first two projects to be funded in this way are an ecological slaughterhouse and a replica Viking village. It is an interesting experiment in local finance for local projects, and so far has been very warmly received by local media and participants. While savers don't, of course, receive any interest on their savings, they benefit both economically and otherwise from the improvements in their local economy and infrastructure as a result of the projects.

Conclusions

The JAK Members' Bank is unique in the commitment it inspires from its volunteers and staff. It provides affordable and responsible finance, and enables its members to have a say in where their money is invested. I have no doubt it will continue to be true to its purpose and values while exploring new frontiers in ethical finance.

Why interest-free banking matters

Does it matter whether a bank charges interest or not? After all, every bank has to charge for its services or it won't stay in business. Interest is simply the way that banks calculate the charge they make for the service they render when they approve a loan and for the risk they take on by doing so. Why shouldn't the charge be based on the amount of money involved, the time for which it's being lent and the demand for money at the time? Doesn't that method of calculation seem fair?

As Ana Carrie shows in her article, even the JAK Bank charges an arrangement fee for approving a loan and then an annual fee every year for as long as that loan is on its books. If these charges were expressed as an interest rate, they would work out at about 3%. That seems cheap until you realize that JAK requires its borrowers to lend it the sum that they borrow for an equivalent length of time. This means that, while they are lending to the bank, customers lose roughly the same amount of interest that they would have paid, net of the 3% service charge, if the JAK had been an ordinary bank and had charged them interest when they were borrowing.

So if the JAK system merely involves people losing on the swings what they gain on the roundabouts, why are the bank's members so enthusiastic about it? One reason is that some believe that the charging of interest sets up a growth compulsion in the economy and that, as perpetual economic growth is unsustainable, the development of a no-interest banking system is a key step towards building a sustainable economy.

The roots of this type of thinking run back to the time when gold was used as currency. Since gold did not increase itself, and very little was being mined, where, people asked, was the extra bullion to come from to pay the interest when both principal and interest had to be handed over at the end of the year? Obviously, the borrower could only obtain more gold if someone else had less, so lending money at interest meant that either the borrower impoverished himself when he paid over the extra or he impoverished someone else. And, as neither outcome was socially desirable, usury, as all forms of moneylending were called no matter how low the interest rate, stood morally condemned by both the Roman Catholic Church and by Islam.

Even though we now use paper currencies, this source-of-interest problem has not gone away. Since almost all money in circulation is issued on loan, the money to cover interest payments can only be obtained by borrowers if other borrowers have borrowed sufficiently more. Moreover, the necessity to pay interest on these additional borrowings means that the economy needs to expand if the proportion of world income which is paid over in interest to the lenders is not to increase.

But let's look at this argument a little more closely. How much is 'sufficiently more'? Not all the interest paid over to the banks gets withdrawn from the stock of money in circulation. Some of it is returned to the stock right away by being paid as interest to the people from whom the banks themselves are borrowing money. Some returns by being paid to cover the banks' operating costs, such as their wages bill. And the amount paid in dividends to the banks' shareholders goes back into the stock too. So only the fraction of the interest paid that ends up as the banks' retained earnings has to be borrowed back into the system. This is not a serious problem. If inflation was allowed to run at about 2.5% a year, that would be enough to allow the ratio between the level of outstanding loans and national income to be held constant. So, if one has a fairly relaxed attitude to inflation, the charging of interest

Continued...>>

GALWAY COUNTY LIBRARIES

is not a serious component of the growth compulsion. If the JAK bank made a surplus one year and increased its reserves, it would be just as much a part of the problem as its commercial, interest-charging, competitors.

Other members of JAK have more sophisticated reasons for giving the bank their support. Oscar Kjellberg, the development director, is opposed to charging interest because it transfers wealth from the poor to the rich and from declining areas - often rural ones - to more prosperous parts. "That sort of transfer doesn't happen with JAK," he says. "People save with us because they either want to borrow interest-free themselves or because they want to assign the right to an interest-free loan to a relative, a son or daughter, perhaps or to an organization they support. This means that most money is lent out in the same area that it was collected, and, if it's not, it's only loaned in a place and for a purpose which the original saver has approved."

In other words, perhaps the most important reason for backing JAK-style interest-free banking is that it limits a dangerous, destabilising positive feedback built into the present economic system. The feedback occurs because prosperous parts of the world get more investment because better returns can be had from projects there, which makes them still more prosperous, while poorer areas have what capital they possess taken away because no good projects can be found. As a result, the poorer areas fall further behind and people living in them are forced to leave to seek work wherever investment is going on. They take up residence in the expanding areas and add their spending to its rising income flow, generating further investment possibilities. And so the cycle goes on. A major cause of the emigration of young people from rural Ireland used to be that their parents had allowed their savings to be invested away from home. A JAK bank would help prevent a recurrence of that situation.

The JAK bank is a good example of a flourishing cooperative - the lenders and the borrowers and the owners of the bank are all the same people – engaged together in an independent enterprise which serves them all and accords with their beliefs. Although the services provided and the purposes for which loans are made are still fairly limited, these are expanding as Ana Carrie mentions at the end of her article. JAK is one of thousands of small cooperative banks around the world that confound the myth that financial services are best provided by the large capitalist institutions which dominate the mainstream financial services industry.

- Editors

A democracy for an ecological age

Mark Garavan

Economic dogma has limited the scope of political debate and action to such an extent that democratic societies are both unable and unprepared to avert the looming environmental crisis. A completely new system needs to be devised. This paper takes a solutions-based approach to developing a new democratic model for Ireland based on existing institutional and legal possibilities.

Mark Garavan is a lecturer in sociology at the Galway-Mayo Institute of Technology in Castlebar, Co. Mayo, and has been a researcher with the Environmental Change Institute at the National University of Ireland, Galway, since 2000. He was awarded a PhD by NUI, Galway, in 2003 for his thesis 'The Patterns of Irish Environmental Activism'. He is a member of Feasta's democracy group and was responsible, with David Healy, for Feasta's submission to Mayo County Council opposing the development of the terminal in North Mayo to process gas from the Corrib field.

Humanity is in a condition of global ecological peril and a radical restructuring of the contemporary model of representative democracy is going to be required to deal with it. However, it is likely that we will actually have to experience the peril directly as opposed to simply anticipating it before we generate the political will to redress the factors which caused it in the first place. The purpose of this paper is to identify those factors and to suggest how they can be addressed.

Modern industrial society – Ireland's included – is socially and ecologically unsustainable. Data on this is overwhelming and barely needs repeating. A few brief illustrations will suffice. For example, it is now widely acknowledged that human-induced carbon dioxide releases have begun to change the climate rapidly. The Third Assessment Report issued in 2001 by the UN's Intergovernmental Panel on Climate Change stated that average global temperatures may rise by almost 6 degrees centigrade by the century's end. We do not know where this will lead us, whether we are at the start of a runaway climate-change event or whether we can slow it down. What we do know is that this aggressive alteration of the earth's careful balance of natural systems will reconfigure the environmental conditions that gave rise to the complex life-forms presently in existence, including ourselves.

The planet's life-forms face other threats as well. The loss of habitats and pollution from a variety of sources have already caused an extraordinary extinction of species. In 1992, the biologist Edward Wilson estimated that 27,000 species were being lost each year but by the end of 2001, BBC 1's *State of the Planet* documentary warned that the situation was far worse. It asserted that unless radical corrective steps were taken now, up to a half of all the species on the planet would be lost within the next 50 to 100 years. The extermination of a species is irreversible. In truth, we don't know how many species there are so we cannot know definitively just how many are being lost. What we do know is that the reduction of bio-diversity is now occurring on a scale greater than any experienced in the last 65 million years and is a direct consequence of human activity.

Social unsustainability goes with environmental unsustainability. The planet simply cannot provide for western patterns of consumption to be extended everywhere. The world's richest countries, with 20% of global population, account for 86% of private consumption. The poorest 20% account for 1.3%. Nearly 60% of the population of the poorer counties, approximately 2.6 billion people, lack basic sanitation. A third do not have access to clean water. Moreover, it is doubtful whether food production can be increased to meet the needs of an expanding global population in view of topsoil depletion, inadequate fresh water supplies and a rapid decline in the supply of oil.

Since the 1960s, a sustained critique has been mounted on the existing political and economic system on *environmental* grounds, supplementing the plethora of social justice, Marxist and ethical critiques. Initially this environmentalist challenge was led by natural scientists such as Rachel Carson who were alarmed by the emerging evidence of the deterioration and degradation of biological systems. Since then writers and activists from a wide spectrum of theoretical perspectives have joined in. A common theme can be identified in the various contributions. It is that our ability as humans to *relate ecologically* to the natural world about us is deeply impaired.

This inability finds itself reflected in, and accentuated by, the dominant western worldview. This is the product of elements of Cartesian dualism, of the mechanistic science of Newton, of an anthropocentric conception of god, of the valuing of particular forms of knowing. This broad paradigm has worked itself out within a raft of self-referential social sciences. The negative ecological consequences of this have been most apparent in modern economic theory which is predicated on a series of assumptions such as its treatment of natural resources as non-cost income, and in classical political theory which has privileged the concept of nation-state sovereignty.

The consequence is that, enclosed within ever-expanding and apparently successful social systems, those with political and economic power no longer comprehend the fragility or limits of the wider natural setting within which we must operate. Their apprehension of the world has become phenomenologically suspect. Nowhere is this more apparent than in the use of GDP as a measure of material well-being. GDP is merely a record of the value of traded goods and services within a territorially-bounded economy. It ignores pollution, resource depletion, bio-diversity loss and even real levels of human well-being.

But if the evidence of unsustainability and dysfunction is so apparent, why do the electorates of the 'democratic' world not insist on change? Part of the answer must be that not enough of us see the need for change because the western economic and political system continues to give the appearance of being successful. Furthermore, it is difficult for many of us to imagine what an alternative society might look like. Another part of the answer is that the political mechanisms by which change on the scale required can be effected are under the control of powerful state and corporate interests who do not want any alterations whatsoever.

2. The contemporary democratic context

While there are a number of possible democratic models, the historically-dominant form has been that of the liberal nation state. In this model, citizens periodically elect representatives who make laws that are agreed to bind all. This democratic form has given rise to political parties that offer sets of policies and programmes to citizens at election time which they undertake to implement during the life of the representative assembly or parliament.

From an ecological perspective, this model has a number of structural flaws which reflect the cultural assumptions current in 18th and 19th century Europe and North America at the time it emerged. Liberal democracy is predicated on the sovereign hegemony of the nation state, which asserts a claim to absolute jurisdiction over a territorially-bounded space on behalf of a culturally-distinctive set of people. Consequently, the democracy that has emerged limits representation to present citizens over a certain age and explicitly excludes from representation people living outside the state's borders, future citizens of the state, future people living outside its borders, and all other life-forms, present and future, both inside and outside its borders. In other words, the nation-state is based on a form of representation which is contracted in terms of space, time and species.

However, leaving this to one side, the difficulty now facing us is that even the limited version of representative democracy offered by the contemporary state has ceased to function effectively at a time when we need popularly-responsive mechanisms of governance more than ever. Democracy is decaying at both poles of the democratic process – in the quality of representation (supply) on the one hand and in the engagement of citizens (demand) on the other. Both of these poles have become degraded and, rather than co-existing in a state of tension and mutual alertness which is their ideal state, they have declined into atrophy and apathy. The result of this has been that the formal political space of the liberal state has been abandoned as an arena within which change might be brought about. It has effectively conceded to the *status quo* of unsustainable policies.

At the supply end of the equation, three features are responsible for the de-democratisation. The first, and most important, is the dominance in public discourse of a certain version of economic rationality. This rationality elevates the functioning of a theoretically-imagined free market economy to be the epitome of sound social behaviour. Concepts such as competition, efficiency, free choice, privatisation and many others have been elevated to a non-problematic status as guarantors of prolonged economic growth and social well-being.

Within this rationality, there is less and less room for collective forms of decision-making that might run counter to its hegemony. The logic of the free-market is asserted to be the most rational logic available – anything else becomes, *ipso facto*, irrational and potentially dysfunctional. The claim made is that each individual pursuing his or her own maximum utility results in optimum social well-being. The state's role is merely to ensure the best environment within which this rationality can proceed. As a result, the rules of a particular economic language game have overwhelmed our ability to speak politically in any other credible way. Those who attempt to do so can be charged with being unreasonable, unrealistic, and even dangerous. The effect of this ascendancy on public discourse has been to close down the capacity of public representatives to speak credibly in any manner. They have become caught in an intellectual box beyond which they cannot manoeuvre.

But, even more alarmingly, this box is not just a theoretical construction. The second factor degrading democratic responsiveness is that power has effectively shifted from visible, accountable persons and institutions to invisible, globally-diffused sites and systems. The control exercised by globalised capital over the increasingly inter-dependant national economies has resulted in power being based upon the ability to control financial resources. Capital flows, investment decisions, currency speculations, and other choices exercised by large corporations directly affect employment levels and wealth levels in individual nation states. This is the power that keeps the box in place but, rather than resist this *de facto* ceding of domestic control, nation-states have accelerated the loss of power by creating international bodies such as the World Trade Organisation which legally binds them into the free trade regime. The result is that, irrespective of who is elected to *de jure* leadership positions within states, politicians can do little substantive policy making, i.e. nothing outside the limits of the box and certainly nothing on the scale required by the current ecological crisis.

Finally, in the last couple of decades, elected representatives have presided over the dismantling of the state's domain of concern, voluntarily in the west but often compulsorily elsewhere to meet the conditions of international loans or in response to military interventions. The dismantling has taken two directions. First has been the deregulation and privatisation of large areas of the economy that were formerly publicly owned, such as transport and electricity provision. Secondly, the state has increasingly devolved decision-making powers from democratic institutions to a variety of administrative bodies. Nowhere is this latter tendency more apparent than in the environmental policy-making area where questions of environmental impact have been determined by pollution-control agencies, environmental impact assessment procedures and 'scientifically'-grounded risk assessments. Environmental concerns have become shunted away from political fora and reduced to a series of technical problems to be processed by administrative bodies. The result has been the reduction, de-politicisation and domestication of environmentalism's alternative models and critiques.

In short, the supply of the representative function within nation states has been degraded by the dominance of free-market economic imperatives, the acquisition of effective power by private corporations, and the privatisation and bureaucratisation of the state. This supply contraction has met with, and in large part has itself influenced, a corresponding decline in the demand for representation from electorates. The demand contraction is an understandable response to the public's realisation of the limits of representative effectiveness. The growing loss of belief in liberal democracy is summed up in commonly-occurring phrases such as – 'It makes no difference who you vote for', 'They are all the same', 'They are all puppets who can do nothing anyway'. This assessment by electorates is confirmed by revelations of political corruption, which have swept many western states in recent years. As a result it has become apparent that the formal channel of exercising democratic power grounded on votes exercised by citizens has become outflanked by informal channels of influence, resting on financial power and political funding (licit and illicit) by the corporate few.

The consequence has been a further significant impetus to the de-politicisation of the public sphere, with the category of citizen being progressively replaced by that of consumer. The drama of politics has degenerated into a theatre of the absurd as powerless and homogeneous political representatives seek to cajole votes from disengaged, atomised individuals whose focus has become increasingly centred on the domain of their own personal autonomy. The electorates of the west now largely expect nothing from the political system, least of all the possibility of a vision of social transformation being translated into a politically-realisable project.

3. What must now be done

Given this context – social and ecological unsustainability and democratic decay – what then is to be the role of an engaged civil society? Despair and despondency, while understandable, will not get us anywhere. We are surely challenged to renewed forms of activism in defence of our humanity and planet. I want to suggest three steps to be taken at once.

The first is to create new networks de-linked from the present system, what Rudolf Bahro[1] used to call 'liberated zones'. These would be economic, social, political and cultural spaces outside the logic and control of the present economic and political system. They might involve local trading systems, new currencies, acts of self-governance, reclamations of civic space, communal self-reliance. These networks may be based upon face-to-face contact, as in traditional geographical communities, or they may utilise the possibilities created by the internet for virtual community and long-distance liaison. The point is to bring people together now to create real, existentially-viable alternatives and support networks in order to begin the process of

constructing a new, sustainable society. No limit, bar human imagination and ingenuity, can be placed on what these networks may be like or upon what their de-linking activities might be. The challenge to de-link now in every way possible appears to provide a key focus for a new and committed activism.

Secondly, the movement for change must be political. De-linking must not be the same as opting out. Our brothers and sisters and fellow species cannot be abandoned to their fate. Activists must re-enter the political sphere with radical critiques of the present system. This is in order to hasten the downfall of the system. The quicker it's gone the better will be the opening conditions for a new model. A political programme centred on policies of sustainable survival needs to be developed to which all strands of progressive opinion subscribes and constantly puts before electorates. What mainstream opinion requires above all is an extension to the limits of its economic and political imagination so that it comes to realise that, as the participants in the World Social Forum have been asserting for the last three years from Porto Alegre in 2001 on, 'another world is possible'.

Finally, and perhaps most importantly of all, we must develop the new ideas that will inform the ecological society. The present system with its assertions of rationality needs to be de-mystified. New ideas and social models will draw on the knowledge gleaned from all the de-linked networks and experiments mentioned above. The coherence and viability of these ideas are crucial because we may yet cling to one hope – that as the nation-states collapse economically and environmentally, they will reach out and clutch onto these new policies in desperation and reconfigure themselves sustainably to ensure their own survival. The task of idea-formation is not just one for a narrow band of 'intellectuals' – it is for all who have engaged in a praxis of dissent and de-linking. Indeed, the ideas that we may formulate now will only be provisional. We cannot know what will work and what will fail in the future – the ecological context that we must incorporate into future governance and economic activity ensures that learning and reflexivity will be an essential attribute of every alternative model.

4. Towards an Irish model of ecological governance

In the final part of this paper I wish to take up the challenge posed above and to move beyond the generalities of 'oughts' and ideals to sketch what the contours of a putative Irish eco-state might look like. I will draw on the Irish Constitution of 1937 in order to argue that models for democratic systems that aspire to environmental sustainability can be both flexibly conceived and yet institutionally available in order to be properly embedded within existing cultural and political contexts. I am not proposing an *ideal* political structure but, rather, suggesting a *possible* model for immediate application.

We are not of course starting from scratch. A considerable body of work has been done on what the desired alternative green world might look like. In general, green conceptions of a sustainable economic and social model have organised themselves around a number of key points such as communitarianism, participative democracy, communal self-reliance, and ecologically-sensitive, human-scale technologies. The assumption is that these principles, if allowed to determine the political and economic order, will invariably produce a sustainable society.

There is little doubt that that might be so. However, while these principles are a necessary condition for ecological well-being, they are unlikely to be a sufficient condition. It is likely that we will need interlocking systems of governance in order to balance potential problems which might arise given that we are dealing with human constructions. For example, a community-based government is vulnerable to authoritarianism (especially towards minorities or deviants from norms), and introspection, and potentially to non-compliance with wider ecological standards. Therefore, a further level of governance, such as a reconfigured state, may be required as a corrective to ensure equity and compliance and to *institutionally* represent the interests of non-participating members of the broadly-defined ecological community i.e. other communities, future citizens and other life-forms. But states also need an inter-state mechanism to ensure that they comply with internationally-agreed norms. To solve the environmental problems facing us we will need binding international agreements. In short, we need multi-level government to ensure that no one defaults, either locally or nationally, from the constraints of acting sustainably.

The Irish State can be reconfigured in this way pretty quickly using the constitution as it stands without any further amendment. Indeed, this reconfiguation could be offered as part of the programme of a radically re-politicised environmental movement. The goal of the reconfiguration is to remove the structural flaws built into the liberal state by re-ordering the balance of its representative weight towards the non-participating interests of future generations and other life-forms and towards maximising democratic participation. The point is to re-align democratic principles with ecological principles in order to better ensure ecological outcomes.

4.1 Local government

There is no doubt that good ecological governance must be primarily local governance. This argument, which centres on reconnecting people to place, creating self-reliant communities and reducing to a minimum transportation and long-distance trade, has been convincingly made in the environmental literature and does not require re-elaboration. The Irish Constitution permits a radical restructuring of decision-making towards the local.

Article 15.2.1

The sole and exclusive power of making laws for the State is hereby vested in the Oireachtas: no other legislative authority has power to make laws for the State.

Article 15.2.2

Provision may however be made by law for the creation or recognition of subordinate legislatures and for the powers and functions of these legislatures.

It is clear from this provision that extensive amounts of law making can be devolved to local units of governance. These units are described as 'legislatures', i.e. law-making bodies. The powers and functions of these legislatures can be set by the Oireachtas. Furthermore, the Oireachtas may not only create such bodies, it may also *recognise* them. This implies that de-linked self-governing units are entirely compatible with the existing constitutional structure of the State and may be facilitated by the State following their formation. What this shows is that a radical switch to local governance and sustainability can be legally accomplished *immediately*.

4.2 Legislation

The Constitution permits considerable latitude regarding how law is made by the Oireachtas. There are no stipulations regarding the types of legislative stages that Bills must pass through before becoming law. The present practice is for Bills to go through five stages which differ largely according to the time each allocates for debate and amendment. It is therefore possible to have an *ecological or sustainability* stage that would in particular enshrine the precautionary principle in any piece of legislation. Such a stage would oblige the Oireachtas to discuss the Bill under this criterion. Such a stage may also be processed by sub-committees of the Oireachtas which would permit direct participation by groups representing environmental and other interests.

It is also possible to provide the Seanad with a specific brief on environmental matters. The constitutional practice has been for the Seanad to review legislation coming from the Dail. In addition, the Taoiseach's eleven Seanad nominees could be selected so as to represent specific ecological interests. Furthermore, some of the Seanad's five electoral panels could have environmental bodies and organisations added to them as nominating bodies, in particular the panels pertaining to national culture and professional interests, agriculture and allied interests, and industry and commerce. Furthermore, the Constitution permits these panels to be elected by much wider constituencies than they are at present. Thus they may be directly elected by the people under Article 18.10.1.

Finally, there is provision for direct participation in law making by the electorate under Article 27. This provision applies to Bills deemed to be 'of such national importance that the will of the people thereon ought to be ascertained' (Article 27.1). This possibility is triggered by a petition, comprising a majority of the Seanad and not less than one-third of the Dail, addressed to the President who makes the final decision. In the context of the technological possibilities opened up by electronic voting one could anticipate an ecologically responsive state being more amenable to such forms of direct democracy.

4.3 An Environmental Council

Betraying its roots in the vocationalist/fascistic 1930s, the constitution also makes provision for the establishment of councils representing social and economic interests.

Article 15.3.1

The Oireachtas may provide for the establishment or recognition of functional or vocational councils representing branches of the social and economic life of the people.

Article 15.3.2

A law establishing or recognising any such council shall determine its rights, powers and duties, and its relation to the Oireachtas and to the Government.

It seems entirely possible that this provision permits the establishment, or *recognition,* of an Environmental Council that could be granted extensive powers and duties, including a supervisory function in national ecological policy formation, ensuring conformity to ecological norms, legislative inputs and above all in articulating at a national level the ecological interests of future generations and other species. This Council may be directly elected by the people, or indirectly by the local units of government, and may be made subject to recall by the electorate.

4.4 Ecological Courts

Finally, it is also possible to make use of the law and courts to further ensure ecological sustainability. This could be done through an Act which establishes new environmental rights and corresponding duties or elaborates existing ones. Such an Act could be supplemented by the formation of a specialised Ecological Court which could adjudicate on matters that may contravene ecological principles enumerated in the Act. These provisions could replace, or add to, existing Special Area of Conservation designations, Environmental Impact Assessment procedures and various planning assessments. Furthermore, an Environmental Ombudsman could also be created along existing models to process complaints under environmental legislation.

There is already a personal right recognised by the Irish courts which could provide for a much expanded set of juridically processible rights. Under Article 40.3.1 the State 'guarantees to respect, and, as far as practicable, by its laws to defend and vindicate the personal rights of the citizen'. In a case brought in 1965[2] against the validity of adding fluoride to the public water supply, the courts held that while it was not proven that this was dangerous to the health of the individual, there was nevertheless a right to

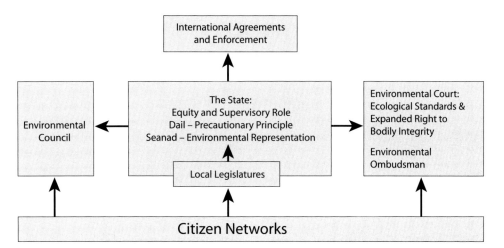

| Citizen Networks |

bodily integrity implied by Article 40.3.1 even though not explicitly mentioned there. The recognition of this right opens up considerable environmental possibilities which could be expanded in a Bodily Integrity Act. The High Court defined the right as follows:

> I understand the right to bodily integrity to mean that no mutilation of the body or any of its members may be carried out on any citizen under authority of the law except for the good of the whole body and that no process which is or may, as a matter of probability, be dangerous or harmful to the life or health of the citizens or any of them may be imposed (in the sense of being made compulsory) by an Act of the Oireachtas (Kenny J).

This definition was endorsed and expanded in the Supreme Court.

> … I see no reason why the principle should not also operate to prevent an act or omission of the Executive which, without justification, would expose the health of a person to risk or danger (O'Dalaigh J.).

It seems clear that there is a basis here for a greatly expanded set of environmental rights based on existing case law and supported by legislation which would permit legal challenges to any attempt by the State to expose the health of any citizen to even the risk of danger. The ecological implications are obvious.

In summary then, a reconfiguration of the Irish political system that may be required in the immediate short term might result in a model with the following general features (see above).

Such a political infrastructure would be complementary to a new economic infrastructure based on local trading systems operating with local currencies, supplemented by national and international currencies.

5. Conclusion

While we cannot be overly prescriptive about the appropriate models for ecological governance, we do need to have some preliminary working ideas in position as new models may be required at relatively short notice. It is in that spirit that this paper is offered.

We cannot know the conditions in which the new model will be introduced. It may be at a time of widespread social chaos and state authoritarianism. If so, there is little doubt that the lives of many millions more people will be in danger than is the case at present.

The development of new social models for an ecological age is now the most pertinent task for the contemporary environmental movement. It is a political task to be undertaken with a new, enriched understanding of politics that defines its aims as that of furthering *the fulfilment of human interest by integrating it with the interest of the total earth community*. That task is open-ended – it can be learnt and refined only as we go along and its outcome is unclear. What is involved here is not just tinkering with an economic and political system. It is nothing less than the construction of a new civilisation.

Endnotes

1 Bahro, Rudolf (1986). Building the Green Movement. GMP Publishers.
2 Ryan V. Attorney General 1965.

Political economy should be the name of the game

Margaret Legum

Too many aspects of economic life have been insulated from political control.

It is time we consigned to history the idea that economics is an arcane, highly complicated discipline, understandable only by brilliant minds who have engaged in long years of study. A huge confidence trick has been perpetrated upon the people of all countries. We are expected to believe that political issues may be decided only within esoteric economic constraints to which only the educated few have access. Margaret Thatcher encapsulated that belief as TINA (There Is No Alternative).

This ideology accounts for the decline in democracy - growing voter apathy, cynicism about politicians and politics, desperate street protest and a culture of hopelessness. What is the point of joining a political party and voting if you cannot thereby influence people's access to the fruits of the economy? Why bother if employment, the rate of interest, the burden of debt, the price of your currency, investment in schools, clinics and utilities - who gets what for doing what - are all beyond the reach of politics? These are all the stuff of economics. And they all involve decisions made in the political arena on the basis of political values.

So what happened? Why has politics given way to a particular kind of economics that creates the same kind of society worldwide? Why do elected governments everywhere pursue much the same economic policies, regardless of the political policies they promised before elections? Tony Blair's Labour Party was swept to power on an unprecedented wave of revulsion against the previous governments' promotion of huge inequality and the decimation of the British industrial base. The basic thrust of economic policy has continued under Blair.

The same applies all over Europe, Asia, Africa and the Americas. Democratic elections in Eastern Europe produced policies creating obscene wealth for the few, alongside mass poverty, destitution and 'ethnic' fighting over scarce resources between people who had lived peacefully together before.

In South Africa, the ANC, with its roots deep in egalitarian political values, was joyfully elected to promote redistributive development. It promised an economics that would match the political miracle to benefit everyone. Today we have even more people living in helpless destitution; redistribution of access to utilities is undermined by poverty; utilities are privatised to foreign companies; and at the top galactic incomes are earned. Street protests multiply.

Why? I am not cynical enough to believe that ANC leaders − and left leaders everywhere - have been seduced by sticking their own noses into the top trough. The answer is that the Thatcher government did something that does, indeed, tie the hands of all governments, so that politics has become subject to a particular version of economics. That was the way to give political inevitability to an economic system that favours a particular sector of society. It was a political act, justified by an untruth − that economics can be removed from politics

That something was innocently named 'the deregulation of capital'. It meant that accumulated money − capital − was allowed to roam the world in search of the most profitable way to accumulate more. It follows that all governments − all politicians − are now required to woo capital or lose it.

The way you do that is to keep wages low and limit the activities of trade unions, so as to attract footloose entrepreneurs. You maintain a low tax base − rich people do not like taxes − so government revenue falls. You keep inflation low and interest rates high, regardless of the effect on growth. You lose employment by opening your markets to cheap foreign goods. You limit government activity, including subsidised government services; and you make your own assets available to the international private sector. Above all, you do not control capital coming in and going out, allowing the exchange rate to fluctuate and speculators to speculate – creating thereby difficulties for your own importers and exporters. You allow your own capital to be listed on stock markets overseas.

You do all this not because it helps to develop your own employment, markets, growth and wealth base – far from it – but because if you did not you would be in worse trouble. The Big Boys, as they say, can pull the plug on your economy while capital is unregulated.

This really has to stop. One terrifying aspect of capital deregulation is the potential for catastrophic financial implosion. Over 90% of currency transactions are purely speculative. The amount of debt world-wide – international, national and domestic – is over three times the value of goods and services everywhere. The last time footloose capital ruled the world was the 1920s; and it ended in the hideous depression of the 1930s, followed by a world war.

Perhaps, frighteningly, that crash has to happen before capital can be brought to heel by elected governments. Then democratic political dissent, based upon political economy, will become the basis of a revived democracy.

But understanding of the current dynamic is now widespread within civil society internationally. The 'Battle of Seattle' began the international process of uniting in opposition to the current world economic order. Anarchists apart, civil society everywhere has adopted the idea that governments must be put back in charge. Democracy cannot happen if unaccountable people and forces -like 'the markets' - in practice make policy.

The question is how this is to be done. There are governments that have defied the capital markets to assert control over their own economies. Notably, the government of Malaysia brought itself out of free fall in 1998 by closing its capital markets, setting its own currency price and stimulating its own economy – in the teeth of opposition by the international financial institutions. China – and to some extent India – keep some control over their exchanges; and in different ways so have Chile, Singapore and Peru.

But more vulnerable and poorer countries, especially in Africa, have felt unable to follow suit. Their governments have, rightly or wrongly, been less courageous. There is no doubt that an internationally-supportive mechanism would enable more governments to take charge.

International capital domination would be reduced by reform of the Bretton Woods financial institutions, now wholly controlled by the richer countries in whose interests footloose capital operates. Their reform would allow international agreement on the control of capital, leaving defiant countries less exposed.

More radical and long-term is the idea of an international clearing agency that would manage transactions between countries in their own currencies. This is based upon the proposal by the British economist J.M. Keynes at the original Bretton Woods conference. He also proposed that both creditor and debtor countries should pay into his Clearing Union a penalty – like a rate of interest. That would provide an incentive for all countries to preserve equilibrium in their balance of payments.

Keynes wrote at the time: 'In my view the whole management of the domestic economy depends upon being free to have the appropriate rate of interest without reference to the rates prevailing elsewhere in the world. Capital control is a corollary to this.'

Margaret Legum helped found, and is a key figure in, SANE, the South African New Economics Foundation. She studied economics at Rhodes University and Cambridge. She and her late husband, Colin, were banned from their home country, South Africa, in 1962 after Margaret had launched the call for international sanctions against the apartheid regime. She now lives in the fishing viiilage of Kalk Bay outside Cape Town and works as a lecturer and journalist.

On productivity

*a Socratic dialogue between
a Buddhist Lama (BL) and
a Mainstream Economist (ME)*

Nadia Johanisova

BL: I have come to ask you a question.
ME: Well, go ahead. But I only have five minutes.

BL: What is productivity and why is it so important in your culture?
ME: Well, that's an easy one. Productivity is a measure of how many outputs you produce with a given amount of inputs. You try for higher productivity in order to get a higher profit.

BL: Could you give me an example?
ME: A factory tries to produce as many cars with as few people as possible.

BL: Excuse me, 1 still do not understand. What are the inputs in this case and what are the outputs?
ME: Well, the outputs are the cars and the inputs are the people, but we do not call them that.

BL: What do you call them?
ME: We call them labour.

BL: That is very strange. But why does this factory try to produce as many cars as possible? Are cars such a good thing?
ME: Well – yes. Cars are very useful. For example, a car takes me to work every day so that I do not have to walk.

BL: You do not like to walk?
ME: To tell you the truth, I love to walk, but I can't really afford the time. 1 would be too unproductive.

BL: So what do you produce?
ME: I produce – er – economic theories.

BL: Like the one about productivity?
ME: Well, yes.

BL: Let us get back to your example. I have heard that cars pollute the atmosphere.
ME: That is true, but it is only an externality.

BL: What do you mean by externality?
ME: I mean that the productivity theory never expected such a thing to happen. Products according to this theory are all beneficial to humankind. Our philosophers explained that to us two hundred years ago. Life in cultures which have low productivity tend to be nasty, brutish and short. But an emphasis on productivity has led to the accumulation of capital and to expanding production possibility curves, we have been able to produce more and more things and this has made our lives more pleasant, more interesting than those in traditional cultures. We are now happier. At least that is what our theory says.

BL: I have been in your country but the people – or labour as you call them – do not seem to be happier than in my country. They seem to have much less time to do the things they really enjoy.
ME: That is because they have to make money to be able to buy the things which make life worth living. Our people are not only labour. They are also consumers, which means they do a lot of shopping.

BL: But if they spend all their time working to make money and producing things to be more productive, and then shopping, when do they actually enjoy life? When do they find time to be together, to take a walk, to enjoy nature?
ME: Well... some of them, usually the ones who made a profit because their factories were productive, buy a house in the country when they retire. There they are far from the pollution of the city and can really start enjoying life. 1 look forward to such a future myself one day.

BL: So productivity makes most people work harder and produce more and more strange things, such as cars, which often destroy the environment. They can't afford to take a walk because they have to be productive, but then some of them, the ones who thought up ways of being even more productive, get a chance to stop being productive and enjoy life in their old age. Well, friend, you have not persuaded me of the merits of productivity. Have you ever considered, as a society, becoming less productive as a path to greater happiness?
ME: To tell you the truth, that has stopped being an option.

BL: What do you mean?
ME: Our country has signed agreements with other countries saying we will do nothing to stop them importing their products to our country if they can produce them more productively - with cheaper labour or fewer environmental constraints, for example. So we need to be productive to compete with them.

BL: And why did your country sign such agreements?
ME: Isn't that obvious? So that our people can buy things more cheaply than would otherwise be the case.

BL: But if someone else produces these things which you need, what will your labour do?
ME: They will have to accept a lower wage packet or maybe part-time jobs in services.

BL: Will this make them more happy?
ME: No, but it is a price we have to pay for making the whole world a more productive place.

BL: You mean – the world will be producing more and more things with less and less inputs?
ME: Yes.

BL: And by inputs you mean people?
ME: Er – yes.

BL: Do you get the feeling that somewhere along the way, people have become a means to an end? To the end of producing ever more things? Most people here are not happy, have no time to enjoy life and nature is suffering from externalities. All this, it seems to me, is caused by the product of economists such as you – this theory of productivity. Maybe you economists should have been less productive in the first place!

Nadia Johanisova teaches new economics at the Masaryk University in the Czech Republic

Book Reviews

Introducing a
new model of democracy

JOHN BARRY

Gaian Democracies – Redefining Globalisation and People-power
Roy Madron and John Jopling
Schumacher Briefing no. 9 Green Books for the Schumacher Society, 2003
ISBN 1 90399 828 X £8.00

Feasta members have written four Schumacher Briefings. This one, by John Jopling, one of Feasta's founders, and Roy Madron, an expert in systems improvement and participatory planning, investigates the kind of democracy required to enable human societies to make the many changes needed to achieve social justice and sustainability.

Imagine a democratic world as complex, adaptive and flexible as the ecosystems with which it interacts. It is made up of millions of engaged, active citizens connected together in a global network of democracies that transcend the nation-state, all organised around the twin goals of sustainability and global/social justice. Imagine further that the internal principles of the network are decentralisation, maximum diversity and 'people-power', which together operate as the organising principles of society characterised as a form of 'social learning'.

A pipe dream? Another form of 'green utopianism' or 'greenprints' for a future that will not happen? Well, think again. *Gaian Democracies* is a bold, innovative book that argues that in these times of increasing global economic and ecological disaster, the desirable is now the necessary.

The book embeds democracy in the complex natural and human systems in which the economy and polity are based. It not only takes on the forces organising 'globalisation' and shows their underlying principles and all-too-evident flaws, but, more importantly, it offers an alternative. Taking its lead and inspiration from the anti-globalisation slogan, 'another world is possible', Roy Madron and John Jopling offer a positive political agenda for an earth-based and human-scale democratic political project of renewal and systemic change. As they put it, "the Gaian democracy paradigm reflects our still-

growing understanding of concepts such as organisational dialogue and learning, soft-systems, cybernetics...complexity and chaos theory, symbiosis, inter-dependency and diversity and, of course, Gaia" (p.132).

Their explicit adoption of a 'systems methodological approach' to analysing the political, economic and environmental problems of contemporary global societies is innovative and a welcome addition to the emerging literature on the alternatives to globalised and globalising capitalism. This book demonstrates the utility and insights to be gained from seeing human societies, polities and economies from a 'soft systems' perspective.

Analytically, it adds an important distinction between 'wicked' and 'tame' problems. According to the authors, 'tame' problems are those that arise from linear systems, have definable outcomes and can be conclusively 'solved'. Examples of tame problems include getting rid of a computer virus, or putting a man on the moon – you know what to do and know when you've done it (pp.40-41). 'Hard systems' thinking and approaches – those drawing on engineering, technology and mechanics – are suited to such problems.

'Wicked' problems are of a different order and kind altogether. They are non-linear, have no definitive 'solution', or 'right' answer, are dynamic and change over time and as a result of intervention. They cannot be defined clearly and "The problem-solving process ends when you run out of time, money, energy or some other resources – not when some perfect solution emerges" (p.42). The vast majority of the problems we face in the 21st century are 'wicked' problems which require 'soft' rather than 'hard' systems solutions and methodologies.

Now, a number of important conclusions follow from this (on the face of it) simple four-fold model – soft/hard systems thinking and wicked/tame problems. The first is that applying hard systems thinking to wicked problems will not only not work (and therefore be a waste of resources and time), but will in all likelihood only serve to exacerbate the existing problem and/or create new wicked problems. In short, applying a technocratic 'solution' to a 'wicked' or non-technocratic problem, or indeed approaching a complex, wicked problem using a 'problem-solving' (as opposed to a 'problem coping' approach or mentality) will fail.

In relation to the natural world, the authors rightly point out that, "Natural systems cannot be controlled with hard systems thinking" (p.57). Yet this is the dominant approach we find in (western) societies and its institutions in science, economics and politics. Examples of this vary from 'technocratic' approaches to 'crime' – such as the installation of CCTV cameras or issuing of identity cards, to increasingly medical and pharmaceutical approaches to health (including, worryingly, mental health). What is even more disconcerting is that the dominant paradigm prescribes that the solution to the problems caused by technocratic and 'hard systems' thinking is...more hard-systems thinking and technocratic approaches! Like the fabled lance of the Greek mythical hero Achilles, technology and hard-systems thinking are held to be able to 'heal' the wounds they themselves have caused.

The dominant 'worldview' or 'paradigm' for dealing with problems in modern societies seeks clear, definite 'solutions' rather than seeing a lot of the problems we face (especially ecological ones) as problems we cannot 'solve' or get rid of (due to their intrinsic complexity, interrelatedness and 'fuzzy' boundaries), but as ones for which we need to develop 'coping mechanisms'. That is, we need soft-systems methodologies to cope and learn to live with 'wicked' problems and minimise their negative impact on human interests and well-being.

This raises a second important point – 'hard' systems thinking is closely associated with an elite, top-down, 'expert' based form of thinking and acting, It is generally non-democratic, whereas a soft-systems approach is implicitly democratic, amenable to bottom-up and participatory involvement of all those with an interest in the problem, not just those who have 'expert' knowledge. Wicked problems do not typically require 'expert' knowledge, but rather require knowledge gained from experience, an ability to learn from and with others and to be open to new ideas. And since knowledge is power (especially in our increasingly knowledge-based society), if the knowledge, wisdom and experience we need to deal with wicked problems is not the preserve of an elite, expert minority (which is not the say we do not need such hard-systems experts), then it follows that 'people knowledge' (or vernacular learning and knowing) is what we most need to deal with the vast majority of the problems we face. Democratic systems rather than non-democratic ones are more likely to be successful in dealing with the problems we face. This is where 'Gaian democracies' come in. As the authors rightly suggest, "the global-scale issues now facing the whole of humanity are all 'wicked' problems, calling for governments to tackle them through soft-systems approaches" (p.52).

In relation to the democratic project the authors outline, one of the many interesting issues they discuss is the vital importance of 'liberatory leadership', as an oft-missing piece of democratic theory and practice. While they rightly seek to reconfigure democracy as a form of self-organisation (rather than control) (p.35), they are also to be commended for explicitly recognising the centrality of leadership to any viable alternative democratic political project to 'globalisation'. Too often, radical democratic thinkers and activists have shied away from the issue of leadership, wrongly associating it by definition with hierarchical, non-democratic or repressive/authoritarian principles or potentials. Yet, it is clear that effective democratic projects, whether one looks at it historically or in terms of the examples around the world today of successful democratic experiments, require effective leaders.

The authors cite some examples of liberatory leadership in the contemporary world, from the 'participatory budget' process in Porto Alegre in

Brazil, under the leadership of the Workers Party (pp.21-22) to examples from the business world – Visa International (pp.17-18) and the Semco Corporation (pp.18-19). Liberatory leadership is characterised by aiming to release and utilise 'people power' based on forms of dialogue, participation and learning between leaders and led. Indeed, it struck me how a lot might be learnt from the various innovative, 'soft-systems' (and therefore 'democratic') thinking and acting going on in the business world – not the first place I, and many others, I suspect, would think of looking for inspiration!

These democratic models see decision-making as a form of collective and institutional learning based on self-reflexive/recursive modes of organisation. They are thus in keeping with the innovative democratic and social scientific thinking associated with Jurgen Habermas and Ulrich Beck, with developments within 'deliberative democracy' and with work on the theory and practice of 'greening' democracy and active citizenship.

Don't run away with the idea that the book simply seeks to develop attractive but utopian models. The authors discuss in great detail the origins, dynamics, principles and institutions/actors of 'The Global Monetocracy' (Chapter 3) which they see as the main obstacle to the creation a global network of Gaian democracies. Taking a systems approach rather than a conspiracy one, they offer a forensic analysis of this purposeful, elite-dominated network which controls the current neo-liberal project of destructive globalisation. The book argues that the debt-based money system not only gives financial institutions (such as the World Bank, the IMF and private multinational banks and other financial corporations) great power, but also acts to drive the global economic system as a whole towards ever-destructive economic growth. As they put it, "In systems-thinking terms, the growth imperative imposed by the debt-money system is a positive feedback mechanism – a vicious spiral" (p.71).We need negative feedback mechanisms (democratic political ones rather than financial economic ones) to change this.

However, it is not simply the global debt-based money system (and the dominance of the US dollar in the global economy) that needs to be tackled. From a 'Gaian democratic' perspective, we also need to change the 'nation-state' system

and the notion and practices based upon the foundational idea of 'national sovereignty'. The reasons for this are many, but principal among them is the claim that "The principle of national sovereignty is inherently conflictual and competitive...under the cloak of national sovereignty, the nation-state provides the executive and legislative support required for the monetisation and corporate ownership of the entire human and natural worlds" (p.79). The continued existence of nation-states and 'international non-society' ensure that there is no democracy at the global level – which suits the global monetocracy perfectly.

Central to the continued existence of the corporate-state rule is the manufacturing of consent together, I would suggest, with the deliberate lowering of expectations by governments, something that is best exemplified by the Blair administration in the United Kingdom. As the authors put it, "Opinion-moulding has become the prime skill of both partners in the big business-government coalition" (p. 96). Equally, the active manufacturing of consent can be measured not just by active affirmation of state rule (through such mechanisms as elections – in which less and less citizens participate), but also by passive acceptance, and silence as opposed to 'voice'. In the modern representative democratic world, sullen silence or even alienation from the political system is perversely counted as consent or even more perversely as happiness.

If there is one criticism I have of this otherwise excellent 'primer for democratic thinking and acting' it is the issue of agency and strategy. Simply put, I would suggest that the authors need to write another book outlining how they think their ideas could be put into action to help fulfil the promise that 'another world is possible'. While they are of course extremely positive about the democratic resistance, energy and innovation that characterises the World Social Forum and what they call the civil society movement (CSM), as offering real hope in challenging the global monetocracy, they caution that "the evidence shows that the CSM is not, and will never be, capable of" making another world possible" (p.102). However, they do not, in my view, really offer a convincing or sustained argument to back up this statement, due perhaps to the fact that the chapter dealing with this issue is the shortest in the book (pp.99-106).

For example, I found it odd that while the authors have rightly criticised the failures of representative democracy as a systemic part of the problem, they then proceed to criticise the civil society movement (anti-globalisation/global justice movement) for failing to participate in liberal/representative democracy. They criticise the movement on the grounds that, "There is no discussion of even the possibility of founding powerful new political parties, fighting elections, winning office and forming governments with a mandate for fundamental economic and social change" (p.106). This would be to work within the existing political system, a reformist approach that they have elsewhere dismissed as inadequate to the task. Yet perhaps the authors are working with a too-narrow concept of the 'political' here, and fail to see the synergies possible between direct action politics outside the existing liberal democratic framework, and innovative, challenging methods of working with, in and through the institutions and practices of liberal democracy. Politics, especially democratic politics, as the authors will only be too aware, cannot be associated simply with elections, political parties and parliaments.

Another criticism I had was in relation to the connection between the democratic project they so eloquently articulate and the question of global/social justice. Perhaps this was more a failure of communication rather than principle (or perhaps in my own reading), but I did feel that a more nuanced approach was perhaps needed in relation to the issue of distributive injustice. For example, the authors state that, "If 'everyone' is responsible for the problems generated by the system, then 'everyone' is also responsible, somehow, for helping to find ways of tackling them – a profoundly democratic implication" (p.38). However, this of course fails to note the 'injustice' at the heart of the global economic system – namely that it is clearly not the responsibility of 'everyone' for either the maintaining of the system itself or the social, economy and environmental problems caused by the system. The issue here is that of power, and the realisation that responsibility is in proportion to power. This means that the powerful, those with the money, political influence and cultural power bear the most responsibility, in terms of being the 'cause' of the problem. So while it may be that we all have our part to play in finding democratic solutions to 'non-democratic' problems, this is not the same as saying everyone is responsible for the problems of the system they are part of.

However, such quibbles should not deflect in any way from this excellent and important book. Indeed, since it is written in a spirit of dialogue and communication my comments should be read in a similar spirit, as someone who was both informed and more importantly inspired to continue the task of learning new ways of thinking and acting to cope with the global and local problems we face in the crucial decades ahead.

Dr John Barry is Deputy Director and Reader in Politics at the Institute of Governance, Public Policy and Social Research, Queen's University, Belfast.

How the media limits the range of public debate

DAVID YOUELL

Free to be Human
David Edwards
Green Books, 1995
ISBN 1 87009 888 9 £9.95

Unconventional ideas find it hard to get mentioned in the mainstream media. A giant filter system keeps us uninformed, confused and, above all, passive.

For anyone curious about why things are the way they are in the world, this book is a good place to start looking for the answer. How we arrived at where we are today is another story, but why we seem so incapable of addressing with any great urgency the enormous problems now threatening humanity and, indeed, all life on Earth, is the subject of *Free to be Human*.

This is a book about the powerful forces working to keep the truth from us. It's about the giant filter system that ensures we remain uninformed, confused and, above all, passive, so that we do not notice the chains that keep us hitched to the goals of the powerful business and political élite in their feverish pursuit of the irrational values of corporate consumerism.

But this is not a book about consumerism. In an eloquently-made argument, it takes in philosophy, literature, religion, psychology, human rights and the environment, as well as politics and the corporate world, to support the central premise: that we are not free to do as we wish - only to do what is required.

Such a wide range of subject matter might give the impression that *Free to be Human* is a heavy tome but that's not the case. In under three hundred pages, David Edwards shows clearly and in a most compelling way, how the thought-control and disinformation processes of the totalitarian state envisaged by George Orwell, when he wrote his famous *Nineteen-Eighty-Four* (in 1949) are not only well-established in modern society, but are even more pervasive and insidious than Orwell predicted.

"Because the filter system acts to maintain a framework of beliefs that are essential to corporate capitalism but utterly superficial, inadequate and absurd as an answer to human life, the search for more adequate answers is limited, and effectively stifled as far as the majority of the population is concerned". In this reference to the framing conditions of society that keep us conforming, Edwards argues that not only do we not see the possibility of alternative answers, we don't even perceive that there is a question any more. We simply accept the *status quo*, as being how life is.

What exactly are these 'framing conditions' that keep us so meekly subservient, like donkeys lashed to a treadmill?

David Edwards draws widely on the work of other authors and thinkers in constructing his argument, including Noam Chomsky and Edward Herman's *Manufacturing Consent* in which the authors propose a hypothesis which they call their 'propaganda model'. This model concerns the way the media works to mobilize support for the special interests of the state and private sector élite, while marginalising thoughts and actions that are less supportive, or opposed to, such interests.

The model is not just about the capability of dominant interests to lightly influence the general direction of the media, which undoubtedly is a distinct possibility from time to time but is, in fact, a "dramatically-effective system of control" by which those dominant interests manipulate media behaviour to ensure it only serves their goals and objectives. It is a far tighter system of control than anything imagined by Orwell.

A key point of his proposition is that the system is facilitated by, and only possible due to its invisibility. It is perhaps the ultimate security system: because it has every appearance of complete freedom, very few feel any need to challenge it!

The transparency of the control system is central to Edwards' argument. Most people would accept that there is at least the possibility that those with power in politics and business - including the media business - could exert influence over what appears or doesn't appear in the media. But no one would believe that *everyone* working in newspapers, in radio and television stations all over the world, is part of a huge conspiracy to misinform.

And of course, there is no conspiracy. And journalists and editors everywhere robustly refute any suggestion of bias or influence whenever it is made. 'No one tells me what to write!' they protest loudly. But no one *has* to, Edwards would argue. The system takes care of it.

To try to explain how the system works, the author returns to an old chemistry experiment used in schools to show how crystalline structures like snowflakes form almost perfect, symmetrical shapes without any apparent control or design. Basically, it works like this.

If you place a square frame like a box lid, on a table, and pour over it a stream of tiny balls, it will eventually and inevitably create an almost perfect pyramid shape. This is because the most stable resting position for each ball is one that contributes to the structure. Those that settle like this, build, while those in less stable positions either move to a more stable position or bounce out. No one is in control. The pyramid shape is simply the inevitable outcome of the framing conditions of round objects falling onto a square frame.

The experiment is a good analogy for understanding why certain ideas and their promoters are strongly supported by the media, while others barely feature. Given the fact that for the most part, the media institutions have themselves become part of BigBusiness with shareholders to satisfy, and advertisers to court, they must support the framing conditions of maximised economic growth fuelled by mass production and by mass consumerism – in order to survive.

As news and information and ideas and people are constantly poured over this economic framework, the ones that support the framing conditions stick, and those that don't, disappear off the radar. It's as simple as that.

Returning to the question posed at the top of this review - why are we so incapable of addressing the important issues of our day - readers may now see that the media corporations have no interest in investigating the root causes of the serious problems facing humanity, such as ozone depletion, global warming, famines, drought, disappearing resources and so on, because that would mean questioning the framing conditions of our society, which would threaten the structure of the pyramid, effectively attacking the ground upon which they themselves stand.

Instead, the 'news' we get is at best a distorted version of reality, and at worst it can be nothing short of lies. And the whole illusion is kept in place by a series of reality filters that make sure there is no critical thought or deep questioning, or even doubt expressed about the sanity of the framing idea that puts the economy before society. Money before Life.

These filters include the size and concentrated ownership patterns in the media. Anyone can start a newspaper of course - if you happen to have a few million to spare. In other words, the huge investment needed acts as a barrier to new outlets for alternative voices coming on stream.

Then there's advertising. Advertisers have extraordinary power to influence what gets in and what's left out. And they use it. Or threaten to use it, which often is enough.

Government and corporate bodies have deep pockets when it comes to the distribution of promotional material, so the source of news also constitutes a filter. As the focus is increasingly on the media business's bottom line, costly news-gathering resources have become thin on the ground so there is an ever-heavier reliance on PR hand-outs. In December 2003, an academic research project in the US found that 40% of news content there comes from PR sources.

Then there's flak. Flak comes in many shapes - letters, phonecalls, speeches, petitions, publications, even law-suits. Just as state and corporate power tend to assist supportive media, the same flak machines aim to undermine unsupportive media.

And finally, the creation of an 'evil' of one sort or another. At one time, communism was enough to justify political or corporate behaviour abroad, or control critics at home. In another era the 'savage' Red Indians, or the treacherous British would have been a convenient *bête noire* to keep us believing the story. And, haven't we heard a lot about a certain war on terror in recent times?

All of these reality filters work to distract ordinary people from asking awkward questions, and ensure that we conform to the framing conditions of society, and stay in buying mood.

Edwards suggests that our assumption that we live in a free democracy goes unquestioned for the same reason as does our understanding of what we mean by freedom and democracy. And we don't truly know, because this assumption is never questioned - publicly. And therein, the author suggests, is a general law of social life: wherever we find an unchallenged social goal, we are in the presence of a great lie, supported by power.

Why should we care about any of this?

The link between media behaviour and the sustainability issue is absolute but inconspicuous. As the willing cheerleader for BigBusiness and its goal of economic growth without limits, business and the media need each other. And those of us who are interested in changing the gameplan need to be acutely aware of the distortion this alliance creates in every aspect of our lives, that results in a constant sidelining of the core issues concerning sustainable living.

In David Edward's words, we need to "master the art of intellectual defence, if we are to challenge the deceptions of a system that subordinates people and planet to the drive for profit."

Free to be Human contains many powerful ideas. I have merely sought to focus on the central issue of the role the media plays in maintaining the illusion that we are free. But as the author of this thought-provoking work reminds us, there is often no greater obstacle to freedom than the assumption that it has already been fully attained.

This is a wonderful, informative and absorbing book. I cannot recommend it highly enough.

David Youell is a partner at downey youell associates, an organisational development practice working at the intersection of communication, values and culture. Website www.dya.ie

MediaLens
David Edwards runs MediaLens, a media watchdog service, with David Cromwell, the author of *Private Planet*. MediaLens' subtitle is "correcting for the distorted vision of the corporate media" and it issues an excellent e-newsletter reviewing current British newspapers and television. www.medialens.org

From economic aristocracy to economic democracy

ADRIAN MACFHEARRAIGH AND CATHERINE ANSBRO

The Divine Right of Capital - Dethroning the Corporate Aristocracy
Marjorie Kelly
Berrett-Koehler Publishers Inc., 2001
ISBN 1 57675-125-2 (hb) £18.99
ISBN 1 57675-237-2 (pb) £13.99

The corporate sector is the most powerful human force shaping the world. Who takes its decisions is therefore of crucial importance. So why does almost everyone accept that shareholders have the sole right to do so? asks the 2003 Feasta lecturer.

Before communities around the world can become sustainable, business practices must become *democratic* rather than *aristocratic*. That is the main message of *The Divine Right of Capital*, an excellent analysis of the way the business and economic systems operate and how they can be improved.

The book's author, Marjorie Kelly, has a long history of involvement in the economics of sustainability. She is the cofounder and editor of *Business Ethics*, a U.S. magazine that has focused on new approaches to responsible business practices since 1987.

In the course of her editorship, though, Kelly has changed her mind about how such practices can become established most effectively. Initially she believed that change would come about because progressive businesspeople were voluntarily transforming capitalism by supporting corporate social responsibility, which entailed actions such as better environmental stewardship, family-friendly policies, employee profit sharing and good corporate citizenship.

However, after monitoring a decade of this type of 'change', Kelly saw that it was merely cosmetic. While acknowledging that some visionary business founders had brought about important changes in a small number of firms, these progressive practices quickly died out once the business was sold on. Moreover, these few responsible businesses were not bringing about systemic change within the general corporate community, which continued following the goal of maximizing profits for shareholders, regardless of the impact on employees, the environment or the public good. Kelly became convinced the problem was systemic, the result of historical and legal factors. She now believes that deep and lasting change in business

practices will not come about until we change the legal factors that guide how businesses operate. *The Divine Right of Capital* outlines these factors and shows the way to bring about real, deep-down change in business practices and in local and global economies.

For example, the book emphasises the overwhelming influence that "fiduciary duty" has on a way a company is run. Currently, in Ireland as elsewhere, this "duty of trust" placed on a company's management is almost always limited to maximizing financial returns to the shareholders. Other parties linked to the company–employees, environment, and local and global communities–are not considered except to the extent that a failure to act would risk financial liabilities that would reduce shareholder profits. Thus, as the law stands, if boards of directors were to consider factors like employee well-being, environment, or public good in their decision-making, rather than shareholder profits, they could be sued by shareholders for not upholding their duty of trust in looking after their financial interests. As a result our present style of accountancy only evaluates financial bottom lines and profits. This has created a system that ignores the full impact of business activities.

Kelly points out that this current system is fundamentally aristocratic and inherently undemocratic in nature, a holdover from medieval times. She gives a fascinating presentation of the social structures, privileges and power held by the elite ruling class in Medieval Europe. Throughout the book she builds up a compelling comparison of our present system of wealth distribution, commonly called economy, and the social system of Medieval Europe. This comparison gives rise to the recognition that our current system is an Economic Aristocracy.

According to Kelly, this Economic Aristocracy has six principles:

i) **worldview** – it aims to pay shareholders as much as possible and employees as little as possible;

ii) **privilege** – shareholders, just like nobles, claim wealth they do little to create;

iii) **property** – a corporation, like a feudal estate, is a piece of property, not a community, and can be owned and sold by the propertied class;

iv) **governance** – corporations have an aristocratic governance structure which implies that those who own the corporation are the only group entitled to vote on decisions determining the future of the corporation;

v) **liberty** – this is preserved for the property owners only;

vi) **sovereignty** – corporations assert they are private and the free market will self-regulate them, just like barons asserted they were independent of the Crown.

Kelly shows that since medieval times, laws permitted change from a political perspective but not from a wealth one. As a result, laws governing economic and business behaviour continue to preserve age-old wealth inequalities. So, while in the political sphere, aristocracy was eclipsed by democracy, the world of wealth and property has remained untouched. As a result, while we would never tolerate medieval practices in our current political system (imagine "King Bertie" ruling by divine mandate, without public representatives or elections), we have not recognized our economic system for what it is: *an historical anachronism of an inherently aristocratic nature.*

Kelly therefore proposes that our economics must become *democratic*. This is what will bring about systemic changes that support ethical businesses. She proposes six principles of Economic Democracy to counter each of the six characteristics of the Economic Aristocracy:

i) **enlightenment** – all persons are created equal and therefore the economic rights of employees and the community equal those of the owners of capital;

ii) **equality** – the wealth created by a company does not only belong to its shareholders but to all those who create it. Community wealth (e.g., natural resources) belongs to us all;

iii) **public good** – public corporations are more than pieces of property or private contracts, they have a responsibility to the public good;

iv) **democracy** – a corporation is a human community and like the larger community of which it is a part it is best governed democratically;

v) **justice** – the wealthy may not claim greater rights than others and corporations may not claim the rights of persons;

vi) **(r)evolution** – just as the people have the right to alter or abolish government it is equally their right to alter or abolish the corporations that now govern the world. Kelly puts the 'r' in brackets was we have done to emphasise that this principle is an evolution with the spirit of a revolution.

Kelly points out that our unquestioning attitude towards the current system is a major factor holding up our progress to a more sustainable future. In medieval times no one questioned the right of the king or the aristocracy to rule, or their right to collect taxes and other wealth from the peasants and/or middle classes who created it. Everyone just accepted that this was the divine right of the monarchy. In a similar way, we have accepted without question company laws that enshrine the rights of the Economic Aristocracy to create more wealth for themselves that is not of their own making.

Kelly's book presents eye-opening facts from up-to-date sources and is so interesting that we both found it hard to put down. Moreover it is beautifully written in a style that makes it a very easy read for general readers and economists alike.

Pointing out the changes in business law that have recently been made in Europe and some states in the USA, the book will provide its readers with important information about the legal changes we need to focus on politically in order to create a culture of responsible and sustainable business activity. It equips us to embark on a journey to install democratic principles and breathe life into the heart and soul of a new kind of economy.

Catherine Ansbro is a director of start-up businesses in the fields of solar energy, astronomy research and education, and 3D imaging systems. She is currently participating in the Sligo/Letterkenny Enterprise Platform Programme (CEIM). She is Deputy Chair of the Irish Green Party's National Council and a member of its Economic Policy Committee.

Adrian MacFhearraigh lives in Donegal and has a background in electronic and telecommunications systems design. He is an active Donegal Green Party member committed to developing ideas, policies and technologies to benefit dynamic, sustainable, high quality human lifestyles.

Transforming 'top-down' corporations into democratic networks

PATRICK MANGAN
AND ANNE BURKE

A New Way to Govern - Organisations and Society after Enron
Shann Turnbull
New Economics Foundation
ISBN N/A £4.99

The more complex a business becomes, the more important it is that it adopts a complex, devolved governance structure that enables its staff to manage without a central direction. Just like the human body, in fact.

The collapse of large and apparently sound corporations such as Enron, which at one time was the world's biggest energy trading company, illustrates that severe problems can arise with the command and control management structures which are the accepted norm for large organisations. Dr. Shann Turnbull is best known for his book *Democratising the Wealth of Nations* which advocates employee share ownership and land trusts[1]. In his new book, Turnbull, the principal of the International Institute for Self-governance and an Australian with a Harvard MBA, applies his knowledge of governance to analyse the failures of management and accountability in what he describes as "top-down" corporations. He identifies three fundamental weaknesses in their structure:

- The tendency of power to corrupt when it is concentrated in a few individuals.
- The difficulty in managing complexity, particularly as an organisation grows.
- The suppression of normal human checks and balances, supposedly for the benefit of corporate efficiency.

Turnbull suggests that new forms of organisation are needed to avoid these pitfalls and that the solution may lie in "network governance", where power, responsibility and decision-making authority are delegated to those best positioned to decide. He believes that organic organisations with the ability to self-replicate and self-manage may hold the key to resilience and robustness,

attributes which Enron manifestly lacked.

Organisational networks such as the human body link diverse and competing systems by maintaining the functions of each component while preventing the domination of any one component over the others. Built-in feedback loops and the limits imposed by competing systems ensure that the sum is greater than the parts. Turnbull argues that if a highly complex organisational structure like a human can be managed effectively by its component systems then this model should provide some lessons for good corporate governance. He also compares organisational networks to the way ants work through complex networks without a CEO and yet can achieve extraordinary results.

The version of the capitalist system which developed after World War II in a period in which environmental issues were not a concern, is neither equitable, ecologically sensitive nor efficient. This may be partly due to the management theories upon which it is based. Much of today's command and control theories are based on colonial practices, which are totally inappropriate in the 21st Century.

According to Turnbull, the unitary board of directors of a large corporation has absolute power over the organisation which the directors are meant to serve. They both set and mark their own exam papers, which hardly bodes well for shareholders or the public. It is "the directors who determine the size of profit which the company reports, irrespective of whether the

---

1   The complete text can be downloaded from
http://cog.kent.edu/lib/TurnbullBook/TurnbullBook.htm#1%20%20%20%20Introduction

financial reports conform to accounting standards".

Since the value of many assets are assessed subjectively, current accounting procedures are sufficiently flexible to allow accounts to be manipulated. Profits are therefore based on subjective assessments of value. So are liabilities, which must raise serious concerns about the value of accounting and audit procedures if deception is part of corporate culture. The integrity of auditors must be compromised if they are hired and fired by the directors on whom they are reporting.

Even when the directors have been shown to have "failed the exam" they may not be accountable to the shareholders as they also control the annual general meeting. Turnbull goes on to say that "the reliance of governments and regulators on non-executive directors to protect investors, or even creditors, is naïve and dangerous".

He notes that various attempts at reform were made in the 1990s by Cadbury, Greenbury, Hampel, and Turnbull himself. However, he feels these reforms were inadequate and although widely promoted around the world, merely lull minority investors into a false sense of security.

Turnbull suggests that current company design can be corrected by making focused changes. The basic steps he suggests are:

- Establish stakeholder panels
- Establish a stakeholding council to bring together different stakeholders into one forum
- Establish a senate to act as arbiters
- Set up a community governance board representing the "unofficial" stakeholders.

The structure Turnbull proposes is more complex than conventional structures and he suggests that the more complex a business becomes, the more it needs a matching complexity in its governance. Among his proposals are:

- Businesses should become self-financing as the current capitalist system over-rewards investors.
- Equity investors should be phased out
- Replace shareholders by members reflecting stakeholding interests
- Accounts in general contain too little information, due to compression of data.
- Don't police, transform

He illustrates the way that these panels, councils and boards can work together in practice by profiling Visa International, the Spanish co-operatives controlled by the Mondragon Corporacion Cooperativa (MCC) and the loose conglomerations of companies called keiretsu in Japan which organize around a single bank for their mutual benefit. The companies sometimes, but not always, own equity in each other.

While Turnbull's proposals are a distinct improvement on current corporate management practice, they are only a starting point for the development of more democratic organisational structures. For example, he still acknowledges the role of the managing director and board of directors and fails to suggest that they may not be appropriate in a truly democratic organisation where authority is delegated to a well educated staff capable of managing a complex and diverse structure without a central authority directing operations,. The book also fails to develop his suggestions on self-organising institutions, on the amoeba-like splitting of enterprises when they grow too large, on decentralising of decision-making to staff, and on the development of corporate or staff learning networks.

So, while the book suggests changes to the present management and governance structures of large corporations, it fails to design a new governance structure.

Overall, though, it is a rewarding book which will stimulate your thinking on what companies are about, who they exist to serve and who should benefit from organisational profits.

Patrick Mangan is a lecturer at Letterkenny Institute of Technology and a founding member of the Irish Institute for Sustainability Education.

Anne Burke lectures in Financial Auditing and Corporate Governance at Letterkenny Institute of Technology. She was previously employed as an auditor in the public sector.

Dig where you stand:
a message of hope

NADIA JOHANISOVA

Soil and Soul: People versus Corporate Power
Alastair McIntosh
Aurum Press, London, 2001
ISBN 1 85410 802 6 (hb) £17.99
ISBN 1 85410 864 6 (pb) £12.99

Traditional cultures were ways which communities had developed for living sustainably in their own place. They still have great relevance today, as a Scottish philosopher and campaigner found.

Alastair McIntosh (b. 1955) is difficult to pigeonhole. Is he primarily an activist, championing the cause of Hebridean islanders against absentee landlords and battling superquarries? An academic lecturing about human ecology? Or is he really deep down a mystic who gets his strength from old Celtic whorls, sacred wells and the roaring of the sea?

In fact, as you will find when you read his book, he is all these things and more, which is what makes the book so interesting. He starts off with a vivid account of his own childhood on the Isle of Lewis in the Outer Hebrides. The local doctor's son, he grew up with a leg in two worlds - the world of his parents, who groomed him to blend with the "higher classes", and the world of the local fishermen and crofters, whose vernacular economy was just beginning to fade. He describes in what to me is the most moving part of his book, the traditional culture of the islands with its complex ecological and social links. Nutrients were recycled through composting human and livestock waste and, in the oldest houses which had no chimneys, even the soot caught in the thatch went back to the fields each spring. He does not idealise the old days. They were hard. But at the same time, a complex "alternative economy" system of mutuality, reciprocity and barter ensured social security, and work was interwoven with song and even dance in a way difficult to imagine today.

With the advent of modernity, this system began to unravel. In one of the most poignant passages of the book, McIntosh describes a recent conversation with an old islander who still weaves fabrics on his old hand loom. He had asked him why he does not sing as he weaves:

"Ah well...there was a time when I was younger and you'd hear somebody walking through the village singing to the rhythm of your loom as they went past. And then when they'd get a bit further on and pick up a different loom's rhythm, they'd change the song to suit that one."

"So why not now, John? Why do you never hear people singing when they're weaving?"

"Oh well...we'd be embarrassed! People expect it to sound like it does on the radio or television now, and if I started singing they'd laugh."

Music is a recurring theme throughout the book. So is Scottish history. McIntosh describes his own gradual awakening to the reverberating impact of the defeat of Gaelic culture at Culloden and especially of the Highland clearances, whose importance was played down in his school days not only by his teachers, but by the islanders themselves.

"What are these ruins really, Tommy?" he asked one day in the mid-seventies as he walked around a group of deserted houses in Lewis with his friend, who served as head stalker for the rich hunters who came to the island to shoot. ' "Just something from the old days." And he went very quiet. It felt inopportune to enquire again.'

One of the most important insights of this book is the tracing of intergenerational and international impact of traumas such as the Highland clearances, which involved the eviction of half a million people from their homes in the nineteenth century to make way for sheep. Those who lost their roots in this way had several choices. Either they could emigrate to America and in their turn help to evict the native people from their lands. Or they could retain a vestige of their warrior culture by becoming soldiers. The irony of the Highlander regiments quelling "mutinies" in India becomes painfully obvious in this light.

As a third choice, these people could migrate to the big cities and become a kind of "cannon-fodder" for the Industrial Revolution, and McIntosh speaks of the descendants of evicted Highlanders still living in squalor in Glasgow tenements today. The burden of cultural trauma often leads to internalisation of the blame for what happened and may erupt into lateral violence - violence against friends, family, or oneself. As the author emphasises, this is not a phenomenon confined to Scotland. In fact, his own understanding of the dynamics of power and powerlessness in Scotland was sharpened through his conversations with local people in Papua New Guinea, where he worked on issues of land ownership in the rainforest.

This dynamic of power and powerlessness is another important strand in the varied tapestry of Alastair McIntosh's book. In a chapter entitled "By the Cold and Religious", he discusses the role of Calvinism in shaping the values and exploits of the emerging British Empire. As in other parts of the book, he complements this with his own experience as a young boy:

> ...At other times kids were thrashed for not knowing their religion. This punishment was undertaken with the tawse - a thick leather strap with two fingers of fizzing fire. The more sadistic teachers carried theirs around like a holstered gun under the jacket...

Between the two world wars, children in Lewis were punished for speaking their own language, Gaelic, in the school playground. In this, as in many other places throughout the book, an analogy with the plight of Native Americans is apparent.

> The Circle is broken and I cannot raise a tune
> The faeries have left and they will not return
> When the faeries danced on the land the Circle was whole
> And then you could raise a tune

These words were composed and sung in Gaelic by an islander after he had seen American Indians on television speaking of their culture as dying because the Sacred Circle had been broken.

It is with recapturing the sense of the sacred, the "real religion" which survives in the taproots of Gaelic culture and in our hearts as well that a

large part of this book is concerned. In a crucial chapter entitled "The Womanhood of God", McIntosh attempts to disentangle this authentic spirituality from the "cold" aspect of religion in collusion with worldly power. This authentic religion has more in common with "mythos", the world of feeling, metaphor, poetry and story, than with "logos", which embraces logic, reason, causality and explicit order. We can find it in the teachings of Jesus as well as in parts of the Old Testament which, however, are seldom chosen as sermon subjects. While both mythos and logos are necessary if we wish to understand the world and change it for the better, our culture with its emphasis on the latter has damaged logos itself from lack of a nourishing context, and it has become a desiccating parody of what passionately fired-up reason could actually be.

McIntosh was working at the Centre for Human Ecology at Edinburgh University when he became involved with two important Scottish campaigns in the nineties: The Isle of Eigg Trust campaign, which eventually succeeded in wresting this small Hebridean island from feudal into communal ownership, and the struggle to protect a mountain on the Isle of Harris from being turned into a gigantic superquarry. This latter campaign has been successful so far, although as the book went to print, success was not yet certain, and there is now talk of pressure to open a similar superquarry elsewhere in the Scottish Highlands.

Activism propelled McIntosh to deepen his own spirituality. It led him to see activism as a kind of latter-day shamanism, involving an ability to 'step outside of existing social programming to glimpse a wider panorama and new options...[see] where consensual reality has become dysfunctional...[and step] into the "world" again, to sound the alarm, to nourish growth and to point towards cultural healing.' He studied liberation theology and Celtic Christianity and he returned to the islands of his childhood as a pilgrim, fishing 'near-forgotten fragments of history from long-overgrown pools of local knowledge' to understand the stories behind the mountain he had set out to save.

In the process, he found new leverage and strength for his struggle and developed a strategic framework for activists who might otherwise either 'sell out or burn out'. Seeing the wider context of your struggle is essential, he says: 'Never be so vain as to expect to reach the stars, but do set your course by them.' An important guiding star for him is the reconstruction of a co-operative society with people linked to the land and to each other through responsibility and respect, such as the one he had been privileged to witness in his childhood.

Spirituality proved a potent ally in the struggle to put a stop to the superquarry plans at Harris. Stone Eagle, a leader of the Mi'Kmaq' Indian Nation who was himself involved in campaigns against superquarries in Nova Scotia, was persuaded by McIntosh to fly to Harris to testify at a public enquiry about the feasibility of the project. A description of the interaction of the media and the people of Harris with Stone Eagle makes gripping and sometimes humorous reading. Another dimension was added by the Calvinist theologian Donald Macleod, who spoke at the inquiry of the need to honour God's creation. 'Do we have God's mandate to inflict on Creation a scar of this magnitude that might detract from Creation's ability to reflect the glory of God?' he asked. The speeches did not impress the inspector in charge of the enquiry, but they had an impact on public opinion, especially in Harris: many islanders stopped supporting the project after hearing them.

According to the book, it was McIntosh's activism which led to the "eviction" of the Centre for Human Ecology from Edinburgh University in 1996. The description of this bitter fruit of his struggles and of the recent progress and aftermath of his campaigns in the last few chapters is perhaps too tedious and detailed, thus diluting what would have otherwise been a well-blended cocktail of past and present, mythos and logos. At its worst, the book tends to slip into a hard-to-believe visionary optimism ('Even when you're losing the battles...you'll invariably end up winning the war').

However, it remains a powerful, well-written and well-researched book. McIntosh is a courageous and independent thinker who has taken his own advice to 'dig where you stand' and dredged up treasures as well as monsters from the mud of Scottish and Gaelic history. He forges new links between activism, spirituality and traditional culture and adds seasoning in the form of his own experience, sharing his mistakes and doubts along the way. At its deepest level, this is the book of a rebel. Let us understand our own true history, our own true religion and our dreams, he seems to be saying, in order to have strength to change things for the better. Only then will the salmon return. Significantly, the salmon, which no longer returns to dammed streams in Lewis, is, of course, a symbol of spiritual knowledge in Celtic mythology.

Nadia Johanisova is a Czech environmentalist and university lecturer in human ecology and new economics. She studied at the Centre for Human Ecology in Edinburgh in 2001/2. E-mail: nadia@volny.cz

The mistaken turning on humankind's path

Jonathan Dawson

The Spell of the Sensuous
David Abram
Vintage 1996
ISBN 0 67977 639 7 £14.00

The Other Side of Eden: Hunter-gatherers, farmers and the shaping of the world
Hugh Brody
Faber and Faber Ltd 2000
ISBN 0 57120 502 X £9.99

The way our ancestors regarded the world may have a lot to teach us about where, and why, our thinking went wrong and how it can be corrected. We need to feel as much a part of nature as they did.

A man leaves his home in American academia to immerse himself in the world of shamanism in Bali and Nepal. After some time, he finds himself becoming ever more deeply immersed in the natural world. Encounters with condors, with spiders, with rocks and grasses, recounted in spell-bindingly beautiful prose, are full of meaning to him. His habitual feelings of duality – of self set against other, of humankind set against the rest of the natural world – are progressively dissolved. In a fundamental sense, he feels himself to have truly come home.

Then, he leaves Asia and returns to the country of his birth. Within a short space of time, his feelings of oneness with the world around him evaporate and he finds himself once again back in a primarily man-made environment, looking out at the rest of creation as a stranger.

What happened? If the state of non-separation and identification with the natural world, apparently so accessible to our aboriginal ancestors and neighbours, is our natural state of being, how did he so easily lose it? Further, how have we collectively as a species so easily lost it? These are the great questions at the heart of David Abram's *The Spell of the Sensuous*.

All the tracks he follows, and there are many, lead him to what he posits to be the single most important technological innovation our species has achieved: the phonetic alphabet. Drawing on extensive anthropological literature, he demonstrates that the way oral, pre-literate

cultures experienced the world is radically different from our own. To begin with, time was (is) experienced as cyclical in nature, with great, repeating mythological stories defining the cycle of the year. No meaningful distinction was made between time and space. Story and meaning derived from and were tied indissolubly to place: the body of wisdom developed by a community, often in the form of songs and stories, represented its store of wisdom on how to live well and sustainably in its own, unique place.

Then, in the wake of the agricultural revolution, as human societies grew in size and complexity, scripts emerged. At first, the symbols were clear representations of the natural world (Egyptian hieroglyphs, Chinese ideograms). However, the trend was towards ever-greater abstraction and the Jews (the People of the Book) became the first people to develop a phonetic alphabet, largely (but not completely) divorced from reference to the non-human world.

With the development of widespread literacy among the Jews, 'a new sense of time as a non-repeating sequence (of events) begins to make itself felt over and against the ceaseless cycling of the cosmos' and history was born. Written down and thus recountable at will, stories become divorced from specificity of place. And between people and their earthly environments is inserted a human artifact that bears no direct relationship to the non-human world – the alphabet. The natural world becomes an object of (progressively more abstract) study rather than the sensuously experienced root and locus of all being. And the illusion of separation of people from the rest of the natural world grows apace.

And then there is the breath, the means by which humans participate in the great intermingling with all other beings in the all-enveloping air. For aboriginal peoples, Abram shows, the air is the sacred and 'thoroughly palpable medium in which we (along with the trees, the squirrels and the clouds) are immersed'. He suggests that the sacredness of breath for the Jews is the reason why their alphabet includes only consonants, the vowels being the breathed, sacred spaces between, the very name of God, the ultimate mystery.

When the Greeks adopted the Jewish alphabet wholesale and, not having the spiritual sensitivities of the Jews, introduced letters to represent the vowels, the last gap through which the natural world and a sense of the sacred might breathe is closed off. The alphabet becomes entirely airtight and self-referential. Now, humans can relate to each other and reflect on the world around them without any reference to the source of what was, for our aboriginal ancestors and neighbours, the source of all life and meaning – the sensuous earth.

Here, Abram introduces his most radical and exciting idea. For the pre-literate Greeks of Homer's time, the term *psyche* referred, in the words of the Milesian philosopher, Anaximenes, to the 'breath and air (that) hold together the entire universe and give it life'. By the time of Socrates (who lived at the beginning of the period of mass literacy among the educated classes in Greece), *psyche* has been isolated and imprisoned within the individual, human skull; the source of 'mind' is enclosed and privatised, and man left alone and lonely, cut off from the natural world and the great enveloping mystery. (Here, another pearl of poetic insight: the melancholy of exile that fell over the Jews and that remains with them still, suggests Abram, attaches itself not just or even primarily to the fact of physical exile, but rather to a much more deeply felt exile from the sensuous earth imposed on them by their adoption of the alphabet.)

For Hugh Brody too, in *The Other Side of Eden*, the Jews were centre-stage at the pivotal moment of our dislocation from the natural world. He describes Genesis as the farmer's version of history in which humans are forever exiled, cursed to bear children in pain but instructed to multiply, dominant over animals and the rest of the world but struggling to survive on harsh land and needing to move on to pastures new when it becomes exhausted. Hunter-gatherers, he asserts, would be astonished by this myth; for them, 'everything is founded on the conviction that home is already Eden and that exile must be avoided'.

This leads him to the startlingly useful insight that our habitual way of regarding hunter-gatherers and farmers has turned reality on its head. As he sees it, it is the hunter-gatherers who are entirely wedded to place and to the stories that bind them to it, to the point where, in Brody's words, those responsible for their displacement from their lands must be considered guilty of cultural genocide. It is the farmers who are rootless wanderers, finding it damagingly easy to obey God's instruction to 'Go forth and multiply....swarm through the earth and hold sway over it.'

The Other Side of Eden is a hymn of respect and affection to the indigenous people of North America (primarily the Inuit) among whom Brody has worked for many decades, and whose interests he has represented in numerous land rights trials. It is a deep meditation on how hunter-gatherers see and experience the world and what their vision has to teach us 'moderns'. In the loving descriptions of every-day life of the peoples among whom he moves, it is the perfect companion volume to Abram's more theoretical treatment of the same subject. Both works resonate with a deep-in-the-bone feeling of remembrance, beyond all romanticised nostalgia, for how we all once ancestrally lived on this earth.

Other than being lovingly crafted books and cracking good reads, what relevance do they have to the myriad predicaments in which we find ourselves today? I see three ways in which they can serve us.

First, they provide a refreshingly new and persuasive analysis of how we got into the mess in which we find ourselves. To remain happy, balanced and powerful, ours is a species that needs stories that make sense. These books provide just such stories, helping us understand the roots of our dislocation from the natural world and the dire consequences that have followed. It is easier to feel compassionate towards and even hopeful about the future of this lost, destructive species having read its story in this way: its deviance seems less of a malignant design fault, more of a simple missed turning on the path.

Second, they offer a startlingly simple but powerful critique of twenty-first century rational thought and its effects. Many of the stories of indigenous peoples, suggests Abram, appear to us strange, simplistic and, even if we are too polite and culturally sensitive to say so out loud, just plain misguided. But how are we to judge the validity of a people's stories, he argues, if not by how well and sustainably they enable us to live on this earth? By this measure (surely the only one of lasting value), it is our own stories, our own ways of understanding the world that are clearly unbalanced.

Finally, and perhaps most importantly, they give us access to new ways of thinking about and experiencing the world that are full of potential for liberation of the type that shifts paradigms. The notion, for example, that 'mind' or 'intelligence' may reside not in the skull but in the enveloping air (and that this may have been the commonly-accepted belief for the great majority of human history!) is ripe to bursting with the potential for revolution.

True, few are likely to choose to spurn further use of the alphabet as a result of reading these books – they are much more likely to increase our appreciation of the joys of reading and send us scurrying back for more! Nonetheless, whole new sensibilities and ways of dreaming into the world become accessible where none had been apparent before; the value of silence and long moments of meditative exposure to the natural world sing out to us from the pages. If solutions cannot emerge out of the field of thought that create the problems in the first place, these books make accessible to us much, new, fertile territory. New stories lurk here that might just be the saving of us all.

Brody too asserts the primacy of story. 'The world is also shaped by stories.....Many hunter-gatherer ways of knowing the world have disappeared, along with hunter-gatherer languages. These are rich and unique parts of human history that cannot be recovered. If the words are gone, so are the stories. A particular shape is lost forever.....Each such case represents a harm that is inestimable: the cumulative loss of language constitutes a diminution in the range of what it means to be human'

The deep love for what we have lost that is evoked by these books fuels a surge of passion to fight for that which remains.

Jonathan Dawson is Executive Secretary of GEN-Europe (the Global Ecovillage Network). He is also a story-teller and sustainabilty educator and lives at the Findhorn Foundation community in Scotland. Email: jonathan@gen-europe.org

How ideas spread and develop

JOHN JOPLING

Enabling Innovation - a practical guide to understanding and fostering technical change
Boru Douthwaite
Zed Books, 2002
ISBN 1 85649 972 3 (pb) £15.95
ISBN 1 85649 971 5 (hb) £49.95

Why are some technological innovations widely adopted whilst others struggle? And what light does the answer to that question throw on how we should seek to spread radical ideas?

Even though this book is about the best processes for developing technological innovations, its relevance runs far beyond its subject. Everyone interested in how ideas develop and spread will find it fascinating.

If you ever wondered whether we need more innovations at all in view of the problems they've created in the past, I don't think you will continue to do so when you've read this book. Douthwaite says that given that our natural resource bank is becoming exhausted and the world's population is increasing, new technologies are needed if per capita consumption is not to fall to disastrous levels.

The book therefore argues that the crucial question is not innovation or no innovation but the process by which innovation is developed. It proposes a theory, 'learning selection', to explain why some innovations have been developed successfully and others haven't. The word 'selection' has echoes of Charles Darwin's 'natural selection' and, sure enough, the way into understanding what 'learning selection' means is via Darwin's theory of evolution. Here's Douthwaite's neat summary:

> Natural selection is at the heart of Darwin's theory of biological evolution. It is the process by which, because of constant competition for the necessities of life, only the fittest individual plants or animals, those best suited to their environment, survive. Differences between individuals in a population arise because of random genetic mutations and sexual reproduction; if any of these differences proves advantageous, it will enable those possessing it to produce more offspring. Some of the offspring will inherit the beneficial trait and produce more offspring too, and so, over time, the genetic composition of the population will change.

So today's world is the result of lots of 'selections.' Natural selection, Douthwaite points out, consists of three mechanisms:

- **Novelty generation.** As a result of random genetic mutations and sexual recombination of differing genetic material, differences between individual members of a species crop up from time to time.

- **Selection.** This is the mechanism which retains random changes that turn out to be beneficial to the species because they enable those possessing the trait to achieve better survival and breeding rates. It also rejects harmful changes.

- **Diffusion and promulgation.** These are the mechanisms by which the beneficial differences are spread to other areas.

The development of a new technology often starts when someone has a bright idea. That's novelty generation. If someone then makes use of the idea, that's selection. And when others take it up, that's diffusion and promulgation. The point that Douthwaite makes is that one should see these three mechanisms as part of a single learning process in which everyone involved - researchers, manufacturers and users - have important parts to play. 'Rather than natural selection, let us call this whole interactive and experiential learning process learning selection' he writes.

In his Foreword, Niels Röling, the professor of innovation studies at Wageningen University in the Netherlands summarises learning selection thus: 'the book argues that successful innovation is based on ...mobilising creativity among people who are willing to run with a brilliant idea, even if it is still flawed and underdeveloped. The fact that [the idea] is underdeveloped is a boon, so long as the various agents in the system are invited to improve upon it.'

Nothing very extraordinary in that you may think but in fact this book is paradigm changing stuff. Douthwaite has enunciated a theory that embraces the diversity of place, human experience and people as an integral part of achieving successful technical innovation. It's new thinking, the first time anyone has put forward, and precisely described, a comprehensive theory on these lines. The contrast is between this 'co-development' model, involving people 'learning by using' and 'learning by doing', and the conventional 'consultancy' development model is huge.

Douthwaite shows that, for developing new technologies, the 'co-development' model works best. In the course of his post-doctoral research on how post-harvest agricultural equipment was developed and adopted in the Philippines, he began to realise that

> agricultural equipment was more likely to be beneficial to more people if the people who benefitted could understand it and adapt it to their local needs. Moreover the agricultural technologies that were most widely adopted were exactly the ones that had been most adapted. This link between adoption and adaptation had some far reaching implications. In particular, it showed that contrary to the standard view that agricultural extension is the job of 'spreading the message to achieve diffusion and adoption of the innovation by as many small holders as possible', it is largely about helping farmers to understand and innovate.

That realisation led him to enquire if similar conclusions held good in fields other than agricultural technologies. The book is an account of that enquiry. It starts with grain dryers in the Far East and then moves on to wind turbines, (why did the Danes succeed in developing good turbines while the Americans, who spent more money, did not?) IT (Linux versus Windows), LETS (local exchange trading schemes) and biotechnology (the Green Revolution and its legacy). And a thoroughly readable and extremely informative account it is.

The practical implications of the 'learning selection' theory are discussed throughout the book. For example, it seems that each new technology needs to have a 'product champion' to push it forward but this person needs to be 'low at the ego end' so that he or she can incorporate other people's ideas. A 'healthy mixture of top down and bottom up' generally seems to work best, too, but there are horses for courses. And different forces are important at different stages. The idea that people in different roles can be equal partners in technology development is fully explored. The strengths and roles of the public and private sectors are discussed in an unbiased way. The impacts of the profit motive and patent laws are spelt out.

I wasn't sure why it was thought necessary to have ten pages on the history of money to introduce the chapter on LETS. It seemed more than the reader needed to know in order to be able to follow the discussion about the money system's development. Not that the history wasn't beautifully written, but it took one's mind off the subject of the book. But the LETS story itself was fascinating. What a refreshing change to be asking not: 'which LETS system is best?' but: 'what are the lessons to be learned from the LETS story about what processes of development work best in practice?'

Although a technology can be regarded as a success if it is widely adopted since that means a lot of people are making use of it, the incompleteness of this measure surfaces in the chapter on the Green Revolution. By the standard of widespread adoption, the Revolution was a success but Douthwaite quotes Vandana Shiva: 'The Green Revolution has been a failure. It has led to reduced genetic diversity, increased vulnerability to pests, soil erosion, water shortages, reduced soil fertility, micronutrient deficiencies, soil contamination, reduced availability of nutritious food crops for the local population, the displacement of vast numbers of small farmers from their land, rural impoverishment and increased tensions and conflicts.' To which he adds: plus high levels of external inputs involving large amounts of energy nearly all of which comes from fossil fuels, which are running out.

'The decision about which R&D paradigm to use should not, however, be based purely on the question of which model can produce the highest number of adopters in the shortest period of time' Douthwaite writes. 'Instead the decision should be determined according to which model is likely to produce the more beneficial impact in terms of peoples' qualities of life, sustainability and the protection of the natural environment.' That's about the nearest one gets to

Douthwaite's idea of what constitutes 'success.' A fuller discussion is left for another day; and will require another book, or books.

The great value of having an intellectual framework is that it enables comparisons to be made between very different sorts of technical innovation. Once you have a model, it's extraordinary how it suggests the questions that need to be asked and provides a mental sorting system for dealing with the answers. I have no doubt that many people working in the fields covered by the case studies will find Douthwaite's insights useful; but in proposing a comprehensive theory of successful technical innovation, he has provided a framework which can, and will, be used in many other fields.

Niels Röling ends his Foreword by explaining that a 'praxeology' is a theory that regulates the thinking of practitioners in a particular field. He goes on: 'I believe that Boru Douthwaite has developed the kind of brilliant incipient innovative praxeology that innovation managers will run with, learning and selecting as they go.'

That's enough to justify giving the book ten out of ten, but for me it's not the end of the story, since it's a book that sets one thinking. It confirms that it's not enough for us to have bright ideas about what needs to be done. We must become information managers studying the processes by which successful change is achieved, with 'success' being measured in terms which include wider sustainability issues. I'll definitely keep coming back to this book.

John Jopling is a retired barrister, a co-founder of Feasta and co-editor of the *Feasta Review*. He lives in Kerry.

Let's use Gandhian principles to select which economic tools to apply

FRANK ROTERING

Inclusive Economics: Gandhian Method and Contemporary Policy
Narendar Pani
Sage Publications, 2001
ISBN 0 76199 580 3 (hb) £38.08

> *We mustn't expect simple, linear, cause-and-effect economic theories to work predictably in a world affected by millions of individual interactions. Whatever the theorists say, if an approach works, it's valid. And Mohandas Gandhi left us with a complete set of criteria to judge if it works or not.*

It's true - you really can't tell a book by its cover. I initially assumed that the "Inclusive" of Pani's title referred to people, and that Gandhi would be tapped for his principles of austerity and Swadeshi - the notion of village self-sufficiency. "Inclusive", however, refers to economic theories, not people. Gandhi's austerity is rejected, and Swadeshi plays only a minor role. What, then, is this book about?

Narendar Pani is Senior Editor of *The Economics Times* of Bangalore, India's technology capital. He has a PhD in Economics, worked for the *Deccan Herald* in Bangalore for five years, has written several books and government reports, and was a Research Fellow at the Indian Institute of Management. From this CV, Pani strikes me as the type of educated journalist who, if he lived in London, would be writing conservative, informative articles for *The Economist* magazine.

Inclusive Economics is about the methods used to formulate economic policy. The book is consistent with my expectations of Pani, but adds a strong moral dimension.

Pani begins his book with an event that shook the economics profession to its core: the Asian currency crisis of 1997. Not a single economist fully foresaw this event, and the *ad hoc* explanations offered after the fact remain unsatisfactory. Pani's view is that an unanticipated event of such magnitude points to fundamental problems with economists' policy tools. His implied question: how can we create policy that avoids such disasters in the future?

Pani's explanation of the failure to anticipate the Asian crisis is that economists filtered a complex reality through their narrow theories. This was a breakdown not of the theories themselves, but of a theoretical approach to economic reality. Pani believes that this reality is too convoluted, too protean, and too subtle for any present or future theory to grasp. What is needed is not better abstractions or more robust mathematics, but an entirely new approach to economic reality.

Pani refers to this new approach as an "inclusive method". The method is based not on a particular theory, but instead specifies the criteria for choosing which theory or theories should be applied in formulating a particular policy. In Pani's words: "This inclusive method thus need not present a completely different set of economic theories. It only needs to present a different method of using economic models." (p. 27)

In other words, Pani feels that the required economic theories are already out there. What is needed is a flexible approach that applies now this theory, now that one, according to concrete analytical requirements. His inclusive method will help the analyst match the theory to the situation.

This is where Gandhi enters the picture. Until his assassination in 1948, Mohandas Gandhi was a social and political activist of extraordinary effectiveness. Early in life he defended the rights of Indians in South Africa, then returned to India and worked for independence and social justice – especially obliteration of the odious caste system. He was not a profound theorist but developed far-reaching ethical principles based on his reading of the Bhagavadgita.

It is this successful application of simple, broad principles to an impenetrably complex reality that attracts Pani to Gandhi's method. The book is really a proposal to shift Gandhi's approach in the political realm to the troubled economic realm. Following are the key principles of Pani's transplanted method.

1. Judge actions by their consequences. It is irrelevant if an action is rooted in a specific theory or ideology. What matters is its impact on people and society. "The validity or otherwise of an action would be determined by the goodness of both the action itself and its consequences." (p. 55)

2. Judge consequences by their impact on individuals operating within society. It may surprise those who decry the standard economic focus on individuals that Gandhi held a similar view. He felt that the individual, not the group, should take precedence in policy formation. However: "... the individual is not an island. He or she interacts with other individuals in a society." (p. 66)

3. Consider a policy's consequences for everyone on earth.

4. Guard against unintended consequences. It is not enough to carefully formulate and implement an economic policy. If the results are adverse, we should modify it immediately.

5. Ends cannot justify the means. If the means are not moral, the ends cannot be moral either.

6. Subjective judgments are indispensable. The aim is not to avoid subjectivity, but to improve the subjective judgments that must be made.

7. Include all factors. Part of the inclusiveness of Pani's method is a comprehensive consideration of all aspects of a situation, not just several purportedly significant ones.

8. Use participant observation as well as secondary data. The analyst cannot confine analysis to published facts and statistics. He or she must venture into the field and share the experiences of those for whom the policy is being created.

9. Resolve conflicts through bargained consensus. Gandhi strongly opposed class warfare and always strove to resolve conflict through negotiation rather than through violence or coercion.

10. Focus on local resources and the local population. That is, adhere to the principle of Swadeshi.

Pani summarizes as follows: "As the Gandhian method opposes the reduction of reality into a single model, its method of intervention in the economy is necessarily more pluralistic. Its focus on consequences makes it open to any instrument that is available at a point of time to achieve a particular consequence. Its inclusiveness implies that the analysis cannot be restricted to a few factors, no matter how important they may be." (p. 122)

Inclusive Economics provided me with a useful overview of the theory behind policy formulation. As someone whose focus has been on economic theory, I learned much from Pani's discussion.

I have two major objections to Pani's thesis. First, I don't believe all the required theories are already out there, waiting to be filtered through Pani's sieve. Second, I doubt that a vague set of principles based on Gandhi and the Bhagavadgita will gain many adherents in the West.

My own perspective on economic theory has been published on the Feasta website, and is summarized in this *Feasta Review*. In brief: standard economics was developed for capital rather than for humanity, and has limited applicability to human well-being and environmental integrity; a new economic theory is therefore required. Pani's orientation is purely conventional, and I doubt that he would even consider the possibility of an alternative economic conception. His broad, inclusive approach to policy formation may well have value, but it should be opened to a wider range of economic theories. Conventional pluralism, in my view, is hardly pluralism at all.

I was surprised at Pani's pedestrian prose and lack of passion. I had expected Pani the journalist to produce a lively book, with at least a few memorable phrases. I found none in almost 200 pages of text, possibly because of intrusions from Pani the academic. And why the lack of emotional involvement with his profoundly moral project? Perhaps this was squeezed out by his editors. If so, a disservice was done to this insightful and progressive mainstream thinker.

I recommend this book only to those with a strong interest in economic policy and a well-developed immunity to academic verbiage. If your eyes glaze over when people mention Karl Popper's criterion of falsifiability, I suggest you read *The Economist* instead.

Frank Rotering lives British Columbia and makes his living by teaching courses on computer software in Canada, the U.S., and the U.K. He studied economics at Simon Fraser University in Vancouver.

Corporations and America's Founding Fathers

JAMES BRUGES

Unequal Protection: The rise of corporate dominance and the theft of human rights.
Thom Hartmann
Rodale 2002
ISBN 1-57954-627-7 $15.95

American corporate law is based on a fraud. How did this come about and what can be done to reverse it?

Trade-dominance by the East India Company aroused the greatest passions of America's Founders – every schoolboy knows how they dumped the Company's tea into Boston harbour. At the time in Britain virtually all members of parliament were stockholders, a tenth had made their fortunes through the Company, and the Company funded parliamentary elections generously. Parallels with US political life today are hard to miss and the Founders must be weeping in their graves.

After independence, corporations received their charters from states and the charters were for a limited period, like 20 or 30 years, not in perpetuity. They were only allowed to deal in one commodity, they could not hold stock in other corporations, their property holdings were limited to what was necessary for their business, their headquarters had to be located in the state of their principle business, monopolies had their charges regulated by the state, and all corporate documents were open to the legislature. Any political contribution by a corporation was treated as a criminal offence. Corporations could, and often did, have their charters removed if the state considered that their activities harmed its people.

Railroad companies, opening up the interior, became the first monopoly corporations. They had traditionally been referred to as *'artificial persons'* and when the Fourteenth Amendment gave all *'persons'* equality before the law they desperately tried to claim that it applied not just to slaves but to them as well. They eventually succeeded with the *Santa Clara County* vs. *Southern Pacific Railroad case.*

Hartmann tried to find why this particular case had suddenly reversed eighteen years of consistent ruling by the Supreme Court that corporations did *not* have the rights of human persons. He found that textbooks only quoted the headnote not any details. He eventually unearthed the original records in Vermont only to find that the judge had specifically stated that the case did *not* relate to corporate personhood. The headnote had been written a year later by a person whose life had been with the railroads, but by then the judge was too ill to check it. This mistaken or fraudulent headnote is still used in court as a cornerstone of corporate law. It set the road to corporate tyranny.

Hartmann believes that reversing the *Santa Clara* case would be the first step to subjecting corporations once again to the control of the people. The federal government, each state, each township, could then regulate corporations to the benefit of its citizens and help local economies to flourish. Indeed, in California local governments have already passed laws that deny corporations the status of persons while in Pennsylvania some townships have forbidden corporations from owning or controlling farms in their communities. Hartmann ends the book with model ordinances to rescind corporate personhood.

I believe that this ties in with George Monbiot's suggestion that every corporation should be subject to *mandatory* fair trade rules and have its licence to trade removed by a national government if its activities are considered to harm communities.

James Bruges is the author of what is probably best brief introduction to sustainability issues, *The Little Earth Book*. He is a retired architect and lives in Bristol.

Making energy the basis of our money supply

BRIAN DAVEY

Not by Money Alone - Economics as Nature Intended
Malcolm Slesser and Jane King
Jon Carpenter Publishing
ISBN 1 89776 672 6 (pb) £11.99

*Calculations based on current market prices tell one nothing about
a project's long-term sustainability. Its costs and benefits in energy terms
would be a much better guide.*

The basic idea of this book is that economics, although useful within limits as a way of understanding the world, has become a dangerous encouragement to self deception when it comes to understanding humanity's relationship with nature. The contribution of nature to economic activity, including its capacity to supply materials and to act as a sink for wastes, cannot be measured through money. Economics, the authors say, can tell us where people would like to go, but we must supplement this with calculations based on physical science in order to tell us where they can go. An action can only be economically feasible if it is also physically feasible and conceptualising our options solely by examining market processes, measured with money variables, can never tell us this. What is lacking is a physical method of quantifying the economy to parallel the monetary quantifications to be used in policy. So the authors argue that energy units must be used as indicators to guide policy if development is ever to be "durable" - the term they propose to substitute for the degraded concept of "sustainability".

Energy is the motor force of all productive activity. It largely accounts for the massive productivity of our industrial economies. The time has long gone when people were employed for their labour power, where that term could be considered a description of a physical expenditure of effort. Labour is now almost exclusively decision making and payments to people are for the management of resources - not for the physical energy that they put into the labour process. A horse could do the physical work of six human beings. A hundred horse power tractor can do the work of 600. The energy

that drives it is its fuel - the muscular effort of its driver in steering is miniscule. Like virtually everyone else in an industrial economy, the tractor driver's main function is to make decisions.

A simple example helped me to take in the distinction between decisions about durability (sustainability) based on economic measures, involving slippery monetary valuations, and decisions based on physical measures. The authors compare two investments - one in a wind turbine and another in a diesel generator - to see which option is the more sustainable investment. Making and running both types of generator can be considered in physical terms and in economic terms. The comparison in physical terms involves looking at the energy in MegaJoules that is involved in making and running each of them - over and against the energy that they each generate over their 20-year lifetimes. The economic decision is based upon the monetary costs arising from constructing and running each of them compared to the monetary revenues arising from the electricity that they generate.

The chief difference, of course, is that, after production, the wind generator requires no further (paid for) energy inputs to run it, but the diesel generator requires further purchased inputs of diesel energy. The authors show that only the physically-based calculation can tell which is the sustainable investment. The diesel generator may appear to be "more economic" here and now - but only because the price of diesel is low and an assumption is being made that currently low oil prices will be stable over the next 20 years. In reality we cannot know what the price of diesel will be. If oil prices rise, which seems likely given what is known about the prospects for the depletion of reserves, it will probably not be the best option, seen in hindsight. An economic calculation based on current market prices tells one nothing about a project's long-term sustainability.

Of course, many economists might protest that when the price of diesel rises that will encourage the switch from investment in diesel generators to investment in wind turbines and the market, informed by price signals, will be working properly. But it doesn't help us to make decisions today and if a switch to renewables is left too late it will become less and less feasible because there will be less and less available energy both to sustain our high consumption lifestyles and to provide the power required to manufacture and install the equipment needed by a new renewables-based economy.

Slesser and King were part of the team that developed the ECCO model for energy forecasting purposes. Its unique feature, compared to other economic models, is that the main technical energy and resource parameters are included and computed as part of the total picture. Using ECCO it is possible to calculate what the effect of switching from fossil fuel and nuclear power generation to power generation from renewables will be on other dimensions of the economy - for example the implications for consumption, employment, imports and exports.

That enables the authors to be confident that many solutions commonly put forward to address sustainability issues are, on deeper examination, not practically feasible. Thus Greenpeace comes in for some criticism because it is simply too optimistic about what is involved in a switch from an oil- and nuclear-based economy into one based on renewables. Using the ECCO model "a dynamic analysis of the investment requirements for renewables demonstrates that it would take a considerable time, maybe a century, to achieve a renewables-based economy".

Energy is the key to addressing other environmental issues too – like the depletion of raw materials and the use of the environment as a sink. In regard to the latter, the authors argue plausibly that energy use per unit of land area is probably the best indicator that can be used for policy purposes to measure the burden different nations are putting on their natural environments compared to the other possible indicators of population density, or GDP per land

area. In regard to raw material depletion, although optimists point to the immense mineral resources still available on the planet, making them practically available requires energy expenditure in mining and extraction - and the energy available to do that is itself on the brink of decline. On this, Slesser and King confirm the analysis made by Colin Campbell and colleagues in the Oil Depletion Analysis Centre - that we are nearing the peak for conventional oil, while the peak for gas is a few years behind.

Armed with their analysis, the authors explore a range of policy instruments which could be used to enable and oblige us to live reasonably comfortably both within technical constraints and within the limits that they have highlighted. This includes ideas like Personal Energy Rights and/or the Unitax on primary energy sources or a local fuel based so-called Ulitax. These would replace taxes on income. Slesser and King are concerned that these are administratively feasible and they show how they would work. Their assertion, stated briefly early in the book, is that "With our ability now to analyse and understand the system, it should not be beyond our powers to create a durable economy and environment by legislating for appropriate negative feedback loops, like the checks and balances of a democratic legal system." Their discussions towards the end of the book are an attempt to grapple with how that might be done and how, if only the mental model used by the public as citizens can more accurately reflect the realities of the physical world, we can "cajole our politicians" into this.

Here I part company, at least to a degree, with the authors. The book was published in 2002, before the Iraq oil war, and I wondered if they would write it in the same way now. All the way through their book, Slesser and King acknowledge repeatedly the forces and vested interests working against the adoption of their ideas. Against these vested interests they raise a voice of reason and of moral protest - an argument about the awful consequences of global decline if no preparations are made for it. Since its publication we have seen the USA, with Britain following behind, lying, stealing and killing to get access to oil supplies.

Because the oil interests are so highly integrated with the arms interest and military logistics, these same interests appear to be profiting highly by the accumulating chaos that they are, in large part, causing. In that sense, the people who King and Slesser deplore, those who say that "to be successful we will have to be more ruthless with each other", are already driving the political and economic process. On the other hand, large sections of the population are becoming aware of the energy crisis, indirectly, through the horrified knowledge that it has motivated the war politics of their leaders, leaders who can no longer be trusted. If there was ever a politician that could be "cajoled" it might have been Michael Meacher, but he is no longer the British environment minister and look at his views now!

What this suggests to me is two things. Firstly, that the problems that this book raises require more than new government policies. It requires new government systems and new concepts of democracy, as well as new information and media networks which we will have to develop out of, and during, the crisis as it evolves. Secondly, we are already entering the period of chaos that the book predicts would occur if we do not act. It is too late, the chaos is under way. Accordingly, the changes in the government system and policy will be developed less to prepare for, and to forestall chaos, and more as emergency ad hoc measures to cope with it. An important part of that will be people acting independently of government to support each other at a local level, as best they can, sorting out improvised energy saving, food, transport and rationing arrangements while counterposing a higher citizens' ideal to the viciousness that is becoming prevalent at the level of policy. This book may provide such a citizens' movement with some broader orientation as to why things are in such a mess. Those who are lucky enough to survive the social chaos in intact communities, if indeed any such communities do survive, will perhaps be able to make use of the economic concepts and tools described in this book in building a more sustainable (durable) form of human civilisation.

Brian Davey trained as economist but has worked mostly in the Nottingham community and voluntary sector. He is currently the development worker for a mental health project with a community organic garden.

Jane King and **Malcolm Slesser** have both participated in Feasta events and Feasta sponsored the creation of an ECCO model of the Irish economy. Copies of this are available on a CD from the office.

Participatory democracy is good for you

"We, the People"- Developing a New Democracy
Perry Walker
New Economics Foundation
ISBN N/A £4.99

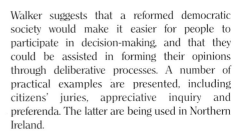

Perry Walker, the development director of the New Economics Foundation's democracy programme and a member of InterAct, the participation network, leads his readers on a journey which begins with a 1774 speech by Edmund Burke. In this, Burke argues that public representation should be seen as powerful people speaking their minds on what they think is best and not bowing to the will of the people.

During the journey, Walker explores the poor state of democracy in western society, highlights problems and suggests new ways of thinking about democratic processes. He says that the decline in public participation in democracy has had social costs. These include the reduction of complex issues into "zero sum" situations in which one group wins at another group's expense

rather than working out "win/win" collaborations.

Walker suggests that a reformed democratic society would make it easier for people to participate in decision-making, and that they could be assisted in forming their opinions through deliberative processes. A number of practical examples are presented, including citizens' juries, appreciative inquiry and preferenda. The latter are being used in Northern Ireland.

I found this an insightful book which made the abstract concept of democracy more accessible and real. With plenty of real world applications it is a bargain at £4.99, or you can download it free from the NEF website at www.neweconomics.org

Patrick Mangan (see p176)

The problem with the money system and competing solutions

BRIAN LESLIE

The Future of Money: A new way to create wealth, work, and a wiser world
Bernard Lietaer
Century 2001
ISBN 0 71268 399 2 (hb) £18.99
ISBN 0 71269 991 0 (pb) £9.99

Money - Understanding and Creating Alternatives to Legal Tender
Thomas H Greco
Chelsea Green 2001
ISBN 1 89013 237 3 (pb) £14.95

The build-up of debt caused by the way currencies such as the dollar, the euro and the pound are created threatens the global economy. Alternative currencies can only offer a partial solution.

These two books, both published in 2001, envisage an economic breakdown because of the inherent faults in the money system. Anyone with concern for a sustainable future for humanity and for the environment on which it depends should study their message. The increasingly-desperate competition and conflicts around the world have many contributory causes, but just one common one: money and the scheming to maintain the power which the control of its creation gives to the banks.

Both authors start by faulting the current official money system but differ in their conclusions about its future. While Lietaer views its collapse as inevitable in the short term, Greco is content to list its flaws. Both propose 'alternative' or 'complementary' currencies to compensate for them.

Contrary to the popular myth still fostered by many banks and politicians, banks do not lend their depositors' money. They create new money when they grant a loan or overdraft and now some 97% of the money in circulation was created in this way. This means that money must constantly be created to replace that being repaid to the banks. This gives the banks power to decide who will get it, and for what purposes - a point not brought out in either book.

Both authors identify the interest charged on the bank loans which are the basis of virtually all modern money as a cause of the serious

problems they expound. Lietaer summarises the problems with interest as follows:

- it indirectly encourages systematic competition;
- it continually fuels the need for endless economic growth; and
- it concentrates wealth by taxing the vast majority in favour of a small minority

As a result, both books view the absence of interest charges as one of the strengths of the alternative currencies they suggest, although Greco nevertheless proposes to use the interest paid on investments of official money to cover the operating of some of his proposed alternative money systems. Neither author sees the exponential growth of debt around the world as a major problem.

Lietaer sees four megatrends converging in the next 5-20 years: monetary instability, the 'age wave' (the increasing average age of the population), climate change and extinction of biodiversity, and the information revolution. In seeing the 'age wave' as a problem of provision of needs, he ignores the huge increase in productivity over the last century and the grossly wasteful use made of it. If better employed, this productivity would decimate the employment necessary to meet needs. He sees the information revolution as a problem because it is 'destroying jobs', but does not consider this as a benefit denied to society by its failure to distribute income better and easily solved by introducing Citizens' Incomes. Discounting the possibility of reform, he sees complementary currencies as the means of moving to 'sustainable abundance'.

He notes that climate change and the extinction of biodiversity threaten 'sustainable abundance' and that monetary instability prevents economies making the drastic changes needed to achieve it. However, he dismisses the possibility of reforming the official money system and fails to consider the effects of the debts generated by the way money gets into circulation. The growing magnitude of total debts - national, business and individual − leads to increasingly desperate, destructive competition. Moreover, since these debts can only be repaid with official money, alternative or complementary currencies are severely limited in how far they can compensate for the problems created by official 'debt-money'.

Greco is more concerned with the details of current and potential alternative currencies, devoting much of his book to descriptions of current examples and a selection of past ones, their strengths and weaknesses, and theoretical possibilities and recommendations for future systems, several of which are his own proposals. He notes that alternative currencies start and are most successful at times (and in places) when the failings of official money are having the greatest impact, and mostly discontinue when conditions improve. The Swiss WIR is the only long-lived example he quotes. For those contemplating starting a local or alternative currency, his book has much to recommend it.

Greco divides historical money systems into 'commodity', 'symbolic' and 'credit' money, but in declaring as an "essential fact" that "money has a beginning and an ending; it is created and it is extinguished" he exposes the limitation of his thesis. While this is true of all the official and alternative currencies he describes - all of which are 'symbolic' or 'credit' systems - it is not true of all money, current or past - or potentially, future.

Both books contain a wealth of interesting facts about, and examples of, alternative currencies plus thought-provoking ideas and proposals. Only Lietaer, however, addresses the issue of international monetary exchanges. I believe his Terra is a promising idea for an international currency, not least because it would be independent of governments and take its value from a 'basket' of real, traded goods.

I do not share Lietaer's pessimism about the possibility of achieving monetary reform - an issue Greco does not even address as he sees complementary currencies as making it unneccessary - despite the failure of its advocates to achieve it to date. His assessment of the invulnerability over the past century of the vested interests manipulating and controlling the current system is indisputable but the mounting instability of the present system and its impending collapse make the possibility of forcing reform much more realistic.

In the 1930s the movement for reform was growing rapidly until war became the solution to the depression. There is never a shortage of money for warfare! Today, again, the fundamental problems generated by the financial mechanism have grown to the point where its instability is widely recognised and the movement for reform is growing fast. This makes effective challenge much more possible as well as vital.

The history of the past few centuries can be explained in terms of the nature of the money-creation mechanism and the deliberate manipulation of that system to suit powerful companies and the banks which funded their development. Greco regards the recent change to 'credit' or fiat money - going off 'the gold standard' - as the ultimate debasement, and as the cause of inflation. He is well aware of the power deriving from the issuance and control of the money supply but cannot accept the fact that its divorce from any commodity-base to become pure credit makes it possible for the first time in history to create and control a national currency for the benefit of society, as proposed by James Robertson and Joseph Huber in *Creating New Money*, among others.

The power and profit banks derive from their privilege of controlling the issue of money must be removed. The sole power to create or destroy national money should be in the hands of a credit-creation authority under democratic control and mandated to monitor society's needs and to maintain the money supply at the level needed to allow trading, saving and investment without serious inflation.

A vital point, however, is that all the money in circulation should have been spent, not lent, into circulation. This means that all new money should be credited to the Treasury's account so that the seigniorage - the profit from issuing it -

is gained by the nation rather than any individual or business.

What gives national monies their special advantage over complementary currencies is the fact that only they are acceptable for payment of taxes and legally recognised for the settlement of debts. As long as they function tolerably well, they are the preferred medium of exchange. The only way to eliminate the debts that have built up as a result of the present way of issuing currencies as interest-bearing loans is by creating and issuing enough debt-free (and therefore interest-free) national currency to retire all the debts. If this was combined with the payment of Citizens' Incomes and switch from income tax and VAT to land-value, pollution and resource taxation, there should be little need or demand for local or alternative currencies. However, until then, or in the absence of reform, these currencies are likely to become of increasing importance to survival.

Brian Leslie is editor of *Sustainable Economics,* the bi-monthly newsletter of the green economy working group of the English Green Party.

Preserving the the planet means scrapping capitalism

DEREK WALL

The Enemy of Nature
Joel Kovel
Zed Books 2002
ISBN 1 84277 080 2 (hb) £45.00
ISBN 1 84277 081 0 (pb) £15.95

*If economic growth has caused the sustainability crisis, why do rich countries
still pursue it? Is it required because of the way money is put into circulation,
as suggested in the previous review, or is the Left correct to blame
the nature of the capitalist system?*

In this convincing but testing text, Joel Kovel argues that economic growth is ecologically unsustainable and leads to alienation because it fuels social injustice,. It has made us the hungry ghosts of Buddhist mythology by creating a world where the work we do makes us sick and we consume so as to try and salve that alienation. We therefore need to replace capitalism with a new system based on production for use rather than exchange.

To promote the message in *The Enemy of Nature*, Kovel once stood as a Green Party member for a New York Senate seat and challenged Ralph Nader for the party's presidential nomination. His academic career has included a period as professor of psychiatry at the Albert Einstein College of Medicine. He has written numerous books and articles on psychiatry and politics including a seminal study of white racism. Like many other US Green Party members, he has a lengthy pedigree stretching from the 1960s as a New Left and civil rights activist. In the 1980s he produced one of the best-known peace movement texts *Against a State of Nuclear Terror*. His path to the Green Party began 1988 when his home in the Catskill Mountains was affected by a severe heat wave, which ruined his garden and made him conscious of the greenhouse effect.

Kovel believes that the ecological crisis is already with us and the world is being unpicked eco-stitch by eco-stitch. Since the early 1970s when reports such as *The Limits to Growth* and *Blueprint for Survival* were published and Earth Day introduced, the human population has nearly doubled, the population of vehicles more than doubled, paper consumption has quadrupled and fish stocks are in crisis.

He vigorously attacks the notion of unlimited economic growth and shows convincingly that growth, far from being an accident, is an essential part of the modern capitalist economy, observing "One way of seeing this is in terms of an economy geared to run on the basis of unceasing accumulation. Thus each unit of capital must, as the saying goes, 'grow or die,' and each capitalist must constantly search to expand markets and profits or lose his position in the hierarchy."

Hostility to multinationals is not enough, he says. Capitalism is not a conspiracy but a process based on commodity exchange. To survive, we exchange commodities to generate the cash to get more commodities, money sticks to our hands and we become dominated by the need to accumulate cash to meet our needs. The 'distortions' of debt, the dislocations of 'free' trade and all the rest are conjured up by the basic atoms and molecules of commodity production.

The Post Office makes a profit if more junk mail is posted and I earn a wage if people buy my books rather than getting them from the library. Doctors thrive on ill health and criminologists only receive a pension if deviant acts continue. The capitalist economy needs waste and destruction to survive. So Kovel urges us to sweep away commodification and directly produce what we need and share. We should construct a pleasurable - even lazy - form of socialism based on the needs of people and the rest of nature. Decommodification of the world leads to the re-enchantment of nature, he says.

Kovel challenges Greens to re-examine the implications of their critique and is critical of types of socialism that ignore the need to sustain nature. He synthesises the more philosophical and radical elements of green politics and Marxism. He examines how ecological ensembles of sustainable production are possible and looks to the communal tradition of religious groups such as the Bruderhof for hope.

While stressing the economic roots of the crisis, he is keen to show how a variety of causes interact with capitalism to drive us towards catastrophe. Alarmed perhaps by his own boldness, Kovel notes

> Growing numbers of people are beginning to realize that capitalism is the uncontrollable force driving our ecological crisis only to become frozen in their tracks by the awesome implications of the insight. Perhaps optimism is appropriate. There is a difference between the impossible and the merely difficult. In fact, the very notion of sensual use rather than an economics based on enslaving accountancy values has a seductive charm. I am not one to minimise the importance of strategy and the difficult debates we need to have about moving to a qualitatively different kind of society but nonetheless the implications of sustainability are to be enjoyed.

Let's borrow all we need from libraries, grow our food, build our houses, teach our sons and daughters to cook and enjoy life instead of being imprisoned by unfree labour and boring consumption. Let us read the novels of John Cooper Powys, practice our zazen and live fully in the world!

In short, Kovel argues that ecology demands anti-capitalism. And anti-capitalism suggests, perhaps, a pagan appreciation of our real, material, living world, an appreciation that brings us back to the necessity of struggle.

This is perhaps the best book I have read on green economics in my quarter century of activism. It needs to be read, reread, its message repeated, networked and acted upon. It is beautifully written. The core message is simple but of great importance: our economic system wrecks the environment, thrives on injustice and allows abstract and alien process to control human life. It shows in some detail why we are destroying the world and how we can stop. Above all, it provides a course of practical therapy to get to ecology, justice and liberation.

Derek Wall, like Joel Kovel, is an eco-Marxist. He teaches political economy at Goldsmiths College, London, and stood in the 2004 European elections as a Green Party candidate for the South East Constituency. His book, *Babylon and Beyond: the economics of anti-capitalist, anti-globalist and radical green movements* is to be published in 2005 by Pluto Press.

A shopping list of solutions, but none nearly radical enough

GILLIES MACBAIN

Eco-economy - Building an Economy for the Earth
Lester R Brown
Kogan Page 2003
ISBN 1 85383 826 8 (hb) £17.99
ISBN 1 85383 904 3 (pb) £14.99

The New Economy of Nature
Gretchen C Daily and Katherine Ellison
Island Press 2002
ISBN 1 55963 154 6 (pb) £11.50
ISBN 1 55963 945 8 (hb) £19.50

*Assigning money values to the environment is not likely to stop its destruction.
Nor will treating a long list of problems one by one suffice.*

I offered to review these books because of their titles. I hoped to find authors who shared my own intuition that the global economy of the future must follow and mimic the patterns of nature, and of life itself, to become a cyclical and sustainable system. When I had read them I felt rather like a malt whisky drinker asked to adjudicate between red lemonade and Seven-up. These offerings are just not strong enough for my taste, but I will do my best to describe them for those who would like to get them out of the library. (I presume Feasta members would do nothing as consumerist as actually buying a book, unless to add to the insulation qualities of a book-lined study.)

Lester R Brown was the founder of the Worldwatch Institute. He is now president of the Earth Policy Institute which produces this book, a series of four page earth policy alerts, and brief eco-economy updates, all of which can be downloaded for free at www.earth-policy.org

The Worldwatch Institute was founded in 1974. The author lists the causes for concern at that time - shrinking forests, expanding deserts, eroding soils, deteriorating rangelands, disappearing species, and the early signs of collapsing fisheries. Can he now tick off the problems tackled and solved? No. The list is still there and has to be added to - rising carbon dioxide levels, falling water tables, rivers running dry, ozone depletion, plus rising temperatures and the other effects of global warming.

These concerns are all the result of a rising global population, with increasing technical mastery of their environment, burning up non-renewable reserves of energy and expanding their economies exponentially, all of this taking place within a finite planetary biosphere.

The book was published in 2001, and it may be that future historians will record the period 1974 – 2001 as a time of innocence, when environmentalists allowed themselves to assume that a more restrained and equitable sharing of the resources of the Earth would follow in due course upon their exposition of the problems.

Brown ignores two most vital questions. The first is how to return the population of the Earth to a level that can be sustained by a global economy that does not use resources faster than they can be renewed. The second, how to deal with the historic tendency of nations and alliances to go to war to confiscate, or defend, vital sources of energy. In mediaeval times this meant land. In modern times it has meant oil, gas, and minerals.

For an environmentalist to protest that that is not his problem would be no more acceptable to me than an industrialist making the same denial of responsibility for environmental pollution. War, like acid rain, often falls upon people far away - but both are side effects of the industrial hunger for consuming fossil energy. Innocence is an illusion. Start a car, or switch on a light, and you are part of this consumption.

Lester Brown works his way through a list of signs of stress in the world's climate, forests, fisheries, soils, and species. He then moves on to a list of solutions to these separate problems, but it is a list. No doubt he understands the interacting complexity of the world, - ecological, industrial, social, economic, and financial - but his well-researched work is to me no more than an environmental laundry list, linear and pedestrian. It is as though the problems can be solved individually and separately, without any changes to global culture - political, economic, philosophical, religious, or otherwise. This I do not believe.

In spite of this there is one paragraph from this book which has stuck in the mind. It is headed 'Learning from China.' China is topical. China is developing very fast. Decisions are being made as to the future of China as an industrial giant, perhaps even the successor of America - as America was the successor of the British Empire and her Victorian period of industrial dominance. So will China catch up with American levels of consumption?

No. For China to match America in per capita beef consumption would require the entire American grain harvest. For China to match Japan in fish consumption would require the entire world fish catch. For China to match the American level of oil consumption would require the entire world's oil.

So that is not going to happen. But Lester Brown does not tell us what is going to happen instead.

The second of these books is *The New Economy of Nature* by Daily and Ellison. One of the women authors is a scientist, the other a journalist.

I do not really understand this book; better to say so than to pretend. Firstly, I do not understand why it is a book. I get information from newspapers, radio, e-mail, and discussion groups. This book could easily have been a couple of interesting articles in a weekly publication - perhaps it once was. Or a couple of radio talks. Do you know how much radio you can buy for twenty pounds sterling? (the book's price). Quite a lot. It is not a book I want to own for reference.

One of the themes of the book is making protection of the environment profitable. That means putting a money value on certain environmental initiatives. As an opponent of putting a money value on things that used to be free and natural, such as clean air and water, I am not the best person to assess the authors' account. Nor am I impressed by their breathless enthusiasm that all is going well. After all, George Bush got into power - and all is not going well. Short term policies are in the ascendant, everywhere you look.

The best account in the book is of New York City buying up its own drinking water catchment area, instead of building enormous filtration plants. This was common sense. Spend a billion dollars to keep the area clear and unpolluted and to compensate the owners of second homes and the developers. Sounds a lot of money until you assess the cost of the filtration plants, which would be billions more.

If New York had thought of this at a time when the upstate watershed was still wild and free of second homes, they could even have done it without the billion.

Free Ballygowan for Gotham city ?

I can relate to that.

Many regard **Gillies Macbain** as Ireland's foremost dark brown thinker but he describes himself as a wheelchair van driver and organic farmer. He lives in a tower house in County Tipperary and is currently assembling the articles he has written over the years into a book.

I've seen the future and it's powered by the sun

EAMON RYAN TD

The Solar Economy,
Herman Scheer,
Earthscan, 2002,
ISBN 1 85383 835 7 £17.99

An Irish politician finds that a book written by one of his German counterparts makes him want to become an engineer when he grows up

The *Solar Economy* starts with a withering critique of the present fossil fuel economy. It lambasts those politicians who leave long-term planning to international stock markets that never look beyond the next quarter. It describes the risks posed by the lengthy supply chains needed to transport dwindling fossil fuel resources to run outdated combustion machinery and a dysfunctional agricultural system. It predicts not only increased international conflict as power blocks squabble for the remaining fuel reserves but also the concentration of wealth in fewer countries and hands.

Such warnings have been heard for at least thirty years and they seem to be having less and less effect on our collective conscious and our will to change. It is as if someone had been highlighting the fact that the King has no clothes for so long that we have become comfortable and complacent about the naked truth of our unsustainable economic model.

But Scheer is not simply foretelling doom if we carry on as we are. He presents a sweeping vision of what the renewable alternative could and should be like. His vision penetrates beyond the obvious potential of photovoltaics, wind power and biomass to explore the ways solar solutions will change every aspect of our economy and lives. Its realisation involves not just putting a few PV panels on our societal roof, but changing the plumbing, wiring and the basic building blocks of our society to build a renewable future.

A key step in that direction will be the development of new energy storage technologies for use by intermittent renewable power sources like wind. A lot of attention has been paid recently to storing energy from the wind by using surplus electricity from wind turbines to electrolyse water to provide hydrogen for use in fuel-cell-powered vehicles. My own hunch, however, having read Scheer's overview of the emerging technologies, is that innovations in areas such as compressed air cylinders may be a better bet in the near future. Unlike battery technology there are no messy chemicals and test cars already have a range of 200km using a compressed air cylinder which is lighter and more compact than any battery in existing electrical vehicles. In my dreams I am already scheming to open the first compressed air re-energising station on the Ring of Kerry to power all those coaches flying along the road.

Indeed, this book will make most of its adult readers yearn to become engineers when they grow up. It is a rallying call for technologists to save the planet by designing ways to store the energy provided free of charge by the sun. As I write, I am sure an engineer in a small lab or a garage somewhere is putting the final touches to a prototype energy storage system that will mark this new century in the same way that Henry Ford's production of the Model T marked the last.

In response to a question in the Dail in 2003, Minister of State John Brown cited the storage of renewable energy as a major problem; he said "In America, they are investing approximately $27 billion on hydrogen fuel research to deal with this matter. One can therefore see the enormity of the storage problem and the financial implications of dealing with it." What a terrible pity the minister's advisers had not seen the positive side to that statistic and insisted that Ireland be in the forefront of similar research. It was unfortunate that the recently-established Science Foundation of Ireland was not given a special remit to fund new sustainable technologies, as has happened in several other countries.

One of Scheer's central convictions is the need for our society to return to the land. He believes that the development of a solar economy will see the location of energy sources and the accompanying storage industries in diverse and often peripheral locations. He claims solar technologies will also bring an agricultural revolution which will have dramatic consequences for rural life. His vision is not of a return to a medieval world of subsistence farming but rather the promotion of what he calls "real biotechnology" to develop the new applications to which biological materials can be put. For example, in place of pesticides he sees the possibility of using sugar-enriched ethanol, and instead of plastic pipes ones made from organic fibre. He insists that local farmers rather than multinational companies holding genetic patents should control the development of new biotechnologies.

The flight from the land of recent years is understandable when one considers how sudden market vagaries or crop failures have broken so many farmers. The heartbreaking isolation of such a situation is less likely when there is a diversity of sources of rural economic wealth. In a solar-powered world, people would be able to depend on income from renewable energy production as well as from crops grown to replace the petrochemical products of today.

The "futurist" movement in the 1920s and 1930s was characterised by paintings of trains and cars moving at great speed. If Herman Scheer was to paint his own futurist vision I think he would do so with paintings of a rural landscape in which people were working at their cleverest to reap the most sustainably from the land.

Herman Sheer is an SPD member of the German Parliament and he is wise to all ways in which the twists and turns of the regulatory process can have a profound effect on the development of the renewable energy industry. Industry sources here can only look on with envy to the political support that has helped bring about the development of 16,000MW of wind power in a country that is positively becalmed compared to our own windy island.

In his economic analysis he rails against the tendency to ignore the marginal long-run fuel costs in the assessment of competing energy projects. The positive news is that the cost of electricity from the wind is now sneaking below that from the cheapest alternative, combined cycle gas power stations. We are at a unique moment when we can either harness the development of technology to create a more equitable and cleaner economy or else face a series of unpredictable crises as our fossil fuels run out. The former process will require not only good engineers to make the necessary technological advances but also political support to ensure we take the right steps forward. Having thought about it again, perhaps those who read Scheer's book will, besides becoming engineers, have to be more political when they grow up as well.

Eamon Ryan, TD, is the spokesperson on energy for the Irish Green Party.

GALWAY COUNTY LIBRARIES

Few reasons to be cheerful, thanks to declining supplies of oil

MICHAEL LAYDEN

The Party's Over
Richard Heinberg
Temple Lodge Publishing, 2003
ISBN 1 90263 645 7 £11.95

Humanity's development path is going to be thrown into reverse in the next few years by oil and gas shortages. The prospects of contraction and dislocation are frightening.

It is easy to understand why Richard Heinberg wrote this book. Mankind has faced many challenges in the past but few as complex as the current one. We have not used the thirty years since the twin wake-up calls of the first OPEC oil crisis and the publication of the seminal work *The Limits to Growth* to reduce the demands we makes on the planet. So, having failed to take the easy steps that would have been required a generation ago, our species motors towards a major dislocation caused by the imminent end to the era of plentiful cheap oil.

"I am reasonably cheerful and optimistic by nature," Heinburg writes. "However, as anyone would, I find this picture of the future to be deeply disturbing. Everyone I have met who understands population and resource issues comes to essentially the same conclusions and has to deal with the same emotional responses - which typically run the gamut from shock, denial, and rage to eventual acceptance - and a determination to do whatever is possible to help avert the worst of the likely impacts."

So this book is clearly not entertainment. It is meant to alarm, educate and perhaps inspire individuals to make a difference in this most terrible struggle our species will increasingly have to face. Heinberg approaches his subject in a logical and well-thought out way.

- He identifies civilisation's dependency on fossil fuel resources
- He shows the vunerability of our civilisation to minor disruptions in energy availabilty
- He examines the various projections of the imminent onset of peak oil and other fossil fuels.

- He looks at the political and geopolitical realities of oil and resources historically and currently
- Finally, he ponders some of the potential solutions or policies which could be implemented to mitigate the effects of these real limits to human economic and social expansion.

The book is an amazingly brave work and it is unusual to see anyone trying to pull so much material together from so many different specialisms and technologies. It is only 242 pages long and because the material within it could easily have been expanded to fill at least five more volumes of the same length, it should be seen as an appetiser rather than a main course. It has the feeling of a work in progress and I would think of it as self-study guide rather than a traditional text. Although a college lecturer, Heinberg is more of a magpie than a traditional academic: he has picked a wide range of little gems from different internet discussion groups and publications. There is an excellent bibliography which is strongly web-based.

This is not a book which many members of the general public will pick up and read to the end. It will not be particularly useful in swaying people who are in active denial about the crisis. However, anyone trying to get a grasp on how dependent on oil and how vulnerable modern civilisation is will find it very useful indeed.

I found his account of the evolution of technology and the four basic classifications of tools in Chapter 1 particularly useful because it develops into a wide discussion of complex societies.

Chapter 2 covers energy use in the modern world and Chapters 3 and 4 provide what is probably as good a summary of the entire energy sector as one will ever get in 80 pages. It covers oil reserves, other fossil fuels, nuclear, and renewable energy sources. His summaries of the energy fields where my expertise lies are reasonably accurate and based on the best information available to the public. On the other hand, I think that his sections on biomass, hydrogen and the conservation of energy are too sparse. These chapters could be supplemented by reading books such as Feasta's *Before the Wells Run Dry - Ireland's Transition to Renewable Energy* and, because of the importance of oil depletion, Colin Campbell's *The Coming Oil Crisis*.

Chapter 5 covers the likely consequences for sectors of the economy such as agriculture and

Chapter 6 discusses strategies to deal with the crisis. Again, both are excellent primers but I suggest that readers might turn to *Natural Capitalism* or David Fleming's *The Lean Economy* before reading *The Party's Over* in order to understand some of the alternatives. Both *Natural Capitalism* and *The Lean Economy* are optimistic books which introduce readers to the terrible waste in our society. If people study them first, their reaction after reading The Party's Over will, I hope, be one of anger and not despair.

In summary, I think this is an excellent book and a very useful reference work for those interested in sustainability. It provides an extremely good, thorough summary of many of the key components of the inevitable contraction and dislocation of society if we continue on our present course.

Michael Layden is an engineer based in Arigna, Co. Roscommon where his family mined coal for many generations. His career has evolved from coal mining through wind energy to rational energy use. His work is increasingly devoted to what he terms 'the alternative dimension of sustainability.'

GALWAY COUNTY LIBRARIES

Time for the next agricultural revolution

TOM CAMPBELL

Agri-Culture: Reconnecting people, land and nature
Jules Pretty
Earthscan, 2002.
ISBN 1 85383 925 6 £14.95.

Ecologically-sound farming techniques - like planting beans in maize fields or raising shrimps in rice paddy - can produce more, and better, food than industrialised methods.

Something is wrong with our agricultural and food systems, Jules Pretty writes at the start of his latest book. Despite great progress in producing more food, millions of people remain hungry and malnourished, while others are eating too much or the wrong sorts of food. The wrong policies have also had enormously negative consequences for the natural environment. Can anything be done to rectify this situation? Yes, Pretty says, and throughout the book he spells out how an agriculture based on ecological principles and in harmony with people, their societies and cultures, can provide the world with both sustainable and productive farming systems.

Pretty makes the point that ecological farming systems are not necessarily new but that they are now beginning to spread and develop an impact in both the industrialized countries of the North and the 'developing countries' of the South.

His early chapters present the evidence to support the contention that industrialized agricultural systems as currently configured are deeply flawed. They certainly produce more food per hectare and per worker than ever before but only appear 'efficient' if we take no account of harmful side effects or 'externalities' - such as the loss of soils, the damage to biodiversity, the pollution of water, the harm to human health, and the disappearance of the family farm. Food appears cheap because these costs are difficult to identify and measure. Likewise the subsidies and export credits given to agricultural commodity producers in Northern producer countries, has meant that farmers in West Africa and elsewhere have had

their markets destroyed. In order to enhance efficiency, modern agriculture has created 'monoscapes' and the poorest, particularly in developing countries, have lost out.

Drawing on the findings of the largest-ever survey of sustainable agriculture in developing countries conducted by the University of Essex where he is based[2], Pretty shows how these initiatives, if spread on a larger scale, could feed a growing world population that is already substantially food insecure without harming the environment. Evidence from South America, Asia, China, and Africa shows that sustainable farming systems are having an impact not only on local communities but further afield too. The study surveyed 208 projects and initiatives. It found that nine million farmers have adopted sustainable agricultural practices and technologies on 29 million hectares.

Some projects which added a new productive element (such as fish, or shrimps in paddy rice) to a farm system were able to substantially improve the farm family's food consumption or increase its local food sales without reducing the cereal yields per hectare. Better water management such as water harvesting and irrigation scheduling had a similar effect. The inter-cropping of legumes such as the velvet bean, or mancuna, with maize, plus controlling pests such as weeds or insects with minimum, or zero, pesticide use, plus introducing locally-appropriate crop varieties and animal breeds led to, on average, a 93% increase in food production. In many cases, it was the synergy created by these improvements rather than any

---

[2]   For a summary report of the University of Essex SAFE-World research project see:
    www2.essex.ac.uk/ces/ResearchProgrammes/SAFE47casesusag.htm

single intervention on its own that led to the overall increase in productivity. These findings are enormously significant, he says, as they counter the prevailing view that agro-ecological approaches offer only marginal opportunities to increase food production, and that industrialized approaches represent the best, and perhaps the only, way forward.

Pretty gives many examples throughout the book to illustrate how these productive and diverse sustainable farming initiatives are having a positive impact on people's lives and the environment. His research for the book brought him into contact with such practices as zero tillage and soil conservation farming in Brazil and Argentina, organic horticulture and land husbandry in Kenya, community-led water harvesting in the drylands of India, and the adoption of IPM (Integrated Project Management) by farmers' field schools in Bangladesh, to mention just a few.

Pretty's definition of sustainable agriculture is a farming system that seeks to make the best use of nature's goods and services without damaging the environment. It does this by integrating natural processes, such as nutrient recycling, nitrogen fixation, soil regeneration and natural pest control, within food production processes. It minimizes the use of non-renewable inputs that damage the environment or harm the health of farmers and consumers. It makes better use of farmers' knowledge and skills, thereby improving their self-reliance, and it makes productive use of people's collective capacity to work together to solve common management problems.

One reason that the present agricultural systems are failing, he argues, is because they have separated themselves from consumers. Industrialized countries have celebrated their agricultural systems' production of commodities, yet family farms have disappeared as rapidly as rural biodiversity. At the same time farmers themselves have received a progressively smaller proportion of what consumers spend on food. Reconnecting sustainable systems of production with consumers is essential, he argues, and he illustrates how this is already being successfully done through farmers' markets, community supported agriculture, the 'slow food' movement, box schemes, urban organic agriculture projects (such as those found in Cuba) and farmers' groups.

None of these alone will provoke systemic change, though regional policies and movements are helping to create the right conditions. Pretty advocates two interrelated concepts which are important for rethinking the future of agriculture and can help this process of reconnecting people, land and nature. The first, 'bioregionalism', the integration of human activities within ecological limits, is a concept likely to be already familiar to readers of the *Feasta Review*. The second - 'Food-sheds' is new to this reviewer. It describes "self reliant, locally or regionally-based food systems comprised of diversified farms using sustainable practices to which consumers are linked in the bonds of community as well as economy" - the idea of giving an area-based grounding to the production, consumption and movement of food. Farming must reorient itself as a multifunctional activity with diverse environmental and cultural connections.

Pretty devotes an entire chapter to the GM controversy as he says it is impossible to talk about agricultural transformation without assessing biotechnology. He believes that certain biotechnological applications (if treated on a case-by-case basis) may have the potential to offer some contributions to sustainable agriculture in the future but that serious questions need to be asked first:

- Who produces such technologies and for what purpose?
- Are they likely to benefit poor and small farmers in the developing world, and, if so, how will such farmers have access to the technology?
- What are the adverse effects on the environment, on human health and food security? What of the fundamental ethical issues?
- How reliable are the regulatory systems and standards to control such technologies?

The final chapters focus on the need to develop social learning systems and to increase ecological literacy if we are to develop not only sustainable agricultural and food systems but also a more sustainable economy and society. A person's knowledge of nature and the land usually accrues slowly over time, and cannot be easily transferred. Yet, according to Pretty: "the immediacy of the challenge means that we must move quickly in order to develop novel and robust systems of social learning that build up relations of trust, reciprocal mechanisms, shared values and rules and new forms of connectedness". Great progress in developing new forms of 'social capital' is already being made through the actions of hundreds of thousands of groups (particularly in developing countries) engaged in collective watershed, agro-forestry, microfinance, and pest management. These collective and participatory systems can also promote significant personal changes.

Despite this, the necessary transformation of global agriculture will largely depend on the radical reform of the institutions and policies that control global food supply and also on fundamental changes in the way we think. The time has come, believes Pretty, for the next agricultural revolution.

This is an elegantly-written, compelling and highly-relevant book, especially in the light of the challenges facing European farmers as a result of the current CAP reform, but also in view of the consequences of the rapid 'modernisation' of agriculture in the developing countries of the South. As such it deserves to be read widely by anyone involved or interested in farming, food and rural landscapes.

Tom Campbell teaches courses in Environment and Development, and Sustainable Livelihoods, at the Development Studies Centre, Kimmage Manor, Dublin. He also serves on the Executive Committee of Feasta.

Getting back to eating local foods

Bringing the Food Economy Home - Local Alternatives to Global Agribusiness
Helena Norberg-Hodge, Todd Merrifield and Steve Gorelick
Zed Books 2002
ISBN 1 84277 233 3 (pb) £13.95
ISBN 1 84277 232 5 (hb) £39.95

This book comes from ISEC, the International Society for Ecology and Culture, a non-profit organisation that promotes locally-based alternatives to the global consumer culture. That sums it all up. For example, it contrasts a Thanksgiving Day meal in the past when all the ingredients came from the farm or surrounding countryside, with the situation today when all the food can come from one vast company, which itself, rather than the farmer, absorbs the greatest proportion of the money the consumers pay.

The book despairs at conventional agriculture in the US - vast, polluting, exploiting – and draws hope from the slow, steady re-growth of human-scale farming and small farmers' markets. Part of the re-growth is due to Community Supported Agriculture (CSA) which involves consumers paying for their produce in advance to the farmer at the beginning of the year. In North America there are some 1000 CSA schemes in operation. Farmers' markets are another solution and,

largely as a result of both approaches, about 5% of British farmers, 15% of German and U.S. farmers and 25% of French and Japanese farmers now sell direct to consumers.

A lot of the alternative picture the book paints seems so very good: the development of small communities, more jobs, better health, the avoidance of vast monocultures, increased crop diversity, absence of overproduction, and more trust, honesty and integrity. The book is packed with statistics that will prove invaluable for anybody making the case for a sustainable future for agriculture, and the wider case for the re-localisation of our economy. It has a cheering collection of 'Things That Work' boxes and a long section of useful contacts.

While it is impossible to predict the future, it will be very interesting to read this book ten years hence. I believe that by then a lot of the suggestions will be in widespread use.

Ivan Ward has farmed organically in Wexford since 1986 growing grass, wheat and oats, and keeping sheep, cattle and horses. He now realises that organic production is not enough and is looking towards selling direct to the public and Community Supported Agriculture.

Highlights from The Feasta Review No. 1

Irish economists' views on sustainability

The first *Feasta Review* opened with a survey of Irish economists' attitudes. Their views fell into two groups, those who believed in economic growth and those who gave priority to ecosystem viability.

> *"It is not an easy matter for anyone to switch from one paradigm to another as the process involves a complete re-assessment of all the things they thought they knew".*

'Uneconomic growth' – as defined by Herman Daly

Professor Herman Daly, Senior Economist in the Environment Department of the World Bank from 1988 to 1994, and well-known for promoting the concept of a 'steady-state' economy gave the first Feasta Lecture under the title *Uneconomic growth in theory and in fact*. Even taking a very anthropocentric approach, at some point, economic growth is bound to become uneconomic, it makes us poorer.

> *"If growth really is uneconomic now, then we have to face very radical kinds of solutions to fundamental problems".*

Daly threw his authority behind Feasta's founding belief in largely self-sufficient local economies, a world community which is a 'community of communities'.

> *"Globalisation tends to convert many difficult but relatively tractable problems into one big intractable global problem".*

Corporate rule or democracy?

Feasta's second lecturer was David C. Korten, author of *When Corporations Rule the World* and *Post-Corporate World*, in which he had analysed the destructive forces of corporate globalisation and global capitalism. His lecture addressed the cultural dimension of the situation.

> *"The challenge before us is to transform a global society dedicated to the love of money into a global society dedicated to the love of life and the continuing exploration of its possibilities".*

In the next paper Korten described how, in a world in which natural wealth (land, for example) is not unlimited,

> *"property rights are being used routinely to justify the exclusion of those without property from access to a decent means of living".*

The last Korten piece came from a talk he had given in 1998.

> *"We live in a world being pillaged by the institutions of global capitalism to enrich the few at the expense of the many.... We must replace the global capitalist economy with democracies and market economies".*

Radical tax changes explained

James Robertson, co-founder of The Other Economic Summit (TOES) and of the London-based New Economics Foundation (NEF), spelt out a programme of radical changes in the taxation system and government spending to create

> *"a new social compact for a new era of equitable and sustainable development"*

Colin Campbell predicts oil production peak

In March 2000 Colin Campbell, world expert on oil depletion, warned that conventional oil is already peaking, non-conventional oil will peak before the end of this decade and gas in about 2020. These were statistics governments and mega-corporations had been careful to hide from us.

"It is difficult to penetrate the many layers of denial and obfuscation that envelope their pronouncements. We need the skills of a detective to determine whether we are dealing with ignorance, culpable ignorance or fraud and deception".

Why the present economy is doomed

David Fleming (whose 2001 Feasta Lecture is reproduced in the present Review) described the heavy dependence of the current world economy on both fossil fuels and growth. End the expansion of the availability of fossil fuels, and what happens?

"There will be serious economic contraction and destabilisation. Unless the installation of alternatives to replace both oil and gas moves ahead at an extraordinary speed, the destruction will get rapidly worse, as the supplies of oil, and then gas, go into decline. The market economy, in its present form, will not survive this sudden loss of cheap and abundant energy."

Ireland 'unprepared for energy crisis'

Kevin Healion reviewed Ireland's energy requirements and readiness (or lack of it) to cope with the expected downturn in oil and gas availability, and the consequences these may have on price.

"A long term steep increase in oil prices could force us into ways of running things that are very different from those at present".

GALWAY COUNTY LIBRARIES

Town and country – a new relationship

To avoid the overuse of hydrocarbons, and also of phosphorous ores, another natural substance in limited supply on which we are dangerously dependent, the Swedish ecologist Folke Gunther recommended a close integration of agriculture and settlements.

"Small settlements integrated with agriculture should be created in the hinterland of urban areas"

Curbing capitalism by carbon rationing

Lothar Mayer, Chairman of the German Schumacher Society, analysed the incompatibility of capitalism and Nature's ecosystems. His remedy is to adjust the way the economy works by a system of carbon dioxide rationing.

"Just as the consumer nowadays automatically pays VAT with any purchase, he or she would in future be charged at the point of sale for all the carbon dioxide released during the manufacture of the goods or the provision of the services he or she is buying"

Reducing the risk of climate change

Tradable quotas at the international level is a component of Contraction and Convergence (C&C), the international negotiating framework for addressing climate pioneered and championed by Aubrey Meyer, founder of the Global Commons Institute.

"The choice we face is between making determined, drastic changes now, or doing nothing. There is no middle road."

Copies of Feasta Review No. 1 are available from the Feasta office for €15, £10 or $20, surface postage paid.